Living
Chicana
Theory

Living Chicana Theory

Edited by
Carla Trujillo

Series in Chicana/Latina Studies

Third Woman Press
Berkeley

Published by Third Woman Press, Berkeley, Calif.
Copyright © 1998 by Third Woman Press.
All rights reserved.

Manufactured in the United States of America.
Typeset by Berkeley Hills Books, Berkeley, Calif.
Printed and bound by McNaughton & Gunn, Saline,
    Mich.
Printed on acid-free paper.

Cover art: *The Pomegranate*, by Maya González, acrylic
on masonite.

Permissions: See page 445, which is an extension of the
copyright page.

First printing 1998
10 9 8 7 6 5 4 3 2 1

Library of Congress Cataloging-in-Publication Data

Living Chicana theory / edited by Carla Trujillo
        p.   cm. -- (Series in Chicana/Latina studies)
    Includes bibliographical references.
    ISBN 0-943219-15-9 (alk. paper)
    1. Mexican American women – Study and teach-
ing.   2. Mexican American women – Social   conditions. 3. Feminism – United States.   4. Mexican
American lesbians.   I. Trujillo, Carla Mari.
II. Series.
E 184.M5L58 1998
305.48'868'72073--dc21   97-38523
                                                CIP

Excerpt from the play *Real Women Have Curves*, by
Josefina López

Ana (age 22):

I always took for granted their work to be simple and
unimportant. I was not proud to be working there at the
beginning. I was only glad to know that because I was
educated, I wasn't going to end up like them. I was going to
be better than them. And I wanted to show them how much
smarter and liberated I was. I was going to teach them about
the women's liberation movement, about sexual liberation
and all the things a so-called educated American woman
knows. But in their subtle ways they taught me about
resistance. About the battle no one was fighting for them
except themselves. About the loneliness of being women in
a country that looks down on us. With their work that seems
simple and unimportant, they are fighting . . . Perhaps the
greatest thing I learned from them is that women are
powerful, especially when working together . . .

Contents

Introduction

Carla Trujillo

> Survival is not an academic skill.
> —Audre Lorde

I grew up very well trained to serve men. I knew how to tune in to their thoughts, feelings, and needs. I could serve them coffee, make tortillas, and cook their breakfast just the way they wanted it. I learned intricate New Mexican recipes from my mother and aunts and could keep a house spotless. When I was seventeen, I was so good at cooking and making desserts that my uncle commented that I would someday make a great wife. My life, in short, had focused on making men the center of my universe. I was taught that nothing else mattered. Happiness and comfort were only for men. And if we didn't have enough work to do in caring for our father, my sister and I had our little brother—a creature made helpless by the attentions of our mother—to attend to. Though my sister and I resisted every way we could, there was little escape from the house doctrine.

My father was adept at controlling every aspect of our lives. He determined what we did and where and when we would do it. Our very thoughts, even when we were certain they were our own, were influenced by him. The food we ate, the subjects we spoke about, the happiness, or lack of it, in the home were dictated by his moods. Our existence was literally defined by him. It wasn't until I left home for college that I tasted life without him. When I left the state for graduate school, I felt for the first time happily and completely on my own.

Once I tasted freedom, I vowed never again to let anyone tell me what to do. My continual rebellion against authorities in graduate school, the Catholic Church, and in my jobs was all part of the baggage I carried from eighteen years under the reign of "the king of the castle." I continued to explore who I was by doing things never allowed before, thinking in ways that were my own, dressing, eating, behaving, and speaking anyway I wanted. I sought and found my personal sense of power and, pleased by the results, encouraged my sister and mother to do the same.

As I grew older, I met Chicanas who described their pasts as similar to my own. I met others who had gentle fathers with wonderful upbringings. Still others said it was their mothers who were the strong ones and the women who had the say-so in the family. It was good meeting Chicanas who had backgrounds different from mine.

Sensitized by my past, I began with time to see and understand much about how power relations are constructed in our country. Each time I got involved in a local women's movement or in activities in the Chicano *movimiento*, or even a discussion of the "proper" stages of moral development in human beings while in graduate school, I realized that other people, whether or not they meant to, were continually attempting to disengage my voice; demean my gender, race, or class; and define my reality. The lesbian movement was not exempt. I encountered countless Euro-American women who recited the rules about how my culture, my color, my politics were supposed to fit into theirs. In all these groups, graduate classes, and coalitions, I met people who wanted me to shut up and do what I was told. Rarely did I encounter openness to different options.

While the "training" I received from my parents taught me to take whatever I was given, I quickly realized that people either disregarded or took advantage of me when I didn't speak up. Patient and polite at first, I gave people the benefit of the doubt, the opportunity to consider whether we could learn from each other. But my frustration at not being heard would turn to anger if I saw that I, or someone I respected, was being disregarded or insulted. This left me with no option but to confront them and call them on it. What I often saw around me was how completely invisible and disregarded women of color often are. Often, we're there for someone else, and no one's there for us, as Sandra Cisneros says in her essay "A Woman of No Consequence/Una Mujer Cualquiera":

I've always been la otra. The other woman. Even when my lovers didn't have a wife. Even when they didn't climb out of my bed to climb that same night into another's. I've been la otra. The one they sought when the one at home didn't understand them.

It's not to say I understood them any better. But they didn't need to understand me, understand? That was the difference.

As I sought to validate my own voice and presence in the world, I became dismayed with the attitudes displayed toward me by those women and men whom I thought of as my colleagues. I was a Chicana activist, and that made me a troublemaker. I was a feminist, which designated me as "difficult" by those in power or as a "sellout" by those without it. And because I was a lesbian, I was automatically labeled a man-hating heterophobe. I believe that many of these inaccurate assertions occurred not only because of stereotyping but because I was a woman who spoke up for myself and for others who couldn't.

I have been at a loss to understand why many of us work so hard not to offend people who step on us. My mother thought it best that I be quiet and complacent. What's the point of that? It only served to keep me oppressed. Yet, unfortunately, speaking up sometimes has a price. In a chapter from the recently published anthology *Chicanas/Chicanos: At the Crossroads* (edited by David Maciel and Isidoro Ortiz), Ignacio M. García refers to "a small but influential number of Chicana scholars" as "gender nationalists" who, in his opinion, "find the lurking 'macho' in every Chicano scholarly work." He believes that these Chicanas seek to change the direction of Chicano Studies (which is true). He further exposes his own homophobia by stating, "The lesbian Chicana scholars have even gone so far as promoting the idea that homosexuality is an integral part of Chicano culture." Another Chicano professor, at a 1990 National Association for Chicano Studies (NACS) conference, publicly denigrated a Chicana scholar on her work because she spoke about diabetes and alcohol addiction in the Chicana/o community. He continued by claiming she was trying to get "Chicanos to stop eating their frijoles" and vowed not to let her "take away his beer." The Chicano editor of the

San Diego community newspaper, *La Voz de Frontera*, physically threatened a group of feminista Chicanas when they refused to kowtow to the veiled threats in his newspaper. A well-known Chicana scholar called five women "lesbian terrorists" when they challenged the homophobia of people who refused them women-only space at a NACS workshop. Then there are the ubiquitous stories of Chicana/Latina scholars who aren't considered for tenure-track positions because they're out lesbians, or simply strong women.

"The struggle continues," Chicana feminist colleague Yvette Flores-Ortiz says. I know it does, but for once I'd like to see what would happen if *every* Chicana spoke her mind and stood up for her rights and embraced the fire and philosophy of "Xicanisma" that Ana Castillo, among others, speaks of in *Massacre of the Dreamers.* I fantasize about the changes we'd see: Chicanas in positions of authority working to redefine the theories and curriculum of the educational system; organizing for political empowerment, demanding and receiving validation for our voices and entitlement to our place in society, achieving equality in all arenas; and, at the very least, expecting sexual satisfaction. No longer would I see Chicanas putting up with the arrogance or insecure posturing of sexist men or the complicity to it by some of the women. I could go on.

Recently, I have witnessed some people making efforts to deal with their sexism, racism, and homophobia, in response to others' speaking up publicly about these issues at great risk to their friendships, their careers, and often their lives. I saw amazing things happen after people spoke up: heterosexual "vatos" speaking out against homophobia and sexism, lesbian women reading about love at a NACCS[1] conference, and heterosexual women publicly stating that from now on, they're going to be "Chingona Chicanas." On top of this, fire has ignited among many Chicanas. On the University of California's Berkeley campus in 1987, the anti-apartheid movement was in full swing. The students from Movimiento Estudiantil Chicano de Aztlán (MEChA), among others, had taken over the Chancellor's office. The police, about to storm in, issued a last call to the protesters to leave or face arrest. The men from MEChA agreed that they thought it best if the women left. So they yelled out, "All right, all the women have to go!" The women yelled back, "Hell no, we aren't going." They stood their ground, and when the police stormed in, all of them got arrested.

The national Chicana/Latina organization, Mujeres Activas en Letras y Cambio Social (MALCS), has just celebrated its twelfth anniversary. At the yearly summer institutes, the women meet, hold plenaries, and present papers on issues pertinent to Chicanas and Latinas in this country and through-out the world. One of the goals of MALCS is to teach and empower women to combine activism with scholarship. Other Chicana/Latina feminist groups have sprung up across the country, passing on some combination of business and lead-ership acumen. In the past few years, more published books and plays by Chicanas (and some Chicanos) portray the Chicana as an active agent, rather than as a superficial ap-pendage to a man.

The voices in this anthology continue the spark ignited more than twenty years ago by Chicanas demanding not just equality but entitlement. This collection of essays and perfor-mance pieces addresses Chicana consciousness, theory, and practice in ways not spoken of before. Many of the contribu-tors, including **Teresa Córdova**, in "Power and Knowledge: Colonialism in the Academy," present a cogent analysis of a system that favors those who quietly comply. **Deena J. González** has the courage to speak the truth in "Speaking Secrets: Living Chicana Theory," in which she gives an excel-lent critique of the "fallout" from being a Chicana feminista. While Deena focuses specifically on the experiences of intel-lectual practice and its complex interrelations, the subtitle of her essay, "Living Chicana Theory," presents an excellent title for this anthology, which I gratefully acknowledge.

The contributors write theory across various disciplines, yet seek to examine its coexistence with consciousness and practice. Their works verbalize and criticize our collective ex-perience in the context of the culture of Mexican descent, but go beyond criticism to attempt social transformation. **Sandra Cisneros** comments on how she sees women considered as expendable objects for the personal gain of others (usually men). **Emma Pérez** introduces us to her position as a "strategic essentialist," which she deems necessary because it "thwarts cultural and political suicide."

Yvette G. Flores-Ortiz addresses the necessity of and begins the process of creating a Chicana psychology in "Voices from the Couch." In "Chingón Politics Die Hard," **Elizabeth "Betita" Martínez** examines the disappointing continuation of male domination in the Chicana/o movement at a twentieth anniversary reunion. In a performance piece, **Alicia Gaspar de Alba** "interviews" Sor Juana Inés de la Cruz, a woman centuries ahead of her time, about her life and philosophies. **Cherríe Moraga** gives a compelling account of the life-and-death struggle she and her partner faced in the premature birth of their infant.

Lara Medina explores the evolution of religion from traditional practices to new Chicana spiritualities in "Los Espíritus Hablando," a series of interviews with Chicanas. My own essay presents recent reconstructions of La Virgen de Guadalupe by Chicana lesbians who challenge and change the classically defined images of her. **María-Socorro Tabuenca C**. writes as a *fronteriza* who elucidates the concept of the border in consciousness and location in the writing of Chicanas and Mexicanas from the El Paso-Juárez area. **Gloria Anzaldúa**, in her essay, "To(o) Queer the Writer—Loca, escritora y chicana," speaks about the overlapping, "multiplicitous" nature of identity as working class, Chicana, queer, and writer:

> I have the same kinds of problems with the label "lesbian writer" that I do with the label "Chicana writer." *Sí, soy Chicana,* and therefore a Chicana writer. But when the critics label me thus, they're looking not at the person but at the writing, as though the writing is Chicana writing instead of the writer being Chicana.

Yvonne Yarbro-Bejarano looks at the images conveyed by Chicana lesbian photographer Laura Aguilar, who "invites us to rethink/re-vision Chicano and its bodies." In this, she joins other artists and writers in theorizing and representing the queer colored body as part of the *we* that calls itself *Chicana/o.* Being different yet wanting to conform is examined in "Tomboy," a performance piece by **Mónica Palacios**, excerpted from *Deep in the Crotch of My Latino Psyche.* **Antonia I.**

Castañeda gives a cogent analysis of the history and politics of violence against women, and **Verónica Guerra** examines the evolution of the Chicana voice, in particular how that voice is represented as silent versus silenced. **Chéla Sandoval** explores the meaning of a politics of resistance and proposes "oppositional mestizaje" as a new coalition and method of resistance. **Norma Alarcón** speaks on the issue of *indígena* representation in relation to the racialized "Chicana" subject, and **Aída Hurtado**, in "The Politics of Sexuality in the Gender Subordination of Chicanas," chronicles the role of women in El Teatro Campesino and elucidates how intra-group sexism is structurally imposed in Chicano communities. **Yolanda Chávez Leyva** gives a poignant examination of the paradox of silence between families and their Chicana/Latina lesbiana daughters. **Barbara Renaud González** ends the book with "Mother's Day," a tribute to the shattered dreams of her mother.

This anthology seeks to construct theory, examine consciousness, and comment on its practice as *we* each see it, and not as it is seen, defined, or constructed by anyone else—especially the "daddies" in society who continually strive to tell us what to do and how to think. In this anthology, twenty-one women continue the process of validating our own existence and creating theory in new ways, through fiction, performance, lecture, and essay. In my call for papers, I asked contributors to submit essays that not only create theory but also address the secrets, inequities, and issues many of us confront in our daily negotiations with a system that often seeks to subvert our very existence. These essays take risks because they utter truths that many in the past have been too fearful to speak. It is my hope that the issues raised in this anthology will not only further the scope of Chicana theory but will also open a dialogue that is absolutely necessary if we are to make any real progress in the future.

Note

NACS is now called NACCS, the National Association for Chicana and Chicano Studies.

Power and Knowledge:
Colonialism in the Academy

Teresa Córdova

In the struggle to give voice to our experiences, working-class people of color encounter multiple mechanisms to silence us. More particularly, we encounter silencing when our voices speak of resistance to injustice–both against ourselves and our peoples. And yet, colonization is the historical legacy that continues to haunt us, even today. The ability to effectively promote justice requires vigilance so that we may immunize ourselves against the paralysis that comes from being silenced. The ideas in this essay provide me with strength to carry on in the face of efforts to suppress a voice which I know speaks "truth to power." My story takes place within academia, an arena that was targeted by the social movements of the sixties and seventies to open its doors to those who had previously been denied access. It is with these movements in mind that I proceed.

Power and Knowledge

Despite claims of universalist objective truth, power and knowledge are intimately connected. The University is a central location for establishing knowledge as a discourse of power, where the power to decide what is considered truth or not, is tied to the power to legitimate that truth (or nontruth). As Michel Foucault reminds us,

> Each society has its régime of truth, its "general politics" of truth: that is, the types of discourse which it accepts and makes function as true; the mechanisms and instances which enable one to distinguish true and false statements, the means by which each is

> sanctioned; the techniques and procedures accorded value in the acquisition of truth; the status of those who are charged with saying what counts as true. (Foucault 1977, 131)

It is important to remember, however, that this "régime of truth" is connected to class interests, where knowledge serves a legitimation function to maintain those interests, particularly those tied to the logic of capital. Enforcing a particular concept of truth, therefore, is intended to reinforce particular class interests. The University as an institution is a key arena where "legitimate" knowledge is established. While discourses of power may have qualities of constraint and repression, they are not, nor have they ever been, uncontested. Indeed, the process of determining what is "legitimate knowledge" and for what purpose that knowledge should be produced is a political debate that rages in the University. Our presence, as working-class people of color (especially women of color), in an institution which values itself on its elitist criteria for admission, forces the debates and challenges previously sacred canons of objective truth. Our presence, therefore, and the issues we raise, threaten the class legitimation function of the University. It is probably for this reason that our presence here is so complex—and so important.

Colonialism

I accept the assumption that "all relations are relations of power" (Touraine 1981), and am therefore analytically compelled to understand the dynamics of social relations as relations of power. This notion is compatible with the observation that the University is an arena of struggle over the definition of what constitutes legitimate knowledge and the legitimate function of the University. I am, therefore, interested in understanding the ways in which social relations within the University shape definitions of the University.

Using colonialism, or colonial relations, as a metaphor to understand relations within the University has made sense to me for a number of years, as I have observed, even within a single department, individuals who play the roles of colonizer or patron, missionary, overseer or gatekeeper, carpetbagger, and rebel. With the possible exception of the rebel, each is contributing to a system of exploitative relationships that exists within the walls of the "ivory tower." It is bold to speak of these relationships, since silence and compliance are so critical to maintaining them. It is in the course of speaking about them, however, that we learn even more about how and why they persist.

Colonial relations serve the exploitative needs of colonialism—to appropriate the resources of those they colonize, whether it be land, minerals, water, taxes, or people. While force is often applied to impose these unequal relations, ideology attempts to convince people of the appropriateness of their respective roles. Detecting the ideology of colonial social relations is a critical step towards changing them.

Thus, it is not sufficient to speak of identities of race, class, and gender, but we must also speak of identities towards power. To what extent does any one of us identify with the forces of domination and participate in relations that reinforce that domination and the exploitation that goes with it? Or conversely, do we identify with the efforts to reverse patterns of domination and seek instead, healthy, sustainable relations?

The challenge of these questions is even more critical as we move into an era of global restructuring that is bringing with it new and increased forms of exploitative relations. Increased social inequality and polarization characterize the restructuring economy (Morales and Bonilla 1993; Goldsmith and Blakely 1992; Ong, et al. 1994). The discussion here, therefore, is not purely academic, but suggests that the choices we make about how we will identify with power have far-reaching implications for our people.

Thus, I use colonialism as a vehicle to assess power relationships and to articulate how ideology functions to reinforce colonial relations of power within the academy. I rely a great deal on the work of Albert Memmi, who wrote *The Colonizer and the Colonized*. It was published in 1965, but still continues to offer some enduring and compelling insights.

The Academy

The University is an unfriendly place for us. The many issues that we encounter include our low numbers in the University, an ethnocentric curriculum, double standards, assumptions of our inferiority, harassment, unfair evaluations, lower pay, and bypassed promotions. These are our daily experiences and are reflected in our daily conversations. Further articulation of these issues can also be found in Joy James and Ruth Farmers's *Spirit, Space and Survival,* a book about African American women; *Broken Web: The Educational Experience of Hispanic American Women,* edited by Teresa McKenna and Flora I. Oritz, on Latina women; a special volume of *California Sociologist* edited by Gloria Romero and Lourdes Arguelles, on people of color in academia; and Patricia Williams's *The Alchemy of Race and Rights.* There is plenty to be read of people who express the pain of trying to survive in the academic environment. Retention literature also suggests that alienation, not incompetence, is the number one reason for students leaving the University. Leaving the University isn't our answer. The question is how can we stay and make it a better place for us to be. If we do it right, the University will not only be a better place for us but a better place. There are certainly others in the University who would also like it to be a healthy environment. These people are often our allies.

Alain Touraine (1981) writes about the shaping of society as "the self production of society." I think of the University in the same way, that is, the self production of the University. If one of the major functions of the University is a legitimation function, then it is important that we see the University as contested terrain and the process of construction of the University as an arena of struggle. Thus, I have chosen the topic "Power and Knowledge: Colonialism in the Academy."

Vehicle for Personal Survival

I came to these issues through personal experience and the struggle of being a working-class Chicana in the context of a hostile environment where I face pressure to define my way of being as inferior and to achieve success by obsessively imitating the colonizer in the hopes that he (often she) will accept me. Thus, this essay is an analysis of my survival, of my "roots and resistance" (Córdova 1994b). The following is my discourse of resistance and my refusal to accommodate. This is a momentary glance at my own process of freeing myself from the colonizer. Yet, more than personal struggle, it reflects the struggle of my communities and my connectedness to my communities. I write this paper knowing that it "crystallizes" many of the conversations we have had among ourselves: It is saying out loud what we have been saying to each other. It is an assessment of the process of conflict of the colonizer and the colonized–a "choreography of conflict" (Sennet 1981). It is the story of the entanglement of the patterns of colonial relationships. The breaking of this entanglement is necessary for the termination of colonialism.

My purpose, therefore, is to use metaphors of colonialist relations to describe power relations within the academy for the purpose of challenging those relations. Without that challenge, justice is impossible. I will address the colonizer's construction of the University, describe some colonial relations within the University, and then discuss the discourse of resistance and ways in which we can challenge colonial relations.

The Colonizer's Construction of the University

If we begin with the notion that the University belongs to the people whose taxes sustain it, then we can describe the hegemonic control of the University as usurpation, a primary feature of colonialism. The usurper, however, must convince himself as well as those from whom he steals of his legitimacy:

> How can usurpation try to pass for legitimacy? One attempt can be made by demonstrating the usurper's eminent merits, so eminent that they deserve compensation. Another is to harp on the usurped's demerits, so deep that they cannot help leading to misfortune. His disquiet and resulting thirst for justification require

the usurper to extol himself to the skies and to drive the usurped below the ground at the same time. In effect, these two attempts are inseparable. (Memmi 1965, 52-53)

It is no surprise, therefore, that the colonialist construction of the University involves the exaltation of the colonizer as superior and the rest of us who dare to enter its domain inferior. So much so that we are told that our very presence in the University has resulted in the diminution of its excellence.

There are at least three canons of the University that enable the colonizer to define himself as superior and therefore deserving of a privileged position within the University. Nagueyalto Warren refers to these icons as a "holy trinity of the ivory tower" (Warren 1993).

First in this trinity of icons is the notion of objectivism, which attempts to separate the "academy and that which it examines." Because of alleged detachment, "objectivity" is equated with accuracy. Defining one's perspective as "objective" suggests its unbiased and superior representation of truth. This is in stark contrast to any subjective interpretation. Thus, a dispassionate "objective" assessment of our experiences is presumably superior to the biased, subjective interpretation from our own point of view. The legitimacy to define our own identities is appropriated through the ideology of objectivity. Meanwhile, the University maintains its intimate connection to the military-industrial complex (Soley 1995).

A second academic icon is the "sanctity of the curriculum," which declares the centrality of the Western experience as the basis of legitimate knowledge. Literature, history, philosophy, and so on are viewed from a Eurocentric perspective that claims itself as universal while it disallows other epistemologies or cosmologies. The end result is a rationale for a white supremacist position and the legitimacy of certain ideas at the exclusion of others.

The third icon of the trinity is the "cry for standards." Every country club has its criteria for admission. The elite University is no exception. Research, however, has demonstrated the cultural bias of many of the so-called measures of excellence, exemplified by standardized tests such as SATs or GREs. Nonetheless, "minorities," in the battle for admission, are seen as below standard, ill-equipped to handle the University, the inferior being, the "other," who is without history, literature, or culture. Defining the standards of excellence from a Eurocentric perspective immediately builds in a systematic bias despite the claims of universal objectivism.

Adherence to the icons is the basis for rewards within the ivory tower. The "detached" scholar, of whatever color or class, who carefully abides by and promotes the canons of the ivory tower, is most readily rewarded with the status and privilege of a well-behaved steward of the system.

The construction of the University by the colonizer is actually the construction of the colonizer's superiority and therefore our inferiority. The sense of entitlement, using the standards of manifest destiny, allows the colonizer to define the standards of access to the University, the appropriate intellectual activity of the academy, and the basis for reward and recognition.

Choreography of Conflict Over the Icons

Entry into the academy by a critical mass of working-class people of color was paralleled by a conscious understanding of the importance and politics of our presence. The creation of Chicano, Black, Boricua, and Native American Studies and associations reflects this awareness. The Preamble of the National Association for Chicano Studies, founded in 1972, states the following:

> We recognize that mainstream research, based on an integrationist perspective which emphasized consensus, assimilation, and the legitimacy of societal institutions, has obscured and distorted the significant historical role which class conflict and group interests have taken in shaping our existence as a people to the present moment. Our research efforts are aimed at directly confronting such tenuous images and interpretations and challenging the structure of inequality based on class, racial, and sexist privileges in this society.

In shaping the form of this challenge, the Association holds that our research should generate information that can lead to effective problem-solving action. Our research should address itself to the pressing problems and issues affecting our communities. . . . Accordingly, the Association also recognizes the broader scope and significance of Chicano research. We must not overlook the crucial political role of ideas in the construction and legitimation of social reality. (NACS 1992)

Puerto Rican scholars reflect similar perspectives in their philosophy that shaped the formation of the Centro de Estudios Puertorriqueños at Hunter College in New York City. Statements reflect awareness of the history of colonialism in Puerto Rico, the conditions that gave rise to migration to the United States, an awareness of racism, and an awareness of the University as an arena of struggle. They state:

Departments of Puerto Rican Studies are not simply places of learning but new and valuable institutions for our community. We believe a proposal such as the present one must convey as lucidly and emphatically as it can the urgency of our need, the sacrifices that have been made to underwrite our emerging presence in the university and the seriousness of our purpose. To create new knowledge and quickly and comprehensibly transfer it to a long denied community is the principal goal of all our effort undertaken within the university. (Bonilla 1993)

Despite what seemed to be the promise of these disciplines, colonial relations within the academy continue to remain strong. The emergence of these perspectives and of our presence was met with an even more concerted effort to punish our defiance and obtain our compliance. We need to honestly examine the ways many of us have been brought "under control" and as a result, betray ourselves, our people, and the vision of a better world. Sometimes we unwittingly participate in our own demise.

Liberal Multiculturalism

Colonialist ideologies are often sophisticated in their subtleties. Ideologies of multiculturalism, "political correctness," and "preferential treatment" keep alive the "choreography of conflict" over the construction of the University. Who has access to the University, what should be taught, and who should be rewarded continue to be questions for debate.

Not everyone who complies with a system does so willingly or knowingly. There are many well-intentioned people who have responded to the demographic presence of "minorities" by calling for a pluralistic "harmony" and a tolerance of difference. Multiculturalism has been the banner for the consolidation of various Black, Chicano, and Native American Studies programs under the umbrella of ethnic studies, the rise of tolerance workshops; multicultural celebrations; and so forth. While one can see allies among the idealists who promote multicultural tolerance, research has already suggested the limitations of this approach (Duster 1995). More to the point, pluralistic naiveté tends to ignore the fundamental realities of power and hierarchy. Antonia Darder, a working-class Puerto Rican academic, states the following critique of multiculturalism:

> Most of the work that has emerged out of traditional theories of multiculturalism has simply replicated, albeit in a more sophisticated and evolved manner, a melting pot philosophy–a philosophy that is devoid of understanding or respect for the cultural integrity of subordinate groups and which is driven by an obsessive need to construct a false sense of social unity, without addressing the social conditions which have fueled intense cultural and class divisions in this country for almost 500 years.
>
> Lip service is paid to inequity, yet these theories do little to directly challenge or alter the existing relations of power that virtually remain unchanged. The consequence is that members of the dominant culture still retain the majority of decision making power in the world of multiculturalism and the discourse principally emanates from a Eurocentric world view. Meanwhile, the liberatory discourse of people of color continues to reside at the margins and is deemed as suspect by many mainstream intellectuals. (Darder 1991, 82)

Many are willing to tolerate cultural diversity to the extent that it does not disrupt the mythic harmony and unity. Raising difficult issues of domination/subordination is done by "difficult" people who make uncomfortable those who thought they had found refuge for their privilege in the rhetoric of "cultural diversity."

Charges of Balkanization and Infringement

Liberal education is founded upon the Enlightenment principles of reason, inquiry, and academic freedom. The alleged result is the objective pursuit of knowledge for the common good. Liberal multiculturalism, claim conservatives, replaces these values with ideology, closed mindedness, and the infringement of First Amendment rights. The alleged result is the fragmentation of an otherwise harmonious society. Naysayers of "multiculticulturalism" are lamenting the "illiberal education," the "closing of the American mind," and "the disuniting of America" (D'Souza 1991; Bloom 1987; Schlesinger 1992).

They charge the destruction of democratic foundations of the university, the Balkanization of America, and the tyranny of "political correctness." At issue is the question of how to deal with an increasingly diverse society. Ethnic and Women Studies programs, affirmative action, and so on are particularly targeted as destroying the foundations of liberal education and a democratic society. Worst of all, goes the argument, the imposition of "political correctness," racial preferences, and idiosyncratic curricula reflects an unreasonable obsession with race and nearly replicates the oppressive *ancien régime,* thus making it impossible to have a truly diverse society which comes from "unity." Included in their analyses are prescriptions for how diverse cultures should get along—a more conservative form of multiculturalism (McLaren 1994). They should get along, these conservatives argue, by submerging their identities and becoming "American."

Liberal multiculturalism, they worry, will replicate the recent conflicts in the Balkans where several distinct cultures were forced together for the purpose of an economic ideology, in that case communism. Does the argument against distinct cultural identities implicitly suggest that U.S. cultures should be merged together for the purpose of an economic ideology, in this case capitalism? Is the point, that liberal multiculturalism is bad for capitalism? In reality, this so-called unity came as a result of violent conquest. Allowing these "diverse" cultures (i.e., peoples of color) to remember their histories reminds us of their conquest, of their colonization.

In this sense, "Hispanic" is the colonizer's response to Chicano, Boricua, even Latino identities. Chicano identity reflects an understanding of 500 years of conquest, of connection to indigenous roots, and to dreams for justice. Puerto Rican identity recognizes the history of the island, the treatment of its "surplus labor" whenever its economic base was shifted, and the genocide of its indigenous people. The term Latino was created to bring together Chicanos, Puerto Ricans, and others whose similar history contributed to their socioeconomic position today. By identifying their similar histories, they establish a basis for mutual coalescence. The term Hispanic lumps groups together without articulating their histories. Their histories and cultures are no longer relevant as they are submerged into something called "Hispanic culture." Government agencies, marketing firms, and *Hispanic Magazine* are the definers of Hispanic culture. All of a sudden, everyone is Hispanic: Europeans, Sephardic Jews, white South Americans, and Filipinos. Chicano and Puerto Rican working-class identities are left out of this construction—and so are their histories. Indigenous and African roots are submerged in favor of Iberian ancestry. If the world has to deal with our "diversity," it is much easier to do so with the less-threatening, reconstructed identities as "Hispanics." Yet, in challenging this construction we are accused of imposing a "politically correct" ideology that is "narrowly nationalistic," while they continue to count the many "Hispanics" among their list of underrepresented faculty, staff, and students.

In expressing their concern that they are the victims of "political correctness," the colonizer is now the victim, afraid of the big bad people of color. It is the colonizer's rights that are being infringed upon when he is asked not to engage in cultural genocide, hate crime, hate language, and so on. Colonizer as victim constructs us as perpetrators. This is the redefining of our protest against racism, as the infringement on their First Amendment rights.

It is precisely these perspectives that make their way into campus debates via forums and campus newspapers. These are the debates of today. While the discourse may vary, the fundamental question of who and what has legitimacy within the University remains. These debates have the impact of shifting the attention away from the fundamental issues of power and hierarchy within the University. Through this conservative form of multiculturalism, the colonizer is frantically seeking to secure his authority as the noble protector of democratic ideals as he attempts to deny that the unity he claims we should embrace is based on violent conquest.

From Universalism to Postmodernism

While pluralists debate over issues of "diversity," postmodernists compete to define "difference." Postmodernists share with multiculturalists their search to reconcile their own identities with the asserted presence of third world people throughout the world. More to the point, "third world" peoples, or the "margins" (both are colonial constructions), have initiated the attacks on the so-called universal truth of the Western world. Nonetheless, postmodernists, in their effort to restructure meaning in an era of global restructuring, have inserted important theoretical challenges into Western discourse:

> Postmodern social theory has much to offer the critique of colonial discourse within educational research since it assumes the position that the age of modernism was characterized by the geopolitical construction of the center and the margins within the expansive hegemony of the conqueror: it is marked by the construction through European conquest of the foundational "I." (McLaren 1994, 182)

While postmodernists did not invent this critique of Eurocentric constructs, they have advanced the critique through their influence on debates within literary criticism, feminism, critical pedagogy, cultural studies, and, increasingly, other disciplines as well. Along with the critiques of modernism comes the notion that social "facts" are social constructions; social reality is mediated by one's positionality; that identity is tied to location (subjectivity); and that meaning is unstable and connected to the advanced capitalist construction of consumerism. Postmodernists are disturbed by the failed Enlightenment promise of autonomous action by individuals and the failed promise of agency of the "I." How, postmodernists wonder, can agency be restored without replicating injustices of totalizing universalism?

Postmodernist theorists are interested in deconstructing meaning as it relates to power relations in the era of advanced capitalism. Yet, for some, the emphasis on contextually shaped meaning and situationally shaped subjectivities does not leave open the possibility for a narrative that transcends individual narratives. In the effort to avoid oppressive declarations of the universal, we are left with multiple subjectivities. This relativism precludes the existence of "truth" and welcomes all subjectivities. All truths are equal. Thus, a new form of liberalism is born that makes impossible the establishing of a politics of liberation.

It's probably no coincidence that truth has been declared dead at a point when scholars of color, building on 500 years of indigenous, anti-colonial, civil rights, and nationalist ideas, are speaking "truth to power." This version of truth, the one that names the specifics of historical oppression, is granted permission to coexist with truths from other positionalities. *You may have your truth, and we will keep ours. But if you dare to challenge the relative nature of truth, that is, my truth, then I call you terrorist and threaten your existence in graduate school, indeed your life.* In other words, in this postmodernist construction of truth, universalism is replaced with relativism. Thus, they say, *We have no objective notions, all we have is relativist notions.* All truths are equal. A recent controversy over the interpretation of a short story exemplifies the point. *If you want to say that you think it's racist that a black man is depicted stereotypically as a rapist, that's OK, you can say that. But we don't think so. We need for you to accept that it is OK for us to say that it's not racist for a black man to be depicted as such. As long as we can agree that we have our relative separate truths, then we can live in harmony ever after.*

If we challenge further their interpretation, we are defined as infringing upon their free rights, their right to have an opinion. We then become defined as terrorists. And our lives, literally, and our ability to operate in the realm of academia become threatened. It's rather similar to the "political correctness" tactic of conservative multiculturalists. The bottom line is that many of them are so afraid of us, that they whimper at the sounds of our voices. In reality, our "difference" is more than they can bear. Relativist postmodernism is their effort to control our "difference" in order to maintain their comfort and privilege.

Another strand of postmodernism is more concerned with the transformative potential of restructured meaning. This "resistance postmodernism," as Peter McLaren calls it, includes the writings of allies like McLaren and Giroux; "postcolonial" and "subaltern" critics like Homi Bhabha and Gayatri Spivak; and people of color like Emma Pérez, Chéla Sandoval, bell hooks, and Cornel West. For them, the postmodernist agenda is to move beyond deconstruction to reconstruct liberatory meaning. For some, this progress has been slowed until the resolution of postmodernist dilemmas of the universalism versus the local. Interesting debates, but perhaps still fundamentally contoured by the discourse of domination. It still remains imperative that theorists engage in liberatory practice alongside those already engaged in such efforts, in order for theory to successfully reflect counter hegemonic meaning.

The ideological debates over "diversity" and "difference" stem from Western philosophical concerns, but are reflective of realities created by Western domination of the world. The ideological debates within the academy help inform our understanding of the power relations within its walls.

Colonial Relations: Colonizers Who Claim to Refuse

There are many in the University, including multiculturalists and postmodernists, who are capable of expressing their objection to the mistreatment of "minorities." In many cases, we find allies among this group. On the other hand, there are others who use this guise as a further means to exploit and/or control us.

There is a chapter in Memmi's book where he talks about the colonizer who refuses. I call this section, "Colonizers Who Claim to Refuse."

The Colonizer as Protector: Paternalism

> Whenever the colonizer states in his language that the colonized is a weakling, he suggests thereby that this deficiency requires protection. [It's for your own good.] From this comes the concept of a protectorate. It is in the colonized's own interest that he be excluded from management functions, and that these heavy responsibilities be reserved for the colonizer. (Memmi 1965, 81-82)

So for your own good, you don't need to be involved in the decision making: we'll take care of it for you and relieve you of the burden. We may often find ourselves in situations where, because of our lower status within the University, we are not allowed to participate—formally—in setting its policies. But we are told not to worry. *Trust us. You can't participate, but don't worry; you are our protectorate; we will take care of you; we will make sure things are done in your interest, though you don't have the right to sit at the table and be involved in defining that interest.*

Patron/as and missionaries will decide what is best for the "noble savage." An implication of this relationship is the assumption of inferiority of "the savage," who needs saving but isn't entitled to determine his/her future. This infantilization is not entirely unlike the Marxist assumption that sees us only as duped masses unable to think clearly and in need of vanguard intellectuals to lead us. They expect us to be grateful for their concern for us, and express shock when we don't respond accordingly.

In academia, we see the rise of missionaries, expressing their concern for "disadvantaged people," who get admitted into programs to study us; but the savages, with their "uneven" records, are deemed unqualified to enter the same program. We can barely stand the patronizing attitude with which they deal with us, so impressed with themselves, as they claim that "some of their best friends are 'minorities.'"

Academic Tourism: The Discovery and Appropriation of the Study of Race

The study of racial "minorities" is currently in vogue. Yet this supposed interest is paralleled by the erosion of Chicano, Native American, Puerto Rican, and Black Studies programs. This fascination with us may have its altruistic reasons but is often motivated by financial incentives and the opportunity to build careers from studying us. This academic tourism involves objectifying and commodifying us, even with the supposed concern for our subjectivity. It generally results in our being pushed aside as "ideological" and "political." Meanwhile the scholarship of people of color gets "replaced with more 'legitimate' voices who become the 'experts' called upon to speak on behalf–and instead–of disenfranchised communities" (Córdova 1994a, 243).

Antonia Darder describes this phenomenon as it relates to the concept of "border studies":

> Hence, the notion of "border crossing" supports the unentitled rights of a person from outside a cultural community to name and voice for that cultural community and to appropriate the knowledge without an actual understanding of the cultural genealogy that informs its meaning and intent. And all of this is done in the name of intellectual study, research, and theoretical discourse. (Darder 1991, 83)

Academic carpetbagging ignores our own articulations, including those used in the formation of our Studies programs. Old ideas get stated as new ones, but using language that serves to maintain privilege and hegemonic advantage. We even know of cases where Anglo faculty will use "minority" graduate students to collect data that they would not otherwise be able to obtain, and then turn around and deny that graduate student access to the data, even after it had been initially promised, calling it "mine." Stories of this kind of theft are rampant, as are stories about edited volumes of appropriated literature and poetry. This carpetbagging uses our plight to build their careers. Only rarely do we find a true ally.

In recent years, we have seen the proliferation of books

being written and edited about us and certain of our writers becoming acceptable "stars." Throughout, the colonizer controls the spigot and the establishing of the "experts" who define us. Foundations and think-tanks still find it easier to award money for policy analysis of our communities to both whites and nonthreatening "minorities." These people become ordained the "policy experts" who presumably have more understanding of our communities than the people who live there. Nonminorities and minorities who function as brokers need to honestly examine the assumption about the communities they are building their careers studying: To what extent does their privilege shape their analyses?

We need to beware of not only the colonizer who pretends to refuse but also the colonized minority whose primary motivation is to seek the approval and rewards of the colonizer. The colonial relationship between the overseer and the colonized is one of the more disturbing and insidious. We have been silent about it far too long.

The Confusion of the Colonized

The colonizer seeks our compliance and sometimes obtains our service. How is he able to convince us to support his agenda? He begins by trying to dehumanize us:

> What is left of the colonized at the end of this stubborn effort to dehumanize him? He is surely no longer an alter ego of the colonizer. He is hardly a human being. He tends rapidly toward becoming an object. As an end, in the colonizer's supreme ambition, he should exist only as a function of the needs of the colonizer, i.e., be transformed into a pure colonized. (Memmi 1965, 86)

> We should add that he draws less and less from his past. The colonizer never even recognized that he had one; everyone knows that the commoner whose origins are unknown has no history. (Memmi, 102)

> The most serious blow suffered by the colonized is being removed from history and from community. Colonization usurps

any free role in either war or peace, every decision contributing to his destiny and that of the world, and all cultural and social responsibility. (Memmi, 10)

The negation of who we are, our history, our past, and our culture leads to "internal colonialism," characterized by defining ourselves in the eyes of the colonizer. Once this self-hatred occurs, we respond by trying to prove that we're OK, to prove our acceptability:

The first ambition of the colonized is to become equal to that splendid model and to resemble him [the colonizer] to the point of disappearing in him. By this step, which actually presupposes admiration for the colonizer, one can infer approval of colonization. But by obvious logic, at the very moment when the colonized best adjusts himself to his fate, he rejects himself with most tenacity. That is to say that he rejects, in another way, the colonial situation. Rejection of self and love of another are common to all candidates for assimilation. Moreover, the two components of this attempt at liberation are closely tied. Love of the colonizer is subtended by a complex of feelings ranging from shame to self-hate. This fit of passion for the colonizer's values would not be so suspect, however, if it did not involve such a negative side. The colonized does not seek merely to enrich himself with the colonizer's virtues. In the name of what he hopes to become, he sets his mind on impoverishing himself, tearing himself away from his true self. The crushing of the colonized is included among the colonizer's values. As soon as the colonized adopts those values, he similarly adopts his own condemnation . . . Within the colonial framework, assimilation has turned out to be impossible. The candidate for assimilation almost always comes to tire of the exorbitant price which he must pay and which he never finishes owing. He discovers with alarm the full meaning of his attempt. It is a dramatic moment when he realizes that he has assumed all the accusations and condemnations of the colonizer, that he is becoming accustomed to looking at his own people through the eyes of their procurer. (Memmi, 121-123)

The confused colonized person, by accepting internal colonization, lives in fear of the colonizer's disapproval. To obtain this approval requires extreme caution in how s/he relates to the rest of the colonized. They deem it necessary to patrol the behavior of the colonized, hoping that s/he will not do or say anything to rock the boat; to carefully tread in our midst; or to simply avoid associating with anything or anyone potentially "controversial." The confused colonized can be described as one of three types: the enforcer (overseer), the impostor, or the wimp (i.e., the "chicken shit").

The Overseer

The confused colonized receives most rewards from the system when s/he enforces the colonizer's rules. In this case, our own people will accept the role of the overseer who demands compliance by the colonized of the rules of the colonizer. The overseer is embarrassed by the *rasquache* behavior of the colonized who refuses to imitate or to assimilate. The threat of this refusal elicits a brutal response by the overseer, who needs to justify him/herself to the colonizer while s/he defines the colonized as inferior. We can observe, therefore, the many confused prodigals who enforce the rules of the colonizer in their role of the overseer in the academy. These very people engage in a process of silencing. They police compliance, sometimes better than the colonizer himself.

When I first came to New Mexico, I was struck by the amount of racism, very blatant as well as subtle, on this campus. When I was commenting on the racism I observed *and* experienced, I was told, "Those of us who have been in New Mexico for a long time are used to racism." In other words, what she was saying to me was, *Why are you calling attention to something about which we are very comfortable?*

When I shared this story with another colleague, he just looked at me and stared. He then spoke about his experiences with racism, and with tears filling up in his eyes, he looked at me and said, "I can't get used to that. How can you get used to racism?"

For the confused colonized to say to me that those of us who have been here for a long time are used to it, she was saying one of two things: *I am colonized and like it that way,* or, *I am an overseer and am comfortable with the power and the privilege that come from my own colonizing situation.* It's the confused colonized becoming the colonizer.

Some of us become so concerned about receiving the approval of the colonizer that we even take on his job of enforcing the rules of the colonizer and get very involved in the policing of compliance. It is these very people who will say to us, *You are destroying harmony. We were fine until you started raising these issues.* In reality, it is their sense of comfort and privilege that we are destroying. It is also these overseers who are threatened by us and work hardest to define our refusal to accommodate as problematic. In some cases, they try to destroy our reputations and our careers, so desperate are they to hold on to their denial. The overseer works on behalf of the colonizer. We need to hold the overseers among us accountable—they are the ones we call the sell-outs.

The Impostors

The impostors are the ones who pretend they are our friends—when it is convenient for them. They walk among us when they feel it is safe, commenting upon our paraphernalia, smiling, nodding seemingly in agreement, using "progressive" phrases, and being nice to us when the colonizer and the other overseers aren't watching. But when it comes down to it, they will fight us on fundamental justice issues and on issues of inclusion and democracy. Ultimately, they will speak to us as though we are beneath them, reinforcing their sense of superiority over us. Their arrogance is on display only in the back room, as they continue their charade of friendship.

They don't stand with us on the tough issues: in fact, they too act as overseers and appropriators. While they are pretending to be one of us, they are setting themselves up to speak on our behalf and promote themselves as researchers of our resistance—again attempting to take away our right to speak for ourselves. In order to be one of us, they have to take risks and stop taking the easy way out. Writing about our resistance does not make them one of us. Until they take risks, they don't have the right to sit with us while we celebrate the victories of having spoken. They will sit with us while we celebrate, intruding on our union, and then return to sit at the colonizer's table, proud to be there. They are confused enough to believe that they can "play both sides."

The Wimps–or the "Chicken Shits"

Courage is difficult to find, especially in the context of re-pression. Undoubtedly, fighting for justice is exhausting. Cour-age, integrity, commitment, and forthrightness are necessary to fight for justice: but precisely because they are so impor-tant, ideology constructs these qualities as problematic. Lack-ing these qualities, the wimp is particularly intimidated by directness, regardless of the style in which that directness is expressed. The softest, most tactful voice still elicits trembling on the part of the wimp who is afraid s/he will have to take a stand. S/he hides behind the myth of neutrality, not knowing that the hottest place in hell is reserved for those who remain neutral in times of crisis.

It is impossible to engage in the struggle for justice with-out some sort of conflict. At a panel entitled "Chicana Stories from the War Zone," at the 1995 Conference of the National Association for Chicano Studies, Yolanda Broyles-González stated, "The war zone is where we live when we challenge injustice." Once we "take up residency in the war zone" we recognize that efforts will be made to discredit us, to discredit our legitimacy. We understand, nonetheless, that our efforts are important. While we take risks for justice, others hide.

In the same panel, Deena González made a point she makes so often (see also González 1991). Specifically, she chal-lenges those who refuse to be "out." She makes the point in relation to the closeted lesbians who remain silent while out lesbians do the work of interrupting homophobia and heterosexism. She also makes the point more generally about those who choose closet politics, while leaving the dirty work to those who are willing to be out. They are not covering our backs while they ultimately side with the colonizer through their fear to stand against him. On the contrary, Deena González argues, "We should speak about what we are, who we are, and what we stand for."

She and He Who Refuse to Be Colonized

One of the first things we need to do in order to refuse to be colonized is to detect the mechanisms by which they attempt to silence us. They attempt to define what constitutes legitimate and appropriate forms of resistance. When they tell us how to behave, they are using mechanisms to silence us, mechanisms to keep us from effectively resisting against our dehumanization.

Choosing Resistance over Silence and Compliance

One of the most empowering things we can do is articulate the mechanisms of silencing: the discourse of silencing, the discourse against giving voice, the discourse against resistance. We are told, for example, that we are *direct and confrontational,* that we are *difficult,* that we are *irrational, too emotional—too angry.* We are told we are disrupting harmony, and we are given blatant backlash for our resistance to the colonial situation. It is important to be vigilant and recognize when this form of ideology is operating. Chicana feminism, in my point of view, is the move away from silence, giving voice to our experience. More importantly, Chicana feminism is the refusal to participate in colonial activity.

Emma Pérez, in her wonderful essay "Sexuality and Discourse: Notes from a Chicana Survivor," expresses this point:

> The law of the white-colonizer-father conditions our world in the late twentieth century. Our challenge is to rebel against the symbol of the white father and affirm our separation from his destructive ideology to create a life-affirming *sitio.* But before defying the law of the father, it is necessary to understand why we are so stuck and so addicted to the perpetrator of destruction. Why do we uphold the law of the white-colonizer-European father, knowing the extent of damage and pain for Chicanas and Chicanos? (Pérez 1991, 169)

Chicanos impose these laws on Chicanas; middle-class Hispanics impose them on Chicanos/as; white women on women of color, heterosexuals, on lesbians and gays, and so forth. Pérez tells us we need to break the addiction to the patriarchal power that destroys us. We need to side with those who attempt to defy the social-sexual power of the patriarchy, rather than turn our backs on those who have the courage to resist. Indeed, we need to join that resistance to form a collective community that is free of the colonizer's power over us.

Strengthening Ourselves

We can refuse colonization by strengthening ourselves. The most common characteristic of being colonized is "rejection of self and love," which is "common to all candidates of assimilation." The love of the colonizer replaces the love of ourselves. "Love of the colonizer is subtended by complex feelings ranging from shame to self-hate." Internalized colonialism is really shame: it's self-hate. Colonization kills spirituality. "Colonization distorts relationships" (Memmi, 121). What we need to do is heal from the brutalities of colonization: We need to heal from the brutalities and pain of the University environment. Women of color writers speak loudly about a pain that we cannot ignore. We do a lot of damage to one another because of the colonized pain that we feel inside: the pain that tells us that we are not good enough, the pain that constantly drives us to seek approval from those that hurt us the most. We turn too much of this pain toward ourselves and one another. The stories are seemingly endless of how the spiritually sick among us are draining our energy and our efforts. The more we can do to strengthen ourselves, the more we can resist the colonizers' definitions of us. Let us assert ourselves with passion.

Internal strength and balance does not mean individualism. On the contrary, centeredness makes room for a collective spirit and the commitment to community and humanity. Too many of us are motivated only by what will benefit us personally, thus making it even easier to do the work of the master. Both selflessness and selfishness make us vulnerable to self-destruction.

Refusing Colonialism: "Thinking Globally, Acting Locally"

Colonialism feeds upon the brutalities against those it colonizes. We see these results in the faces of undocumented, segmented, and worn-out labor; residents of disinvested neighborhoods; mothers of children born without brains; under/ unemployed parents who can barely, if at all, sustain their families; alienated youth and adults addicted to alcohol, drugs, or violence. Global restructuring is making all these problems worse, making our resistance against this dehumanization all the more important. We can resist at every level: in our households, our workplaces, our organizations. As the Republicans force more decentralization of regulations and privatization of services, our local community involvement becomes more critical. We need to continue our earlier efforts to establish collective, truly democratic, humane ways of treating one another. Let us not confuse what is authoritarian and what is democratic.

Valuing Humanity and Community

Why is our presence such a threat to colonialism within the University? Colonialism feeds upon dehumanization. If we build local communities, where humanity and humanization is our main priority, then we can challenge the nature of colonialism and colonial relationships. "They" do not want us at the University because of the potential that we have to fundamentally change the nature of this institution. That is, to fundamentally challenge its foundation as an elitist institution that produces knowledge to maintain military-industrial conflicts, rich-white-male-elite power, and the maintenance of people of color in "their place." It is this potential that we need to build on: the potential of making the University a bastion of humanity, an arena where knowledge is disseminated and produced for the benefit of people.

Our strategy and our struggle against colonialism should be to replace it with the struggle for community. The University is set up to detach us from community–from our community and a sense of community. Part of humanization is to build community and all that involves. Building community opposes domination and injustice. In this effort, we can find allies and build coalitions. Coalitions become critical for our survival.

The Discourse of Resistance

This discourse of resistance requires that we redefine what constitutes legitimate resistance. All of the discourses of domination, including "political correctness," postmodernism, multiculturalism, and gatekeeping, are trying to determine what constitutes legitimate response, legitimate resistance. *We* need to take control of defining what constitutes legitimate resistance. The attacks on our Studies programs tell us that we have no right to insist that our history, our literature, our cosmology, our knowledge should be legitimate knowledge. "Political correctness" is telling us that we have no right to object to abuse, that we should shut up and take it. Accusations and divisiveness have charged that we are causing Balkanization as a way of saying that our legitimate existence is only through the eyes of the colonizer, through his definition: *Why don't you just accept what we call you? Why don't you just accept how we define you?* Rumors that define us as "irrational," "hard to get along with," "direct and confrontational," "difficult," "angry," or "fearsome" are methods used to define what is legitimate resistance. That is, it is the colonizer, and his overseers, who are most threatened by the act of speaking "truth to power." We cannot allow the colonizer, or those who serve him/her, to define what is appropriate resistance, for s/he shall always tell us to behave. They do the most outrageous things and then tell us how we are supposed to react to them.

We need to reinvigorate the ideals we expressed when we developed Chicano Studies. As we redefine what is legitimate knowledge, we must ask, For whom are we doing theory? When "theory is not rooted in practice, it becomes prescriptive, exclusive, elitist" (Christian 1990, 340). How we frame questions becomes important. Do we frame our questions in the literature for the purpose of "advancing" the literature, or do we reframe our questions in the community, based on the needs of those communities? We must develop methodology that allows for *our* subjectivity: involvement in our communities, not detachment. As Emma Pérez recently reminded us, our passion should be our motivation (Pérez 1995).

We need to challenge the notion of society as a whole, glued together by consensus or total domination, rather than in the process of being shaped. We need to avoid a discourse of victimization, another colonialist construction. Our history is more than elite behavior. In fact, part of redefining what constitutes legitimate knowledge is insisting on the inclusion of resistance as interactive with the forces of domination. Resistance has been a factor in the shaping of history. Our destinies are defined in interaction, that is, in an interactive process of conflict.

We've defined conflict as something that we should not engage in and thus leave it to others to take the risks—and the blame. Conflict is deemed pathological, problematic, destructive, and somehow exceptional. (Conflict certainly can be destructive when it is thoughtlessly done for the wrong reasons.) Conflict should be seen as central, as necessary: personally, theoretically, and politically. We are, in fact, warriors engaged in the ideological battle over the construction of knowledge. What we need to do is not reject that conflict but learn how to effectively engage in it. We need to embrace it—to see the rise, the development of knowledge and the University as a process and the shaping as the process of conflict. While we need to be selective about which conflicts we engage in (choose our battles), we need to be strategic about how we engage in them. Our role is to think of how we can strategically engage in that process of conflict, "tactical subjectivity," as Chéla Sandoval calls it (1991, 14).

All of this is ultimately for the purpose of humanization. The foundation of colonization is dehumanization. I believe our work here, our purpose here, is for the humanization of the University and making the University accountable to the community.

Note

This paper was originally presented at a Brown Bag luncheon at Women Studies, University of New Mexico, March 28, 1994. Excerpts were also presented at the Chicana panel, "Gender, Power, and Institutional Backlash: Chicana Stories from the War Zone," at the 1995 Conference of the National Association for Chicano Studies, Spokane, Washington, April 1, 1995. I wish to thank the many people who participated in the formulation of this paper. I especially acknowledge Miguel Angel Acosta for his incisive contributions.

Works Cited

Bloom, Allan. 1987. *The Closing of the American Mind.* New York: A Touchstone Book.

Bonilla, Frank. 1993. "Brother, Can You Paradigm?" Unpublished article.

Christian, Barbara. 1990. "The Race for Theory." In *Making Face, Making Soul: Haciendo Caras,* edited by Gloria Anzaldúa, 335-345. San Francisco: Aunt Lute.

Córdova, Teresa. 1994a. "Refusing to Appropriate: The Emerging Discourse on Planning and Race." *Journal of the American Planning Association* 60, no. 2 (Spring): 242-243.

___. 1994b. "Roots and Resistance: The Emergent Writings of Twenty Years of Chicana Feminist Struggle." In *The Handbook of Hispanic Cultures in the United States: Sociology,* edited by Felix Padilla, 175-202. Houston: Arte Público Press.

Darder, Antonia. 1991. "The Establishment of Liberatory Alliances with People of Color: What Must Be Understood." *California Sociologist* (in a special issue entitled *Culture and Conflict in the Academy: Testimonies from a War Zone,* edited by Gloria Romero and Lourdes Arguelles) 14, no. 1-2 (Winter/Summer 1991).

D'Souza, Dinesh. 1991. *Illiberal Education: The Politics of Race and Sex on Campus.* New York: Vintage Books.

Duster, Troy. 1995. "They're Taking Over! And Other Myths About Race on Campus." In *Higher Education Under Fire,* edited by Michael Bèrubé and Cary Nelson, 276-283. New York: Routledge.

Foucault, Michel. 1977. *Power/Knowledge: Selected Interviews and Other Writings 1972-1977.* New York: Pantheon Books.

Goldsmith, William W. and Edward Blakely. 1992. *Separate Societies: Poverty and Inequality in U.S. Cities.* Philadelphia: Temple University Press.

González, Deena. 1990. "Malinche as Lesbian: A Reconfiguration of 500 Years of Resistance" Plenary Address at the 1990 conference of the National Association for Chicano Studies, San Antonio, Tex. Later published in *California Sociologist* (in a special issue entitled *Culture and Conflict in the Academy: Testimonies from a War Zone,* edited by Gloria Romero and Lourdes Arguelles) 14, no. 1-2 (Winter/Summer 1991).

James, Joy and Ruth Farmer, eds. 1993. *Spirit, Space and Survival.* New York: Routledge.

McKenna, Teresa, and Flora I Ortiz, eds. 1989. *Broken Webs: The Educational Experience of Hispanic American Women.* Encino, Calif.: Floricanto Press.

McLaren, Peter. 1994. Preface by Paulo Freire. *Critical Pedagogy and Predatory Culture: Oppositional Politics in a Postmodern Era.* New York: Routledge.

Memmi, Albert. 1965. *The Colonizer and the Colonized.* Boston: Beacon Press.

Morales, Rebecca, and Frank Bonilla, eds. 1993. *Latinos in the Changing U.S. Economy.* Newberry Park, Calif.: Sage Press.

National Association for Chicano Studies (NACS). 1992. Preamble to *Critical Connections between University and Community,* edited by Teresa Córdova. National Association for Chicano Studies.

Ong, Paul, Edna Bonacich, and Lucie Cheng. 1994. *The New Asian Immigration in Los Angeles and Global Restructuring.* Philadelphia: Temple University Press.

Pérez, Emma. 1991. "Sexuality and Discourse: Notes from a Chicana Survivor" in *Chicana Lesbians: The Girls Our Mothers Warned Us About,* edited by Carla Trujillo. Berkeley: Third Woman Press.

____. 1995. "Technologies of Desire." Plenary Address at the 1995 conference of the National Association for Chicano Studies; Spokane, Wash., March 30, 1995.

Romero, Gloria and Lourdes Arguelles, eds. 1991. *California Sociologist* (special issue entitled *Culture and Conflict in the Academy: Testimonies from a War Zone*) 14, no. 1-2 (Winter/Summer).

Sandoval, Chéla. 1991. "U.S. Third World Feminism: The Theory and Method of Oppositional Consciousness in the Postmodern World." *Genders* 10 (Spring): 1-24.

Schlesinger, Arthur M. Jr. 1992. *The Disuniting of America: Reflections on a Multicultural Society.* New York: W.W. Norton and Company.

Sennet, Richard. 1981. Foreword to *The Voice and the Eye*, by Alain
Touraine. Cambridge: Cambridge University Press.

Soley, Lawrence C. 1995. *Leasing the Ivory Tower: The Corporate
Takeover of Academia*. Boston: South End Press.

Touraine, Alain. 1981. *The Voice and the Eye*. Cambridge: Cambridge University Press.

Warren, Nagueyalto. 1993. "Deconstructing, Reconstructing, and
Focusing Our Literary Image" in *Spirit, Space and Survival*,
edited by Joy James and Ruth Farmer. New York: Routledge
Press.

Williams, Patricia J. 1991. *The Alchemy of Race and Rights: Diary of a
Law Professor*. Cambridge: Harvard University Press.

Speaking Secrets:
Living Chicana Theory

Deena J. González

Speaking secrets is never easy. In many cultures, it is considered bad form because secrets stigmatize families and community, separate one from loved ones, and leave bad impressions . . . "What makes Chicana lesbian feminists 'unattractive,'" one colleague whispered conspiratorially to me–because I pass as a Chicana femme, "is that they keep talking too damn much about who they are, what they want, and how they want it. Enough!" Below, I address the politics of comfort and the revelations of discomfort that permeate our Chicana feminist discussions nationwide. I am not entirely convinced that revealing secrets or describing them is a good strategy or even necessary, but I feel that if we are to change the institutions of higher learning in this society, spaces need to exist for new dialogues borne in feminist praxis, women-of-color discussions. I am equally uncomfortable discussing some of these issues only in a national, and not an international or global, context. It is their insidious nature nationally that keeps us from focusing attention on similar situations globally. But I do it because I trust that out there listening may be some thinkers and artists who can translate these kinds of remarks into a new political/activist agenda and because Chicanas–one of the most severely underrepresented groups in the professoriate–will recognize the value of new languages and a better discourse community.

Many Chicana feminists have assessed difference, usually as explorations of the boundaries or conflicts lying between majority or minority voices. A theme unifying these essays, reports, and manifestos across the three decades of their creation is the presumption of a united Chicana feminist voice and the marked absence of (named) differences among Chicanas. The avoidance of such topics as tension, contradiction, ambivalence is unsurprising, considered in the context of oppression, of hegemony, of colonization, or of our fragile condition in the apparatus of the university. Examples or evidence of our marginalization abound: fifteen Chicanas hold Ph.D.s in the discipline of history, three in economics, five in anthropology, ten in political science, and many of those degrees were received across a span of two recent decades. Our situation in the academy is not improving radically or rapidly. Chicana feminists explain some of the causes as structural or institutional, others as attitudinal and historical. Regardless of origin or impact, however, the evident lack of a major presence in the research environment also shapes the feminist debates surrounding difference.

Differences among Chicana feminists split recognizably along familiar seams: separatists and non-, lesbian/feminist and non-, male-identified and non-, tenured and non-, and working-class or non-. To explore all of the ruptures would be difficult because evidence for many is based on hearsay, anecdote, gossip, and innuendo; below, however, I argue that each of the divergences marks a special place along the road of accommodation within academic environments as Chicanas have sought to craft an identity built on the contrary historical principle of sameness and on the contemporary (uneasy) recognition of differences.[1] Our contradictions are really thus not as alarming or unusual as institutions might have us believe, but they are likely to worsen before they improve.

Chicano scholars have usefully depicted the role of stagnation and dissension, of tension and acrimony, among students, politicians, and other groups, linking these trends to the "ultimate" failure of the movement or group.[2] This is one of the first pieces to suggest that Chicana feminists, too, display a wide range of group ideologies and identity politics, positive for some, negative for others–"lesbian terrorism" as one of our dissenting colleagues labelled a particular form of intervention during one of our National Association for Chicano Studies (NACS) conferences. In the face of an historically stipulated or manufactured unity, as *la causa* or *el movimiento* (the [la]she/[él]he dyad) required, many have recognized that cohesiveness based on shared academic purposes is unachievable.[3] But this essay or document seeks to understand differently; difference, that is, not as group dynamics but as a measure of the vast gap between image and reality, or past and present, and as a system for recognizing and reorganizing behaviors and values that do not now fall—and perhaps have never fallen—neatly into manageable categories of analysis.

The charge of lesbian terrorism is an interesting case in point because it was made after the annual meeting of NACS where only four Chicana lesbians were presenting papers and a tiny group (fewer than fifteen of the nearly one thousand registered participants) charged the Association with specific acts of homophobia. Other than a panel at the Riverside Conference in 1981, no other gay/lesbian-content panels had ever appeared at NACS. Doubt about the debate, about the accusations and negative interpretations of their signficance, at the 1990 conference continue to haunt the Chicana lesbian feminist participants, particularly those who feared being "outed." The result was a stifling of dissent, a loss of consideration for jobs ("We hear she doesn't get along with other Chicanas" was a charge levied against my application for a job), accompanying the more generalizable, but still painful, recognition that the Association needed remediating.

What happened at NACS in April 1990, in Albuquerque, was a necessary disrupture in the process of implementing a Chicana feminist process in the academy and community, and deciphering it here suggests the need to plot it historically against other divergences. As professors Alma García and Teresa Córdova have described in previous separate pieces, a process within the Chicano Studies Association had begun unraveling after 1982, when Mujeres en Marcha, a UC Berkeley group of graduate students plus one lonely assistant professor, organized a panel addressing sexism in the Association (or Ass-ociation, as many of us fondly recalled).[4] Several barriers had been removed along the way since then, many thought by 1990, and perhaps gays and lesbians could anticipate a more senisitized audience, capable of dealing with lesbian separatism, lesbian feminism, lesbian-identified politics. After all, a NACS conference in 1984 was dedicated to Voces de la Mujer: but at that gathering and subsequently, little organized lesbian participation existed. One problem originated in the title of the conference on women, chosen by many Chicanas as well as Chicanos: The depiction of "woman" in the singular, and the pedestal-creation tone of tracts that continued to abide the male authority ("la" Chicana, "la" mujer, in which, as many Chicana lesbians notice, "she" usually signifies the heterosexual, preferably maternal, woman) suggested an unpleasant remedy to NACS's institutionalized sexism and homophobia. Which Chicana exactly did the conference have in mind? Certainly not its Chicana lesbian activists.

Seven years later, the same contentious 1990 conference featured Emma Pérez's famous plenary on Chicana sexuality from a lesbian perspective, but the Ass-ociation stood ready to defend the rights of all its participants, especially homophobes, suggesting that lesbian voices could be used and even heard, but that our bodies were another matter. Remarkably, our allies were few and the hostilities vented, many. In that conference, men declared that a workshop which did not allow men (lesbian-organized and on homophobia) should be forced to disband, presumably by men pounding at the door.[5]

The threatened action came as a shock to the lesbian organizers of the panel/workshop, who had never seen so much academic interest in lesbian feminism from the men of NACS. The workshop went along without external disruptions; not lost on lesbians was the point that the male-identified women and closeted lesbians in the audience themselves assured, in fact, a set of public contestations where the real issues—to be in or out of the closet—were subsumed to dialogue peppered with heartfelt (but missing-the-mark) statements like, "I like to think that I try to treat all people fairly . . . ." The internal antagonisms stemming from ambivalences about the tone of the discussion made clear the point that among a pluralism of feminist expression, some types of feminism, some types of lesbian rhetoric and analysis—especially the quiet kind—were to be abided, and others not.

Psychologists currently working on data collection among communities of color might well evoke their concept of "idioms of distress" to understand these next reflections about Chicana feminist expressions in NACS.[6] In the same Albuquerque conference, a panel of six Chicanas presented for the first time an organized review of Chicana feminist presence in the Ass-ociation. No lesbians were mentioned, and when I raised the issue against the context of erasure and invisibility, as well as our decided if unacknowledged presence (my own, Emma Pérez's, Gloria Anzaldúa's in Ypsilanti in 1983, and so on), the silence and awkwardness were apparent. One panelist determined, "Well, we really fucked up," while another's response was, "I did have comments here in the margins, but because of time . . ." The irony that some of the panelists appropriated gay/lesbian/queer discourse to describe Chicana feminists as "coming out of the closet" would not be lost on the critics of the panel and its implicators. Referenced were such groups as the Colectiva, a Berkeley Chicana collective of the late 1970s, and Mujeres en Marcha, another Berkeley Chicana/Latina organization of the early 1980s. Each of those groups had a lesbian presence and sustained a specifically woman-identified ideology at certain key moments in their histories, but this was lost to the NACS presenters examining the history of Chicanas in the Ass-ociation. In an extended commentary, I issued the suggestion that such panels attempt next time to incorporate a "sexed" analysis of the important contributions Chicanas had made to the organization itself by looking closely at the ideological representations as well as the particular presence of lesbians and bisexual women in NACS. I argued that sexuality was still operating at the border of the holy trinity most Chicana scholars deployed: race, class, and gender or sex. My commentary was not particularly well-received, nor was my analysis appreciated. In fact, I received mail from many Chicanas who were puzzled by the depth of hostilities expressed and the multitude of anxieties unleashed when some were "challenged to confront homophobia." All were marked by a concern to "move beyond" this painful stage.[7]

As the cliché would have it, things merely worsened. At the MALCS meeting held in the summer of 1990, at UCLA (the Mujeres Activas en Letras y Cambio Social organization hosts its annual meeting on a university campus each summer) similar issues surfaced, and included this time the difficult negotiation of a white woman's presence on a panel. (White women are not excluded from MALCS, but are asked to respect the panel spaces as workshop or working zones for women of color; they are invited to the plenary sessions or public sessions). The organizing/site committee for the conference specifically requested that the white woman be informed of this policy and invited to the public session, but the MALCS site coordinator instead chose to follow the advice of the University's attorney and of other staff by including the woman as presenter. When several MALCS members stood outside the session and informed the white woman as well as the other participants of the subtle but important difference between attendance and presenting, between public sessions and workshops, many registrants became uncomfortable and began discussing MALCS's "exclusionary" tactics.

The points of view escalated so greatly that by the end of the day, rumors were flying that the participants were being "terrorized" by [mad/raging] feminists who wanted to declare MALCS a "woman-of-color-only" zone. This was not exactly the case, because the Institute, as it is frequently called, receives university support, and cannot in any technical sense, then, refuse to admit anyone. The organizing site committee had, however, attempted to follow the bylaws and work within them. Too few Chicanas yet understood the matter of our colonization and of what would happen if MALCS were to open its doors to white women, all men, or all women of color. The bylaws stipulated that women of color could present their work in panel, workshop, or artistic fashion, and register for the entire conference, *and* that men respect these guidelines by attending only the larger, public sessions. Lesbians and women-identified policies were called out of order by many of the attendees, and many missed the point about the need for a space freed from male and white gazes.[8]

The impact of the gaze was not a literature many Chicanas at MALCS knew, although we could say that the material condition of the gaze was in fact "known." Many at the conference attempted to explain the issue as approach, position, politics, or policy, and the business of explanation itself became wrapped up in the need to "reach undergraduates," an issue that was under much discussion even in the conference planning. MALCS originally had been conceived as a space for newly completed Ph.D.s, Chicanas/Latinas in the academy, with a decided focus on the survival of faculty. Subsequent to the UCLA conference, the focus of MALCS changed toward undergraduates, with faculty attending not to work with one another but to reach across areas. Because I came from an undergraduate teaching college, this became one of the reasons I would eventually decide to leave MALCS. My concern up to that point had been to organize Chicana faculty, and I had worked to recruit into the academy over thirty Chicana/Latina undergraduates in intensive, individual contact at Claremont and throughout the country, in speeches, at conferences, in meetings, and as a reviewer of undergraduate fellowship applications. Several Chicana faculty in MALCS claimed to share the same view, but none voiced this viewpoint at the UCLA meeting.

Since the beginning, coincidentally, MALCS had been under pressure to justify its stances, and the summer workshop of 1990 remained true to that history. The chagrin of a visitor from México had been evident some years earlier when the issue of women-only space had surfaced at a business and by-law meeting in Davis, California: She explained how startled she was to hear us debating this theme (*tema*) in 1988, when in Mexico City a decade before no one had disputed the need for their group's autonomy (from men). At that gathering in 1988, the lesbian feminists deduced that MALCS's members were not yet interested in detailing a women-only site, much less a Chicana/Latina-only site.

The responses of many MALCS attendees suggested that Chicanas were still uncomfortable in women-only or women-of-color-only zones. Afraid to be labelled "separatist," their arguments masked nicely the basic homophobia that also dominated the discussions. The real fear, Emma Pérez, Antonia Castañeda, and I argued, lay in the charge of "lesbianism," conceived of, in this context, as ideology and not entirely as sexual practice or performance. Some would call our policies and politics acts of aggression subsequently within the MALCS Summer Institute. That conceptualization permeated all of the workshops and brainstorming sessions that sought to "make right" the so-called exclusion of one white woman. So much attention to the presence of one person threatened momentarily the existence of the entire organization, and our fragility in the academy was clearly specified by these discussions; the bulk of the rhetoric focused on questions like "What are we going to do . . . become like South Africa with an apartheid system?" or "Why can't we all just respect our differences?" These questions, I offer, suggested the extent and range of our colonization as they sought for an erasure of differences or a denial of them through the liberal dogma of "treating people well." The white woman involved–some might say "trapped"–by *our* process threatened and initiated later a grievance against MALCS, despite receiving a letter of apology from the MALCS chair.[9] Only the gallant efforts of a number of feminist scholars at UCLA who understood the significance of the stand taken saved the organization from a lawsuit. Today, the ideology and praxis might not be so readily supported because concepts like "reverse" discrimination or racism permeate the academy and academics are specifically fearful of these charges.

The events at MALCS and in NACS in the 1980s and 1990s suggest an interesting development in the bumpy demarcations that map Chicana feminism as it appears on the conference scene over the past two decades; multiple interests have been raised and discussed at each juncture. No group or set of groups emerges feeling elated or at ease. Dis-ease is, in fact, rampant. These remarks serve to decipher the meanings embedded in the discomforts of the present, and offer some possible hope to the matter of living a problematized Chicana, lesbian/feminist identity, recognizing that those who are most outspoken will suffer academic ostracism, and worse.

I am aware that I write this in a decade when Chicano student nationalism, indigenism, and heterosexism appear again to be increasing. Although Chicano scholars have called nationalism abiding and important, even necessary, a sustained critique of its explicitly misogynist and homophobic tradition has yet to be made. My concern arose about the strong linkages between the silencing of women and nationalist Chicano politics again while speaking at conferences like the one in 1992 at California State University, Northridge, where a group of Chicana feminists organized around an incident with the Theta XI fraternity who had passed around and sung a song called "Lupe's Song," a truly offensive document that has been circulating in the manuals of some fraternities at the Berkeley and Davis campuses of the University of California for over two decades. The song is a diatribe against Mexican women, pulling out as it does every offensive stereotype we live with— "Mexican whore," "hot-blooded, cock-sucking," is in one stanza; "she finished her life in a welter of sin" is another line; and at the end of the so-called song, Lupe is dead in her grave, her body being consumed by maggots, and still, the initiates sing, she is "crying for more." Chicanos and Euro-American administrators were united in their misunderstandings of the significance of such aggressions against Chicanas/Mexicanas. Objectified in this way, Lupe had become, for the Chicana students on the campuses who launched protests against this racist misogyny, their mothers, grandmothers, sisters, and cousins.[10]

Similarly, we have much to fear from some of the new brand of Chicano nationalism that floats across universities these days. At the University of California, Santa Cruz, a Chicana activist was raped by several Chicanos who claim to be all for Aztlán. The details of that, as well as the muggings of Chicanas at UC Davis and at UC Irvine have yet to be told, but it is clear that Chicana undergraduate activists have cause to be alarmed for their safety on campuses, especially when they speak out against Chicanos or against the white fraternities. A few years ago, another Chicana graduate student at UCLA was the victim of an obsessed Chicano professor from another University of California campus, and despite legal counsel, evidence including lovesick messages penned on official University stationery, as well as notes delivered through florists, she could do nothing to keep the man away from her until her lawyer threatened legal action. The harrassment began when she discussed job possibilities on the campus where he taught; he pursued her, following her into the classroom. The University of California, Riverside, chose not to pursue the charges, despite the evidence and meetings with several Chicana academics. At Arizona State University, a grievance against a visiting Mexicanist was launched by a student, but stopped when he returned to his home campus. From the University of California, Santa Barbara, students called recently, at the annual meeting of the National Association of Chicano

Studies in Spokane, for an investigation into a professor who was charged (but never convicted) of sexual harrassment/assault at an Ivy League school where he was visiting. Student newspapers report these "incidents" regularly, as they do date rapes and other assaults, but few cases are ever heard and most are suspended.[11] We could continue with the evidence, much of it "unsubstantiated" in the actionable sense of the word, but passed from Chicana to Chicana, campus to campus.[12]

The link between woman-hating and woman-bashing is today stronger than ever, and I raise it because it must also serve as our basis for new forms of confrontation and solidarity. Within our ranks, we have problems, and outside of our communities, we face many of the same hostilities Mexican women faced in the nineteenth century and indigenous women have faced since Europeans first landed on these lands. Rape, battery, abuse, and violence are aspects of the vicious cycle of conquest and colonization, and they affect us daily in the institutions where we reside. Women who refuse the favors of men, or resist sexual harrassment, have been labelled "frigid" and subjected to harsh reviews and public criticisms. One Chicana wrote a work reviewed by a senior Chicano colleague, someone the author had rebuked, and the review labelled her "a poor scholar." All she could do was to ignore the review, but she never stopped thinking that the criticism was based on more than her scholarship.[13]

Suggestions on Woman-Identification

Billy Tipton, who passed through his life mostly as a man but was biologically/genitally a woman, and countless others before him/her, offered in death a message about life's ironies and inconsistencies. Tipton's wife claimed to reporters that neither she nor their adopted sons knew that he was "genitally" female. FTMs and MTFs provoke re-readings of the gender and sexual codes, occasionally of the racial idiom: Catalina de Erauso in the fifteenth century passed as a man to fight in a war, and soldaderas in the Mexican Revolution changed their appearances or inverted their gender or sex. Mostly, the

early twentieth-century warriors adapted their dress or presentation to suit their purposes and reverted to the traditional
codes when ordered or upon returning home.[14]

Transexuals and transgendered personalities and activists,
as well as transvestites, offer an interesting counter-discourse
to the entire issue of identification because they evidence how
so much of sexual–like cultural or racial–identification is encoded, hidden, masked, learned, and "achieved." Ultimately,
the transgendered suggest, sexual orientation and sexual identity can be said to be acquired, conceded, or performed.[15] Contemporarily, non-transgendered Chicana activist/feminists argue tenaciously–because the odds against our cultural and racial self-identification are historically stacked to begin–that
our identity cannot be so easily shed or willfully adopted.
Despite some access to hair dyes, skin treatments, plastic surgery, and so on, few Chicanas can mask their physical appearances to "pass" as non-mixed-race people. Those who can
frequently go on to adopt other outer-defining characteristics,
clothes and hairstyles especially, to distinguish themselves from
the Euro-American crowd. Sexual orientations are different
that way, because some can indeed be rearranged, and the
legacy of such rearrangement enjoys a long, interesting, and
whimsical history. Sor Juana Inés de la Cruz asked her mother
to cut off all her hair and requested to be sent to the university
disguised as a boy.[16]

But even identification as Chicana has been adopted by
some late in life. Just as gay/lesbian is not an identity "raised
into," Chicana is a cultural identity rarely fixed in early childhood. One Chicana lesbian writer, who achieved fame in the
1980s, actually came to her identity as a Chicana in the course
of her writings in that same decade. Although many would
have us believe that the term Chicano/a acquired its popularity in the 1970s, many Chicana feminists did not even begin
to deploy it until much later. This, naturally, caused older activists dismay. Chicanas struggling within Chicano organizations in the 1970s, as students, workers, and activists, wondered where these same spokespersons had been all along in
the period of "repression," as one has categorized the post-
1960s era.[17] While it is easy for scholars new to Chicano Studies to dismiss these questions as "nationalistic" or to suggest

that the inquisitors are evoking a more-Chicana-than-thou attitude, the point is missed that the interrogations bear relationship to matters of trust and to historical memory—in a way to making the secret public. To say that Chicano identity today is fluid and changing, or always has been, and that it should be understood unbound by categories of authorization politics, can be liberating, but not necessarily for those who have borne witness to a struggle of survival and now, see a concomitant appropriation of that heritage.[18]

Some Chicanas/os who have renamed themselves in previous lives used their Anglicized names or refused to accent their appellation, to demonstrate their mainstream allegiances. Others in the process of self-discovery returned to their family names, while some shed their given identities (the custom of switching a "Juan" to "John" was popular especially in Catholic schools in the 1950s). Gloria Anzaldúa's rejoinder in *Borderlands*, the fear of losing identity or misplacing it, thus is laced with an understanding of this history of being misnamed.

Granted, experimenters against tradition, many activist Chicanas recognize, have historically been ostracized and scrutinized as defilers of their traditions, dismissed entirely or expunged from the historical records. Still, the most acerbic among us also raise the spectre of people's newfound identities as evidence of a culture willing to accept without scrutiny spokespersons whose messages suit the (mostly capitalist and still neocolonialist) agendas at hand; liberals and women who teach Euro-Americans about racism are particularly welcome in the "multi-culti" agendas of the moment. A pluralist multiculturalism thus emerges, but one still not missing its ironies or contradictions and dismissive of radicals just the same. One minute Richard Rodríguez (self-pronounced, Raw-dree-guess) is an ordinary American; the next, a Mexican-American starving for lack of memory or feasting at the scholarship trough—not as a man but as a "scholarship boy." People of color do indeed need to concern themselves with infantilization, but not of this variety. Rodríguez remains boy or son, and adulthood eludes him. This is perhaps the saddest testimony of our times for a man whose mestizaje abides his history.[19]

Perhaps some identities can be more readily outgrown than

others, but neither Tipton nor Rodríguez offer us happy news in this regard; each live(d) through their respective fantasies, but do they really "escape" history? The question suggests an exploration of racial history and of what women-of-color scholars now identify as an important ingredient in identity studies, the significance of racial memory. The theorizing suggests this: as we are sexed, we are also raced, historically, materially, concretely.[20]

Historically, in Mexican societies, female identity coexisted with racial/cultural identities that fluctuated, remained unsettled, but were rarely articulated. Femaleness tended to be situated and fixed in paradigm dramas of medieval and post-medieval periods: Virgin, martyr, witch, whore were the points on a quadrant within which women's behaviors, attitudes, images, even values and beliefs, were plotted. Daughter, mother, grandmother, and widow were kinder, if utilitarian and realistic, affectional plottings of the same. But disjunctures occurred: in 1519, Malintzin Tenepal, the woman of many names—Malinche, Malinalli, Doña Marina—spawned new myths. Where did this linguist/diplomat belong? She became symbolic for a reason. Across the centuries, Native/indigenous, mestizo/mulatto, criolla women of Mexico aborted traditions, becoming emblematic in ways that historians have only recently explored. Their journeys of survival, like ours of discovery or recuperation, are crucial because through them Chicana identities contemplate a fluid history unlike that which the earlier paradigms allowed.[21]

Female identity and racial or ethnic identity operated together historically, as they do today, but this does not mean (then or now) that they are permanently conjoined. Class and social location shaped these identity formations, and women were as bound in the past as we are today by structures and ruling ideologies, even when we try to acknowledge class privileges. Who we are as women, as lesbians, as feminists, as Chicanas, or as Latinas of many mixed backgrounds, suggests Gloria Anzaldúa, should not inhibit our working together, but by the same token, we cannot continue to pretend that we agree on things or that the world treats us all the same. Color, dress, speech, our writing, our art, our service all mark us differently, and some few of us walk the world in privilege while many, many others get dismissed, depreciated, or disciplined. Control of language—in this case, still, English—assists mobility, geographic, sexual, and economic. This is why writers like Emma Pérez, Cherríe Moraga, Alicia Gaspar de Alba, and Gloria Anzaldúa (listed backwards alphabetically by surname, simply to demonstrate the point), become so crucial to the project of painting a Chicana identity. The ability to speak, think, and work within the English language, and to do it well, finally provided a ticket into mainstream/hegemonic feminism.[22] The contradictions of in/out/or shadowspaces remain, as they did in 1980, when a group of Latina lesbians in San Francisco quibbled with the authors of *This Bridge Called My Back* around issues of appropriation and visibility. "So that they never again can say that we do not exist." was how one supporter of the anthology put it, when questioned about the racial and sexual politics of the underwriters of *Bridge. Bridge* and other volumes, including *Compañeras, Haciendo Caras,* and *Chicana Lesbians,* magnified the dilemmas of a situated policy of identity, while they also made, indeed, the invisible, visible. And the debate raged throughout the 1980s as Latina lesbians of the Bay Area revealed in a survey that they were uncertain whether more exposure or revelations truly "made any difference."[23]

The Latina lesbians I interviewed (who numbered twelve) in a lengthy survey, and the interviews conducted with this "convenience" sample, made emphatic statements regarding their sexualities (practiced, assumed, and given), their racial/political concerns, and their coming-out processes, as Latinas and as lesbians. The conflation of identities, in fact, marked their searches for an "authentic" identity, and they had no trouble detailing its configuration. Many had participated in the conferences of the past decades, including the "First National Hispanic Women's Conference," in San José, California, in 1980, and in various meetings of the National Women's Studies Association, as well as Women's Music Festivals in Northern California and the Midwest. Each said that they preferred all-women's gatherings to mixed ones, and few had heard of NACS or MALCS. The results suggest the confinements of the academy, and yet, Latinas, Chicanas, lesbians and non-, signal the importance of such gatherings as historic, if difficult. Without these "popular" gatherings, many academic Chicanas would have little material upon which to base our existence inside the institution. The conclusion forces a question the critic Angie Chabram poses: "How do we incorporate 'the' popular in our work and what does it mean to speak of, or to, 'the' popular?"[24]

On the Politics and Policies of Location

Perhaps the debates at NACS in the early 1990s surrounding the too-evident lesbian-feminist presence (one plenary session on Chicana sexuality/lesbian identity in 1990; two years later another plenary session dealing with Chicana/Native spirituality, Chicana/Native race identification, and Chicana lesbianism, in 1992; two panels on Chicano/a gay/lesbian issues; several out-lesbians and gay men who actually registered for the conference; the first Lesbian Caucus meeting within the Association) could be assessed for their sexual politics primarily, but then the particular positions articulated in the Conference's homophobic rhetorical styles would be lost. Chicana lesbian feminism at NACS and at other conferences in the new decade of the nineties suggests other possible readings of the events at the congress and for the Chicano/a academic community as we near the end of the century.

First, many listeners clearly remained convinced that a Chicana lesbian feminist is merely a Chicana feminist who has sex with women. Several explanations support the reasoning. Few courses, faculty, or programs advance an articulate, analytical argument about sexuality that lodges it in categories beyond "preference," usually interpreted to mean sexual preferences. When we are "raced," we are not "gendered." When we are "gendered," we are not "sexed." Newer works, and even those in the 1980s–like Gloria Anzaldúa's *Borderlands*–plotted a narrative of lesbian identification that ran contrary to what lay in the popular imagination, but it was read in its desexualized state. Few reviewers of the book insist as a starting point that its author is a Chicana lesbian; fewer deal explicitly with the bottom-line woman identification that shapes the book. Through her lesbian, Chicana, borderlands identity, Anzaldúa performs a multilayered play against history, philosophy, and literature, but these are all situated on a foundation of lesbian identity that eludes the majority of academics. Few critics, Chicano and non-, appreciate her scholarly activism. In fact, philosophy, history, literature all could become the organizing basis for interpreting Anzaldúa critically, but according to at least one gay Chicano critic, her history is suspect.[25] In such ways, works by Chicana lesbians in malestream circles are on the one hand appropriated (as references) and on the other hand, dismissed (in coded language and without supporting evidence—it is not merely the criticism I take issue with here, it is its method). At UCSC's History of Consciousness graduate program, which uses Anzaldúa's *Borderlands* as one of its primary texts, Gloria was presumably denied admission because she "was not theoretically sophisticated."[26]

We are not discussing here entirely the denial of Chicana identity or even of lesbian identity. Rather, having been placed on the playing field, so to speak, we are now to be viewed as deficient on other grounds; in this case we might offer as explanation the issue of language domination, English, but also facility in an academic tongue and simultaneously, *one* academic discipline. Traversing borders makes for a good conference, but it-is-not-for-hire becomes one of the criticism's many messages. Interestingly, on the other hand, the Chicana writers whose sexuality can be seen to organize efforts to reinterpret all Chicano sexuality (read as all male sexuality) become iconographed as spokeswomen for movements in which they were absent, either by choice or by exclusion.[27] Whereas most heterosexual critics conveniently overlook that many Latina lesbians have been writing about (their) sexuality for years, including Alicia Gaspar de Alba, Juanita Ramos, Emma Pérez, and Carla Trujillo, their work is rarely cited. Why? An answer may reside in the field of vision Spivak spins in her interviews, where interrogated identities, radical departures, and anything that might complicate a grid remain in forlorn corners and where the spectre of irreducible differences does not equate with knowledge, while reducible differences do.[28]

Other answers reside in the lack of attention given small presses without long-running reputations in feminist studies.

Another, however, has to do with the very messages different Chicana lesbian writers relay. Not all are equally popular, or "easy" to understand. What underlies this process is the even larger, nagging problem that has to do with the lack of context, historical and contemporary, critics especially face in attempting to place any Latina lesbian's work. Two choices appear to dominate: The old historical archetypal drama–the virgin, martyr, witch, whore–becomes the principal way of deciphering the language of lesbian texts; *or* women with new messages are relegated primarily to footnotes, or left "unread," that is, uncited, which means not invisibility, but opposition by dismissal, and this supercedes a critic's other concerns. Either way, Latina lesbian text remains unsituated, unrecovered, and maligned; meanwhile, to demonstrate familiarity with some Chicana/Latina writers, a few works make their way into footnotes and bibliography or into our presentations. One critic also explained to me that he was hesitant to discuss lesbian texts because he felt that as a non-lesbian he might miss the point, or err. Such rigorous honesty, however, is rare.[29]

Insider appropriation and exploitation are more common than we like to think. Cherríe Moraga's work is an excellent example of the pedestal-creation process that accompanies the more famous Chicana lesbian writers (*famous* meaning for the moment in university classrooms across the country). It is interesting that Moraga's explicit references to her sexuality, sensuality, desires, and butch-femme melodramas are one example of what makes her work popular, but too many students tell me that those aspects of her work remain undiscussed in favor of attempting to *explain* her identity. Another probable explanation about Moraga's fame, one Chicana lesbian professor has said to me, is that as long as her message can be the only one presented before a class, or comes to that classroom from the distant reaches of the kooky Bay Area, it is palatable. Again, the iconography based on the solitary voice or example begs the question Why this one and not others?[30]

The search for multiple visions and reenvisions of Chicana lesbian identity needs also to consider the role lesbian sex traditionally plays in heterosexual circles. In fact, most works, with the bold exception of Cherríe Moraga's, a few selections in *This Bridge Called My Back*, or some poetry in Juanita Ramos's

anthology, were decidely shy about overt sexuality or cognizant that a dominant discourse community could not be
counted on to "read" sex in any way this side of tit-illation/
elation. The point seemed to be that to discuss vividly, passionately, or explicitly how lesbian love, romance, lust, and
sexuality operated was to break a silence, feed hungry heterosexual desires, and miss the mark entirely. The heaviness of
profound silences is again notable.[31]

Cultural feminism and bourgeoise feminism all along had
been attempting to say something about lesbian relations:
Women loving women is a revolutionary (romantic, cultural,
political) act *and* is better for women than heterosexual relations. This was one of their conclusions. What lies neglected,
of course, are the insiders' debates about butch/femme (the
doubtful laments about whether femmes are really heterosexual lesbians, untrustworthy, and so on), about anonymous
sex, about class privileges, about academic versus non-aca-
demically trained or situated, about community-based/non-
profit workers versus the professionally clustered. Still to come
in the 1990s' Chicana lesbian communities of Aztlán, were
the S/M debates, or desire's mappings, the "new" family arrangements (nuclear, extended, three-ways, with or without
males?), and the matter of the younger, "Queer"-identified,
who sounded in rhetoric, ideology, and approach very much
like 1970s bisexuals. Their dress reflected the throwback, and
between it, grunge and punk/new age, the costuming nature
of gay/lesbian/bi/transgendered/queer identities, their
"performativity" as it were, took their turn down the runway;
"unpeggable" was one characterization of the multiple array
of values and styles displayed by younger gays and lesbians;
"positively undecipherable" was flung their way more than
once.

Veteranas have made valiant efforts to keep up, but as one
(Chicana lesbian) physician told me, "I see in the ER where
some of the new sexual and marital arrangements lead–violence, fear, abuse. It doesn't seem like an advance." She was
addressing especially the results of S/M sex, of drugs and dangerous sex practices, and of assaults based on different domestic arrangements. That any of these so-called new lists of
abuse can be linked directly or indirectly to new sexual prac-

tices is inconclusive, but in the minds of many health practitioners and care providers, that idea remains popular. Crucial
to their analysis as well is the absence, silence, or invisibility
of a counter-discourse that is widely acknowledged or received.

On Misogyny Among "The" Chicano

I have never been fond of isolating solitary Chicanos, as was
popular during the late 1960s and 1970s. "El" pachuco, "su"
ruca, "la" jefita were constructions drawn from popular forms
of addressing the zootsuiters, their girlfriends, and their mothers. Still, I have been tempted to participate in an inversion of
a different sort by singularizing *a* Chicano (male) and stripping him of his misogyny. What I say next can be read as
manifesto, as a call to action, and certainly as an effort to confront publicly issues without attacking personalities or the
people behind them. This is also instructive, as a display of
how Chicana lesbian feminists might begin modelling new
methods of survival, certainly necessary in the hostile environment of the academy for students and for untenured faculty, as well as for the severely underrepresented, that is,
Chicanas who chair departments, Latinas who receive adequate research support, and Latina administrators. It derives
from a sense of helping others by dislodging them from comfortable moorings by pointing out that words have meaning
and that our language, printed or spoken, carries responsibilities.

It was recently brought to my attention that two Chicano
(gay) academics were gossiping about me and severely undermining my standing as a Chicana historian. One said to a colleague of mine that I had been instructed in the uses of footnotes, in the differences between primary and secondary
sources, and had been told that some of my sources were "un-
reliable" or "untraceable." Such words, to historians, are of
course cause for serious concern. The Chicano making the
charge was grateful to have been spared such embarrassments,
he told my colleague who had offered criticism designed to
"fix" his citational style. As a person who has spent over ten
years on said manuscript, two of those double-checking all of

my sources at each of the three archival repositories I use—because all of them employ different numbering systems and many of the documents are not microfilmed in the original projects of recovering these sources—I took grave offense at the charges, let alone at their patriarchal, authoritative rendering. The remarks were made indirectly, with malicious intent, and they caused me to reevaluate how woman-hating operates in this society, how it infects and incarcerates Chicanos as it obliterates Chicana scholarship. Granting passing remarks such weight, other Chicana colleagues believe, is important because what circulates as fact is frequently based on erroneous information that works its way into decisions affecting people's lives: fellowship applications, research allowances, and job interviews.

The ironic and horrifying thing about the implications of such charges of my work is not that they were made at all—not the least important issue is that as a Chicana from New Mexico, my honor and name are being insulted by such innuendo—but that it appears to have originated from someone who is frequently denied positions at Ivy League schools and is the subject of an "attack" via the Internet on a book he has written on New Mexico. In other words, what has been said off-handedly about me is said about him, except that the criticism of my work is quiet while his is public. My position when I was mailed a copy of the discussion from the Internet (to which I did not then subscribe) was to understand immediately the racial, homophobic implications of the attack on his credentials and to do what I could to halt them, by calling the sender and by obtaining information on the public denouncements and academic criticisms of the book which served as the topic of the controversy. My aim was to interrogate the gossip and cut through it by presenting to anyone, when I was asked about it, the substance of the criticisms and his specific responses to them. In other words, I made efforts to understand the nature of the discussion before participating in it in any way.[32]

Many Chicana feminists practice forms of situated criticism, with our intentions as clearly delineated as we can make them at select junctures. It is not the case that we cannot criticize one another; rather, we tend more to resist the effort to dehumanize and demonize one another in the ways some might expect. Chicana lesbians—versed and raised into a different social and political ethic—tell me that they expect from colleagues fair treatment, but agree that too many Chicano men in the academy occupy their positions of authority as chairs of departments, as "blind" reviewers, or as consultants by relying on the privileges which surround them: misogyny, sexism, heterosexism, and class or color, to name a few. Demonstrated evidence of the double scrutiny Chicanas receive exists: Some Chicanos consistently call publishers to "verify" evidence of contracts whenever a Chicana is reviewed for promotion in phone calls that are explicitly driven by the hope of uncovering a lie; whether they do the same for their male colleagues is unknown, but it has come to be increasingly identified as a Chicano practice.

The message consistently from those who determine fellowships, positions, and the like is "Chicanas Beware," or so many of my colleagues tell me. At a conference, one Chicana recently hired in a prestigious position said that she refuses to take on some of the more well-known Chicanos because she fears what they will do. In that sense, we practice a disingenuous, if strategic, politics of location. It is understandable, yet troubling.

Hostile interactions are common among academic Chicanas and Chicanos. Gossip and innuendo are sometimes all that remain to verify our importance, and in periods of heightened discrimination, these practices presage others. The issue here is not about landing the top jobs, for these are systematically denied us anyway; holders of prizes and fellowships are repeatedly taught the lesson in and by the academy that "good enough" is insufficient. Among Chicanas, the climate worsens and fear of repression increases. Several Chicanas have charged Chicanos with plagiarizing their work (none of these charges have been made public); several Chicanas have lost academic jobs because Chicanos have branded them "troublemakers." The few Chicanas in positions of visibility, as department chairs or as academic deans, frequently experience accusations of unfairness ("'she' threatened my tenure" has been levied against some, or "she never returned my materials" and so on).[33]

The historical record is silent on the subject of our internal dissension, but I raise it because I believe that undergraduates and graduates, a new generation for the academy, must practice new ways of living, of apologizing, and of confronting. Ask how many tenured Chicanas chair departments in universities (at last count, four, none of these in the University of California system), how many head Chicano or Latino Studies departments (five), and the evidence makes clear the need for developing a method of outlining our concerns. Interestingly, we live in an era of silence where few people bother to question the gossip mongers or detractors with, Why are you saying this about another Chicana? or, Why, in particular, have you chosen to tell *me* this?

Such questions more than others force speakers to think about their social responsibilities, about the implications of words on people, about images and politics. One colleague suggests that these expectations of the academy are unrealistic; after all, he says, entire books have been written about the role of gossip and innuendo and slander in the profession of history—why would anyone stop or practice a different way of being "academic"? This question and others like it point out the necessity of "discovery," something that academics also practice; many, for example, share confidential material with each other or across state lines to make decisions in hiring or promotion. Not all practices result in an undermining of reputation or in character assassination. My interests are not so naive as to believe that the institutional climate can be overhauled in some utopic vision of institutionalized responsibility, but these remarks are made to detail how a Chicana lesbian praxis within an institutional climate might come to be valued or recognized.

Such insights and methodologies occur to me at every important juncture in academic life: the first review, job interviews, and reviews for promotion. During my tenure evaluation at Pomona College in 1990-91, I learned who my friends were, and I lost many colleagues and others I had also once considered friends and collaborators. At the very end of the review process, the College Cabinet, made up of a quorum of all the full professors, decided that they wanted to send a message about scholar-activists. Many were in receipt of a long-winded letter a colleague had written anonymously to the Board of Trustees. So similar was the language of this letter to another that he had been sent previously, that the President of the College stepped in and confronted the effort to undermine my tenure by conversing with its author and the trustees. Clearly, the boundaries of professional and ethical conduct were being violated in my case; one week later, the Cabinet voted overwhelmingly to accept the tenure decision that all of the other College committees below theirs had already approved. Had I not had intervening feminist colleagues or administrators sensitive to the challenges people of color routinely present to guardians of institutions, I would have become involved in long and disruptive litigation.

We learn from distraction that what we are doing is right, especially if it receives undue attention. Secondly, assaultive criticism in the academy traditionally has been prized; although in men and women of color, its rewards are often illusory. Still, the lessons are numerous and crucial if we are to solidify our presence and sustain friendship in the academic theatre.

Marking a Chicana presence is cruical to our survival, but it also establishes other important linkages to institutions that have traditionally excluded us. The business about our tenure cases, controversial or not, becomes woven into the fabric of insitutions, and students routinely inquire about them when other controversies emerge. The effort among some is to keep alive "history," an effort I applaud, but among others, it is also a tactic designed consistently to remind us that some do not welcome our presence.[34]

Many Chicana academics at academic institutions, especially the elite ones of the country, remain congnizant of a particular irony: We are sometimes hired to remind dominant actors and actresses of their inhumanity—in other words, as guestworker, in a previous generation as bracero, in another as soldadera; before that, we were called "Malinche" (Malintzin Tenepal), "treacherous" (Sor Juana), and "shrewd" (La Tules). Activist scholars provide fodder for some, and we would be foolish to deny this. In Chicano circles, Chicanas can offer blistering, even obliterating, critiques against our Chicano critics because of our cultural intimacy or sense of historical memory; gay, lesbian, bisexual, or straight, we share an elemental and historical journey that does not forgive our transgressions so readily. "Lorena was Latina," is a slogan many Chicana colleagues say they would like to post on their office doors to scare away woman-haters. But taking up the knife or gun, history also has shown us, is a temporary solution. Hating men because some of them hate us offers us a spirtually bankrupt future, and many Chicanas refuse that favor as well.

Conclusions

Woman identification is feared and often confused with lesbian identity; it is difficult to create a lesbian identity without some woman identification, but not all women-identified women are lesbians.

Chicanos are as misogynist today as they were in the 1960s, and many of the beneficiaries of Chicano Studies programs in this country turn around and disparage Chicanas at every opportunity, when they are not busy harassing them or plagiarizing their work. I say this because it needs to be said for the record and understood as part of the historical pattern of woman-hating. Not all Chicanos are the same, but many allies are strangely silent on the topic of the annihilation of Chicanas.

To deal with these issues in an academic environment, and break the cycle of violence into which we have been socialized and accommodated, means that we must begin to name our fears, to acknowledge that we cannot move forward alone, and that each step we take to tell secrets moves us one step closer toward what bell hooks and others term a liberatory, transformative life. This is the task of our generation, to not fear others' truths, to listen and act in the best way we know against woman hating, and to force the authorities to reckon with our honesty and frankness.

Notes

1. I will, on occasion, digress and grant history concessions in this essay, because its lessons for Chicana identity have yet to be un-

packed. See my "Chicana Identity Matters," in Antonia Darder, ed., *Culture and Difference: Critical Perspectives on the Bicultural Experience* (New York: Burgen and Garvey, 1995).

2. For traditional Chican*o* interpretations, see Carlos Muñoz, *Youth, Identity, Power: The Chicano Movement* (New York: Verso Press, 1989); the older work of Mario Barrera, *Race and Class in the Southwest: A Theory of Racial Inequality* (Notre Dame: University of Notre Dame Press, 1979), and his more recent, *Beyond Aztlan: Ethnic Autonomy in Comparative Perspective* (Notre Dame: University of Notre Dame Press, 1988). For a truly "off-the-wall" set of conjectures, based on no cited sources or thorough understanding of Chicana feminist discourse, see in David R. Maciel and Isidro D. Ortiz, *Chicanas/Chicanos at the Crossroads: Social, Economic, and Political Change* (Tucson: The University of Arizona Press, 1996), the essay of Ignacio García, especially pages 190-192 and footnotes 24 and 25. For a gendered analysis of some of the same material, see Dionne Espinoza, "Nationalism, Gender, and Chicana Cultural Resistance," 1996 Ph.D. dissertation, English, Cornell University.

3. For an example of the critique, see Angie Chabram-Dernersesian, "I. From You: The Manifest ChicanO to Us: La Nueva/The New ChicanA," in Lawrence Grossberg, Cary Nelson, and Paula A. Treichler, eds., *Cultural Studies* (New York: Routledge, 1992), 81-95.

4. Several essays trace Chicana feminist writings. See Alma García, "The Development of Chicana Feminist Discourse, 1970-1980," *Gender and Society*, vol. 3, no. 2 (1989), 217-238; Teresa Córdova, "Roots and Resistance: The Emergent Writings of Twenty Years of Chicana Feminist Struggle," in Felix Padilla, ed., *Handbook of Hispanic Cultures in the United States: Sociology* (Houston: Arte Público Press, 1994), 175-202. Also see, on Chicana lesbian feminism, the review essay by Alicia Gaspar de Alba, "Tortillerismo: Work by Chicana Lesbians," *Signs: Journal of Women in Culture and Society*, vol. 18, no. 4 (Summer 1993), 956-963.

5. Several women volunteered to act as "guards" and to explain the necessity of women's-only space to men wanting to enter the session. The entire issue might have been avoided had the program listed properly that this was a workshop and not a panel, something the organizers of the conference attempted to remedy as the situation unfolded. One result of the contestations is that the Lesbian Caucus was formed later in the conference, in a motion "sponsored" (a requirement in NACS) by the Chicana Caucus. Several participants walked out in protest of the motion, one angrily objecting on grounds that "she brought her children to NACS." The discourse and the emotions revealed the level of homophobia which continued in NACS and manifested itself in the annual meeting once again

in San Jose, California, in 1993, where Chicana lesbians walking through a hotel lobby were harassed and physically attacked during the conference. In 1995, a student receiving one of NACS's prizes for best essay accepted the award in "women's" drag and was left a note from a "Christian" under his hotel door specifying that he "could change" but that he was still "loved." At the same meeting, the Gay Caucus changed its name to the Joto Caucus. It and the Lesbian Caucus now provide meeting space and allocated time for gays/lesbians/bisexuals/transgendered members of NACS.

6. See, for example, the work of psychologist Dharma Cortez on Puerto Ricans and NuevoRicans.

7. One letter from an undergraduate suggested that my remarks were important, but that "we should learn from one another and not criticize each other publicly." Similar logic and arguments were once the hallmark of public Chicano discourse, especially in the nationalist movements of the 1960s and '70s, when Chicano men hegemonically insisted on a silencing of differences.

8. See MALCS bylaws, unamended, from the UC Davis, Summer 1987 Institute, Article VI, Section 4 which differentiated the public/private sessions in principle: "All plenaries and keynote sessions are open to the public as well as to registered members," and which was to follow the voting sections. Distributed in the packets of the 1990 Institute were 1987 bylaws missing this and at least one other section, the MALCS Declaration, which was different from its Preamble. Notes on the side of the bylaws as we were writing them in 1987 included (for the attorneys who would be looking them over) "Shall we specify here that workshops or panels are for MALCS members *and* women of color only?" The site committee at UCLA never reviewed the current bylaws in its planning meetings.

9. The correspondence between then-chair of MALCS, Professor Margarita Melville (who was not on the site committee) and the complainant is interesting. I was faxed a draft of a letter to the complainant, Susan Wilhite, Department of Education at UCLA; in response to specific points MALCS apologetically attempted to negotiate the principle of women-of-color zones, or spaces, "sitios y lengua," as Emma Pérez deploys the terms, and traditional American liberalism, including the exclusion/inclusion divide. For work detailing this specific Chicana feminist praxis, see Emma Pérez, "Speaking from the Margin: Uninvited Discourse on Sexuality and Power," in Adela de la Torre and Beatríz M. Pesquera, *Building With Our Hands: New Directions in Chicana Studies* (Berkeley: The University of California Press, 1993), 57-71; in expanded version, Emma Pérez, "Sexuality and Discourse: Notes from a Chicana Survivor," in Carla Trujillo, ed., *Chicana Lesbians: The Girls Our Mothers Warned Us About* (Berke-

ley: Third Woman Press, 1991), 159-184. The Ombudsman, Nancy
Barbie, called me after meeting with the site coordinator for MALCS
that year, Angelina Veyna; at the meeting, the fact that Wilhite had
been listed on the program and had then been "prevented from
speaking" or, in my version, been asked to withdraw her participation, was discussed. More phone calls ensued, one between Angelina
Veyna and myself, on August 14, 1990, where I was told that the
MALCS chair, Margarita Melville, was asking Veyna to "defer to
her," in this matter, another between Melville, Antonia Castañeda,
and myself on August 16, 1990, and then the fax transmissions to all
involved up to this point. The Institute had carried the title: "Conflict and Contradiction: Chicana/Latina Empowerment in the 1990s
and Beyond."

10. I am working on a manuscript about "Lupe's Song." For a chronology, see "'Lupe' Sixteen Years Later: Why Fraternities Continue
to Degrade Women," *La Gente*, vol. XXIII, no. 1 (October/Novem-
ber 1992), 9.

11. The Yale and UC Santa Barbara student newspapers covered
the charges and reported on the concerns of students on those campuses, and so did *The Chronicle of Higher Education*, December 9, 1992;
on Yale, see the *Yale Daily News*, December 9, 1992, page 2, which
reported that graduate school dean, Judith Rodin, was forwarded
the findings of the grievance board and "preparing" to convene the
University Tribunal. See also the open letter to the provost, Judith
Rodin, by undergraduate Karen Alexander, January 14, 1992, *Yale
Daily News*, page 1, and a follow-up in the same newspaper, November 19, 1992 and December 4, 1992. See also the *Santa Barbara News-
Press*, January 20, 1993, B1-2, "UCSB historian confirms Yale sex
charge," in which Mario García confirmed the charges and stated,
"No criminal, civil, or academic body has ever found me guilty of
sexual assault." On the unanimous passage of NACS's Resolution
no. 23, at the Spokane, Washington, annual meeting, see NACS
Business Meeting notes, April 1, 1995. The resolution states that the
Chicana Caucus of NACS "unanimously demands that the University of California, Santa Barbara conduct an investigation into the
charges of sexual assault brought against Professor Mario T. García
and into the findings reported in the media and that Yale University
cooperate fully with UCSB so that the investigation be thorough."

12. On the UC Riverside case, meetings with the ombudsmen were
also arranged; the university decided not to pursue formal charges
against the professor in Ethnic Studies.

13. Telephone interview, November 1992.

14. On Tipton, see *Variety*, Obituaries, February 8-14, 1989; *People
Weekly*, Paula Chin and Nick Gallo, "Death Discloses Billy Tipton's

Strange Secret: He was a She," February 20, 1989; *Time,* vol. 133, February 13, 1989, 41; *The New York Times,* vol. 138, February 2, 1989, A18. On Latinas who have practiced transgendered identities, see for Catalina de Erauso, Mary Elizabeth Perry, "The Manly Woman: A Historical Case Study," *American Behavioral Scientist,* (September/October 1987), 87-100. On Mexican women who have passed as men in various periods in Mexican history, see Elizabeth Salas, *Soldaderas in the Mexican Military: Myth and History* (Austin: University of Texas Press, 1990), 23, 33, 71.

15. Many studies, autobiographies, memoirs, and essays address transgendering and genderbending, which is different. Running through much of this work is the interesting notion that sexuality is also concession. See Leslie Feinberg, *Stone Butch Blues: A Novel* (Ithaca, N.Y.: Firebrand Books, 1993) for a recent novel/memoir. The films of the late Marlon Riggs explored these topics along racial/ideological/aesthetic lines as well; see *Tongues Untied* (1989), *Ethnic Notions* (1987), *Non je ne regrette rien: No regret* (1992), and *Black Is—Black Ain't: A Personal Journey through Black Identity* (1995). A good introduction to genderblending/bending is Holly Devor, *Gender Blending: Confronting the Limits of Duality* (Bloomington: Indiana University Press, 1989). On gender's performativity, see Judith Butler, *Gender Trouble: Feminism and the Subversion of Identity* (New York: Routledge, 1990) as well as her *Bodies That Matter: On the Discursive Limits of "Sex"* (New York: Routledge, 1993).

16. On Sor Juana, see Alan Trueblood, trans., *A Sor Juana Anthology* (Cambridge: Harvard University Press, 1988). Also see the writings of Chicana authors and playwrights, Alicia Gaspar de Alba, "Excerpts from the Sapphic Diary of Sor Juana Inés de la Cruz," *Frontiers: A Journal of Women Studies,* vol. XII, no. 3 (1992), 171-179; and Estela Portillo Trambley, *Sor Juana and Other Plays* (Ypsilanti, Mich.: Bilingual Review/Press, 1983).

17. Examples of some of the earlier divisions were traced carefully in the monographs of the early movement; see Marta Cotera, *Diosa y Hembra: The History and Heritage of Chicanas in the U.S.* (Austin, Tex.: Information Systems Development, 1976), and Magdalena G. Mora and Adelaida del Castillo, eds., *Mexican American Women in the United States: Struggles Past and Present* (Los Angeles: The UCLA Chicano Studies Research Center, 1980). See the writings of Anna Nieto-Gómez, including "Chicanas Identify," *Regeneración,* vol. 1, no. 10 (1971), 9; "Sexism in the Movimiento," *La Gente,* vol. 6, no. 4 (March 1976), 10. Also see Marcela Christine Lucero-Trujillo, "The Dilemma of the Modern Chicana Artist and Critic," in *De Colores Journal,* no. 3 (1977), as well as her poem, "Machismo is Part of our Culture," reprinted in Dexter Fisher, *The Third Woman: Minority*

Women Writers of the United States (Boston: Houghton Mifflin Co., 1980), 401-402.

18. Some Chicano/as who self-identify contemporarily as Chicanos/as, in earlier lives appeared in print with Anglo and non-Spanish surnames or first names; the practices suggest more than ethnic flip-flopping. Rather, some schoolchildren were renamed by Catholic nuns, teachers, and others who did not speak Spanish. Some were forced into English and Anglicized names. I am not suggesting in this section that we forget this history, but that we understand the reasons for a lack of self-specification in multiple contexts which is still necessary in our debates about identity formation and formulation.

19. See Richard Rodríguez, *Days of Obligation: An Argument with My Mexican Father* (New York: Penguin Books, 1992). Chicana scholars, having argued through one decade with figures like Octavio Paz, have primarily chosen not to engage with Raw-dree-guess. Should we, a starting point would be the possessive tone revealed in the title, the twists in the story that derive from patriarch (although somewhat disembodied/disidentified by the son) to gay ("homosexual") son, and the fact that mother figures hardly at all, except as backdrop. Similar self-hatred, this time disguised as a critique of "ethnomania" and multiculturalism, is embedded in the work of Ruben Navarrete, as recently shown in his editorial in the *Los Angeles Times* in response to the Chicano hunger strikers at UC Irvine, November 5, 1995, Opinion Section.

20. One starting point of a sexed, gendered analysis would be to read the works of historian Antonia Castañeda, including "Women of Color and the Rewriting of Western History: The Discourse, Politics, and Decolonization of History," *Pacific Historical Review*, vol. LXI (November 1992), 501-533; "The Political Economy of Nineteenth-Century Stereotypes of Californians," in Adelaida R. del Castillo, ed., *Between Borders: Essays on Mexicana/Chicana History* (Los Angeles: Floricanto Press, 1990), 213-236; and "Gender, Race, and Culture: Spanish-Mexican Women in the Historiography of Frontier California," *Frontiers: A Journal of Women's Studies*, vol. XI (1990), 8-20. Contrast this work with (which is uncited by) Tomás Almaguer, *Racial Fault Lines: The Historical Origins of White Supremacy in California* (Berkeley: University of California Press, 1994).

21. Many Chicana scholars have written about Malinche; see my "Malinche as Lesbian: A Reconfiguration of 500 Years of Resistance," *California Sociologist*, Special Issue, Vol. 14 (Winter/Summer, 1991), 90-97; Alicia Gaspar de Alba, "Los Derechos de la Malinche," in *IV Encuentro Nacional de Escritores en La Frontera Norte* (1989), 145-152; and her poem, "Malinchista, A Myth Revised," in a section on ar-

chetypes compiled by Tey Diana Rebolledo and Eliana S. Rivero, eds., *Infinite Divisions: An Anthology of Chicana Literature* (Tucson: The University of Arizona Press, 1993), 189-271. On colonial women on the northern frontier of New Spain and in the early Mexican period, see Antonia Castañeda, "Presidarias y Pobladoras: The Journey North and Life in Frontier California," in *Renato Rosaldo Lecture Series Monograph*, no. 8 (Series 1990-91), 25-54, reprinted in MALCS, *Chicana Critical Issues*, (Berkeley: Third Woman Press, 1993), 73-94; and by the same author, "Sexual Violence in the Politics and Policies of Conquest: Amerindian Women and the Spanish Conquest of California," in De la Torre and Pesquera, eds., *Building With Our Hands* (Berkeley: University of California Press, 1993), 15-33.

22. The impact of that presence is open to debate and interrogation; see Chéla Sandoval, "U.S. Third World Feminism: The Theory and Method of Oppositional Consciousness in the Postmodern World," *Genders*, no. 10 (Spring), 1-24.

23. Many possibilities exist for interpreting the varied and multiple stances of Chicanas on particular issues; Gayatri Spivak's idea of an unsituated or fluid shadow space is intriguing (derived from some of the work of Victor Turner), as is the notion of pluralizing grids and complicating patterns by "re-facting" history (my arrangement of her concepts). See Gayatri Spivak, *Outside in the Teaching Machine* (New York: Routledge, 1993), chapters 1 and 4. Noted references *for Bridge, Compañeras, Haciendo Caras,* and *Chicana Lesbians* are: Gloria Anzaldúa and Cherríe Moraga, eds., *This Bridge Called My Back* (Boston: Persephone Press, 1981); Juanita Ramos, ed., *Compañeras: Latina Lesbians* (New York: Latina Lesbian History Project, 1987); Gloria Anzaldúa, ed., *Making Face, Making Soul: Haciendo Caras* (San Francisco: Aunt Lute, 1990); and Carla Trujillo, ed., *Chicana Lesbians: The Girls Our Mothers Warned Us About* (Berkeley: Third Woman Press, 1991).

24. My essay on Latina lesbian sexuality, "Latina Butch/Femme," is in process. The Chabram question is from a telephone conversation, May, 1995. On the importance of a realignment with empirical work, see Spivak, *Outside in the Teaching Machine*, 17.

25. See Ramón A. Gutiérrez, "Community, Patriarchy and Individualism: The Politics of Chicano History and the Dream of Equality," *American Quarterly*, vol. 45, no. 1 (March 1993), 44-72. Gutiérrez says about her book, "It is a combination of history (much of it wrong), poetry, essays, and philosophical gems, in which Anzaldúa describes her fractured identity . . ." (63) and "Anzaldúa claims to be a mestiza or mixed-blood lesbian . . ." (63). I am certain that Gutiérrez was not conflating mestiza/mixed-blood/lesbian identities, but readers might compare his analysis to mine by thinking of analysis as relational.

26. Conversation with Anzaldúa, 1990. She is enrolled in a Ph.D. program at UCSC, in literature.

27. Frances Aparicio examines these aspects of the problematic in "On Multiculturalism and Privilege: A Latina Perspective," *American Quarterly*, vol. 46, no. 4, 575-588. On the iconographic tendency, see especially Tomás Almaguer, "Chicano Men: A Cartography of Homosexual Identity and Behavior," *Differences: A Journal of Feminist Cultural Studies*, vol. 3, no. 2 (1991), 75-100, the section entitled, "Cherríe Moraga and Chicana Lesbianism," 90-95.

28. See Spivak, *Outside in the Teaching Machine*; for interviews with her see the same work, introduction, as well as in *The Abject, America*, *Differences*, vol. 2, no. 1, (special issue) 1991.

29. Examining Chicana lesbian text as phase is not terribly promising either. Here, the historian's enjoinder might prove useful: Linking explicit sexualities (the tradition, for example, of Mexicana/Latina women dressing as men, traced across eras and not to fulfill historical voyeurism) would make it easier to read/recover lesbian text and contextualize it as well. For some steps in this direction see the introduction (28-29) to *Infinite Divisions: An Anthology of Chicana Literature*, Rebolledo and Rivero, eds. (Tucson: The University of Arizona Press, 1993), where an effort is made to sustain and "know" literature through irreducible differences, as reflected in the title of the anthology.

30. Some might suggest that perhaps Moraga's voice is judged the best and that explains its use. Popularity is not my concern here. It is the application of these works that needs assessment; solitary confinement—in prison, course syllabi, or at conferences—must be interrogated.

31. Exceptions have been cited throughout this essay; see Gaspar de Alba's "Tortillerismo," in *Signs*, vol. 18, no. 4, 956-963; Trujillo, *Chicana Lesbians*.

32. See on Ramón A. Gutiérrez's *When Jesus Came, The Corn Mothers Went Away*, Bitnet Communications, Richard Jensen, H-Net Central, and Sandra Kathryn Mathews-Lamb, resulting from a meeting of November 13, 1994 at Salt of the Earth Bookstore, Albuquerque, New Mexico. Written commentaries and criticisms by several Pueblo writers, professors, teachers, and cultural workers preceded this discussion and were compiled in *American Indian Culture and Research Journal* (Native American Studies Center, University of New Mexico), vol. 17, no. 3 (1993), 141-177.

33. The scene was codified in the recent courtroom antics of defense counsel in *Rudolfo Acuña v. the U.C. Board of Regents*. After three weeks of testimony, and a filled courtroom, eight jurors unanimously found that the university had indeed discriminated against Profes-

sor Acuña on the basis of age. When an Ad Hoc Committee report listed age references in five sentences, beginning with "Born in 1932" (a fact not listed on any of his application materials), "at age 59," "senior *person*" (my italics), and so on, the university had a hard time proving that it had not discriminated, especially when faculty reports likened Acuña to a dictator and labeled him possibly tyrannical. The university, however, began laying its case for refusing to instate Acuña (he is a professor at California State University, Northridge) by bringing Chicanos from UCSB, who had publicly testified against the hiring, to the courtroom in the last days of summation and then accusing the courtroom public of being "intimidating" and "threatening." Interestingly, no member of the courtroom public, except perhaps myself, had any direct conversation with the defense's witnesses; my remarks were entirely gracious and subdued, but the groundwork was being laid for an appeal or a denial of appointment.

34. An example from my tenure review arose when some used it as a reason to write about college "favoritism" in conservative newsletters like *Heterodox*, where one of my colleagues accused the college administration of bestowing special privileges on me. Other articles in newspapers responded to these attacks, but most often they remain unrefuted. See, for example, student attacks on my teaching (and that of my colleague, Sidney Lemelle, who is African-American) in *The Student Life*, Pomona College, Mark Klauber, "Opinions," February 26, 1993; our department chair's response, March 5, 1993; and Klauber's parting shot, April 30, 1993. I no longer grant interviews to anyone associated with the student newspapers on campus, and I have never received an apology for the unattributed, unchallenged remarks made about my pedagogy, grading techniques, and so forth.

A Woman of No Consequence
Una Mujer Cualquiera

Sandra Cisneros

Keynote Speech, National Lesbian and Gay Journalists Association, Third Annual Conference, February 18, 1995, San Antonio, Texas.

I've always been la otra. The other woman. Even when my lovers didn't have a wife. Even when they didn't climb out of my bed to climb that same night into another's. I've been la otra. The one they sought when the one at home didn't understand them.

It's not to say I understood them any better. But they didn't need to understand me, understand? That was the difference.

So I don't count. Una mujer cualquiera. A woman of no consequence. That's me.

I want to talk about sex, because not only will I get your attention, but because it is the thing we don't talk about in my culture, especially not as women. There is so much left unsaid in my family, in my community. So much that is taboo and not permitted me to say, do, or even think as a woman of Mexican ancestry.

I am a sinverguenza. I am not ashamed to be shameless.

All week I kept wondering what I could tell you that would make you hear me, that would make you listen with more than your ears, allow you to accept what I have to say, and ultimately open your heart and let me in.

I knew I would have to tell you a story, and if I told it well you would grant me the privilege of being quiet and paying attention when I spoke. And if the story was a good one, you would remember it long after you left here. It would change the way you think about women like me, and therefore change the way you look at the world.

I have been the other. The exotic on a white man's arm. The poor girl, the working-class woman venturing out from the barrio, ashamed when people looked her in the eye, recognized her for who she really was when all along she thought she'd fooled them.

A Woman Like Me

There was a way the doorman had of looking at me. Like if he knew I'd just risen from the warm sheets of a narrow twin bed, my girl's bed. And in the bathroom I'd dressed, put on the black puta stockings my lover requested, the black lace garter belt with its rubber tongues and metal on my thighs, and no underpants—no, no, nothing else touching me there, Don't wear anything, understand?—nothing but my jeans pulled over this, and then a big sweater my mother had given me over the lace pushup bra, and then a scarf and then my ski jacket over this and gloves and a hat, all this in January mind you, dressing myself in my mother's house, in the bathroom, the only room with a lock on the door, eating the egg and chorizo tacos my mother had fixed, and thinking I am going to my lover's house, and my mother not knowing about that other part of my life, the man I am in love with, the pleasure he gives me, thinking this while walking over to the bus stop, the metal clasps on my thighs under the thin cloth of my jeans, and the way I am already aroused, as if I woke with a hard-on anticipating the lover I am traveling towards this morning on the Division Street bus, then transferring to the subway, changing trains downtown at Washington Street to the Howard line that would take me north to where his wife was making coffee, enough for herself and then some extra for her husband—and for me, though she didn't know it. And then after riding that train, picture me looking out the window, looking at the other passengers, wondering if they knew where I was going, and then the cold, the terrible cold when you stepped out and walked the four blocks over to the high-rise next to the lake where he lived, and the snow crunching under my boots, those thick boots made for hiking in Alaska, and underneath my jeans and boots and lamb-lined gloves and woolen scarf and hat, underneath all these layers of cloth, my skin, under black lace and smoky nylons with seams that I am wearing for the man waiting for me in a bed still warm from where his wife rose and left it for me. And I pass the doorman of this fancy glass high-rise down by the lake expensive building, and he looks at me with that funny grin he saves for women like me, my kind, he knows who I am, he's met women like me before. And I pretend I don't see him looking at me like that, I pretend I don't know what he is thinking, just hurry past him, up to the elevator filled with old women with white hair, that elevator that smells like white people, how do I explain it, with the smell of their homes, their hair, their food, you have to be not-white to know what I mean. And then the elevator and hoping the white-haired women on that elevator aren't guessing, aren't looking at me, aren't wondering—she is that kind of woman. A woman who climbs into another woman's bed a few minutes after she's left it. A woman who is the darkest rose, the darkest night, the other side of who knows. A woman who is the Niger, the thousand and one Arabian Nights, who is all the Amazon, who is Andalucia, who is the dust of Calcutta, who is Gauguin's Papeete, who is black-tongued and black-haired, the blue-black labia that is I the color of a bruise, la noche triste, is the blood smeared on temple walls, is Chichén rising from jungle, is the beret of cloud tipped on a twin volcano, is the deserts of Tangiers, the Uled-Nayl of your soul, a woman who will take you there, and you have chosen me so different from that woman you share a life with, so other than she, you've chosen me. With you, with you in her bed, your bed, yours, and I don't care, I don't care what the doorman thinks, oh, yes, there, there, love me like that, please. Say you love me, say it. Because I am black Oaxacan pottery, the banks of Ab-i-Diz, the orange water in your tea, my tongue like all the roof ledges of Mexico City studded with glinting glass, the eye of a cenote, the waves rushing against the black rock of Patagonia, the condors against the Andean blue of sky, the Santiago coup, the miners of Bolivia, all the waters of the waterfalls of Uruguay, the Aruba carnival of nights, sticky mango licked from the brown wrists of a girl from Cuba, Caguas, Mayaguez, Medellín, Quintana Roo, say you love me, say it, say it, lapping me up, lapping up the brown caramelo of my skin, say you love me, daddy, please. Yes, yes. Little nip of hurt, pedacito de mi alma, oh, I knew it, I knew you did.

My life of crime began at nineteen when I had an affair with my first married man. I became a sexual outlaw then. My life was a lie, a secret that was at once delicious and terrible, a pact of duplicity; he feared his wife would find out, and I lived in terror my parents would. But it was wonderful to be a sexual renegade, to have a secret, to hold that secret in the mouth and savor it when one was alone. For a Catholic girl like me, it was heaven. I enjoyed being a sexual deviant—I think it was due to being raised by nuns. Sincerely. Don't scratch, and as a result—you start to itch.

Then, I did not identify with that other woman, his wife. She with her expensive silk pajamas hanging behind the bathroom door, her blond hair hairpins on the sink. A woman like that wasn't my sister. I felt no remorse.

Until my parents found out.

I did not want my family to be ashamed of me, yet I had shamed them. It was then the most devastating thing I could've done to them. How could you sink so low? my mother's voice over the telephone, Don't you have any self pride? And for once I was speechless. Because I felt I had dishonored my family I wanted to commit suicide.

As you can see, I didn't. In fact, I went back to my life of crime, again and again. You might say I became a sort of repeat offender, repentant but not reformed. It was a long time before I could brave the words, say them, set them down on paper and write about the kind of woman I was. Not the one I let the public see. Not the private myth I had invented for myself. But the one I really was. It was only when the writing made me squirm and did not make me look good, neither politically correct nor poetically attractive, only then did I know I was telling the truth.

I am in the business of blabbing secrets. I have made a lifetime profession of examining myself to excess. I write about what is taboo for me, not taboo for men or for white women, or even my Chicana friends. I force myself when I write to look at what harms me by my silence—my shames, fear, degradations, terrors, the memories I don't talk about. I know it is dangerous to speak, but sometimes it is more dangerous to be quiet.

I am famous now for being an hocicona, but when I was attending graduate school at the Iowa Writers Workshop I was too afraid to even speak. Partly because I was young, and partly because I was other and didn't know it. What I did know was a terrible sense of shame. The language for that shame I carried with me for many years in the form of things I did not talk about or want known about me; I'm not certain I was aware of it in a conscious way, but it was there nonetheless like a fine shard of glass that had healed under the flesh; poke and it hurt. It did not clarify itself into words until that graduate seminar when we were talking about houses. House, or lack of one, became my madeleine cookie. Once I could name that smudge as shame, as shame of my working-class home, neighborhood, of my doubt about my right to a life of letters, of my fear of not being as good as my classmates, of not being smart enough, I became angry. Fueled with that anger, the poems and stories came in a torrent.

I don't want to be silent again. I want to make up for all those years I was too afraid to speak, and I want to speak for those still afraid to speak. I want to write to change the world with my writing, nothing less. I want to teach the world to be tolerant and compassionate, but in real life I am neither tolerant nor compassionate towards those who harm me, I am not tolerant towards those who would kill me, I am not tolerant towards those who prey on the weak of society, the powerless, the oppressed, I am not tolerant and compassionate towards those who do not understand nor love me.

I have not forgiven that first white man I once loved, and since then I've held a grudge against all white men. I have not forgiven the brown men who have betrayed and continually betray Chicanas. I can't stand the Pope whose decisions so much affects the destiny of women of my class and race. I still don't trust white women unless they first show me they have moved halfway to meet me by learning about my culture and not asking me carry them over the Rio Grande on my back. I am filled with anger. So how can I claim to teach tolerance and compassion when I am so full of my humanness?

Perhaps I would not even be aware of this paradox had I not traveled to Yugoslavia eleven years ago on my first NEA Fellowship. I lived in Sarajevo all of a summer and a month beyond. The Sarajevo I knew was the one of before the war when there was still hope, the city was renewing itself for the oncoming winter Olympics. Such a lifetime since that summer. Our walnut tree dropped walnuts onto the tin roof of the summer kitchen. I remember scrubbing Turkish rugs on my hands and knees, my knees stropped raw. I remember cracking walnuts with a hammer for a cake we were baking. I remember washing laundry by hand. Shops were out of everything, and anything you wanted, cakes, dresses, clean rugs, had to be done a mano and took a lot of time.

Here it was that I met and became good friends with Jasna, a neighbor woman who was to become my translator and good, good comadre not only while I lived in Sarajevo, but the years beyond. Jasna later came to visit me several times in the United States. We worked on translating my stories into Serbo-Croatian. We read books to each other. We washed linen and laughed at the outrageous stories of our lives. When the war began, we did not believe it could possibly arrive at Sarajevo, a city of culture, a city noted for its ethnic tolerance.

The events of history must always strike ordinary people as it has struck me and my friend in Sarajevo. A bit of disbelief, of shock that this thing, this war is happening to you, is happening to someone you know personally, someone with a name who has to get up and go to work in the morning on streets open to mortar and sniper fire, is happening on streets where one sat and drank the daily Turkish coffee in tiny, doll-sized cups.

I remember that beautiful street along the river where the American library once stood. Under the cherry trees one afternoon I read the cat poems of T. S. Eliot. This I remember clearly because a cherry fell from a branch as I was reading and stained the page with an indelible wine-colored "o." It was just a cherry-stain, not blood, but I was horrified; the book wasn't mine. It belonged to the American library across the river on that beautiful street that is now called Sniper Alley.

I left Sarajevo eleven years ago wondering why destiny had taken me there. In retrospect I understand there are no coincidences. When the war broke out and I didn't hear from my friend for almost a year, I lived with the ache of not knowing whether she was alive or dead. The apathy of the world outraged me, but the worst part was knowing I was part of the not doing.

A speech I wrote for an International Women's Day rally in San Antonio broke my silence. Since then I have been speaking out about my friend caught in that city. For a time a group of women friends and I held up signs in front of San Fernando Cathedral here in downtown San Antonio, keeping a peace vigil for an hour each Saturday. People looked at us as if we were crazy. After all, what did Sarajevo have to do with San Antonio?

Little by little, we gave up the signs and began moving inside the church, lighting candles, meditating for peace. It was during one of these meditations that I realized something profound. If I am holding a peace vigil for Bosnia then it is only logical that I cannot be fighting with my mother, or with that artist across town, or with anyone for that matter. If I want peace in Sarajevo, then I must work at being a peaceful person here. I must be peace. I must work towards speaking, writing, acting in peace towards everyone I come into contact with within my world. This is a lot harder than holding up a sign, but it is what my weekly peace vigil has taught me to do in order to save my friend in Sarajevo.

So what does Sarajevo have to do with sex and my talk this morning? I didn't intend to talk about sex today. I had planned to talk about being the Buddha. I wanted to say we need to have tolerance and compassion for each other, for each individual in this room, for every person that comes into our lives, but how could I tell you that and have you believe me when I am not the Buddha?

True. I am not wise. But my writing can be. That is why it is necessary for me to write about the topics that scare the hell out of me, that force me to look closely at my rage and my arrogance, to admit to my pride and my narrow-mindedness, my vindictiveness, and create, write from that place wiser than I am. Only if I am this honest can I arrive at enlightenment. It will take me, like meditation, to the truth, my truth, and teach me, change me. And changing a mind, my own mind, is the route to transformation.

Sometimes it seems there is so much in the world that needs to change, I am overwhelmed before I get started if I think of what I cannot do. I am encouraged and filled with hope when I realize what I am capable of doing as one human being and how much I have done in the forty years I have been alive.

There is pain and suffering in the world, true, but I think we must ask ourselves as writers, as people who have suffered oppression, are we guilty of perpetuating pain with pain, oppression with oppression. Has our fear and our rage forced us to hold knives, pull triggers, to fight evil by being evil.

I am convinced that the power of an oppressed group is its vision, its ability to see pain where others might not see it because they have not experienced it. "Once there is seeing, there must be acting. Otherwise, what is the use of seeing?"– Thich Nhat Hanh. Each of us has witnessed unique atrocities specific to our gender or race or class or sexuality; each of us, and our distinctive visions, is our gift to each other as a group and to the world at large.

When I read what atrocities are happening in Sarajevo, or in East L.A., when I read about gay-bashing, Proposition 187, the apathy and lack of compassion to those with AIDS, I feel ashamed. And yet, if I am mindful, if I am responsible with language, I can create powerful writing from this pain I feel.

As a writer, I know too well the power and repercussion of words. I want to make sure when I speak, when I write, that I am not reacting from anger or pride. Am I examining my anger and pride and using it instead to understand where my anger came from? If I am honest with myself, if I don't bullshit, the reader will know it. And there is power in writing from the truth.

I want to be humane to counter all the inhumanity on the planet. I want to *not* be ashamed to call myself a human being. For the sake of those I love too dearly, my friend in

Sarajevo, my raza, my gay and lesbian friends, my family, it is not enough to write from my ego.

What is a writer's duty? a journalist once asked me. The writer's duty is to be the Buddha. To serve others with wisdom and compassion.

If we can do this, if we can change our reactions to peaceful actions, our anger to insight, our pain to understanding, each day, today, this moment, now, then and only then will we deserve to call ourselves writers, to call ourselves human beings.

Irigaray's Female Symbolic in the Making of Chicana Lesbian Sitios y Lenguas (Sites and Discourses)

Emma Pérez

When I was nineteen, in the mid-seventies, I came out as a lesbian, although like many lesbians I can trace my desire for women back to my mother's womb. I am a native of Texas, a state where homophobia is severe, like racism. To come out, I left Texas, moved to California, and within one month I met the woman of my dreams, the woman with whom I'd spend the rest of my life. We lasted six months. She was a year older than me, and I like to say she left me for a younger woman, a woman of eighteen. When we lived together those first glorious months, we endured a small yellow cottage with a black and white plaid couch, no bed, and no curtains. We slept on a cold, hard floor. One evening, as we finished shopping at a local market, a carload of young white boys barked words they imagined would lure us to them. We shouted we weren't interested, and they replied predictably. They screamed accusingly, "Lesbians!" and we blared, "Yeah, so what?" Luckily, they drove away, and, laughing, we walked to our curtainless yellow cottage feeling exposed to a hostile world but too young and in love to care.

I disclose this personal story to introduce my stand as a strategic essentialist. Deconstructive theorist Gayatri Chakravorty Spivak integrated these concepts when she wrote, "It is not possible not to be an essentialist, one can self-consciously use this irreducible moment of essentialism as part of one's strategy."[1] A strategic essentialist, then, is one who exercises political representation, or identity politics, within hegemonic structures. The strategy asserts countersites within dominant society. As a dynamic process, this tactic gives voices to each new marginalized social or political group, bonded temporarily at specific historical moments. French feminist Luce Irigaray, for example, exhorts women to "break away" into separate spaces as a political strategy to create a female imaginary resisting phallocentric representation.[2] Strategic essentialism is a type of caucusing, with each new caucus making its own rules, agreeing upon its demands, restrictions, freedoms. The process is not permanent or fixed but instead somewhat dialectical, acknowledging irreducible differences within separate *sitios y lenguas* where the resolution of differences is neither desirable nor necessary.[3]

At this juncture in so many struggles for human rights, I essentialize myself strategically within a Chicana lesbian countersite as a historical materialist from the Southwest who dares to have a feminist vision of the future. My essentializing positions are often attacked by a sophisticated carload of postmodern, post-Enlightenment, Eurocentric men and by women who ride in the back seat, who scream epithets at those of us who have no choice but to essentialize ourselves strategically and politically against dominant ideologies that serve only to disempower and depoliticize marginalized minorities. Post-modernists accuse essentialists of being exclusionary and totalizing because we claim identities without regard for others. But as "marginalized others," essentializing ourselves within countersites thwarts cultural and political suicide. We must separate into decolonized third world spaces of our own making. Strategic essentialism is practiced resistance against dominant ideologies that silence and/or model marginalized groups. The modeled minority, aware of the danger of being *the* token, knows that an invitation to the center serves to silence and disempower the group(s) she/he is invited to represent symbolically, individualizing a political cause. To survive, modeled minorities must assert self-identity among their own political, cultural, or social group, or face persistent, lonely fragmentation.

My reply to the more cultivated carload of men and women who accuse me of essentializing is like my reply to the young pestering boys when I was nineteen. I jeer, "Yeah, so what?" This paper is a lengthy rejoinder to the accusation that categorizes marginalized groups into an essentialist camp without regard for the fact that in a postmodern world, where many of us speak as women of color, as ethnic white women, as lesbians of color and white lesbians, as third world people, as physically marginalized people, we construct creative, not reactive, countersites with multiple voices in mostly masculinist, Eurocentric colonizing institutions.[4] I believe, as Spivak argues, that representation cannot take place without essentialism.[5] If we do not identify ourselves as Chicanas, lesbians, third world people, or simply women, then we commit social and political suicide. Without our identities, we become homogenized and censored.

To speak as a woman or, more specifically, to speak as a Chicana lesbian who has inherited a history of conquest and colonization in the Southwest, to speak as myself with other women like myself means that I seek decolonized spaces where discourse can unfold and flourish, where theories of Chicana lesbian representation can be launched among ourselves without the threat of appropriation from those who claim to want our words.

But we have entered a postmodern age, some say a postcolonial one. In the Southwest, however, I often feel we are still embedded in the colonial social relations we inherited in the sixteenth and nineteenth centuries. Postmodernists suspiciously glare at those of us who claim to speak as women, as third world people, or as lesbians. Being a woman, a lesbian, or a person of color does not ensure that one will speak as one, given our multiple identities and multiple voices. There is no "authentic" Chicana lesbian voice. But authenticity is hardly the issue. The real question, I believe, is posed by Nancy Hartsock who plainly and powerfully asks, "Why is it that just at the moment when so many of us who have been silenced begin to demand the right to name ourselves, to act as subjects rather than objects of history, that just then the concept of subjecthood becomes problematic?"[6] Why, indeed.

In the first part of this essay, I engage Luce Irigaray's theory of the female symbolic to argue for *sitios y lenguas* as a matrix of strategic essentialism. In the second part, I introduce examples of invasionary politics as experienced by third world women and Chicana lesbians who grapple with dominant discourses. Briefly and at the end, I exemplify Chicana/Mexicana lesbian representation in Texas/Chihuahua with women who uniformly create social and political spaces.[7] Throughout, I'd like to suggest that safe, decolonized spaces where Chicanas, Mexicanas, and lesbianas interact follow Irigaray's scheme by contributing to a culturally specific female imaginary. A distinct, Chicana/Mexicana *lesbiana cultura* has been in the making, even if occasionally interrupted by exhausting, invasionary discourse and politics. This is also a call for coalition-building with other political and social groups who acknowledge a need for alternative strategies.

Can women speak as women, can Chicana lesbians speak as Chicana lesbians? Do hegemonic voices have to speak for the marginalized? By invoking Luce Irigaray, whose work theorizes a definitive urgency for the construction of the female symbolic, I pose these questions. The French feminist does not want to "create a theory of woman," but instead, she is attempting to "secure a place for the feminine within sexual difference."[8] The female imaginary would persevere without being subsumed by the male imaginary. Women would stop masquerading for and as men.

A critic of Irigaray, Lisa Jardine, discusses the French feminist's strategy, a strategy that initiates female discourse to conceive of the female imaginary. Jardine notes, "Here is Irigaray, speaking the female imaginary, leaving the (male) imaginary to his own devices."[9] Jardine claims that despite the trend to create fresh feminist psychoanalytic theory, the discourse falls prey to what it challenges, the male-symbolic order, and within that order, men argue, "Feminists have got to give us some space."[10] Hence, appropriation of feminist discourse leads to the diffusion of women's language, women's story, her story, her space. I agree with Jardine's main premise, that feminist discourse is appropriated, therefore disempowered. I do dispute a secondary argument about Irigaray. She reduces the French feminist to a biological reading and criticizes her language, a female-centered language which makes Jardine "uncomfortable." Quoting from Irigaray's essay, "When Our Lips Speak Together," where the French feminist pronounces woman's pleasures as plural, Jardine omits phrases from the page because "if it deliberately discountenances the men, we too have always felt a certain uncomfortableness with it (that's why I left a bit of the last passage out."[11] The phrases, which make Jardine and other (perhaps heterosexual?) women uncomfortable, are the following:

> Fondling the breasts, touching the vulva, spreading the lips, stroking the posterior wall of the vagina, brushing against the mouth of the uterus, and so on. To evoke only a few of the most specifically female pleasures. Pleasures which are somewhat misunderstood in sexual difference as it is imagined–or not imagined.[12]

For some women–I would argue for some lesbians anyway–Irigaray's narrative offers a language of desire, even a seductive discourse. She constructs the female imaginary as she negotiates for its creation.

For Lisa Jardine, Irigaray's discourse reduces the theorist to biological essentialism. By placing women, women's bodies, and their sexualities at center, the feminist essentializes to achieve a specific task–the female imaginary. She seems aware of "biology is destiny" arguments hurled against her. However, Irigaray is nobody's fool, not Lacan's, and not that of the women who have come after him to footnote her text and place it in an essentialist category. She also seems cognizant of the female symbolic as a dynamic process, which leads me to the following section.

Why am I, a Chicana lesbian historical materialist appealing to French feminism? Can European feminist paradigms help to reconstruct Chicana (hi)stories? Does the female symbolic lead to an understanding of Chicana lesbian representation? Can Irigaray's discourse clarify the cultural construction of sexuality for Chicanas? I use Irigaray for a number of reasons. I subscribe to her contention that women need to create female discourses; however, as a historian, I have witnessed how women have always created their communities and discourses within phallocentric arenas. My point of departure argues for marginal marginalized lesbians and women of color to continue framing our decolonized spaces and languages, *sitios y lenguas*. We have done so within designated, colonial spaces. But, just as Jardine points out that men appropriate from feminists, women of color face the same appropriation when our spaces are invaded and penetrated, as we are discursively and territorially colonized. We seek decolonized spaces beyond the third world spaces of white women's kitchens and white men's cotton fields where we still find Chicanas.

I look to Irigaray to ask whether essentializing strategies, such as centering women—but in this case lesbians of color—inhibit or enhance social, historical, and cultural analyses. Is a socialist feminist lesbian of color an essentialist because she claims *sitios y lenguas*, spaces and languages, sites and discourses, apart from male-defined and/or Eurocentric arenas? Do essentializing strategies for radical socialist feminist lesbians of color confine us? Yes and no. Essentializing strategies are survival strategies, after all, and often the only means to an end for marginalized groups. These strategies are never the solution, but they are a process for finding and expressing one's multiple voices.

I am also intrigued by Irigarayan concepts because I believe that her probing of sexuality may provide lesbians with a language to decode sociosexual relations and then invert the language at our command. In her essay "When Our Lips Speak Together," she uses transgressive female language. Her essay, as women's erotica, offers a site and language of deconstruction and reconstruction. As a lesbian of color, I borrow from Irigaray the advocacy of female discourses for communities of women of color; as a Chicana feminist, I adopt yet another language, European feminism, to understand how third world women are located by colonialists.

Margaret Whitford outlines two dominant readings of Irigaray: one is a biological reading, the other is a Lacanian reading, whether interpreting or misinterpreting Lacan. But a third, less popular reading is by North American feminists who read Irigaray as a feminist celebrating relationships between women.[13] My own reading probably falls into the second and third categories, although I question what almost appears like an analysis of the universal woman.[14] Instead, I argue for historical, regional, and cultural specificity to celebrate relationships between women. For me, marginalized groups must have separate spaces to inaugurate their own discourses, *nuestra lengua en nuestro sitio*.

Celebrations are hardly an impulse when Euro-American,

Eurocentric women and men, or even men of color, assume they have rights to Chicana lesbiana *sitios*, claiming they must have equal access to our spaces as if social relations are equal between people of color and Euro-Americans or between women and men, as if we no longer lived in a capitalist, patriarchally framed society that continues to dictate hierarchies. Even though postmodern theorists have retired hierarchies, domination, unequal socioeconomic relations, unequal gender relations, and unequal racial relations, all still thrive; and, totalizing as it seems, for the powerless and colonized only a powerful colonizer exists. Subtleties and refined differences among the powerful are lost nuances to the powerless and the colonized.[15]

Invasionary Politics

I would like to present two examples of invasionary politics in the academic community. Invasive or invasionary politics are most often practices under the guise of sisterhood or brotherhood. I want to critique these prototypes of sisterhood to exemplify the problems women of color face in the academy when asked to speak as women of color and are therefore essentialized from above. In the second personal illustration, I outline the political dynamics when Chicana lesbians speak as Chicana lesbians in the academy.

The first case is taken from an essay in the anthology *Conflicts in Feminism.* Marianne Hirsch, one of its editors, exposes her feminist politics and the way in which she came to terms with her racism.[16] She refers to the feminist theory group organized at the Bunting Institute in 1984 where one African-American member and one Chicana member led the first discussion on race and class. She claims she was prepared to accept criticism about her exclusionary practices concerning women of color, but she was not prepared for the women of color to ask, "Why should we talk about this with you? What purpose will it serve?" Hirsch was horrified when the Chicana said that she felt more deeply connected to Hispanic men than to white women. Hirsch responds:

There I knew what to say, I argued back, heatedly, passionately, terrified that if what she said was true I would lose what I had been building–personally and theoretically–for fifteen years. It took a long time for me to acknowledge that I was trying to argue her out of her experience. Her experience threatened me profoundly, and with my defensiveness I was only confirming her point.[17]

She further rationalizes that during the next year, the women in the group built trust by thinking more seriously about the privileged positions of white middle-class feminism. Hirsch also notes that they built "powerful coalitions, even lasting bonds."[18]

Both editors, Marianne Hirsch and Evelyn Fox Keller, theorize that conflict is essential and sometimes even a "source of pleasure" when feminist coalitions between Euro-American women and women of color are formed. I ask, pleasure for whom? If indeed we acknowledge inequality and unevenness, not to mention the cultural biases in a room where two women of color become the moral conscience–the cultural workers for white majority women–then we cannot assume the dynamic is good, enlightening, or pleasurable for the marginalized. Race, class, and ethnic equality is presumed. And I only name a few of the differences reduced by the dream of a common language. Women of color have been invited, but not to discourse with each other. They have been invited as reactors and resisters, who reveal discursive and territorial colonization upon entering confrontations that presume equal sociopolitical relations between first and third world people. Unfortunately, only after abusive conflict do some Euro-American women begin to realize gender consciousness is irreducible and that coalition building is a delicate matter, to say the least. How can this pleasurable conflict be cast so lightly while the social relations between Euro-Americans and people of color in the United States remain historically incongruous? Inequality, historically inherited and materially grounded, impedes pleasure for the person lower on the socioeconomic, racial, patriarchal rung.

The question the women of color posed before Hirsch's group in 1984–"Why should we talk about this with you?"–is the same question many women of color asked through the feminist movements of the 1960s and 1970s, and the question still remains in the 1990s. The practice of invasionary politics is reasserted under the guise of feminist discourse and under the guise of equal opportunity. Marginalized others are silenced, having no rights to spaces to construct creative rather than reactive discourses.

Social scientists and field workers have proven repeatedly that conflict with those who have more socioeconomic and political power places the disempowered in a peculiar position, a distrustful one, but certainly not one in which the colonized voluntarily bond with a discursive and territorial colonizer. The groundwork laid by such discourses can be rather like false intimacies. Chandra Mohanty reminds us, "Sisterhood cannot be assumed on the basis of gender; it must be forged in concrete, historical, and political practice and analysis."[19] The praxis, after all, will serve to liberate us.

Theoretical commonalities, based on gender, do not negate irreducible differences. For one, the hierarchy within a capitalist, patriarchally framed society must be dealt with. And, in an ideal socialist feminist universe, differences would still exist, but they would be respected and admired, not trivialized. A racial economy, which benefits many Euro-American Eurocentric people and harms many people of color, can parallel an argument about a male-centered economy that damages women, an Irigarayan concept. But what is the reality? As a historical materialist, I observe race relations and I observe social relations between women and men. A political, historical, and regional analysis of race and gender relations is imperative. The irreducible differences are centered in multiple *sitios y lenguas*, ongoing processes with little or no resolution. The mistake made within any arena, whether academic or political, is that a common enemy bonds "us" and makes "us" all the same, while "they," the common enemy, are also all the same. But strategic essentialism circumvents totalizing by implementing a political strategy that recognizes that political and cultural bonds and coalitions are based on identities in constant flux. At this juncture, I become a historian searching for specificity, regionally and locally, to ask how inherited sociosexual relations affect people. Historical specificity, then, is compulsory.

The next example of invasionary politics is a personal one about homophobia at home, as Gloria Anzaldúa indicates.[20] When the few Chicana lesbians who are "out" in the academy decided to hold a closed panel at the National Association for Chicano Studies in spring 1990, a panel open to all women—physically challenged, lesbian, heterosexual, bisexual, homophobic, Latina, Euro-American, working-class, middle- and upper-class, and so on—we expected criticism from some of our less supportive female and male colleagues, but we did not expect combat. The gentler comments ranged from "That's separatism" to "What do lesbians want anyway?" The harsher comments I'd prefer not to repeat. When a group of Chicana lesbians proposed the possibility of a lesbian caucus, the response from well-respected, Chicano professors was that "a marijuanista caucus" would have to receive equal time if a lesbian caucus was formed, linking lesbianism to deviance. Later, the men who made such comments denied them and pretended they had only been joking, unaware that lesbian and gay bashing are no more amusing than racial slurs. There were also those who sat passively while homophobic remarks flew.

After I confronted a heterosexual Chicana about her homophobia, she said, I was told, that a workshop open only to women was exclusionary. This "confrontation" would later earn me the title "lesbian terrorist" at a Chicana academic meeting in the summer of 1990. I also challenged Chicano males (one heterosexual and one gay) about their uninformed comments. My gay colleague quickly agreed; the heterosexual man listened and then admitted he had prejudged us. Despite my so-called terrorist tactics, both of these men communicate regularly with me. Along with my call for Chicana/Mexicana *sitios y lenguas*, I also see essentializing strategies as ways to open up dialogue between essentialist camps. (Such conflicts and confrontations, however, are hardly bliss.)

But getting back to the questions of who speaks as a lesbian or can lesbians speak? My experience has been that when Chicana lesbians speak politically, there are efforts to silence Chicana lesbian voices, and any effort to make spaces and create discourses are threatened by invasionary politics. The straight mind also denies the possibility of women's devotion to female-centered sexuality.[21] Heterosexual discomfort permeates critiques of women-loving women. Interestingly, Irigaray is herself a heterosexual, but it is my contention that within her female symbolic she centers women's bodies and sexuality to arouse heterosexual women to awaken from compulsory heterosexuality. In the case of Chicanas, the straight mind mostly disregards lesbian sexuality unless we look to Gloria Anzaldúa or Cherríe Moraga, both of whom are often trivialized because theirs is *just* a lesbian perspective and therefore a marginal one. In either case, the power dynamic I've spoken of earlier in the situations I outlined above is victimizing. Irigaray when speaking as a woman is trivialized; lesbians when speaking as lesbians become the heterosexual's victim discursively.

Those who read lesbians merely as essentialists, or Irigaray as a biological determinist, impose not only a heterosexist critique but reduce the experiences to univocality. I agree with Margaret Whitford's reading of Irigaray, which equivocates the male philosophers who accuse Irigaray of essentialism as the true essentialists.[22] Within a male symbolic, women have two choices: Either practice strategic essentialism or embrace the male symbolic, which mimics women who mimic men who sometimes mimic women mimicking men. The mimicking men are the postmodernists who have entered feminist territory to invade, to appropriate, and to hurl accusations at women who claim essentialist strategies.

Sitios y Lenguas en Tejas y Chihuahua

As representations of Chicana/Mexicana lesbian sites and discourses, I would like to introduce briefly summaries of voices from these communities. I borrow partly from ethnographic methodology presenting anonymous informants. The women did not want to be identified from taped recordings and preferred to talk openly and freely in group sessions. I took notes, but only after the sessions were over.[23] Anonymity for these women is culturally, regionally, and politically critical.

The topics at group meetings included sexual practices; multiple partners; monogamy; aging; mothers; dancing; dress; make-up; AIDS; safe sex; dental dams; lubricants; vibrators; families; married lovers; marriages; leather harnesses; sizes, colors, and shapes of silicone dildos; who did it to whom and how; Catholicism; Protestantism; films; writers; artists; the (not-so-) Free Trade Agreement; the border patrol; daily border crossing; the bar scene; the pickup scene; tequila; racist customs officers; sobriety; butch/femme; coming out; cooking; jealousy; money and class distinctions; cars; fathers; children; and, finally, cultural differences and similarities between Chicanas and Mexicanas.

At one of the livelier sessions, women invented cultural vocabulary, making up words and poems with transgressive connotations. For example, *chingar* (fuck) has phallocentric implications. Tired of the phallologocentrism, the women improvised with *panochear*, from the Nahuatl root, *panocha*, which is contemporary slang for vagina. Instead of using *chingón*, which implies a Herculean man, we invented *panochona*, representing a formidable, impressive, woman, whether lesbian or straight. At another meeting, one of the Mexicanas, whom I'll call Fulana, created the first lines of the following poem and then other women added more lines. Note the Nahuatl sounds.

> *Machácame la panocha*
> *machácamela otra vez*
> *mi panocha machaca*
> *machácamela bien.*[24]

My point is this: The discussions could not have been as open, as free, or as nurturing if "outsiders," for example, non-Latina lesbians, had attended. Cultural affinities are part of the self-naming process. As Chicanas and Mexicanas redefining ourselves, we felt empowered. I do not want to give the impression that we only gathered socially, to talk *tonterías*, nonsense. I only mean to argue that for third-world lesbians, a regionally and culturally specific female symbolic can be constructed in our own spaces. For me, this kind of bonding and nurturing makes it possible to embark upon struggles for social change.

Again, I ask myself, why I, a Chicana lesbian, am attracted to Irigaray's female symbolic, herself a Eurocentric feminist, although cognizant of historical materialism.[25] I find in her work an essentializing strategy, a point of departure for my own essentializing strategies as a historical materialist from a region twice conquered and colonized. I find in her work a method that strips away masks, and I find in her work the suggestion of a solution, the construction of female discourses. Our communities have always had a healthy degree of community separatism, spaces and languages apart from invasion, conquest, rape, and penetration, whether conquest is discursive (of the body of text) or territorial and physical (of the land and body). As an idealist, I continue to envision a future materially grounded in a female symbolic that appreciates irreducible differences.

Notes

1. Spivak, *The Post-Colonial Critic,* 109. In the same interview, Spivak notes that Stephen Heath has also been credited with first using "strategic essentialism."
2. Irigaray, *This Sex Which is Not One,* 160-161.
3. See my essay, "Sexuality and Discourse: Notes from a Chicana Survivor," 159-184, where I define *sitio y lengua* as self-constructed Chicana spaces to create Chicana discourses. This process is also what Homi Bhabha refers to as "sliding ambivalently from one enunciatory position to another" in an attempt to "articulate cultural differences." See Bhabha, "DissemiNation: Time, Narrative, and the Margins of the Modern Nation," 298.
4. See Chéla Sandoval's essay, "Third World Women and a Theory of Oppositional Consciousness," *Genders,* Fall 1991. She argues for third world women's oppositional consciousness as the means by which they have survived dominant feminist spaces.
5. Spivak, *The Post-Colonial Critic,* 109.
6. Hartsock, "Foucault on Power: A Theory for Women?" 163.
7. This is part of an ongoing assessment of Chicana/Mexicana lesbiana voices in the El Paso/Juárez border where I have lived for three years. I thought it necessary to provide a few examples of how Chicana/Mexicana lesbiana *sitios y lenguas* continue to thrive in a unique geographic area where homophobia could kill us, psychically and physically, but our lesbiana discourses nurture and enliven us.

8. Irigaray, *This Sex Which Is Not One*, 159.

9. Jardine, "The Politics of Impenetrability," 66.

10. Ibid., 63.

11. Ibid., 66-67.

12. Irigaray, *This Sex Which Is Not One*, 28. This is a different translation from the one Jardine uses.

13. Whitford, "Rereading Irigaray," 107.

14. I agree with Whitford's analysis that Irigaray is not a pre-Lacanian, but a post-Lacanian. She seems to understand profoundly his patriarchal bias where women are concerned. Ibid., 108.

15. Memmi, *The Colonizer and the Colonized.*

16. Hirsch and Fox Keller, "Conclusions: Practicing Conflict in Feminist Theory," 370-385.

17. Ibid., 383.

18. Ibid., 384.

19. Mohanty, "Under Western Eyes: Feminist Scholarship and Colonial Discourses," 333-358.

20. Anzaldúa, *Borderlands/La Frontera.*

21. Of course, I must cite Wittig, *The Straight Mind and Other Essays*, for her analysis of the "straight mind."

22. Whitford, *Luce Irigaray: Philosophy in the Feminine*, 103.

23. I talked with ten to twelve women over less than a year, meeting with them weekly at first and then sporadically. Sometimes only four or five women would be at a rap session. Half of the women were native to Texas and the other half were native to Chihuahua, Mexico. I spoke with more women from each region but decided to narrow my notes to twelve. I use assumed names, given the delicate topics and their open dialogue. I am taping some women in one-to-one sessions but, again, only anonymously.

24. *Machaca* was redefined as "to embrace, squeeze, or hold firmly and passionately."

25. Irigaray speaks of women as commodities and surplus value for men in both *Speculum of the Other Woman* and *This Sex Which Is Not One*, clearly borrowing from Marx's theories.

Works Cited

Anzaldúa, Gloria. *Borderlands/La Frontera*. San Francisco: Spinsters/ Aunt Lute, 1987.

Bhabha, Homi K. "DissemiNation: Time, Narrative, and the Margins of the Modern Nation." In *Nation and Narration*, edited by Homi K. Bhabha, 291-322. New York: Routledge, 1990.

Hartsock, Nancy. "Foucault on Power: A Theory for Women?" In *Feminism/Postmodernism,* edited by Linda J. Nicholson, 157-175. New York: Routledge, 1990.

Hirsch, Marianne, and Evelyn Fox Keller. "Conclusions: Practicing Conflict in Feminist Theory." In *Conflicts in Feminism,* edited by Marianne Hirsch and Evelyn Fox Keller, 370-385. New York: Routledge, 1990.

Irigaray, Luce. *Speculum of the Other Woman.* Translated by Gillian C. Gill. Ithaca: Cornell University Press, 1985.

___. *This Sex Which Is Not One.* Translated by Catherine Porter with Carolyn Burke. Ithaca: Cornell University Press, 1985.

Jardine, Lisa. "The Politics of Impenetrability." In *Between Feminism and Psychoanalysis,* edited by Teresa Brennan, 63-72. New York: Routledge, 1989.

Memmi, Albert. *The Colonizer and the Colonized.* Boston: Beacon Press, 1967.

Mohanty, Chandra. "Under Western Eyes: Feminist Scholarship and Colonial Discourses." *boundary 2* 12-13 (Spring/Fall 1984): 333-358.

Pérez, Emma. "Sexuality and Discourse: Notes from a Chicana Survivor." In *Chicana Lesbians,* edited by Carla Trujillo, 159-184. Berkeley: Third Woman Press, 1991.

Sandoval, Chéla. "Third World Women and a Theory of Oppositional Consciousness." *Genders* (Spring 1991): 1-24.

Spivak, Gayatri Chakravorty. *The Post-Colonial Critic: Interviews, Strategies, Dialogues.* Edited by Sarah Harasym. New York: Routledge, 1990.

Whitford, Margaret. *Luce Irigaray: Philosophy in the Feminine.* New York: Routledge, 1991.

___. "Rereading Irigaray." In *Between Feminism and Psychoanalysis,* edited by Teresa Brennan, 106-126. New York: Routledge, 1989.

Wittig, Monique. *The Straight Mind and Other Essays.* Boston: Beacon Press, 1992.

Voices from the Couch: The Co-Creation of a Chicana Psychology

Yvette G. Flores-Ortiz

Introduction

The discipline of psychology, born of Eurocentric and male-centered traditions historically, has ignored and silenced the voices of women of color. Furthermore, influenced by notions of patriarchy and Western domination, the theory and practice of psychology have subjugated women by measuring their development, personality, and mental health against a male, white, upper-class model.

The scant literature regarding the psychology of Chicanas[1] is comparative, devoid of class, gender, and cultural analysis. Not surprisingly, Chicanas often emerge as deficient, deviant, or dysfunctional. In the few instances where the culture of origin of Chicanas is considered as a variable of analysis (e.g., Diaz-Guerrero 1955, 1967), a cultural deficit model emerges which blames cultural patterns (devoid of an historical analysis), particularly *machismo* and *marianismo* (the emulation and idealization of Marian traits), for whatever is found lacking in the women. Thus, Chicanas are typically the object, and not the subject, of psychological theory and inquiry. Even feminist psychology, which challenges patriarchal assumptions of the male as referent, generally fails to consider that when women of color are subsumed under the variable of gender, biased comparisons often result. If the subjective experience of class and racial oppression is not considered, Chicanas will appear deficient or dysfunctional when compared to more privileged middle-class white women.

While Chicano scholarship has done a great deal to elucidate the subjective and objective experience of racism and discrimination and their long-term sociological and economic sequelae, few Chicano scholars have extended their analysis of class and race subjugation to the psychology of Chicanos; fewer still have incorporated a gender analysis (Baca Zinn 1982; Garcia 1990; Pesquera 1993; Segura 1993; De la Torre and Pesquera 1993). To date, a psychology of Chicanas that incorporates a social, gender, and class analysis does not exist. Moreover, the disciplines of Chicano Studies and feminist psychology have much to offer towards an understanding of Chicanas and the creation of a Chicana psychology.

This essay offers beginning thoughts on such a psychology, and initial formulations of a theory and practice that gives voice to Chicanas in their complexity as women, as human beings. This essay reflects thinking informed by my work as a clinical psychologist for over two decades and my experiences of immigration to the United States in 1965. My migration to this country as an early adolescent forced me to define myself for the first time in terms of comparisons to an "other." I was no longer the youngest child from a working-class family, situated in an historical past, connected across generations to people from the Americas, Asia, Africa, and Europe. I was suddenly a "Spanish-Speaking, Spanish-Surnamed other" (meaning non-Mexican, non-Puerto Rican, non-Cuban, the only federally recognized categories of Latinos in the 1960s). Unceremoniously planted in an urban Los Angeles middle school two days after my arrival, I quickly became the interpreter for my mother, the cultural broker for the family, the vehicle for the actualization of my parents' "American dream." Over the past three decades I have grown accustomed to the role of interpreter and translator. As a professor, psychotherapist, and researcher, I have tried to give voice to the realities of others who cannot yet do so for themselves. The thoughts reflected in this essay are therefore co-created—the outcome of many hours of dialogue, mutual learning in the classroom, in the community, in the therapy office. Where possible, the voices of mentors, teachers, and sources of inspiration are cited in the tradition of Western social science. The others will know, as they see themselves in these pages, that I have tried to honor their experiences and do justice to their wisdom and their pain.

A Contextual Theoretical Framework for Chicana Psychology

In the 1980s, Chicana writers began to situate Mexican-origin women in the center of Chicano scholarship. Prior to that time, they had been in the margin of the discipline and invisible in psychological literature. Early writings described Chicanas stereotypically, exclusively as the center and heart of the family. Familistic sociology reinforced the perception of women as unidimensional, anchored primarily in the maternal role. Andrade (1982) uncovered the pervasive nature of this stereotype in the social science literature, noting the policy implications of situating Chicanas exclusively in the home. Historically then, Chicana identity has been defined primarily, if not solely, in terms of family roles.

Contemporary Chicanas are multidimensional women, workers, spouses, lovers, mothers. While Chicanas continue to be undereducated, underemployed, underpaid, and devalued (De la Torre and Pesquera 1993), an increasing number are employed outside the home. According to the 1991 census, 44.4 percent of Latinas were in the labor force. Working women thus fulfill multiple roles. The impact of wage labor on the social and family roles of Chicanas has been studied only recently (Pesquera 1993; Segura 1993; Zavella 1984, 1987). Segura's findings on motherhood and employment are particularly noteworthy. She found marked differences between immigrant Mexican women and Chicanas concerning the relationship of motherhood and employment. Chicanas in her sample displayed high levels of ambivalence between motherhood and employment, appearing to reflect a more traditional gender ideology and a desire to "realize the prevailing social construction of motherhood that exalts childrearing over paid labor" (Segura 1993, 139). What is then the psychological impact on women of the perceived obligation to choose between realizing this social construction and maintaining an adequate standard of living? What are the psychological consequences for Chicanas of delayed motherhood or of choosing to remain childless? While Pesquera (1993) has identified the ways in which Chicanas often couch their work identity within the family and gender roles, we still know very little about the psychological correlates of multiple identities.

A Chicana psychology, then, must incorporate an analysis of identity development that is multidimensional and feminist, and which provides a lens sensitive to the sociocultural context. The Contextual Psychology model of Ivan Boszormenyi-Nagy (Boszormenyi-Nagy and Spark 1984), modified by Bernal and associates (Bernal et al. 1982, 1985, 1986; Flores-Ortiz 1989, 1993a, b, 1995; Flores-Ortiz, et al. 1994) offers such a theory and practice. This model proposes that the psychological realities and needs of individuals must be viewed through a systematic analysis of four levels or dimensions: the level of facts, individual psychology, family/ systemic context, and an ethical-relational dimension. Within this paradigm, the individual is viewed in terms of history, culture, and politics. The theorist and practitioner examines how Chicanas are positioned and how identities are constructed in terms of gender, race, class, and sexuality. Moreover, the role and influence of family legacies and relational ethics in the construction and reconstruction of self is examined. Thus the psychology of the individual is understood not in terms of intra- or intergroup comparisons, but in relation to her own uniqueness. A brief review of each dimension is offered.[2]

Dimension of Facts

This dimension includes an analysis of the sociocultural and historical background and their effect on individuals and groups. In addition to circumstances which exist at birth: ethnicity, race, gender, sexuality, physical characteristics and capabilities, the contextual model proposes that historical events, as well as cultural values, beliefs, and traditions influence, shape, and often determine the lives of individuals and families across generations. For Chicanas, analysis of their history of colonization and neocolonization is essential to understand their development as individuals and as a group.

The development of identity for Chicanas must be viewed

through the lens of race/class/culture/sexuality. How a Chicana defines herself ethnically or culturally, even in terms of the label she uses, is grounded in her history in the United States and racial/economic dynamics that foster and maintain class stratification based on color and gender. Chicana identity has been constructed by others who have used labels to categorize her racial composition and to connote her differentness from those in power. Thus efforts to self-define and choose identity labels must be understood through an historical analysis.

An examination of gender highlights the experiences Chicanas share with other women; however, an analysis of race and class factors is essential to comprehend the discontinuities in experience among women of different backgrounds. It is in the analysis of the factual dimension of Chicanas that Chicana scholarship can make its greatest contribution, as it offers both in the humanities and the social sciences the language and method to view Chicanas as subject.[3]

Individual Psychology

Central to understanding Chicanas' emotional and psychological well-being is an analysis of the impact of gender oppression. Here feminist scholarship can inform Chicana psychology. Luepnitz (1988), Baker-Miller (1986), and the Stone Center Scholars (Jordan et al. 1991) among others, have promoted a psychology that views women's development as different from men's (rather than deviating from men's). Women's development is seen as culturally determined and mandated (Baker-Miller 1986). The psychological development of women emphasizes *being* in *relationship to others* and an identity defined on the basis of their *service to others.* Furthermore, while women's identity is tied to providing essential services for family and society, patriarchal systems and structures devalue these roles and find worthy only those functions performed by men.

The social expectation that women perform tasks essential to human survival and the simultaneous devaluation of these tasks create a contradictory context within which women must forge an identity. Psychological theories typically offer explanations of female psychology that reflect the societal overvaluing of males and devaluation of females. It is not surprising that women often emerge as less psychologically fit than men (Baker-Miller 1986).

A feminist psychology, however, values women's contributions as nurturing, affective beings. Moreover, feminist theories view women's traditional focus on mutuality, interdependence, and connectedness as signs of health, balance, and strength and as resources for those she loves, not as the weaknesses of character that male-centered psychological theories have determined them to be.

While feminist writers generally do not elaborate on issues of class, ethnicity, and race, they articulate issues of gender applicable to Chicanas. Moreover, to fully grasp the psychological tasks Chicanas routinely face, an integrated analysis of how race and class impact gender roles must be included in a Chicana psychology (Flores-Ortiz, et al. 1994). The individual psychological dimension thus includes an analysis of women's identities, self-worth, and resilience in the face of patriarchal systems and discriminatory practices.

Family/Systemic Dimension

Within a contextual framework, the world of the family is analyzed as a system developed over time and influenced by history and generational patterns in order to elucidate the rules that govern individual and collective behavior. The multigenerational web of legacies, loyalties, and expectations derived from cultural values and traditions are seen as influencing interdependent relationships and providing a map for the conduct of family members (Flores-Ortiz and Bernal 1989; Flores-Ortiz, et al. 1994).

Both Chicano and feminist scholarship offer additional lenses which help situate Chicanas in the family. An analysis of the family as a patriarchal structure elucidates the roots of family injustice. Examination of the family's adaptation to a history of segregation and discrimination serves to depathologize Chicano family patterns that appear dysfunctional because they differ from social science stereotypes of normalcy.[4] Such an analysis clarifies the relative contributions of class, gender, and racial factors to the creation of balanced and imbalanced family patterns.

Contemporary Chicano families must be seen as systems that have evolved despite a hostile context (Williams 1990). The uniqueness and diversity of Chicano families also need to be examined to better understand the family-role demands Chicanas face (Flores-Ortiz 1993b). A sensitive assessment of Chicana identities must be filtered through this lens. The expectations for identity formation and behavior families hold for Chicanas must be studied. The goal is not to reify the family, as early Chicano scholarship tended to do, but to examine critically the strength and support a family can offer, as well as the ways in which family life oppresses and victimizes women (Anzaldúa 1987; Flores-Ortiz 1993a, 1996). Chicanas' multiple roles within the family; the construction of contemporary family life; the balancing of wage labor, domestic labor, parenting and nurturing, as well as alternative lifestyles, must be viewed through a feminist lens that understands cultural values and expectations, neither reifying nor pathologizing them.

Chicana psychological theory and practice must incorporate an analysis of the interaction of facts, individual psychological characteristics, and family dynamics to promote healthy ways of being and prevent imbalance and injustice within and outside the family (Flores-Ortiz 1993a, b; Flores-Ortiz et al. 1994).

Ethical/Relational Dimension

This dimension examines the degree of fairness, justice, and balance in relationships. Boszormenyi-Nagy and Spark (1984; and Boszormenyi-Nagy and Krasner 1986) propose that ethical relationships are characterized by a fair balance between giving and receiving and between the debts and obligations accrued in the interdependent balance of mutuality. This balance is never static, since giving and receiving necessitates

situations of temporary imbalance (i.e., taking over some responsibilities of a family member who is ill). However, chronic
situations of imbalance ultimately result in unfair relationships.
For example, relying exclusively on women as nurturers de-
pletes women and indebts men to them. As Baker-Miller (1986)
has noted, men ultimately resent and sometimes despise
women because women carry their emotions for them. At some
level, men then become (and feel) dependent on women; de-
pendency being anathema to some, this leads to the devaluation of women's contributions to their emotional health.

Patriarchally based systems have placed on women those
feelings, behaviors, and attitudes which are essential for survival, then devalued these services precisely because women
are identified with them almost exclusively. The recognition
of women as depository of men's emotional needs contributes to feelings of worthlessness in men. Women are subsequently punished for fulfilling traditionally mandated roles.
They are labeled "emotional, passive, dependent," characteristics devalued by men and pathologized by male-centered
psychologies.

Key to a contextual understanding of individual and family psychology is the notion of *entitlement*, the existential realization of having inherent rights and privileges. A feminist
analysis raises the question of whether women, enculturated
within a sexist social system, can ever feel entitled to just and
fair treatment. A contextual practice of psychology seeks the
ways in which she can feel entitled. In the same manner, how
can individuals and groups subjected to discrimination on the
basis of color, language, ethnicity, culture, and sexuality claim
their inherent rights? From a contextual psychological perspective it is critical to understand the *subjective experience of
disentitlement* which is a consequence of oppression and may
be at the root of many human problems (Flores-Ortiz and
Bernal 1989; Flores-Ortiz et al. 1994). Women often speak of
not having rights, of lacking the basic entitlement to think of
themselves first.

Furthermore, psychological theory and practice must strive
to foster entitlement, mutuality, and fairness in relationships.
Without mutuality, unfair, unjust relationships will develop.

Thus, abusive relationships are viewed as byproducts of social systems which devalue women and the nurturing roles they perform (Flores-Ortiz et al. 1994).

The contextual model posits that historical factors, individual psychological characteristics, and family systems are partly determined by the ethics of the larger social context. Violent, unjust societies breed and foster unjust, unfair relationships through the institutions that replicate social norms, including the family. It follows that patriarchal societies and their representative institutions foster dehumanizing social networks. Both men and women are dehumanized by chronic conditions of imbalance; men because they are discouraged (or forbidden) to feel and be connected emotionally to others, women because their self-worth is connected exclusively to being in the service of others. Rigid family and social systems perpetuate imbalance and promote the psychological development of men who cannot give (it is considered unmanly) and women who cannot ask or receive (it is considered unfeminine). It is these conditions of chronic imbalance in family life which result in seemingly cold, distant men and martyred women (Baker-Miller 1986).

Also central to contextual theory are the concepts of *legacy* and *loyalty*. Loyalty, the adherence to familial and social constructions of rules and norms (the shoulds) is the glue that keeps families connected. In situations of social injustice, the family often becomes the sole support for its members. In such instances, family members can become unduly indebted to the family. Concomitantly, the adults may demand excessive loyalty of the younger family members, which can culminate in the sacrifice of individual autonomy in the service of family unity. Women typically are expected to be more loyal to the family than men (Flores-Ortiz 1993a, b), resulting in an imbalance between what they receive from and what they are expected to give to the family. The construction of female identity, then, often is based on what she *should do* and who she *should be*, as determined by family and society.

Legacy, the social, cultural, and psychological inheritance passed from one generation to the next, is viewed as a key to understanding health and dysfunction among individuals. For Chicanas, the cultural legacy of Malinche (Mirande and

Enriquez 1979), for example, has served to foster distrust between men and women. As a cultural symbol, Malinche was blamed for the colonization of the Aztec and became the repository of all that was considered weak, evil, and defeated among indigenous Mexican males. As a cultural symbol, Malinche has been used to blame women for the troubles of men in post-Colombian Mexico and by extension in the colonized southwestern United States. Woman's image as treacherous, deceitful, and above all *disloyal* is personified by the interpretation of Malinche as *la Madre de los chingados.* In one clean swoop, one woman is blamed for the end of the world in Mesoamerica and the beginning of oppression *for men.* While Chicano writers have attempted to reinterpret the conquest and come to terms with the subsequent *mestizaje,* only Chicana feminists have called into question the prevailing interpretations of Malinche (Cotera 1976; Del Castillo 1977).

The facts of the conquest of Mexico and centuries later its loss of lands to the United States, and the attribution of blame to women, helped create a context of unfair relations between men and women and a legacy of injustice for Mexican-origin people in this country which has impacted psychological adjustment and family relations. Similarly, the Chicano movement and the European-American *and* Chicana feminist movements (Pesquera 1993) have made significant contributions to the current positioning of Chicanas.

The Chicano movement called for justice and demanded equity for Mexican-origin people but said little about the rights of women in the community and family, despite the significant participation of women in the movement. In fact, early Chicana feminists were chastised for demanding their rights (Sosa Riddell 1974). This was viewed as separatist and disloyal; often Chicanas were asked to wait with the promise that justice for Chicano men would eventually benefit them. Over twenty years later, Chicana feminists continue to demand fairness, equality, and justice outside and within the family (De la Torre and Pesquera 1993; Flores-Ortiz, 1993a, b).

The unfair blaming of women for the Conquest and neo-colonial status of Chicanos has potentiated unjust relationships between Chicanos and Chicanas. Since women are expected to nurture, they are expected also to accept blame and restore the male's integrity through acts of love and sacrifice. The inherent power differential between men and women further promotes imbalanced relationships. Thus, an understanding of relational ethics and their impact on individual and family psychology is central to promoting emotional health within and between Chicanas and Chicanos.

Key Variables in Chicana Psychology

A feminist Chicana psychology must consider a number of facts to better understand Chicanas' psychological development. As women of color in the United States, Chicanas are impacted by sociocultural legacies, including gender, economic, racial, ethnic, sexual, and religious discrimination. Unlike white European-American women, however, Chicanas are forced to deal with the historical reality that Chicanos also are oppressed. Given the cultural/gender expectation that women be the givers of love, sustenance, and emotional well-being *and* the transmitters of culture, many Chicanas have found it difficult to challenge patriarchy and male subjugation.

Chicanas historically have fought for equality and justice for the group, even though they were unfairly treated by men. United to men by the experience of racism, many Chicanas who raised questions of gender equity were made to feel disloyal, selfish; their commitment to the family and cultural/ethnic group questioned. Their voices often were silenced by the group, the family, and the dominant culture.

Thus, Chicanas must be viewed not only as triple minorities (Mirande and Enriquez 1979), but as women whom others have tried to silence for hundreds of years. Psychological notions of self-esteem, resilience, ego strength, and so forth cannot be divorced from the historical and social context in which Chicanas have been situated and in which they are now actively positioning themselves.

Central to Chicana psychology is an understanding of her relationship to others and to herself, in order to discover how she has survived, coped, and thrived. Chicanas now are writing their history and creating their theories. These texts, through their scholarship and testimony, iluminate the relevant issues Chicana psychology must address.

The next section examines the psychological context of some Chicanas. Utilizing their own voices, I examine how they forged their identities and sexualities, how they confront the "Isms," and cope with injustice.

Pláticas del Diván/Conversations from the Couch: Identities

Male identity has agency; males are defined and define themselves in terms of what they do. Women are defined in terms of their relationships: as someone's daughter, wife, partner, mother, sister, *comadre*, friend. The "I" for women is contextually determined. Moreover, Chicanas are defined and often define themselves on the basis of their appearance and the degree of approximation to a (bi)cultural ideal. The referent may be either the stereotypic "good loyal passive faithful compañera" construction of the Chicano Movement, the "braided tortillera good mother/wife" version of Mexican psychology and Anglo social science, or the stereotypic "blond goddess" construction of Anglo and upper-class Latino media. Given the choices, Chicanas historically have had to forge an identity that either attempted to honor the expectation of loyalty to various stereotypes or was oppositional. In the latter case, Chicanas who questioned the validity of the identities offered as models often were labeled disloyal, assimilated, or the worst insult imaginable a decade or so ago, *femenista*, implying white-washed feminist. Many women did not perceive they had a choice to challenge existing constructions of female identity; the prize to pay was too high.

In the last two decades Chicanas have begun to articulate the need for greater freedom in forging an identity. Despite the growing numbers of Chicanas who speak out, many continue to feel the burden of legacy and loyalty inherent in biculturality: "It's not a comfortable territory to live in, this place of contradictions. Hatred, anger and exploitation are the prominent features of this landscape" (Anzaldúa 1987, preface).

Indeed the psychological landscape for many Chicanas has been one of suppression of self in the service of others. This is an exploitative context that generates anger. However, anger is the one emotion denied most women; it is inconsistent with a stereotype of passivity, submission, sweetness. The fact is most women are angry; they have reason to be. Were they to deny their anger, they would be denying the injustice that surrounds them; that would be psychotic, a denial of reality. Nevertheless, most women do not express their anger. They feel it, but swallow it. The anger is manifested often through diagnosable psychiatric complaints: depression, anxiety, eating disorders, "nerves" (Flores-Ortiz 1993b).

Chicanas who do not attain culturally mandated identities are viewed as deviant; in particular, women who remain childless or who are lesbian. Within a traditional value context, women who do not marry are acceptable as long as they become caretakers of others (aging parents, nieces or nephews), or who serve God (i.e., nuns). Occasionally single, professional women are acceptable if the family views academic attainment as antithetical to marriage (i.e., not beneficial to men).

A Contextual Feminist psychology proposes that mental health for women requires the coexistence of identities without overvaluing one (mother) and devaluing others (independent adult). Moreover, for such a shift to occur, men's identities must be expanded. They must be permitted to explore and express their gentler sides without being punished (Baker-Miller 1986). Until that social revolution occurs, women must continue to speak out, to find constructive channels for their anger, and to challenge the status quo. Mental health professionals as well as scholars must support those struggles, not collaborate with unjust systems that work to put women "in their place."

The forging of an ethnic identity entails conscious and unconscious processes grounded in history, which often reflect forced and untenable choices:

> I look in the mirror and see Mayan eyes, Asian hair, the color of copper. My body reflects a thousand years of history. I am. I walk out the door and become an other, I am perceived as the chola from East 14th; they call me wetback at school. The

homeboys want me to be a certain way. What about what I want? My family wants me to be "American." I don't know what they mean. I am American; qué más Americana que yo? (Rosa, age 14)

Rosa was referred to therapy because she was "having problems with authority." Her parents found her to be disrespectful; her teachers labeled her defiant because she questioned the relevance of readings in her history class. I was asked to "treat her," in other words to help her "fit in" better. But for her to fit in she would need to become less vocal. I, as a psychotherapist, was expected to silence her. A bright, articulate, artistic young woman, Rosa was in a stage of development where questions of identity are central. She knew who she was, but found untenable the demands to become someone else's ideal. Her active refusal to be subverted was labeled by family and society as deviant (disrespectful, defiant). Rosa's inherent sense of entitlement, fostered (until adolescence) by a loving family, was problematic to some of her teachers and male friends. Psychotherapy with Rosa focused on supporting and building that entitlement, not suppressing it. Our dialogues or pláticas addressed choices, alternatives, and avenues to grow and be healthy. Rosa struggled to find balanced responses to the obligations connected to her roles of daughter, student, and friend as she blossomed into an independent young woman with a strong and proud voice.

Some families place excessive demands for loyalty on their daughters, allowing them to define themselves only in terms of their relationship to family:

I owe my father who and what I am; he needs me home, to take care of Mom. I cannot put my needs ahead of his. I owe him, them, my life. I don't have the right to think of me. (Julia, age 30)

The second daughter in a family of three daughters and one son born in the United States, Julia attempted to straddle her world and her parents' immigrant ideals and cultural values. The father had worked two jobs for the past twenty years to afford his wife and children an upper-middle-class lifestyle.

Julia went to private schools, had expensive jewelry and clothes, latest model car. She was the peacemaker in the family, always trying to please her parents. Her father had set the example of sacrifice, and because he "had done so much for her" Julia did not feel entitled to leave home, to marry, to be herself.

Julia, of course, had never been told explicitly that she needed to sacrifice her desires for her family. She "knew" it; she was able to read the cultural prescriptions. The parents reinforced Julia's "knowledge" by labeling her a good daughter, because she too did so much for the family (unlike a sister who was considered selfish). This situation made it more difficult for Julia to express her desire for greater balance between family obligations and individual needs. Furthermore, her inability to be herself contributed to episodes of bulimia. Unaware of her anger, Julia punished her body. Her needs for self-fulfillment were invisible to herself. Recovery from her eating disorder necessitated an exploration of her needs as a woman, as a person, and addressing directly the contradictions in her family roles. This was facilitated by an analysis of her family's context in the United States through a discussion and clarification of the dimensions outlined above. Julia was able to understand how her symptoms were directly related to social and familial expectations. She gradually began to forge an identity that both connected her to her family and manifested her separate, more independent self:

> I always knew I loved women, not just as friends. When I was a little girl I wanted to marry a woman when I grew up. I also knew I couldn't tell anyone. Mom and Dad always wanted so much for us. I knew if I told them I would break their heart. At school my friends would tease me. I tried dating, I even married a man. But one morning I woke up and knew I could no longer deny being lesbian. I had to tell. Can anyone understand the forced choice between family approval and sanity? When I told Mom she cried; not because of shame, but because she knew how the world would treat me. "Twice marked," she said, "Chicana and gay." (Deborah, age 50)

According to Anzaldúa (1987, 19) the ultimate rebellion a lesbian of color can make against her native culture is through

her sexuality, because she then goes against "two moral pro-
hibitions: sexuality and homosexuality."

Through her sexuality, a Chicana lesbian slips in and out
of the interstices of her psychological reality. "It is a path of
knowledge—one of knowing (and of learning) the history of
oppression of our Raza. It is a way of balancing, of mitigating
duality" (Anzaldúa 1987, 18).

Indeed, for Chicana lesbians the question of identity crosses
the borders of race, class, gender, religion, and culture. Issues
of belonging to a culture and family that is homophobic must
be examined with sensitivity. Within a contextual framework,
sexuality is an inherent right. Individuals are entitled to express their sexuality in non-exploitative ways. Thus, it is fundamentally unfair (and unethical) for theoreticians and psy-
chotherapists to support only one expression of sexuality.

Deborah's midlife struggle to forge an identity that embraced and bridged multiple identities was facilitated by a critical analysis of cultural values, the internalized expectations
from her family, and the inherent unfairness of being denied
expression of her sexuality.

Women's rights to their bodies and their sexuality need to
be intrinsic to any discussion of psychological theory or practice. Traditional psychological formulations have viewed
women as sexually incomplete men; such notions have fostered the sexual control and victimization of women. Among
Latinos, the cult of virginity (Bernal and Alvarez 1982) has
served to restrain women's sexuality. The most extreme form
of such domination is sexual violence. Family violence of any
form epitomizes all that is wrong with patriarchal systems
(Flores-Ortiz 1993a; Flores-Ortiz et al. 1994). Thus, women
who are victimized in their own families must forge an identity of survivorship (Flores-Ortiz 1997).

The psychological impact of intrafamily sexual victimization is exacerbated by the cultural dictum that the victims must
hold the secret to protect the perpetrator and keep the family
intact. For Chicanas, this dictum may be reinforced by the
knowledge that males are victimized in the larger society.
Women are in fact tacitly asked to protect men from institutions perceived as hostile to Chicanos (police, judicial systems)
by remaining silent. Moreover, the larger social context ex-

plicitly and implicitly blames women for their own victimization, also encouraging silence. Through this silence men are exonerated and women are held responsible for the abuse they suffer.

Sexual victimization and other types of violence attack the moral and spiritual fiber of women. When her exploitation is rendered invisible and she is silenced, she may compare herself to Malinche:

> I knew it was my fault; how else could I explain my father's abuse? Perhaps I was not smart enough, or good enough, obedient enough, quiet enough, invisible enough. He said he loved me; he provided for us kids. Maybe I just had to pay for the sins of Malinche and women like her. (Flor, age 25)

Flor was sexually abused by her father since age two. The abuse stopped when she left home at sixteen. She told her mother about the abuse and was not believed. Her brothers called her a liar and a whore. She became suicidally depressed. She did not kill herself, she said, because she did not want to cause her mother any grief. She was depressed for many years, but did not tell anyone else about the abuse until after her father's death. She had not wanted him to go to jail. Healing from this abuse took many years and necessitated a historical analysis of the factors that create abusive family systems. Flor also needed to expurgate her guilt and rebalance and renegotiate the mother-daughter relationship (Flores-Ortiz 1993a, 1995). Initially, she had described herself as "an ancestral whore"; years later she saw herself as yet another victim sacrificied to male gods. Ultimately, she saw herself as a survivor who emerged from years of victimization unsullied, whole, with a strong voice.

Psychological theory and practice must understand the sequelae of incest and the conflict inherent in the woman feeling disloyal as she begins to protect and heal herself. Furthermore, the context of Chicano families who abuse their children must be understood along factual and historical dimensions, not to justify the abuse, but to seek culturally congruent ways of healing (Flores-Ortiz 1993a, 1997).

Towards the Future: Survivors Recreating Themselves

Anzaldúa (1987) perceives Chicanas as having two choices: to abnegate and feel victimized and blame others for the victimization (which may be a culturally congruent script), or to feel strong and in control. Furthermore, Chicanas can forge an identity based on a history of domination and disentitlement or incorporate the history of struggle and resistance of the indigenous ancestors and of the women who came before. The latter is a proactive self-ascribed identity that by necessity must be grounded in knowledge of history. The formation of Chicana identity must then be a conscious journey involving a critical analysis of culture(s) and an awareness of the political context of Chicanas and Chicanos.

A Chicana psychology can offer maps for such a journey. A theory that contextualizes Chicanas can facilitate the attainment of emotional well-being and interpersonal justice. Having access to one's history, understanding the facts and how these impact individual and family health, provides women with tools to fight the "isms." Such a psychology, however, depends on dialogue and partnership between scholars and community, between practitioners and clients. In essence, the process of creating a Chicana psychology entails the coconstruction of identities for all those involved in the struggle.

Notes

1. The term Chicana is used to discuss women of Mexican origin and describes the experiences of women who identify with this label. While many of the issues addressed in this paper apply to Latinas, the focus of this essay is exclusively on Chicanas.
2. For a more detailed discussion of these dimensions see Ivan Boszormenyi-Nagy and Geraldine Spark (1984) *Invisible Loyalties*, New York: Brunner Mazel; and Yvette Flores-Ortiz and Guillermo Bernal (1989) "Contextual Family Therapy of Addiction with Latinos." In G. Saba et al. (eds.), *Minorities and Family Therapy*, New York: Haworth Press.
3. See Gloria Anzaldúa (1987). *Borderlands/La Frontera: The New Mestiza*. San Francisco: Spinsters/Aunt Lute Press.

4. See, for example, Yvette Flores-Ortiz, "La Mujer y la Violencia," in *Chicana Critical Issues*, 1993, Berkeley: Third Woman Press; and "The Broken Covenant: Incest in Latino Families, in *Journal of Chicana/Latina Studies* 1 (2) 1997, Berkeley: University of California Press.

Works Cited

Andrade, S. J. 1982. "Social Science Stereotypes of the Mexican American Woman: Policy Implications for Research." *Hispanic Journal of Behavioral Sciences* 4 (2): 223-244.

Anzaldúa, G. 1987. *Borderlands/La Frontera: The New Mestiza.* San Francisco: Spinsters/Aunt Lute Press.

Baca Zinn, M. 1982. "Mexican American Women in the Social Sciences." *Signs: A Journal of Women and Culture in Society* 8 (Winter): 259-272.

Baker-Miller, J. 1986. *Toward a New Psychology of Women,* 2nd ed. Boston: Beacon Press.

Bernal, G., and Ana Isabel Alvarez. 1983. "Culture and class in the study of families." In *Cultural Patterns in Family Therapy,* edited by Celia Falicov. Gaithersburg, Md.: Aspen Pubs.

Bernal, G., and Carmenza Rodríguez-Dragin. 1985. "Terapia Familiar Intergeneracional: Intervención breve en una familia con problemas de alcoholismo y depresión." *Monografías EIRENE* 10.

Bernal, G., Yvette Flores-Ortiz, and Carmenza Rodríguez-Dragin. 1986. "Terapia familiar intergeneracional con Chicanos y familias Mexicanas inmigrantes a los Estados Unidos." *Cuadernos de Psicología* 8 (1), 81-99, Cali, Colombia.

Boszormenyi-Nagy, I., and Barbara R. Krasner. 1986. *Between Give and Take: A Guide to Contextual Therapy.* New York: Brunner Mazel.

Boszormenyi-Nagy, I., and Geraldine Spark. 1984. *Invisible Loyalties.* New York: Brunner Mazel.

Cotera, M., 1976. *Diosa y Hembra: The History and Heritage of Chicanas in the U.S.* Austin, Tex.: Information Systems Development.

De la Torre, A., and Beatriz Pesquera, eds. 1993. *Building with Our Hands: New Directions in Chicana Studies.* Berkeley: University of California Press.

Del Castillo, A., 1977. "Malintzin Tenepal: A Preliminary Look into a New Perspective." In *Essays on la Mujer,* edited by Rosaura Sánchez and Rosa Martínez Cruz. Los Angeles: University of California, Chicano Studies Center Publications, 129-149.

Díaz-Guerrero, R. 1955. "Neurosis and the Mexican Family Structure." *American Journal of Psychiatry* 112 (6): 411-417.

___. 1967. "The active and the passive syndrome." *Revista Interamericana de Psicología*, 1 (4): 263-272.

Flores-Ortiz, Y. 1993a. "La Mujer y la Violencia: A culturally based model for the understanding and treatment of domestic violence in Chicana/Latina communities." In *Chicana Critical Issues,* edited by Mujeres Activas en Letras y Cambio Social, 169-182. Berkeley: Third Woman Press.

___. 1993b. "Level of Acculturation, Marital Satisfaction and Depression among Chicana Workers: A psychological perspective." In *Las Obreras: The Politics of Work and Family,* edited by Vicky Ruiz. *Aztlán* 20 (1 and 2): 151-175.

___. 1995. "Chicanas at Midlife: The interface of race, class, and gender." In *Racism in the Lives of Women,* edited by Jeanne Adleman and Gloria Enguídanos, 251-259. New York: Harrington Press.

___. 1997. "The Broken Covenant: Incest in Latino Families." *Journal of Chicana/Latina Studies* 1 (2): Berkeley: University of California Press.

Flores-Ortiz, Y., and Guillermo Bernal. 1989. "Contextual Family Therapy of Addiction with Latinos." In *Minorities and Family Therapy,* edited by George W. Saba, Betty McKune Karrer, and Kenneth V. Hardy, 123-142. New York: Haworth Press.

Flores-Ortiz, Y., Marcelo Esteban, and Ricardo Carrillo. 1994. "La Violencia en la Familia: un modelo contextual de terapia intergeneracional." *Revista Interamericana de Psicología* 28 (2): 235-250.

García, A. M. 1990. "Studying Chicanas: Bringing Women into the Frame of Chicano Studies." In *Chicana Voices: Intersections of Class, Race, and Gender,* edited by Teresa Córdova, et al., 19-29. Austin: Center for Mexican American Studies, University of Texas.

Jordan, J. V., Alexandra G. Kaplan, Jean Baker Miller, Irene P. Stiver, and Janet L. Surrey. 1991. *Women's Growth in Connection: Writings from the Stone Center.* New York: Guilford Press.

Luepnitz, D. A., 1988. *The Family Interpreted: Feminist Theory in Clinical Practice.* New York: Basic Books.

Melville, M., ed. 1980. *Twice a Minority: Mexican American Women.* St. Louis: C. V. Mosby.

Mirande, A., and Evangelina Enríquez. 1979. *La Chicana: The Mexican American Woman.* Chicago: University of Chicago Press.

Pesquera, B. 1993. "Work gave me a lot of confianza: Chicanas work commitment and work identity." In *Las Obreras: The Politics of Work and Family,* edited by Vicky Ruiz, *Aztlán* 20 (1 and 2): 97-118.

Segura, D. 1993. "Ambivalence and Continuity: Motherhood and employment among Chicanas and Mexican immigrant workers." In *Las Obreras: The Politics of Work and Family*, edited by Vicky Ruiz, *Aztlán* 20 (1 and 2): 119-150.

Sosa Riddell, A. 1974. "Chicanas en el Movimiento." *Aztlán* 5 (1 and 2): 155-163.

Williams, N., 1990. *The Mexican American Family: Tradition and Change.* New York: General Hall.

Zavella, P., 1984. "The Impact of Sunbelt Industrialization on Chicanas." *Frontiers: A Journal of Women Studies* 8 (1): 21-27.

___. 1987. *Women's Work and Chicano Families: Cannery Workers of Santa Clara Valley.* Ithaca: Cornell University Press.

"Chingón Politics" Die Hard: Reflections on the First Chicano Activist Reunion

Elizabeth Martínez

"The Old Chicano Dinosaurs and their High-Spanic offspring will once again engage in organized revelry, militancy and joy with other consenting adults and their offspring," announced the call for the 20th Anniversary Chicano Activist Reunion held in San Antonio, Texas, December 27 to 30, 1989. The call kept its promise to a considerable extent. "Once again" also applied, unfortunately, to some things that we could well do without. Among them, what some call "*chingón* politics," roughly translatable as tough-guy politics (*chingar* means to screw)–an affliction hardly limited to La Raza.

This was the first big, interstate reunion of Chicano activists from the 1960s ever held. According to registration records, 130 people attended, but the actual number was higher. Officially 111 came from Texas, with sprinklings from California, Arizona, New Mexico, Colorado, Indiana, Wisconsin, and Washington. Most participants seemed to be academics or public school teachers, bilingual educators, social workers, union staff members, or employees of government-funded programs and sometimes private industry. Among the nationally known leaders from the 1960s who came were Rodolfo Acuña of California, noted Chicano historian; Mario Compeán, a La Raza Unida (LRU) party leader and now university professor; José Angel Gutiérrez, conference chair; Reies López Tijerina, former leader of the New Mexico land struggle; and Antonio Rodríguez, a Los Angeles-based activist-lawyer formerly in the workers' organization CASA. The fact that these are all men set the stage for what happened at the event.

The reunion call had been issued by Gutiérrez and Event Chair Irma Mireles. Now a Dallas attorney and investment-banking director for a securities firm, in the 1960s and early 1970s Gutiérrez was a student protest leader who went on to found LRU as an alternative to the Democrats and Republicans. The party won stunning victories in Crystal City, Texas, where it took over the city council and school board; it had less success in other states. Today a chapter or two claim to exist, but barely; numerous former Texas LRU activists now work in the Democratic Party. Most of the volunteer cadre for reunion operations came from the LRU network.

Gutiérrez emphasized that the event was a reunion rather than a conference and, as he said, "not intended to decide things but to make it possible for people to confer and make agendas." The list of participants and the discussion sessions were open to any additions, but proponents had to take the initiative. Non-sectarianism would be the order of the day and, in public at least, this held true--for which, *mil gracias.*

The program offered a rich diet of activities, including a "Labor Lunch," a walking tour of the Alamo, a "Chicano Power" rally, an evening of "Chistes Calientes y Cerveza" (Hot Jokes and Beer), a champagne and tamales breakfast, political discussions and panels, a banquet and dance, and a memorial mass for activists who had died, as well as films and book-signing parties. Headquarters was St. Anthony's Hotel downtown, but most gatherings took place at a community center or in restaurants.

When the reunion had ended and the lobby of St. Anthony's returned to being blonde instead of brown, what could one say about it?

Supermachismo Lives

Most striking to this writer were the issues still not dealt with after 20 years--for one, sexism. Discussion chairs, event hosts, and speakers (except those on the topic of women) were overwhelmingly male. In "The Chicano Movement in Hind-Sight," the only panel that aimed to analyze the past, every presenter was male. Sexist jokes and asides could be heard at times even within the formal program, including one "joke" about Chicana lesbians. The reunion offered no child care. One of the new books touted at the reunion was *United We Win*, a history of La Raza Unida Party that fails to discuss the crucial role played by women in LRU; they are present only incidentally. The author acknowledges his omission, but adds nevertheless that overall he's convinced the book includes "the most essential" material.

Reunion organizers had made efforts to recognize women's accomplishments. The featured speaker at the Labor Lunch and guest of honor at the banquet was Emma Tenayuca, the young leftist heroine of the huge Mexican pecan shellers' strike in San Antonio in the 1930s, called La Pasionaria by local people. Male speakers at the Labor Lunch extolled women organizers. The banquet was dedicated to honoring Chicana activists, with a major speech by San Antonio activist Rosie Castro, in which she criticized the way that the role of women has been obliterated in books.

Such efforts would probably not have been made 20 years ago; we can see real progress and it would be wrong to characterize the whole reunion as flagrantly sexist. But too often the merit of those efforts was subverted by other realities, the recognition of women rendered proforma or patronizingly. When the subject of women was not on the official agenda, old-style practices and attitudes reasserted themselves. At the end of the banquet dedicated to La Chicana, a brief on-the-sidelines display of juvenile machismo by two movement "heavies" sent us reeling backward. The banquet itself was billed as a "Tribute" and it is not just sour grapes to say: Tributes are nice but how about something more substantive?

The "Chicano Power" rally was a full-scale celebration of "*chingón* politics," dominated by male speakers in numbers and time consumed, with a special man-to-man show we would like to forget performed by two movement "heavies." During one hour-long address, the (male) speaker turned from the lectern every few minutes to gesture and smile at another male speaker sitting on the stage, and totally ignored everyone else up there, including two women. The seated man would smile back at the first, and on went the spectacle of mutual stroking to the tune of militant rhetoric. Was that trip really necessary, *compas*?

At the meeting to discuss agenda items for a future conference, a mild proposal was made that the ongoing problem of sexism, as seen at this reunion, be included. The clapping of women that followed spoke to the existence of widespread frustration. The men said nothing immediately, except for one, who may have had too much champagne from the tamales breakfast and now protested angrily but not very clearly. A woman present criticized a word he used, "chink," in his outburst. She was one of those strong Chicanas who stand up against both sexism and racism, for they see the connections and know both are wrong ("We were the chinks of the 1960s," she said later). The man, very upset, let himself be led from the room by another man, to stand outdoors on a large terrace. It felt like 20 years ago, and I could hear brothers in New Mexico calling women who took feminist positions *agringada* (gringo-ized). Or just a few months ago, when this writer was chairing a meeting of Mexicans and Chicanos in the Bay Area, the voice of a man arriving late saying, "Oh, so women run things here."

Then, returning to the present, I saw through the big glass wall overlooking the terrace that the man who had left was weeping. *Ay mi Raza*, and what do we make of all this? I think we make of it something that bell hooks has exposed forcefully in *Z Magazine* regarding African Americans: the effects of equating "freedom" with "manhood," of sexualizing liberation. *Chingón* politics does the same.

Aztlán for Whom?

We can begin by looking at the narrow nationalism that usually characterizes *chingón* politics. From the 1960s until now, radical Chicanos have talked about the vision of Aztlán, that semi-mythical place north of Mexico from which the Aztecs migrated south to what became Tenochtitlán, today's Mexico City. As a dream of homeland, a sort of Brown Nation thesis, Aztlán symbolizes, on one hand, the righteous rejection of racist oppression and the colonized mentality which facilitates that oppression. It echoes a very genuine longing not to feel like some kind of misfit, to taste self-respect. On the other hand, the concept is reactionary on issues of race and class relations, beginning with glorification of the Aztecs, who after all maintained an empire and took deadly tribute from the conquered.

Not surprisingly, the concept of Aztlán has always been set forth in ferociously macho imagery. The average Chicano today hardly takes Aztlán seriously as a goal, but he might secretly imagine himself garbed in an Aztec warrior outfit gazing on the naked breasts of some red-lipped princess. If you note the whiff of sexual possession there, it's no accident. Merely as symbol, the concept of Aztlán encourages the association of machismo with domination.

Another reactionary aspect of this nationalism has been to advocate for "the culture" uncritically. For example, in the 1960s many of us glorified the family in its supposedly "traditional" form without examining patriarchal values and practices. The family has indeed served as a genuine bastion of Raza self-defense against a hostile society. But we do not need to defend blindly all deeds committed in its name. We do need to recognize that the Chicano family itself--especially wife-husband relations--has changed over recent generations, with patriarchy yielding significant ground. At the same time research has turned up questions about just what was "tradition," anyway. All these issues call for new thinking found now among academics; unfortunately Chicano political discussion rarely takes them on.

"*Chingón* politics" also defines concepts and styles of leadership in a patriarchal way. In her fine banquet speech, Rosie Castro speculated that one reason histories of the movement have consistently neglected women's contributions "is that we have practiced a different kind of leadership, a leadership that empowers *others*, not a hierarchical leadership." We should extend her perception to say the leadership that empowers others is the leadership we need.

Alas, too often we have had the other kind of leadership, because *chingón* politics expresses a culture of domination--which means not only women but also men are its victims. The rooster both lords it over the hens and fights other roosters for barnyard primacy. The drive to be top-cock in almost any situation can seem almost compulsive, leaving no room for giving or receiving constructive criticism. We should note that these frantic roosters do not come merely in shades of brown; they could or can today be found in the white New Left, Black liberation organizations, Native American groups, you name it.

For years progressive Chicanos have talked about fighting the "colonized mentality" that makes Raza identify with the oppressor and denigrate ourselves. We have thought too little about how that colonized mentality includes the idea that sexuality proves the man. Our history as a people of Mexican origin began with a hemispheric rape, and we carry in us, consciously or not, the idea that to be conquered is to be *chingado* (screwed); that to become unconquered requires dominating--even screwing--others. We have thought too little about how racism and sexism are interrelated, reinforcing structures in a system that identifies domination with castration, that quite literally casts politics in sexual metaphor.

And so the *carnal* who wept outside that window must have thought he didn't know who he was anymore–feeling threatened by criticism from a woman, without a new way to envision masculinity, some kind of despair set in.

Internalized Sexism and More

Among women at the reunion, internalized sexism emerged, for example, when they minimized their own activism and importance. Many of us accept the view of Chicano men as the main victims of racism. If women are brought into the picture, it is most often in some sex-defined role (the Chicana housewife fighting a poverty imposed by racist institutions, the unwanted sterilization of potential mothers, the young Chicana having to get a job because her husband can't). This view thrives, one must emphasize, on a lack of challenging from women.

The problem has deep roots. Many working-class Chicanas, understanding the freedom-manhood equation, consciously choose to take a back seat and achieve their goals in relating to men by manipulation rather than confrontation. Too often their hearts have been broken when a husband or brother or father cannot find work, cannot find respect, and cannot tolerate life except at the bottom of a bottle. Then they, as much or more than men, will insist that the term *machismo* embraces the best and not the worst of manhood. In 1969, at the first Chicano Youth Conference, the women's workshop reported back, "We don't want to be liberated." Now, 20 years later, you could hear one Chicana tell another at the reunion, "This is Texas. We don't talk that feminism stuff."

But there are other ways to survive politically and spiritually. What we must abandon is a manhood that rests on demeaning womanhood, a sense of identity for one that requires imposing nonentity on the other. Some of us said those words in the sixties; the San Antonio reunion suggested how much they need to be said again. The demeaning and imposing can be subtle; gross forms of sexism common in the 1960s *movimiento* are much rarer today. Men who at least intellectually reject *chingón* politics slowly grow in numbers today, I think (more in some geographic areas than others). But the malady persists. In fact, it is likely to draw strengths as poverty and racism worsen, thereby fortifying an all-too-frequent equation of Chicano liberation with sexism in all its forms.

Time Out

Early evening in San Antonio, warming again after a bitter-cold spell. In the hours before the reunion banquet, an activist friend from the 1960s takes a few of us to a magical place known as Burro Land. It's a sort of Chicano beer garden run by a pleasant couple named Rendon; people like to call it Rendon State Park. Lots of space under trees, some picnic tables, a big 1960s-style Chicano mural on the far wall, and a small building in the center where you can buy beer. Another small building stands discreetly at the back; you may enter there only if you do not have papers, says the friend. Probably a joke, but--reserved for the undocumented? Hey!

It's a chilly night, and a big wooden pallet burns nearby, with more pallets waiting in a giant stack. About a dozen Chicanos have gathered around one of the picnic tables. Suddenly two men stand there in full-scale U.S. Air Force camouflage uniforms, Spanish names on their tags. One of them has a guitar and begins to play it, singing, while somebody whispers in my ear, "They're going to Panama. Do you know that 25 percent of the troops Bush sent there are Chicano?"

The Chicano with the guitar sings a song popular in the 1960s whose chorus melodiously repeats, "Che, Che, Che" (as in Guevara), and people join in. The song echoes across Burro Land; so much for the Air Force. Then Manuel from Phoenix asks for the guitar with immaculate Mexican courtesy, and it is handed over. He and his buddy sing a corrido (ballad) that they wrote about a young Chicano killed by police. The passing around of the guitar has begun.

From somewhere, our original GI Joe in camouflage produces an electronic keyboard and starts harmonizing on the weathered picnic table. The fire crackles, the multicolored Christmas lights strung on tree branches overhead sparkle. No man seems to need to put down another, and no fights start despite the growing mountain of empty beer cans on the picnic table. The night is big, and mellow.

They are all men, the players; it is a man's show, and the heroes in too many of the songs are male. Still, this particular night, the men share, they respect, they cooperate. They make beauty, Mexican style.

Meanwhile, in Struggle

As that evening suggested, there are also some good things which haven't changed. On the afternoon of December 29, about forty reunion participants--mostly women--met to talk about past activism, which often turned out to be present activism as well. None of the national "movement heavies" attended, which may have helped people talk about themselves and struggles they had waged. Their comments confirmed that indeed no national "Chicano movement" exists today, but hundreds of individuals and small groups are working at the community level on mostly local issues. Women in particular--Severita Lara, Carmen Zapata, and others--gave sometimes incredible accounts of dogged efforts over long years. Goals ranged from basics like a bathroom to replace the outhouse at an elementary school in a Mexican neighborhood to becoming the first Chicana county judge via more elections, recounts, new elections, and new recounts than one could remember.

As people talked, *chingón* politics vanished from the scene.

This was just ordinary folks fighting for their rights and their communities, full of pride and determination: the reunion at its best.

That same afternoon brought the agenda-planning meeting mentioned earlier. For three hours people spelled out the many issues confronting Chicanos. They included such community concerns as racism in the welfare system and how a woman with one child could possibly live on the Texas stipend of $137 a month. Drug problems and "a phony drug war which doesn't try to offer youth any alternative," as Maria Jiménez, director of an American Friends Service immigration law monitoring project, commented. Alcoholism, stressed as much if not more than drugs. The drop-out rate, youth, AIDS, U.S. policy on El Salvador, worker struggles, media accountability, the need for multiculturalism, not just biculturalism. Ruben Solís of San Antonio raised the issue of class with a now-famous comment: "I know some rich Chicanos who would sooner pick up a little dog on the road than give me a ride. There's a lot of materialism. It's the Gold Card."

The list of issues went on and on, because the biggest reality that remains almost unchanged, if not worsened, is the conditions facing Chicanos.

Antonio Rodríguez and Gloria Romero published an article in the *Los Angeles Times* just before the reunion with some incredible statistics: In 1989, Chicanos were more likely than ten years earlier to be poor. A quarter of all families and a third of all children live below the poverty line today. Since 1970, the earnings of Latino males have declined from 90 percent to 78 percent of what white men with equal training earn. The drop-out rate in East Los Angeles that students protested with "blow-outs" in 1968 remains the same today: 50 percent. At the same time, gains from the struggles of twenty years ago have been dismantled in the 1980s; affirmative action, bilingual education, and Chicano studies fight for their lives in many places.

San Antonio itself reminded us of the racism that exists. In one reunion event, historian Rudy Acuña led a group on a "Mexicans Won at the Alamo Walking Tour." The Alamo, for those who have forgotten, was a fortress besieged and finally taken by Mexican troops in 1836 when Anglos were seeking to grab Texas from Mexico. Aflame with that usual bad-loser spirit, Anglos raised the vengeful cry of "Remember the Alamo!" They rewrote history to turn a long, difficult battle into a massacre and the defeated Anglos--a pack of filibusterers whose leaders included a slave trader and an escaped murderer--into martyred heroes. Now we would hear the true story.

About thirty of us gathered in front of the Alamo, where a sign commands, "Gentlemen Remove Hats," and a plaque on the wall exhorts, "Be silent friend/Here heroes died/to blaze a trail/for other men." Acuña began talking about the fort's excellent defenses, when a stocky, uniformed "Alamo Ranger" bustled up to proclaim repeatedly that he had to stop; he was not authorized to conduct a tour. After we all insisted on the right of free speech, the Ranger finally departed, grimly. The story continued until the Ranger returned accompanied by a solemn-looking civilian whose tag said "Curator." This man asked Acuña what he was doing there. "Talking," the professor answered with dignity. "About what?" asked the curator. For five seconds it felt like *High Noon*; were we all going to be arrested for trespassing on gringo history?

Firmly and with only a slight trace of disbelief, Rudy answered, "The Alamo." The curator nodded faintly and left. Mexicans won the Little Battle of the Alamo that day.

At the reunion, the spirit of activist commitment to fight racism reached beyond Chicano communities to the international level. Maria Elena Martínez, Rodríguez, Solís, and others expressed strong pro-internationalist positions that included support for the struggles of Palestine, Nicaragua, El Salvador, and Cuba. One foggy morning, about 25 reunion participants joined a lively community march of some 300 people toward El Salvador, and one of them spoke there about the need for "a campaign to educate our people so they will protest Panama."

Though it has run strong among Chicano activists, internationalism has not taken deep root in many working-class communities, with occasional exceptions like the sanctuary movement. Even at the reunion, few, if any, people advocated alliances with other peoples of color, or with progressive Anglos. Collective analysis of such problems facing the *movimiento* remained minimal during the reunion.

Where Is the Vision?

Individual comments on accomplishments and errors included Maria Jiménez's view of the Chicano movement as having been full of contradictions, both reactionary and progressive. In particular, she noted, "Our nationalism stayed within the context of the existing structure of society. But actually we were part of a global phenomenon of national liberation struggle." Similarly, Antonio Rodríguez asked why the movement had not done more to change conditions for Chicanos. "Some academics will say it's because of *envidia* [envy], that we couldn't unite." He believed instead that our failure then was because "we didn't see that our struggle is part of a global struggle for national liberation."

Compeán pointed out that "as a result of our work--and people were killed in the struggle--institutions are now opening." Rudy Acuña agreed, but on the other hand, he added, "We haven't changed very much. We have in the White House a man who is the moral equivalent of a Colombian drug dealer . . . We have to get more belligerent . . . We have to come up with a vision that goes beyond brown capitalism."

Most of these comments came from a broadly left viewpoint; other politics could also be heard at the reunion, and in broad strokes they reflected the historical range from accommodation to resistance. But the current "Hispanic" view that sees movement activists as too confrontational and "out of step" did not dominate.

In the arena of electoral politics, the picture was multifaceted. A leading Los Angeles activist considered electoral politics hopeless in that city, because "the Democrats and Republicans can out-fund any independent candidate." A man from East Chicago, Indiana, said of Chicano activism there, "We used to make headlines, now we're more into electoral politics." This must be true of numerous areas; in 1988 Latinos held 3,360 local and state government elected positions, well over triple the number in the 1960s.

Issues of class and the role of middle-class Chicanos surfaced occasionally but were not examined in depth. Rudy Gonzáles of San Antonio called for more recognition of accomplishments by middle-class organizations, more coalition-building. On the other hand, Acuña thought that "the left of the Chicano movement should have gone into organizations like LULAC [League of United Latin American Citizens, born in the 1920s, primarily middle-class] and fought for political space." The president of LULAC had supported Bush on the Panama invasion, Acuña said. He attributed this and other problems to the lack of moral authority in Chicano politics. "I would support a Ron Dellums before I would support any Chicano candidates on the scene now. We failed to build a political culture."

But neither he nor any other man at the reunion spoke about how women could take a leading role in building that culture. For Gloria Romero and other Chicanas, women were crucial. "When I look back at the reunion, I see that the women moved things just as they did in the 1960s. And women raised the issue of sexism; the men were not going to. *Chingón* politics is everywhere, in academia or whatever, and we have to deal with it."

Would the reunion prove to be a launching pad for the revival of La Raza Unida Party? In conversation, a few advocated that step, but they seemed a small minority. José Angel Gutiérrez himself stated in an interview, "Conditions now are different than twenty years ago. Then there was no alternative to the Democratic Party. Now the Democratic Party (apparently meaning certain sectors in Texas) is run by Chicanos who were in La Raza Unida. In that regard there's no need for an alternative party." On the other hand, Gutiérrez added, the idea that Chicanos should have independent political force, leverage, and clout will continue.

Three projects for the future emerged from the reunion: a conference which an agenda planning committee would develop; work to counter the official celebration of the five hundredth anniversary of Columbus "discovering" America, in June 1992; and another reunion in 1994. Where these ideas will be taken is hard to predict. A scheduled meeting of the agenda committee in Austin reportedly had to be canceled when only three people responded.

At least the reunion *did happen,* and perhaps in retrospect it will mark the beginning of new developments. For now it confirmed that mobilizing a new mass movement of Latinos, or just Chicanos, is not on the agenda of the near future. Several reasons for this have been reviewed by Carlos Muñoz, Jr., a 1960s leader and now a professor at Berkeley who published the book, *Youth, Identity, Power.* Muñoz has written about the many variations in culture, race, region, generation, and class among Chicanos (even without including other Latinos!), which contribute to uneven political consciousness and a lack of clarity about identity.

As for the Chicano left, it is in no better shape than anybody else's left. Meanwhile, the people go on slugging: Shortly after the reunion, Levi's in San Antonio laid off a huge number of workers, many of them Chicanas or Mexican women, so it was back to the street with picket signs and learning how to talk to the city council. Promising arenas of action include labor, environmental issues, coalition work, culture, and especially women's writing. The men can go on being *chingón* dinosaurs, if they must--but let us hope you *carnales* find new ways to be strong.

The Politics of Location of the Tenth Muse of America: An Interview with Sor Juana Inés de la Cruz

Alicia Gaspar de Alba

For the past five years, I have been living with Sor Juana in my head, my heart, and my dreams. I have been researching her life, listening to the underside of her words, letting her entrap and guide me through the webs of logic, pun, and metaphor that she so meticulously spun in her writing. She converses with me constantly, but ours has not been a scholarly or critical relationship. She wants me to narrate her story, to write a novel about her through both her eyes and mine. Her vision— that of an intellectual, intrepid seventeenth-century Mexican nun, scholar, and poet struggling against the subjection of her female body—appears in her poetry, her prose and her plays, and is filtered through my vision, that of a twentieth-century Chicana lesbian writer who can claim the choices and identities not available to Sor Juana, even though she constructed them quite lyrically in her "scribblings." It is through our combined visions that I introduce you to Sor Juana Inés de la Cruz.

Biographical Overview

She was born in 1648, in the small town of San Miguel de Nepantla. The third "natural" daughter of Doña Isabel Ramírez, she was baptized as Juana Inés Ramírez, "daughter of the church," a euphemism for a daughter born out of wedlock, the patriarchal institution of legitimacy. From her earliest years, she was attracted to learning, and at the age of three she managed to convince her sisters' teacher to give her reading lessons. At six or seven, as she relates in her famous intellectual autobiography, *La Respuesta a Sor Filotea*, "having learned how to read and write, along with all the other skills of needlework and household arts that girls learn,"[1] she was ready to attend the University of Mexico; all her mother had to do, she said, was dress her in boy's clothing and send her to live with relatives in Mexico City. Because her mother refused to grant her bold request, Juana Inés dedicated herself to reading all of the books in her grandfather's library, despite continuous scoldings and punishments.

Doña Isabel and her three daughters lived in Panoayan, on the outskirts of Mexico City, at the foot of the volcanos, Popocateptl and Ixtaccihuatl. The hacienda belonged to Doña Isabel's father, Don Pedro Ramírez. It is known that Juana Inés felt a strong attachment to her grandfather; not only was he her surrogate father but she was his "consentida," and they shared a love of letters and books that clearly fostered her scholarly nature.

When Juana Inés was eight, her grandfather died and her mother gave birth to her first stepbrother. For reasons that critics can't explain with any certainty, Juana Inés was sent to live in Mexico City with Doña Isabel's wealthy sister and brother-in-law. Critics have wondered what motivated Doña Isabel to dispose of her eight-year-old daughter under what must have been very emotionally abusive circumstances for the child. Some critics have suggested that economic duress was the cause of Doña Isabel's decision; others believe that Doña Isabel's new consort did not like Juana Inés and wanted her out of his way. Yet others surmise that the girl's recalcitrant "oddness," her attachment to books, her curious and hermetic nature, made her mother deeply uncomfortable. One thing is certain: Doña Isabel was not sending her daughter away to school.

Nonetheless, Juana Inés persisted in her pursuit of knowledge. During the eight years that she lived with her aunt and uncle in Mexico City, Juana Inés, with the help of her books and her inkwell, taught herself. She enjoyed visiting bookstores on her own and participant-observing the metropolis around her, renouncing certain foods (such as cheese) that she thought contributed to a slow mind. She learned Latin grammar in twenty lessons, denying herself the pleasure of long hair until she had learned what she had set out to learn, for, in her young but disciplined mind, she saw "no cause for a head to be adorned with hair and naked of learning."[2] In lyrical vignettes, Margarita López-Portillo's *Estampas de Sor Juana Inés de la Cruz* tells that Juana Inés had a male tutor for these lessons, one Don Martín de Olivas, an undergraduate at the university, who also introduced her to the texts of Homer, Ovid, and the like.[3] Perhaps it is he who helped shaped Sor Juana's opinion of male teachers, which she relates in the interview.

In 1664, during Juana Inés's sixteenth year, a new viceroy and vicereine arrived from Spain and moved into the palace in Mexico City. By this time, the rumors of Juana Inés's erudition had already spread throughout the city, and the vicereine, la Marquesa Leonor Carreto de Mancera, devoted patroness of the arts, lost no time in extending an invitation to Juana Inés's uncle to present the girl scholar of New Spain at the court. Sor Juana does not record what the interview was like, but she must have impressed the viceroy and vicereine to such a degree that, from her sixteenth year to her twentieth year, she lived at the palace as a lady-in-waiting to the vicereine. One of the most popular stories about her stay at the viceregal court recounts the time the viceroy sponsored a tournament between nineteen-year-old Juana Inés and approximately forty scholars, including historians, mathematicians, theologians, philosophers, and poets. For the outcome of the tournament, I turn to the words of the viceroy: "In the manner that a royal galleon might fend off the attacks of a few canoes, so did Juana extricate herself from the questions, arguments and objections these many men, each in his specialty, directed to her."[4]

We must remember, however, that those were dangerous times for an intelligent and independent female; the spies of the Holy Inquisition lurked in every household. Literacy for criolla[5] girls was tolerable, even desirable in some circles; genius was another story. Fortunately for Juana Inés, the inquisitors of Mexico did not take her as seriously as the French inquisitors took Joan of Arc; and, later, when her fame was as vast as her knowledge, she had very powerful protectors in the Mexican viceroys, at least until 1690.

It is believed that shortly after the tournament, Juana Inés experienced three months at a Carmelite convent. Her reasons for entering the severely ascetic order of Barefoot Carmelites is unknown, but three months later, she had returned to the palace. In his 658-page biography of Sor Juana, Octavio Paz discounts the theory that illness brought her back to the palace; instead, he believes that Juana Inés was not cut out for the ascetic life. Within a year-and-a-half however, she was signing her testament of faith to the order of Saint Jerome, which was, Paz informs us, "an order known for the mildness of its discipline."[6] The Order was so mild, in fact, that the nuns were permitted to own slaves, jewels, and property. The nuns' cells were two-story apartments, complete with kitchens and parlors. Sor Juana, it is known, had a substantial library, a collection of musical and scientific instruments, and an assortment of souvenirs given to her by the nobles who often visited her in the convent. She also had investments in convent property and owned a slave, a mulatto woman named Juana de San José, given to her by her mother when she signed her temporal vows.

Convent life consisted of a number of rituals, most of which were "repugnant" to Sor Juana, as she confesses in her autobiographical *La Respuesta a Sor Filotea.* Anything that might disturb her studies—be that the seven canonical hours during which the sisters congregated to pray, or quibbling maids in the courtyard, or visits from other sisters during the siesta and recreation hours—interrupted the solitude she needed to concentrate on her research and her writing. Obviously, she had not joined the convent to marry Christ, although it was because marriage was her only other alternative, and because she felt, as she says, "total antipathy for marriage," that she donned the veil. She also deemed the convent the most fitting place to "insure [her] salvation."[7]

A radical feminist analysis of a few of Sor Juana's poems, particularly the requiems she wrote for la Marquesa de Mancera, the vicereine who took her under her wing, and all of the poems she wrote for another vicereine, la Condesa de Paredes, will explain not only why Sor Juana chose to live a separatist life by joining the convent but also why Sor Juana was concerned for her salvation. Both during and before her bride-of-Christ days, Sor Juana was often criticized for being too "masculine," that is, for indulging her mind too much, for speaking out, for reading and writing, for not being submissive to her superiors. Such crimes were punishable by the Inquisition, no small threat to seventeenth-century New Spain, let alone to a woman with an inclination for knowledge and a disinclination for men.

Of course, Nobel laureate Octavio Paz, who is considered (and no doubt considers himself) the foremost authority on Sor Juana, would radically disagree with such a radical feminist analysis. Octavio Paz is not the only one of Sor Juana's critics and biographers to declare that there was nothing "abnormal" (to use their word) about Sor Juana; still, Paz is unique because instead of simply dismissing the possibility, he tries to prove that any traces of "masculinity" which may have surfaced in Sor Juana's character derive from a combination of psychic traumas: melancholia, subjection to the church, compensation for the absent father, penis envy, and, perhaps, even a courtly love affair (with a man, of course) gone awry. Paz draws a complex analysis of Sor Juana's intense friendship with la Condesa, arriving at the conclusion by the way of some very Freudian (and need I add homophobic) logic, that both women were suffering from "an excess of libido," which, moreover, did not have an outlet in the opposite sex. "A different object—a female friend–had to take its place," says Paz. Thus evolved what Paz calls the "platonic love-friendship" between Sor Juana and the Countess.[8]

We are indebted to la Condesa for having the first anthology of Sor Juana's poetry published when she and her husband returned to Spain. The volume was released in 1689, bearing as one of its subtitles *la décima musa de América*, the tenth muse of America. She was not the first "tenth muse," however. The Greek lesbian poet Sappho was baptized with that epithet by Plato 1700 years earlier. It is doubtful that Sor Juana did not know this bit of literary trivia, but Paz would twist his tongue around in his mouth to make us believe that la Condesa's allusion to Sappho (it was la Condesa, after all, who titled the book) was but a baroque compliment to the sublimity of Sor Juana's verse.

In the last five years of her life, Sor Juana experienced first international recognition as a writer and then her fall from grace. Despite the fact that la Condesa and her husband left Mexico in 1688, Sor Juana and la Condesa engaged in a prolific correspondence, which, unfortunately, has been lost to us. Between 1689 and 1691, two volumes of her writings were published in Spain. In 1690, she wrote the *Primero Sueño*, or *First Dream*. *First Dream* is the most difficult, the most tangled, the most arcane of Sor Juana's "scribblings," as she calls her writing. Thanks to Luis Harss, we have an English translation of the work in which he not only translates from Spanish to English but also interprets Sor Juana's imagery, symbolism, and allusions in the context of the scholarly traditions and esoteric mysteries upon which they draw. The gist of *Primero Sueño* is also the gist of Sor Juana's life: In the darkness, she seeks knowledge and freedom, a solitary journey guided by a spirit that is enemy to daylight, a quest for the dark truths within the universe and within herself that ends in failure, in waking up to the light of reason. For me, *First Dream* is a prophetic work, predicting what would happen to Sor Juana with the next five years.

In 1691, she wrote the autobiographical *La Respuesta a Sor Filotea*, which, although published posthumously, created concentric circles of scandal within the clerical community in which it circulated. *La Respuesta* is perhaps Sor Juana's most important work for those interested in the details of her life as well as in her intellectual discourse and writer's craft, but it is also the source of Sor Juana's downfall. It was in *La Respuesta* that Sor Juana revealed the depth and scope of her intelligence and powers of logic. Here it was that she expressed her negative feelings about marriage, her "black inclination" for learning, her rebelliousness as a child, her displeasure with the other nuns who envied and persecuted her for her studies, her indulgence in melancholia, and finally what we could call her feminism, her defense of a woman's right to learn and develop her mind for the purpose of exalting her soul.

La Respuesta was Sor Juana's last manuscript. In 1692, (the same year that the witch craze hit New England), Luis Harss tells us:

> Sor Juana gave away her books and instruments . . . and signed gloomy Church documents renouncing the world and renewing her vows as a nun . . . At least one of these papers—a Profession of

Faith signed "the worst of women"—was written in her blood . . . .
So Sor Juana may have gone through a spiritual crisis, or allowed
herself to be finally bludgeoned into submission.[9]

Once, Sor Juana had called herself both martyr and executioner, and now the very instrument that she had relied on for
liberation was signing her own bill of sale to the church. What
happened? Why did she give up? It is my theory that she was
a victim of an ultimatum. As powerful as her protectors had
once been, she now faced not just her confessor, her mother
superior, and the rest of the convent, but the archbishop of
Mexico and the Holy Office as well. Their ultimatum must
have been quite simple: Either prostrate yourself to the church
or be publicly humiliated in the Quemadero (the place set aside
for burning heretics). After renouncing her books and her studies, Sor Juana devoted herself to nursing the nuns who had
fallen prey to an unidentified plague that scourged New Spain.

Three hundred years ago, on April 17, 1695, at four o'clock
in the morning, the woman who is today hailed as the tenth
muse of America died of plague in a convent in Mexico City.
She was 47 years old and had spent 27 of those years cloistered
in the convent, separated from the world, writing, reading,
learning, fighting for her rights, and hiding—though not very
effectively at times—the spade that her critics and biographers
have called everything but a spade: her lesbianism.

Colonial Feminism

As you can see from the brief biography above, the life of Sor
Juana Inés de la Cruz offers fertile opportunities for feminist
scholarship, particularly for that branch concerned with the
theories and questions that constitute a woman's politics of identity specifically because of her "location in a female body."[10]

In "Relating to Privilege," Aída Hurtado points out that
white women have a privileged relationship to white men and
are, therefore, guilty of perpetrating a similar domination over
women of color as that practiced by white men over white
women. While the white women who were canonized as pio-
neers for women's rights were *married* to (rich) white men,

Hurtado explains, black women who were fighting against the multiple oppressions of race, class, and gender were *owned* by white men. "Relating to privilege," then, breaks down to two primary subordinations: seduction and rejection. White men seduce white women into being their lovers and wives so that they may bear racially "pure" offspring who will inherit and perpetuate the status quo; women of color, on the other hand, are rejected by white men because they would reproduce racially mixed offspring who would threaten the white male privilege.[11] Interestingly, Sor Juana both seduced and rejected white men. Certainly, her beauty, wit, and rhetoric seduced the nobles and aristocrats (not to mention their wives) who sought her company as much in the "galanteos de palacios"[12] as in the tertulias she held in the convent; however, she also rejected white men for the same reasons that white men reject women of color: reproduction. Her rejection of what Adrienne Rich calls "compulsory heterosexuality"[13] meant that she would be nobody's mother, wife, or mistress.

One of the more popular epithets attached to the name of Sor Juana Inés de la Cruz is "first feminist of América." That Sor Juana was considered the "first" feminist implies a class privilege, for if she had not been of the educated class, if she had not had the protection and support of the viceregal court and the ecclesiastical council of seventeenth century New Spain, if she had not entered one of the wealthiest and most prestigious convents, she would not have had the political connections necessary for getting her work published and distributed, solicited and reviewed.

Criollo academics like Paz "validate" Sor Juana's scholarly inclinations as either divine inspiration or masculine identification, both privileges that ultimately subjugate Sor Juana to the clergy and the state and that define for her the role of Hispanic bourgeois intellectual. I propose to reconfigure Sor Juana, not as a Hispanic, but as a Chicana lesbian feminist. There is no sense in denying Sor Juana's membership in the educated class, nor in denying that Chicana lesbian feminists also share that privilege (regardless of our individual class backgrounds).[14] But we must also keep in mind that, as gendered bodies within patriarchy, we share Sor Juana's subjugated condition, her struggles for autonomy, as well as her search for meaning and transcendence through education and cultivation of a personal/ political voice.

The "of America" part of the epithet signifies a nationalist consciousness. Through a literary analysis of Sor Juana's lyrical, comical, and theatrical verses, particularly those using Nahuatl and Negro idioms, María González argues that Sor Juana should not be classified as a writer of the Golden Age, that is, as a peninsular gachupina, but as a Mexican writer with an evolving nationalist consciousness. González believes that in Sor Juana's work we can find a sketch of the Mestizo/a, "[el] nuevo ciudadano que se bullía entre dos patrias: la una lejana y desconocida; y la otra muy cerca a los ojos y al corazón."[15] In this new citizen can be perceived the spirit of Mexican independence that would manifest itself a century later. In Sor Juana, then, we see a model of the nueva ciudadana, that is, a woman of the Americas, product of colonization, employing her agency and her tongue to create an autonomous identity within the confines, and indeed through a methodology, of male sovereignty. Moreover, because her experience is rooted in the soil of the so-called New World (despite her liaisons with the Spanish aristocracy), and because the bulk of her education takes place within the musty covers of European books, she is a product of cultural mestizaje. She is, in fact, a mestiza in Gloria Anzaldúa's sense of the word, a crosser of cultural and (as we shall soon see) sexual borders, a woman deeply immersed in the mirror of her writing and in the Coatlicue State of crisis and restoration.[16]

What remains of the epithet, the "feminist" label, is what intrigues me most. Given Sor Juana's class and cultural affiliations, her keen awareness of and resistance to gender-specific oppression, her empirical career in the camp of what we now know as women's liberation, her continual struggle for survival, her evolving nationalist consciousness, her separatist strategy, and her very postmodern sense of multiple identities, can it be argued that not only was Sor Juana a feminist but, in fact, she was a symbolic foremother of Chicana lesbian feminism?

My main purpose in this interview is to dig beneath Sor Juana's identity as a criolla and as a nun and thus reveal what kind of "sister" she really was. The school of *Sorjuanistas*, of which Octavio Paz is the self-appointed leader,[17] finds it too threatening to entertain the notion that the "first feminist of America," the female Mexican cultural symbol second only to the Virgin of Guadalupe, was, in fact, of the lesbian persuasion. Insists Paz:

> To think that she felt a clear aversion to men and an equally clear attraction to women is absurd. In the first place, because even if that supposition were true, it is not likely that while she was still so young she knew her true inclinations; in the second, because only by attributing to her an intellectual and sexual license more appropriate to a Diderot heroine than to a girl of Juana Inés' age and social class in New Spain could she cold-bloodedly have chosen as refuge an institution inhabited exclusively by persons of the sex that supposedly attracted her . . . It is futile to try to learn what her true sexual feelings were. She herself did not know.[18]

I am convinced, however, that Sor Juana *did* know the contours of her own desire, and I identify her as a lesbian separatist femininst who cross-dressed as a nun to hide, even from herself, what in seventeenth-century Spanish America would have been interpreted as heresy. Despite Octavio Paz's admonition that there are no "documents" to prove her "Sapphic tendencies,"[19] through both her writings and her strategic silence, Sor Juana offers us ample evidence of her "true inclinations." She certainly would not be the first lesbian nun in the history of the Catholic Church.[20]

In her perpetual conflict between reason and passion, we see the enactment of Anzaldúa's Coatlicue State, a particular faculty of the mind characterized by "psychic unrest," in which the multiple layers of a mestiza consciousness interface either consciously or unconsciously, leading from crisis to restoration.[21] It is this repressed identity, this hidden Other within herself, that constitutes the politics of location which Sor Juana and I will construct through our interview. The two Coatlicue states that I try to illuminate in the interview are Sor Juana the mestiza offspring of white male discourse (imperialism) and female subjugation (América), and Sor Juana the lesbian, crosser of spiritual and sexual borders.

I should explain that the theoretical questions put to Sor Juana in the interview are framed within the discourse of white feminism, not because I choose to privilege white feminist discourse over third world and Chicana feminisms, but because, in the colony of New Spain, founded upon the binary opposi- tions of the European "fatherland" and the "virgin" New World, gender oppression was a way of acting out not just male privi- lege, but imperialist dogma. Moreover, what Norma Alarcón calls the "gender standpoint epistemology"[22] that posits women's subjectivity primarily in relation and opposition to men (while ignoring or subsuming the impact of race and class upon that subjectivity), was the cause for which Sor Juana lived and died, colonial feminism.

Although there was no first world-third world dichotomy in the fifteenth through eighteenth centuries, it can be argued that New Spain, because of its condition as a colony of a Euro- pean superpower, constituted the equivalent of a third world country (a legacy that continues under a different master). The hierarchical structure of colonialism applied both vertically and horizontally to the women of New Spain. Horizontally, for every criollo and mestizo there was at least one criolla and a mestiza, each one living out the prescriptive codes of her class and caste. Vertically, of course, the criolla was considered superior to the mestiza. There was, however, a common ground between the classes that applied only to the female gender. Whether criolla or mestiza, women in colonial Mexico were subalterns. Like the land and the indigenous people, women were taken, claimed, owned, exchanged, pillaged, conquered, silenced, dispossessed of their own destinies. As Alan Trueblood says in his introduction to *A Sor Juana Anthology*:

> Woman's subordination was absolute in colonial Spanish America. In the secular sphere she was to be a homemaker, assuring males at all social levels a dependable domesticity that would free them for the careers or labors to which tradition or chance assigned them. If instead of marrying she became a nun, as bride of Christ she had a duty to be completely submissive to His living body, the Church.[23]

Hence, though the hierarchical structure of colonialism cre- ated class divisions among women as much as among men, gender oppression intersected those class divisions and made all women members of the subaltern, invisible class. It is true that Sor Juana was everything but invisible during her lifetime, despite her being cloistered in the convent. For all her popularity, however, and probably because of it, she was silenced by the church and lived in that silence for two and a half centuries after her death. Being silenced, however, is not the same as being silent, and before the final muffling came, Sor Juana left what later became four volumes of *Obras completas*, from which I have drawn for her responses to my questions in the interview.

Lesbian Drag: Sor Juana's Separatist Habit

Aside from its deconstruction of gender oppression, white feminism's radical branch (which Chicana lesbian feminists have adapted to our own ends) offers separatism as a strategy for resisting and rejecting that oppression. Although entering the convent was ultimately a form of subordination to the patriarchal Church, nunhood was essentially a separatist condition for Sor Juana, the cloister a woman-only space. In *La Respuesta* she tells us that she joined the convent to escape the fate of marriage. In so doing, she refused to "become," in Simone de Beauvoir's sense, a woman,[24] that is, to participate in the social construction of her body. She also rejected her essential femaleness, the biological destiny attached to womanhood, which would involve sexual intercourse with men, childbearing, and motherhood. In choosing to become a nun, Sor Juana was, in effect, as Monique Wittig says, refusing "to become (or to remain) heterosexual."[25] Hiding her body under the habit and the veil was the equivalent of cross-dressing as a lesbian.[26] But, since "lesbians" did not "exist" in seventeenth-century América, it follows that Sor Juana also did not "exist." She had renounced her gender and her sex; she did not live "in the world" but rather in a community of other degendered and (supposedly) asexual beings. Moreover, her body was reduced to a *condition*: of servitude, obedience, abnegation.

But Sor Juana also refused to conform to these three requisites of her chosen condition. Habits and vows notwithstanding, the nun's condition was still located in and circumscribed by a body with mammary glands and ovaries. Cinctured, bound, shorn, and veiled as this body was, it was still the kind of body that became a "bride" of Christ, and lived either as a "sister" of all of the other "brides," or as a "mother" superior. As the holiest of holies, her "Husband" was not of the flesh, but His corporeal substitute was the pope, and His emissaries were the good "fathers" of the Church, all of whom started out as "brothers" and became surrogate "husbands," invested with the power to tell His "wives" what to do. A mainstay of this power was the ritual of confession, which, as Michel Foucault explains:

> unfolds within a power relationship . . . [in which] the agency of domination does not reside in the one who speaks . . . but in the one who listens and says nothing; not in the one who knows and answers, but in the one who questions and is not supposed to know.[27]

The vows of chastity, poverty, and obedience functioned as church laws, and any infringement of the laws had to be confessed to the "fathers," who, alone, had the power to mediate and punish, eavesdrop and absolve.

All of the "fathers," "mothers," "sisters," and "brothers" of the (again) mother church were, in fact, a family. According to Chris Weedon, in *Feminist Practice and Poststructuralist Theory*, the family is "the instrument *par excellence* of the oppression of women through male control of female sexuality and procreative powers and [also men's] control of economic power."[28] Hence, heterosexual relationships as defined by the institution of the family were implicit in the nun's condition; moreover, it was a polygamous heterosexuality, on behalf of the "Husband" and "fathers" (naturally), not always sublimated to spiritual terms (read rape). The nun, then, was both woman and female, a wife, after all.

In the first part of *Plotting Women: Gender and Representation in Mexico,* Jean Franco deconstructs what she calls the "religious narrative" of colonial Mexico, as expressed by the "holy" women of the age, equating the visionary confessions of mystical nuns to fantasy literature, wherein the repressed feelings and desires of the nuns had room to transform themselves into ecstatic visions, of not little sublimated sexual content, which was then disclosed to a father confessor. Another function of mystical literature was its transmission of sacred knowledge; even illiterate nuns could "know" and thereby become empowered. In her second chapter, which focuses on Sor Juana, Franco discusses the two domains of discourse that framed Sor Juana's life and choices; the palace was one domain, the convent the other. Franco argues that at court women were allowed some measure of choice, if only in courtly games and rituals, and were thus slightly superior to women in convents. In the religious domain, women's only recourse to discourse was through the hysteria of mysticism; knowledge was transmitted by the Holy Spirit and recorded by the nuns, who were only seen as channels. As a bridge between the palace and the convent, however, Sor Juana exercised the privilege of a courtly lady and suffered the physical/sexual constraints of the hysteric.[29]

Why did Sor Juana choose this paradoxical existence? True, she escaped cohabitation with a man, sexual intercourse, and childbearing, but was she not still oppressed, owned, and socially constructed? Yes and no. I argue that, apart from being a nonexistent lesbian, Sor Juana was also a separatist feminist to the extent that she was aware of her spiritual and intellectual rights which, for a criolla woman in colonial Mexico, could only be fulfilled through separation from the social restraints placed upon her class and gender. The only road to autonomy and fulfillment, narrow as that road was for a woman, came through separation from society, and this meant joining a convent. Although the convent was subject to the patriarchal mandates of the church, it was closed to men and governed, for the most part, by the women living within its walls. As Asunción Lavrin points out, "Reading [in convents] must have been almost universal since nuns were supposed to use part of their leisure time in the reading of exemplary books."[30] And, although an education, per se, was not the goal of convent life, Sor Juana's reputation as a "scholar"; her connections to the viceregal court, the aristocracy, and the ecclesiastical council; her prolific pen; and her indefatigable pursuit of knowledge (arcane, sacred, and secular) all helped Sor Juana to cultivate–

though not without persistent persecution—an impressive literary and scholarly career within the convent.

One of the few biographies of Sor Juana written by a woman is Mirta Aguirre's *Del encausto a la sangre*, published in Cuba in 1975.[31] I find interesting connections between Aguirre's title and the title of one of Anzaldúa's chapters in *Borderlands*. *Encausto* refers to the red ink used by the Aztec emperor to write and sign his royal documents. Aguirre's title implies that Sor Juana's pen once flowed with the prestige of an Aztec emperor, but later, when she renounced all traces of that prestige, the red ink became the blood with which she renewed her vows and called herself "la peor," the worst of nuns. Anzaldúa's chapter, "*Tlilli, Tlapalli*/The Path of the Red and Black Ink," discusses the trials and tribulations of a writer's life. "Escribo con la tinta de mi sangre,"[32] says Gloria, which is both literally and metaphorically how Sor Juana lived and outlived her own life.

What happened to Sor Juana's body during her twenty-seven-year deluge of intellectual activity? Or rather, what happened to her sexuality, to her desire, to her politics of identity? Let's find out. Let's ask *her*.[33]

Interview with Sor Juana Inés de la Cruz

AGA: Sor Juana, three hundred years after your life span, you are hailed across the western world as the "first feminist" and "tenth muse of America" because you were one of the earliest advocates on this continent for a woman's right to an education. What argument did you use to try to convince the patriarchy that women, in fact, owned this right?

SOR JUANA: "Like men, do [women] not have a rational soul? Why then shall they not enjoy the privilege of the enlightenment of letters? Is a woman's soul not as receptive to God's grace and glory as a man's? Then why is she not able to receive learning and knowledge, which are the lesser gifts? What divine revelation, what regulation of the Church, what rule of reason framed for us such a severe law?"[34]

AGA: Your major premise, indicated by the previous set of questions, is that, yes, a woman's soul is rational and yes, a

woman's soul is just as receptive to God's grace as a man's—
that, in other words, men and women are equal in the eyes of
God and should, therefore, be equal in the eyes of society. This
is a revolutionary theory for your times, a dangerous theory
that could lead to an inquisition, a trial, perhaps even a visit to
the stake in the Quemadero.

SOR JUANA: "Reason, just like a sword
                    can be wielded at either end:
                    the blade, to wound to the death;
                    the hilt, to provide defense.
                        "If, well aware of the danger,
                    you insist on using the blade,
                    how can you blame the sword
                    for a choice you yourself have made?"[35]

AGA: Indeed this conviction of yours that women had as
much right to knowledge and self-expression as men, and your
long and unabashed practice of that right, convicted *you* to the
persecution of everyone around you. What was the root of this
persecution?

SOR JUANA: "A head that is a storehouse of wisdom can expect nothing but a crown of thorns . . . [but] I do not wish to say
. . . that I have been persecuted for my love of wisdom and
letters, having achieved neither one or the other."[36]

AGA: But you *were* attacked as well as envied for your achieve-
ments in the field of reason.

SOR JUANA: "Whatever eminence, whether that of dignity,
nobility, riches, beauty, or science, must suffer [the burden of
envy and persecution]; but the eminence that undergoes the
most severe attack is that of reason . . . For no other cause
except that the angel is superior in reason is the angel above
man; for no other cause does man stand above the beast but
by his reason; and thus, as no one wishes to be lower than
another, neither does he confess that another is superior in
reason, as reason is a consequence of being superior."[37]

AGA: Let me try to deconstruct what you've just said. It's
not that you consider yourself eminent in reason and therefore
superior to those who have not developed their reason; you
seem to be saying that human nature is rational and therefore
superior to animal nature, and that as a woman you should not
be persecuted for being rational nor considered inferior in rea-

son because women are human and reason is a consequence of human nature. In fact, it is this rational essence that you use as your primary line of reasoning in your defense of women's rights. Nonetheless, weren't you the target of incredibly irrational attacks?

SOR JUANA: "The most noxious, those who most deeply wounded me, have not been those who persecuted me with open loathing and malice, but rather those who in loving me and desiring my well being . . . have mortified and tormented me more than those others with their abhorrence. 'Such studies are not in conformity with sacred innocence; surely she will be lost; surely she will, by cause of her very perspicacity and acuity, grow heady at such exalted heights.' How was I to endure? An uncommon sort of martyrdom in which I was both martyr and executioner."[38] And the arrows did not stop there. "Even having a reasonably good handwriting has caused me worrisome and lengthy persecution, for no reason other than they said it looked like a man's writing, and that it was not proper, whereupon they forced me to deform it purposely."[39]

AGA: Your father confessor and your sisters in the convent weren't the only ones who accused you of masculinity. I'm thinking, of course, of that Peruvian man who sent you some clay vessels and a letter saying that you should have been born a man. In your reply to the Peruvian, you say something about womanhood that ties directly into what both Simone de Beauvoir and Monique Wittig say about the myth of woman. They say that woman is a creation of the patriarchy, that the institution of heterosexuality turns females into women, that gender is a byproduct of heterosexuality. Would you recite those lines in your response to the Peruvian that begin with your allusion to Salmacis, the magical spring in Greek mythology that supposedly could change someone's sex?

SOR JUANA: "Here [in the convent] we have no Salmacis, whose crystal waters, so they tell,
to nurture masculinity
possesses powers unexcelled.

"I have no knowledge of these things,
except that I came to this place
so that, if true that I am female,
none substantiate that state."[40]

AGA: One of the fundamental concerns of feminist theory is what is known as "subjectivity." Chris Weedon defines subjectivity as "the conscious and unconscious thoughts and emotions of the individual, her sense of herself and her ways of understanding her relation to the world."[41] Sor Juana, what is your sense of yourself, specifically of your body?

SOR JUANA: "I know only that my body,
                not to either state inclined,
                is neuter, abstract, guardian
                of only what my Soul consigns."[42]

AGA: If you are not inclined towards the masculine or the feminine state, and you feel, as you say, "a total antipathy for marriage,"[43] then it seems to me that you are rejecting two of the basic tenets of the patriarchical system: a strictly dichotomized gender order and heterosexuality. If your subjectivity is not constructed by these two very powerful socializing forces, what is it constructed by, Sor Juana?

SOR JUANA: "My dark inclination has been so great that it has conquered all else!"[44]

AGA: And what exactly is this "dark inclination?"

SOR JUANA: "From the moment I was first illuminated by the light of reason, my inclination toward letters has been so vehement, so overpowering, that not even the admonitions of others—and I have suffered many—nor my own meditations—and they have not been few—have been sufficient to cause me to forswear this natural impulse that God placed in me."[45]

AGA: How did living in the convent affect this "natural impulse," this "negra inclinación,"[46] as you called it?

SOR JUANA: "Once dimmed and encumbered by the many activities common to Religion, that inclination exploded in me like gunpowder proving how [privatio est causa appetitus] privation is the source of appetite."[47]

AGA: By privations you don't just mean that convent life provided little time for learning and writing. Weren't you also forbidden to study at one point?

SOR JUANA: "At one time this was achieved through the offices of a very saintly and ingenuous Abbess who believed that study was a thing of the Inquisition, who commanded me not to study."[48]

AGA: But you studied anyway, not in books, but through observation of things around you, particularly in the kitchen.

SOR JUANA: "Lupercio Leonardo spoke well when he said: how well one may philosophize when preparing dinner . . . Had Aristotle prepared victuals, he would have written more."[49]

AGA: Yes, so you told the Bishop of Puebla in your *Respuesta.* What kinds of discoveries did you make during this period of abstention from your books?

SOR JUANA: "Once in my presence two young girls were spinning a top and scarcely had I seen the motion and figure described, when I began, out of this madness of mine, to meditate on the effortless modus of the spherical form . . . I had flour brought and sprinkled about, so that as the top danced one might learn whether these were perfect circles it described with its movement, and I found that they were not, but, rather, spiral lines that lost their circularity as the impetus declined . . . And what shall I tell you . . . of the natural secrets I have discovered while cooking? I see that an egg holds together and fries in butter or in oil, but, on the contrary, in syrup shrivels into shreds; observe that to keep sugar in a liquid state one need only add a drop or two of water in which a quince or other bitter fruit has been soaked; observe that the yolk and the white of one egg are so dissimilar that each with sugar produces a result not obtainable with both together. I do no wish to weary you with such inconsequential matters, and make mention of them only to give you full notice of my nature, for I believe they will be occasion for laughter."[50]

AGA: Padre Antonio, your father confessor, did not intend for you to forswear learning altogether, did he? I thought he was mainly perturbed by the fact that you wrote poetry, scandalous secular poetry that was either commissioned or encouraged by the viceregal court or by the nobles and poets who often visited you in the convent. Didn't Padre Antonio tell your mother superior that, had he known you would write verses, he would have married you off to a man rather than placed you in the convent?[51]

SOR JUANA: "'But, most beloved Father,' I said to him, '. . . whence your direct authority . . . to dispose of my person and the free will God granted me? . . . Vexing me is not a good way to assure my submission, nor do I have so servile a nature that I do under threat what reason does not persuade me, nor out of respect for man what I do not do for God; and to deprive myself of all that can give me pleasure, though it be entirely licit, it is best that I do as self-mortification, when I wish to do penance, and not because Y[our] R[everence] hopes to achieve it by means of censure.'"[52]

AGA: How bold of you to use the word "pleasure" to a censor of the Holy Office, a scout of the Inquisition. Again, Sor Juana, you are preceding feminist theory by three centuries.

SOR JUANA: "What we need is a seminar
with no other aim than showing
not the ways of human learning
but the comforts of not knowing.

"Exempt from need for caution,
taking pleasure in all things,
we'd scoff at whatever threats
the stars' influence brings.

"Thought, let's learn not to know
since so plainly it appears
that whatever we add to our minds
we take away from our years."[53]

AGA: It is well known that you are an autodidact, that after being taught to read and write at the age of three, you were responsible for the breadth and depth of your own education with, as you say, "no other than a mute book" for a teacher and "an insentient inkwell" for a colleague.[54] What is not so commonly known is your opinion of male teachers.

SOR JUANA: "I do not find that the custom of men teaching women is without its peril, lest it be in the severe tribunal of the confessional, or from the remote decency of the pulpit, or in the distant learning of books—never in the personal contact of immediacy."[55]

AGA: You believe that there would have been more educated women in your time had there not been a dearth of older women teachers. Can you elaborate on that?

SOR JUANA: "If a father desires to provide his daughters with more than ordinary learning, he is forced by necessity, and by the absence of wise elder women, to bring men to teach the skills of reading, writing, counting, the playing of musical instruments, and other accomplishments, from which no little harm results, as is experienced every day in doleful examples of perilous association, because through the immediacy of contact and the intimacy born from the passage of time, what one may never have thought possible is easily accomplished. For which reason many prefer to leave their daughters unpolished and uncultured rather than to expose them to such notorious peril as that of familiarity with men . . . For what objection can there be that an older woman learned in letters and in sacred conversation and customs, have in her charge the education of young girls? This would prevent these girls being lost either for lack of instruction or for hesitating to offer instruction through such dangerous means as male teachers."[56]

AGA: One of your most famous poems is the "Philosophical Satire," in which you explore the myth that women are responsible for men's sins. Would you please recite just the first two quatrains of this *redondilla*?

SOR JUANA: *"Hombres necios que acusáis*
           a la mujer sin razón,
           sin ver que sois la ocasión
           de lo mismo que culpáis:
              "si con ansia sin igual
           solicitáis su desdén,
           ¿por qué queréis que obren bien
           si las incitáis al mal?"[57]

AGA: In this poem, you're revealing the "occasion" for sexual transgression, which is men, and thus you contradict the patriarchical ideology that says women are inherently sinful. If women are sinful, you say, it is because men provide the occasion for sin to flourish. By soliciting and inciting women to sin, and then turning around and accusing women of having sinned, men behave the way Satan behaved in tempting Christ. Hence, men are the tempters and women the victims of temptation—another twist on the traditional idea. The seductress becomes the one who is being seduced, solicited, objectified; the seduced, because he occupies the power position as male and as client, is actually the seducer, the cause of women's fall from grace.

SOR JUANA: "Who is more to blame,
           although both are guilty of wrongdoing,
           she who sins for pay,
           or he who pays for sin?
              "Why act so surprised [señores]

at what is your own fault?
Love what you have created
or create what you can love."[58]

AGA: You say you joined the convent out of your own free will, but some of your modern-day critics, and I'm thinking primarily of Octavio Paz, believe that because you were born out of wedlock in a patriarchal society and were thus an illegitimate child no honorable man would marry you, and so your only choice was the convent.

SOR JUANA: "I entered the religious order, knowing that life there entailed certain conditions (I refer to superficial, and not fundamental regards) most repugnant to my nature; but given the total antipathy I felt for marriage I deemed convent life the least unsuitable and the most honorable I could elect if I were to insure my salvation."[59]

AGA: In other words, becoming a nun was the logical alternative for your life; not only would you not have to live with a man and bear his children, but also you would not be out in the street. Rather than lose prestige and find yourself on the road populated by "hombres necios," you would still be protected by an honorable institution of the patriarchy. By joining the convent, you tried to resist being created in the patriarchal image of woman.

SOR JUANA: "I know . . . that they were wont
to call wife, or woman, in the Latin
uxor, only those who wed,
though wife or woman might be virgin.
    "So in my case, it is not seemly
that I be viewed as feminine,
as I will never be a woman
who may as woman serve man."[60]

AGA: Meaning you will never have sexual intercourse with a man, which is what the etymology of "woman" signifies; thus, you should not be considered a woman. Here is another outright rejection of heterosexuality; but the question is, did you reject sexuality? Although you say that your body was "neuter" and "abstract," you painted the bodily proportions of your most excellent friend, la Condesa de Paredes, in a most sensual and highly erotic way. I'm thinking of that poem you sent to Maria Luisa after she left Mexico. Would you recite that

middle section in which you describe la Condesa's throat, arms,
and fingers?

SOR JUANA: "A passageway to Venus' gardens,
                    your throat is as an ivory organ
                    whose music melodiously ensnares
                    the very wind in bonds of ecstasy.
                        "Tendrils of crystal and snow
                    your two white arms incite desires doomed
                    to barrenness, like those of Tantalus:
                    thirst unslaked by water, fruitless hunger.
                        "Your fingers are alabaster dates
                    springing in abundance from your palms,
                    frigid if the eye beholds them,
                    torrid if the soul should touch them."[61]

AGA: And what about the poem you wrote to commemo-
rate a secret that la Condesa confided to you, a secret which
you literally swallowed?

SOR JUANA: "The page, discreetly, will relate
                    how, the moment it was read,
                    I tore your secret into shreds
                    that shreds be not the secret's fate.
                        And something more, inviolate,
                    I swallowed what you had confessed,
                    the tiny fragments of your note,
                    to guard the secret that you wrote
                    and honor thus your confidence, lest
                    even one scrap escape my breast."[62]

AGA: Forgive me if I press the point, Sor Juana, but those
lines are charged with erotic feeling and I have a difficult time
accepting that the mind that produced those images lived inside an "abstract" body. I think what you mean by "abstract" is
the concept of a body that is doomed, like Tantalus, to perpetual temptation and unfulfilled desire.

SOR JUANA: "Let us renounce this argument,
                    let others, if they will, debate;
                    some matters better left unknown
                    no reason can illuminate."[63]

AGA: From which I interpret that being a woman-identified
woman was not rational to you nor your society, but also such

things were "unknown," the choice did not logically exist; hence entering the convent would be the only rational way of hiding an irrational inclination and of exercising an unknown choice.

SOR JUANA: *"Este amoroso tormento*
                    que en mi corazón se ve,
                    sé que lo siento, y no sé
                    la causa por que lo siento."[64]

AGA: Is it that you still find it difficult to talk about your desire, even after three hundred years, or that you don't have the words to name that desire?

SOR JUANA: "Of things one cannot say, it is needful to say at least that they cannot be said, so that it may be understood that not speaking is not the same as having nothing to say, but rather being unable to express the many things there are to say."[65]

AGA: That reminds me of Foucault, who says in *The History of Sexuality, Volume I,* "Silence itself—the things one declines to say, or is forbidden to name, the discretion that is required between different speakers—is less the absolute limit of discourse . . . than an element that functions alongside the things said."[66] In one of your poems to la Condesa, you play with this notion of silence and yet your passion for la Condesa comes out quite lyrically. Would you mind quoting some lines from that work?

SOR JUANA: "I love you with so much passion
                    neither rudeness nor neglect
                    can explain why I tied my tongue,
                    yet left my heart unchecked . . .

                    "And, although loving your beauty
                    is a crime beyond repair,
                    rather the crime be chastised
                    than my fervor cease to dare . . .

                    "Let my love be ever doomed
                    if guilty in its intent,
                    for loving you is a crime
                    of which I will never repent.

                    "This much I find in my feelings—
                    and more that I cannot explain;
                    but you, from what I have said,
                    may infer what words won't contain."[67]

AGA: I understand now why you gave yourself the epithet, *la peor* when you renewed your vows in blood after capitulating at last to your father confessor's and the archbishop's persecution. Not only was that a common way for nuns to debase themselves (as was expected of them) in documents such as testaments of faith but you were also telling the truth, *your* truth, that is. The implication of the epithet, that you were the worst of nuns,[68] can be extended to mean that you also saw yourself as the worst of socially constructed *women*. And you were the worst of women because you refused to be the kind of woman or nun your society and your superiors expected you to be. You rejected their construction of your identity.

SOR JUANA: "If this is a sin, I confess it,
                 if a crime, I must avow it;
                 the one thing I cannot do
                 is repent and disallow it.

                     "The one who has power to probe
                 the secrets of my breast,
                 has seen that I am the cause
                 of my suffering distress.

                     "Well he knows that I myself
                 have put my desires to death—
                 my worries smother them,
                 their tomb is my own breast.

                     "I die (who would believe it?)
                 at the hands of what I love best.
                 What is it puts me to death?
                 The very love I profess."[69]

Notes

1. Sayers Peden, Margaret. *A Woman of Genius: The Intellectual Autobiography of Sor Juana de la Cruz.* Translation of Sor Juana's *La Respuesta a Sor Filotea de la Cruz,* edited and with an introduction by Margaret Sayers Peden. Salisbury, Conn.: Lime Rock Press, 1982, 28. Hereinafter cited as *Genius.*
2. *Genius,* 30.
3. López-Portillo, Margarita. *Estampas de Sor Juana Inés de la Cruz*

(Mexico: Bruguera Mexicana de Ediciones, S.A., 1979), 57-65.

4. Quoted in Octavio Paz. *Sor Juana, or the Traps of Faith.* Translated by Margaret Sayers Peden. Cambridge: Harvard University Press, 1988, 98. Hereinafter cited as *Traps.*

5. In the class and caste superstructure of colonial New Spain, *criollos/ as* were first-generation Spanish-Americans and their descendents born in the colonies.

6. *Traps,* 99.

7. *Genius,* 30.

8. *Traps,* 217.

9. Harss, Luis. *Sor Juana's Dream,* translated and with an introduction and commentary by Luis Harss. New York: Lumen Books, 1986, 7.

10. Rich, Adrienne. "Notes Toward a Politics of Location." In *Blood, Bread, and Poetry: Selected Prose, 1979-1985.* New York: Norton, 1986, 214.

11. Hurtado, Aída. "Relating to Privilege: Seduction and Rejection in the Subordination of White Women and Women of Color." *Signs* (Summer 1989): 833-855.

12. Paz, Octavio. "Juana Ramírez," translated by Diane Marting. *Signs* (Autumn 1979): 80-97.

13. Rich, Adrienne. "Compulsory Heterosexuality and Lesbian Existence." *Signs* 5 (Summer 1980): 631-660.

14. Though it can be argued that not all Chicana lesbian feminists are, in fact, academics, it is the academics who are more likely to claim these three labels as signifiers of their difference and identity. I am, therefore, alluding not to the *empirical* Chicana lesbian feminist whose politics of location is shaped by *experience* and not necessarily framed by terminology or schools of thought as much as to the Chicana lesbian feminist who creates her various identities and political locations through participation in academic discourse communities, particularly the intellectual history of Chicanas. But as Chicana historian Deena González argues, if we extend feminism outside the walls of the academy, Sor Juana is not, in fact, "the first feminist of América." If feminism is primarily about female agency and resistance to male domination, and not necessarily a written discourse, then the "first feminist in América" was the woman who brokered between European domination and indigenous resistance, la Malinche. See Deena González, "Encountering Columbus," in *Chicano Studies: Critical Connections Between Research and Community,* edited by Teresa Córdova. Austin: University of Texas Press, and The National Association for Chicano Studies, 1992, 13-19.

15. González, María R. "El embrión nacionalista visto a través de la obra de Sor Juana Inés de la Cruz." In *Between Borders: Essays on*

Mexicana/Chicana History, edited by Adelaida R. Del Castillo. Encino, Calif.: Floricanto Press, 1990, 252.

16. Anzaldúa, Gloria. *Borderlands/La Frontera: The New Mestiza.* San Francisco: Spinsters/Aunt Lute, 1987.

17. Paz, Octavio. *Sor Juana Inés de la Cruz, o, las trampas de la fe.* Barcelona: Editorial Seix Barral, 1982.

18. *Traps,* 111.

19. *Traps,* 217.

20. In fact, in Judith Brown's hagiography, *Immodest Acts: The Life of a Lesbian Nun in Renaissance Italy* (New York: Oxford University Press, 1986), we learn of one of the first documented cases of a lesbian nun, in this case, a fifteenth-century Italian abbess named Benedetta Carlini. Benedetta's relationship with Bartolomea, another nun, was unwittingly discovered in a church investigation of Benedetta's supposed mystical visions (Coatlicue States?).

21. Anzaldúa, Gloria. "Entering into the Serpent" and "La Herencia de Coatlicue/The Coatlilcue State." In *Borderlands/La Frontera: The New Mesitza.* San Francisco: Spinsters/Aunt Lute, 1987, 25-51.

22. Alarcón, Norma. "The Theoretical Subject(s) of *This Bridge Called My Back* and Anglo-American Feminism." In *Criticism in the Borderlands: Studies in Chicano Literature, Culture, and Ideology,* edited by José David Saldívar and Héctor Calderón. Durham: Duke University Press, 1991, 32.

23. Trueblood, Alan S., ed. *A Sor Juana Anthology,* translated and with an introduction by Alan S. Trueblood. Cambridge: Harvard University Press, 1988, 1.

24. de Beauvoir, Simone. *The Second Sex,* translated and edited by H. M. Parshley. New York: Bantam Books, 1952, 249.

25. Wittig, Monique. "One Is Not Born a Woman." *Feminist Issues* (Winter 1981): 49.

26. My own novel in progress focuses on Sor Juana's veiled subjectivity as a lesbian. Drawing together historical facts about Sor Juana's life (such as the tournament sponsored by the viceroy between Juana Inés and forty scholars of the university and the documented conflicts between Sor Juana and her father confessor), and critical insights gleaned from Sor Juana's own "scribblings," the novel traces the quest of Sor Juana's self-acceptance through a maze of struggles between logic and passion, employing the narrative technique of first-, second-, and third-person perspectives to characterize Sor Juana's multiple selves and conflicts.

See Gaspar de Alba, Alicia. "Excerpts for the Sapphic Diary of Sor Juana Inés de la Cruz." *Frontiers: A Journal of Women Studies* vol. XII, no. 3: 171-179. Reprinted in *Tasting Life Twice: Lesbian Literary*

Fiction by New American Writers, edited by Ellen Levy. New York: Avon, 1995.

See also "Juana Inés." In *New Chicana/Chicano Writing*, edited by Charles Tatum. Tucson: University of Arizona Press, 1992, 1-15. Reprinted in *Growing Up Chicana/o*, edited by Tiffany Ana López. New York: William Morrow, 1993.

27. Foucault, Michel. *The History of Sexuality, Volume I: An Introduction*, translated by Robert Hurley. New York: Vintage Books, 1990 61, 62.

28. Weedon, Chris. *Feminist Practice and Poststructuralist Theory*. Oxford: Basil Blackwell, 1987, 40.

29. Franco, Jean. *Plotting Women: Gender and Representation in Mexico*. New York: Columbia University Press, 1989.

30. Lavrin, Asunción. "Values and Meanings of Monastic Life for Nuns in Colonial Mexico." *Catholic Historical Review*, vol. 58, no. 3 (1972-73): 382.

31. Aguirre, Mirta. *Del encausto a la sangre: Sor Juana Inés de la Cruz*. Havana: Casa de las Américas, 1975.

32. Anzaldúa, Gloria. "*Tlilli, Tlapalli*/The Path of the Red and Black Ink." In *Borderlands/La Frontera: The New Mestiza*. San Francisco: Spinsters/Aunt Lute, 1987, 71.

33. Most of the responses in the subsequent interview are taken from Margaret Sayers Peden's translations of Sor Juana's work, particularly *La Repuesta a Sor Filotea* (orginally published in 1691). Use of the translated material does not constitute Professor's Peden's (or anybody else's) alliance with my view of Sor Juana or my interpretation of her writings. The construction of Sor Juana's sexuality and politics of location is strictly my own.

34. *Traps*, 499.

35. *A Sor Juana Anthology*, 93.

36. *Genius*, 52, 56.

37. *Genius*, 50, 52.

38. *Genius*, 46.

39. *Traps*, 497.

40. *A Sor Juana Anthology*, 31.

41. Weedon, 32.

42. "In Reply to a Gentleman from Peru, Who Sent Her Clay Vessels While Suggesting She Would Better Be a Man." In *Sor Juana Inés de la Cruz: Poems*, translated by Margaret Sayers Peden. Tempe, Ariz.: Bilingual Press, 1985, 23.

43. *Genius*, 30.

44. *Genius*, 42.

45. *Genius*, 26.

46. *Genius*, 43.

47. *Genius*, 32.
48. *Genius*, 58.
49. *Genius*, 62.
50. *Genius*, 62.
51. "Appendix, Sor Juana: Witness for the Prosecution." In *Traps*, 491-502.
52. *Traps*, 501.
53. *Sor Juana Anthology*, 95.
54. *Genius*, 40.
55. *Genius*, 76.
56. *Genius*, 74, 76.
57. The following is my own translation of these lines. For the full text of the "Philosophical Satire," see *Poems*, 29-33:

> Stubborn men who malign
> women without reason,
> dismissing yourselves as the occasion
> for the very wrongs you design:
> if with unmitigated passion
> you solicit their disdain,
> why expect them to behave
> if you incite their deviation?

58. Again, this is my own translation of these lines from the "Philosophical Satire."
59. *Genius*, 30.
60. *Poems*, 21.
61. *Sor Juana Anthology*, 51.
62. *Poems*, 45.
63. *Poems*, 23.
64. *Sor Juana Anthology*, 78.
65. *Genius*, 20.
66. Foucault, 27.
67. *Sor Juana Anthology*, 45.
68. See "Protexta que, rubricada con su sangre, hizo de su fe y amor a Dios la Madre Juana Inés de la Cruz, al tiempo de abandonar los estudios humanos para proseguir, desembarazada de este afecto, en el camino de la perfección," in *Obras completas de Sor Juana Inés de la Cruz: comedias, sainetes y prosa* (vol. IV) edición, introducción y notas de Alberto G. Salceda. Mexico: Fondo de cultura económica, 1957. For the original document in the convent's book of professions, see the Dorothy Schons Archives at the Benson Library's Latin American Collection, University of Texas, Austin.

See also María Luisa Bemberg's filmic treatment of Sor Juana's

life, *Yo, La Peor de Todas* (1990), which was showcased at the twelfth annual Gay and Lesbian Film/Video Festival in Los Angeles in 1994.
69. *Sor Juana Anthology*, 89.

Free At Last

Cherríe Moraga

"Free At Last" is an excerpt from a long essay entitled "Waiting in the Wings," in which I chronicle my own queer story of pregnancy, giving birth, and the first year of mothering. It is the story of one small human being's survival, of life, of thriving in the age of death, the age of AIDS. My son, Rafael Angel, was born prematurely at only 28 weeks of gestation in Hollywood, California, one day before I was to return to my home in San Francisco. He weighed only two pounds, six ounces, and spent the first three and a half months of his life in an intensive care nursery. In the pages that follow I describe those months of near-death and recovery. They are mostly journal entries, interspersed with reflections I wrote later because at the time I was too immersed in the living of the crisis to speak of it.[1] The essay is a poet's journal (I see now in retrospect), for even giving birth does not satisfy the artist's hunger to create. Finally, this is the story of faithfulness between two lesbian lovers (mothers) and the family that sustained us.

7 julio: Midday, San Gabriel, my parent's home

Nothing will ever be the same. I knew our lives would be changed by the arrival of this baby, but the manner of his arrival is as nothing I have known in my life, feeling so awestruck by every moment–Rafaelito's push toward life. (I am afraid to write of these times, afraid somehow language will lessen what I know.)

Today, as I fight off the traces of a cold, I focus on nothing else but purifying myself, that when he begins to draw from my milk tomorrow, it will fortify him, sustain him as his life struggle sustains me. This child is no stranger to me. Possibly because he looks now as he will look eighty years from now, an old man, I already gone. I see in him my mother's aging forehead, my own collapsing chin (once perfectly delineated), the blurring ancient eyes of my grandmother in the years just before her death at ninety-six. But my son's life lies before him and each day the ancientness will obscure itself in ounces of baby fat and he will carry this knowledge of this closeness to death (the other side of life) as a great secret inside of him.

Today I do not visit him. I take the day to recuperate, but every time I close my eyes he is visible right behind my eyelids. No, it is truer to say he is always an image pressed upon my memory, my sleeping and waking life. My mind at times does not serve as my friend. My heart, yes. In that place resides a seamless connection between my baby's essence beating inside those incubator walls and my milk-hard-breasted body. I struggle to overcome this constant fear and anxiety in the effort to discover a deep and unwavering faith for his survival, his fruitfulness, his life.

8 julio

My faith has been challenged. Faith in what? The benevolence of the universe? To whom do I pray? To the impassive face of Indian Virgen that must know something of what I suffer—she, who bore a son, who lost a son? To the broken body of an Aztec lunar goddess that I witnessed whole and womanly two Mexican summers past? Is it her strength—the power of Coyolxauqui—I draw from, a female power potent enough to eclipse the sun? Or is it this Califas ocean, swelling into a rage, yet tender enough to sustain a child's blue balloon afloat for hours. I follow the balloon with my eyes as it dances at the precipice of the breaking waves. These are the ruminations of a fully grown fully unfearful woman. That is not me.

At forty I feel myself respond to the crisis of Rafaelito's sudden entrance into this world as I did as a child of eight, fearing my mother's death. At eight, I prayed endlessly all night long as my mother lay in a hospital bed some fifteen miles away. I dug a crater into the inside of my elbow with nervous nails, scratching . . . scratching . . . scratching. I worried. I worried for her life. I grew superstitious, feared the wrong set of prayers, a forgotten passage, a misdirected look at a plaster saint could mean her death. I prayed and feared always God's punishment, God's closed ears and heart. I kept my sister up at night. I cried. Today, my mother said to me, "Remember hija, it was your prayers that got me out of the hospital." She, too, thought of the child I was thirty-two years ago.

Now, I see faith is not so easy to secure. I am still superstitious as I pour my breast milk into the garden. I fear the wrong gesture, the wrong words might offend those ever-heartless gods. Still, I take the chance, watering the garden earth with my body's milk. I pray as I pour . . . for life, for my baby's life.

As I see Rafaelito grow stronger and healthier each day, I can't make sense of my blessing in the face of the ailing babies next to him, barely clinging to life, hooked up to respirators and IVs. When my mother and I go to Sears to buy nursing bras and newborn infant wear (clothes Rafaelito cannot possibly fit into for months), she tells the young Chicana cashier about my preemie baby boy. The cashier tells us, too, of her brother born premature, now thirteen with cleft tongue and seizures. "He's only grown up to here." She measures off the air at her elbow. I fear hearing her speak of it, fear bad omens lying dormant in strangers' anecdotes. My mother confesses the same fear. "When I was pregnant," she said, "I thought it wasn't good to even look at a deformed child."

9 julio: Sueño

My son has been born but is not fully human in form yet. He is a kind of guzanito in the early stages of development. How gratified I was to awaken to the knowledge of his perfectly human face staring back at me from my arms.

In a later dream, I am to attend some kind of gathering of women, a kind of retreat. When I arrive, I am shocked to see mostly white women dressed in ethnic fabrics. I can't keep face. I don't want to be here. I want to find my sister. I cry and cry and want to return only to my baby's side. I can think of nothing else. Later in the same dream, I am on the phone debating with a man, then a woman over their rights to a piece of my writing. "I don't give a damn," I tell them. "I'll return the payment to you. Don't use my work." I cry to my mother, "I care about nothing but this baby." She understands.

About five days after Rafa's birth, Ella goes home to San Francisco to get "things in order." The plan is she will return in a week and we will spend the summer here in Los Angeles until the baby is well and grown enough to return with us to S.F. We will sublet an apartment and move our work down south for the time (at least two to three months, they tell us). So far, Rafael Angel's condition has been stable, his breathing normal with the occasional "brady" when he forgets to breathe. The nurses tell us it is normal. Their systems aren't in full operation yet. I am awed that even the instinct to breathe is not a given. Rafaelito is also too young to suck. For at least the next five weeks he will be fed my breast milk through a tube down his throat. So, I pump and pump and pump and label and store my milk in the hospital freezer and in my parents' freezer, transporting it in small ice chests each day to the ICN. As I watch the soft white liquid descend through the tube into his pursed mouth, I tell him, One day hijo, te daré el pecho. Ten paciencia. *More for myself than him.*

14 julio

Rafael is transported by Air Ambulance to San Francisco Kaiser. We are not home yet.

Without warning, I arrive one morning at the ICN to be told that Rafaelito is stable enough to be transferred to Kaiser, San Francisco. "Is it safe?" I ask. Yes, they tell me, explaining that a nurse, a doctor, and a respiratory therapist will fly down from S.F. to travel with him. I call Ella right away. Tell her, "Don't bother coming. We're coming up." The private ambulance plane is waiting as we pull up in the ambulance. Rafaelito is rolled aboard in a compact incubator with all the necessary accouterments—heart monitor and oxygen saturation monitor, IV, in place, respirator ready to go just in case. Nurse Bobby is a mixed blessing, cracking jokes the entire way about "Ra-fee-el" already being a jet setter as she passes out the plastic-wrapped sandwiches and beverages, playing stewardess. She relieves me of some of my anxiety, but is a bit more cheerleader than my mood. Still, when she asks if Ella will be there to meet me, referring to her by name, my heart opens to her. She's read the report, *I think.* She knows we are dykes. *And I am relieved that we will have at least one emissary at this new hospital. One less thing to explain. The doctor, a thin bearded Jewish neonatalist, has little to say to me throughout the trip. As I gaze out the porthole window, the view moving from farmland to forest, I hear him making copious notes next to me, his pen scratching against the clipboard. I glance over to the report on his lap, spot the words "artificial insemination."* Everybody knows my business, *I think. Then I ask him, "So, what do you think, Doctor? How's the baby gonna do?"* He answers, almost disappointed, *"Oh, this baby's not even a challenge."* I think that is supposed to encourage me, but weeks later, when Rafael is be being taken into surgery, barely clinging to life, I want to ask him, *Challenge enough for you now, Doc?*

19 julio: San Francisco

> This time is a subtle study in non action as a way of attaining real meaning in your life.
> −*I Ching*

No truer words. I am in the hospital cafeteria again. These days are the hard days. Rafaelito back on a ventilator, blood transfusion yesterday, twenty-four hours non-stop bradycardiacs. Today he is stable, but exhausted. I am exhausted, too, have never lived like this before. So much passes through my mind, so much to write of what I've learned about familia, life, fear of death. But the writing remains in the wings. It takes great effort to move this pen across the page in an attempt to document some thread of what I am/we are experiencing. To document my son's survival. Guerrero, I call him. Warrior boy.

Tede died yesterday.[2] Without his knowing, he has been an intimate part of Rafaelito's life. Tede writing me of angels in his poetry, my choosing Angel for Rafaelito's second name, hearing that Tede had AIDS so close to the news from the geneticists that my baby was a male. Is there a kind of queer balance to this birthing and dying . . . lesbians giving life to sons, our brothers passing? Rafael Angel is the child of queers, our queer and blessed family, laughing with Pablo[3] and Ella after the insemination, sitting on the bed next to me. We just laughed and laughed. Days later, I knew I had conceived, felt that stirring inside me alone in NYC. I wanted no part of NY, wanted only home, Ella's smell, the slow and subtle creation of my child.

Rafaelito came to me effortlessly, our first try at conception. He was, literally, waiting in the wings . . . angel wings, waiting for me to finally decide to call him to this earth. But now I see Rafaelito is not so easily won. He enters this life with a delicate deep strength, as living reminder of the precariousness of our lives. I breathe through the isolette, call to him, to me, to us, to life. "Rafaelito, Rafaelito, quédate aquí, hijo, con nosotros. Tu familia te espera." I call him over to this side. He listens and slowly rolls over toward us.

It is hard to write, harder yet to pray. I am now in the intensive care nursery. Rafaelito se ve tan pálido. They tell me not to touch him today, to let him rest, but I want him to know I am here. I do not touch. I watch. I watch his small ribcage rise and fall, sometimes with such great effort. Then when his chest is still, I search the monitors frantically, always in momentary panic that mi hijo may have forgotten again to breathe. At this hour of the late afternoon, his chest appears almost transparent. Ella arrives.

20 julio

Ella called the hospital this morning to inquire about the baby, having to put up with the usual deterrents: Who are you? No male voice on the line, but a woman, my lover, seeking to know about our son. "Read the damn chart," she snaps back. "I'm the co-mother." "Co-mother," a concept about which even San Francisco hospitals haven't a clue. I cannot comfort her much when she is bruised by the hospital's ignorance. I hear only her telling me Rafaelito has had more bradys. "How many?" I want to know and do not want to know and suffer that I am not there with him at this moment and suffer that I also can hardly bear to see him struggle so to breathe. And still we don't know what's wrong with him.

Tomorrow Ella and I will split shift—me in the day, she in the evening—so he won't be left alone without us. We draw comfort seeing him together, but it seems there is little room for comfort these days. I was heartened by his look of well-being this afternoon, his color richer, his brightening as Ella spoke to him, as I sang to him.

I learn the lessons of motherhood daily. There are no guarantees, only faith. But what is there to believe in other than simply that Rafaelito was destined to come into this life and share it for a time with us? How I want that time to be full and long and rich. How desperately I want his life as I have wanted nothing before in my life. I pray for this as minute by minute these days Rafaelito struggles simply to remember to breathe.

25 julio

I didn't write when the days were the worst, when they rolled Rafaelito's tiny isolette down the corridor into the operating room and he followed our sad gaze (a calm recognition in his eyes) until he was out of sight. I didn't write when they told us the hardest words to hear: "If it is too late we'll just close him up again." Our baby had contracted NEC, the thing we most feared, an infection that literally eats up the intestine, deadly among so many preemies. If it's not caught in time . . . The news of the perforated bowel comes so close to the news of Tede's passing.

In the waiting room one floor below the operating room, we wait for some word. Pablo has just left, or rather we sent him away, somehow knowing Ella and I needed to be alone in this, needed to find private way to stave off this baby's passing. I have brought un rosario, the wooden one given to me by my mother. Ella and I wrap ourselves up together in the deep vinyl lounge chair, we hold each other and pray. Endlessly, calling down the ancestors, the saints, the sinners that have already testified to such moments of stark terror. Audre,

Cesar,[4] Abuelita. Tede stays with us like an angel.

> You were there with us, weren't you, Tede? Irish and ancestor. Our queer recently born ancestor with all the dead Mexican relatives we remembered and invoked. Abuelita who always asked me, "¿Cuándo te vas a casar? hija. Necesitas familia." While my family held me in her lion arms and my son had his guts cut open on the floor just above our heads.

Somehow in the midst of our prayer, it suddenly occurs to me that I have no choice in the matter, that my baby will die or will survive regardless of how tightly I hold him away from death. I suddenly realize that the holding itself is not what Rafaelito needs. He needs to be free to decide. To stay or leave. Oh, how I hoped he would stay, but I couldn't make him. I can't explain the feeling, that moment of saying to Ella—against every instinct in me—"We gotta let go." Wasn't it our vigilance that was keeping him here? In the letting go might he not slip from us completely? *That was the risk, for what did we two know of death? I only knew my holding on so strong would soon crush all the heart I contained and there would be nothing left over to mourn or raise a son. Si es tu voluntad, I find myself saying the unthinkable out loud, passing the decision on to powers unknown. But in that gesture of letting go, I felt Rafaelito move towards us, toward's life.*

Forty-five minutes into a three-and-a-half hour surgery, Nurse Stacey comes in and tells us there was a small perforation. The surgeons removed only two centimeters and the ileosical valve. "He's going to be fine."[5] Soon after, Deborah arrives, "packed for survival." She forms a little altar on the small lamp table from the holy cards and healing stones she has brought. We don't light the incense but place the sage next to the burning candle enflaming the face of la Virgen. My rebozo becomes the altar cloth. We give thanks. Later Estér and Renée show up. Ella has called them. "We need some family with us," she says. When Rafaelito is brought back to the ICN, he is a limp yellow doll, a stripped monkey naked under the glare of heat lamps. He is all wound and he is my son, breathing through a respirator, and so morphined he is feeling no pain. I remember, we get ourselves out of there. We have Japanese food. I drink beer with a vengeance.

*

For the first time since Rafaelito's transport to San Francisco, I've taken the day off, feeling a sore throat coming on. I call the nurse on duty. The news is good. All signs promising that Rafael is recovering well. I think of nothing, no one, but my baby, even as I wash the rugs, dry the dishes, oh yes surely as I pump my breasts; I imagine his miniature mouth opening onto the rose tip. I imagine the earliest most earnest seeking. I imagine his return to la madre from whom he was so abruptly separated, me, my womb, that sweet protection. The world outside, full of enemy.

It is hard to write when there is no one fixed now to be. I am not the same. I don't know how to write of death. I read *The Tibetan Book of Living and Dying,* and I know I am like the majority, how I fear to even name death, that somehow in the naming, it will surely visit me. And yet, I know that this is the next necessary step. Rafaelito's close encounter with death, his tenuous hold on life, his fragile and threatened beginnings, have introduced me to living with the knowledge of death.

26 julio

Is it residual fear (now that my son heals himself) that causes the fire of an unnamed panic to rise up my spine, spilling across the back of my shoulders, flooding my heart, closing down my throat without warning? Susto, es susto—a fear poisoning the blood.

I know the smell of death. It smells of fear. Fear that is the endless hum of plastic tubes penetrating lungs, the size of tear drops, rain drops. He was born the summer when the angel died, a rainless summer, a Southern California dry summer.

The oxygen tube will be removed this morning. I pray for Rafaelito's strong lungs.

1 agosto

All is good news with Rafa, eating now—barely three ccs every two hours, but it is a start, the antibiotics stopped today. He is on his own steam.

The change continues to astound me, how thoroughly mother I feel. There is no way to feel less than this total commitment to the change of this child in our lives. Tonight I am unable to sleep. I rose disturbed by what seems to be again an infection in my system, warding off a sore throat all week. I have felt off balance for months now, since the advent of allergy season. "No one responded," I tell Ella. Throughout the last months of pregnancy, no one took my allergies, my sinus infections seriously. Yet a part of me feels this is what wore me down, eventually causing the rupture of my membrane, the water breaking. We'll never know for sure.

There has been little documentation of my son's entrance and struggle to sustain himself in this world. Few letters scratched upon these journal leaves, only my heart as testimony—a fear as familiar now as my own breathing. Again last night, we watched his energy wane, watched Rafaelito move into his miniature cuerpecito, lay low, and await his own renewal: the transfusion of blood, the rush of antibiotics. This morning I call about his condition and revel in the news of his orneriness, his anger at not being fed. "He's kicking up a storm," Nurse Bobbie tells me. "He's mad we're not feeding him yet." And again, I know my baby will pass through this, regain his health, return to us whole.

And it is a return. His early separation was so radical, the wound of which is salved only in the sudden appearance of a droplet of milk at the lip of my tit, the movement of Rafael kicking against my belly as I hold him hard, swaddled against my chest. His smell. His smell that grew sweet with the rise of milk inside my breasts, that grew sweet with woman-sex. Even my sister tells me, "I love that smell. I'll never forget that smell," knowing it four full times in her life, four babies. She didn't mean some baby wrapped in the newborn warmth of a receiving blanket. She meant birthsmell, the thick-membraned blood-smell passing out between a woman's legs at birth and for a full moon's cycle following. I didn't tell her how close such scent came to that lesbian secret, of how close women came to birth each time we make love to one another and mean it. It is a lesbian sex smell. A mother-smell. A mother-lover, a mother-fucked smell. It is life.

My baby's smell sleeps in every item of tiny clothing–tee shirt, sleeper, knitted cap, and booty–I lay out, fold and shape, and prepare for his arrival. The smell holds an innocence like nothing I imagined, only remembered vaguely in my own once-innocence. Ironically, as my baby grows older, he grows more innocent. He becomes more "baby" and less sabio, less viejito, less my mother's aging face, and instead, the seamless face of hopefulness, of future. But his hands retain the memory. Wrinkled, a map of generations revisited.

He is my poem. El milagro of what has passed and what will go forward. He is history and future, as Tede now knows, as Audre was given the daily glimpse of for fifteen years, battling cancer. Through Rafael I have been given the gift of bearing witness to a soul's decision to take hold of an earthly life. Earth Angel. We have stood on this side calling to him, "Come join us, hijo. Take hold. Be here." This time, we know he is going nowhere but into our arms, into the embrace of this worldly existence. He has made a decision that at twenty-eight weeks we didn't know for sure he would make. Now after five weeks on this planet, we know he will remain with us and "live to be a very old man," as Nurse Rose tells us.

Rose has become our "seer" of sorts, bringing in holy cards of archangels and St. Jude and directives from her recently passed mother, who according to Rose was la mera Croatian curandera in Kansas City. Rose convinces me to make the trip over to the shrine of St. Jude, a mile or so from Kaiser at St. Dominic's Church. The edifice is a massive monument to San Francisco's Catholic elite, but inside I draw comfort from the stale scent of frankincense and the wintry childhood smell of melting votives. St. Jude, "the patron of lost causes." Although his title makes me a little nervous, I follow Rose's directions and make my way up the side aisle to the shrine ablaze with white candles. I slip a five into the metal slit, light five candles, and with each I pray not only for Rafa but for all the babies and their ailments whom I've come to know in the ICN: for Alex that her sleeping limbs will awaken, for Nathaniel that his heart will heal, for Simone that her eyes will see clear and far, for Freddy with Downs, and for all the others whom I've seen, mirroring Rafa's own embattled state–one-

and two- and three-pound human animals with swollen brains and strokes and weak hearts and drug addictions and troubled families, just struggling to hold onto the little life they got.

Leaving the church, I run into a man asking for change and a prayer. For some reason, I tell him that my son is sick and in the hospital. "I guess we both are hurtin'." He says he had a son once. I give him a twenty. I couldn't help it. I give him a twenty to ward off death.

15 agosto

Over six weeks in the hospital since Rafael Angel's birth. Six weeks. And we may have as much as another six weeks ahead of us. Ella and I are beginning to feel the aftershocks of our near-loss of Rafa. The last four days, he struggles against a new infection, a staph infection, brought on by the IV needle implanted into his chest. We worry over what could still come in the next weeks.

I think of little else but him. Ella tells me I'm obsessed, but there is no other response to have. Still we wear each other down. I hear her cry, but I cannot comfort her. I move about as a nervous child. Fear—its violent rush of adrenaline—grows horribly familiar, and I clean and hammer and fill empty boxes and move more furniture and do laundry and wash dishes and dishes... with a vengeance against whom? Against death? Against its residual poison left in my bloodstream? I drown the taste out with tequila, a bottle of wine. I forget. I sleep a dreamless dead sleep to fortify myself for the next day. But last night was different somehow. Last night I dreamed Rafa, a mother's dream. Not desperate, but full of longing for his *return.*

Yesterday, it was harder than ever to leave him in the hospital, to be parted from him. Each leave taking, a violent rupture. I return home empty-handed. Ella and I fight because we are tired and worried. All is an effort, except the spontaneous impulse towards this baby. In my heart, I am not inside this writing at all. I am across the city, my face pressed to the steaming plastic glass of Rafaelito's isolette.

17 agosto

Some change has taken place. The garden flourishes, although Ella battles daily against the onslaught of ants and aphids. Yesterday Rafael Angel looked better than ever, contento, tranquilo. Well-fed, his color took on a richness I hadn't seen since his birth. I can finally visualize his return home: this soul's entrance into this world. I remember the death of Cesar, Audre, Tede, all within the last year. I, too, know I will die. How is it that the sudden appearance of life is the measure of our own sudden passing? Rafael will see a world I will not. And yesterday, for some reason, I remember my parents' years here grow less daily.

*

I will try to write every day, not as yet another chore but as yet another joy, as when I put my baby to my breast and he lives complete as my life's lesson, my teacher, wholly in the present of that suck/and/pull/and/rush of liquid filling his mouth and throat, settling full and sweet at the base of his hunger. His hunger, for now, can be satisfied. The lesson of babies.

21 agosto: Sueño

I awake at 4:30 a.m. from the dream. Rafael is suddenly losing weight. He is down to 600 grams. He won't make it. I am beyond shock, beyond fear. Bobbie is the nurse in charge. She is not alarmed, only in a way acquiesced to his dying. I can't bear it. No one seems to be responding. He is slipping away. The feeling is strangely familiar, one that I had feared so much, laying dormant inside me throughout all these weeks since his birth—a sense of the inevitable finally coming to pass.

*

Waking and writing at this hour, I visualize Rafael Angel in his isolette in the hospital. I wonder if he is awake at this hour, now 5:15 a.m. I realize as he energetically gains weight that with each gram he moves closer to his return to me, to us, to his home. I wonder if the dream is larger than I think. With each gram, he also grows less and less dependent, less mine. He will never be mine and will surely pass away one day, as inevitably as my dream. And I am already parted from this body.

My parents are here to visit. A good visit. Much kindness. They seem quite content. I relish my time with them, the regularity of our meals together: the chicken with rice soup we eat in the late afternoon, their midnight chicken sandwiches, my father's ritual glass of red wine.

The gift of this child is how he has opened my eyes. I see my mother's amazing physical beauty, the quality of her skin, still sensual, seamless (the skin of a fifty year old at seventy-eight). She dresses in front of me, stands bare-breasted without shame. Is it motherhood that has made our bodies finally shameless to each other?

26 agosto: Sueño

In the dream I am on the shore of the mainland. There is an island out in the water. Tidal waves ravage it as hundreds of people rush to the mainland for safety. The tidal waves are huge. I am awed by their grandeur. The people that rush to shore are beach-goer types: white people, young, moneyed. Suddenly I realize my parents are on the island. I worry that they have been consumed by the storm. Then my father appears from out of the water. He is dressed in white. Surfacing from underwater his calm is almost Christlike. He walks toward the shore without fear. I wonder about my mother when suddenly she, too, appears, but her safety is threatened. There are tidal waves surrounding her. I hear a voice. It is the voice of Ella or my sister. It tells me to go in there and save my mother. I am shocked that this has not occurred to me. I know I cannot save her, that it would be a false gesture, that I would surely drown, but the voice insists that I go in there. I awaken.

10 septiembre

I could have held him for two hours in the darkness, in the

silence, simulating that place from where he emerged, not violently but of his own volition. But there was the fear of falling asleep while holding him bundled as he was, the fear of him falling in my arms where his breath might not find release, fear of suffocation, a mother's fear, a mother's guilt as I bring him back into the hospital nursery. The nurse reminds me, "Probably the first time since his birth he had things so quiet." Can I ever make it up to him, those last three months in the womb lost? Then I imagine the endless hours when he will have both silence and darkness and also the warm embrace of my breast . . . when I get him . . . when I get him home.

25 septiembre

Returning from the ocean, I call the hospital, speak with Nurse Rose. She tells me Rafaelito has made me a birthday card. She tells me the story of getting his spindly legs to stay put onto the ink. His signature, a footprint in a card. Earlier today, I came into the ICN and Ella had arranged for a cake to be awaiting me, again signed by Rafaelito. "Felíz cumpleaños, Mamá," it said, and I still marvel at the miracle that someone will soon grow to call me mami.

Today Ella and I walk the beach. It is all I really wanted to do for my birthday, to meditate on the glass wall of wave that crashes onto the shoreline. Sandpipers scurry along the wet sand, burrow their beaks in search of sand crabs. I remember my own childhood, how like the sandpipers I learned to read the signs of where the crabs were buried, bubbles of air cracking the smooth surface of the sand, their soft-shelled bodies hidden less than an inch below. I am too exhausted to write tonight, but I only wanted to record my bottomless joy at the entrance of Rafael into my life, of the ever-awe of what was not present with me, suddenly appearing and residing in my heart.

28 septiembre

I try to dissect the wild scrawl. Ronnie's handwriting. He speaks of his imminent death. Although in good health, he says he considers it constantly since learning he is positive. He asks me not to write of him posthumously as Francisco did of Tede. He wants only to be remembered by his poems, as we all wish, to be remembered by our poems.

But I have forgotten how to write the poem, the play. I read Ronnie's letter where he mentions at least five writers I do not know, but Bob Kaufman was not one of the unknown to me, and I dream of doing nothing other than reading until I know them all, until I have something to write again. These days I feel I never fully inhabit the hours. With Rafael, I feel always that I am missing him, even while watching his small sculpted "African head," as Myrtha calls it, as he sucks my breast. I don't realize my utter frustration at the length of his hospital stay, now going into the fourth month. I don't fully absorb the recent news that there may yet be another blockage in his intestine, another cut-and-paste job on the operating table on Friday (what was to have been a "routine operation").[6] I don't know my own anger until I hear myself raging on Deborah's answering machine, "There is nothing to fear but fear itself," I shout, "and it is consuming me!" I cling to Rafaelito, hold my ears against bad news. I am that stricture, that blockage between him and all that threatens him.

The prognosis is good for his recovery, but I grow weary of the low-level fear that runs concurrent with my life: that always, around the corner, there will be another problem that the doctors failed to mention. I worry over how much intestine will be lost, over the pain Rafaelito will experience. I worry that he must go hungry for days without my milk to sustain him.

The next few weeks are to be the last leg of this journey, and suddenly I grow afraid of how dependent we have become on the women who have nursed Rafa through these last three months: Rose, Stacey, Bobbie, Sue, Gurline, Donna, Terry, and others whom we never met who watched him throughout the night while we slept or tried to sleep.

Three months. Hard to imagine such a length of time, even in retrospect. But it is not our dependence on them that I fear so much as the loss of the connection. These nurses have become our family, the only ones who have known intimately, on a daily level, the heartache we endure. I know some of these women have even come to love Rafa, thinking of him as "their baby" and getting some serious attitude when he's not listed as one of theirs for the shift. Seeing them fight over him tells me how attached they've become, and maybe, without admitting, they've even become a little attached to us. With no man in the way, Ella and I have sat with these women 'til 11:00 p.m. on Saturday nights, shooting the shit about their love lives—their crazy jazz musician boyfriends and soon-to-be marriages in the midst of a Yugoslavian civil war. We've befriended the one dyke couple in the nursery, after it took me nearly two months to figure it out. We've talked politics, sex, fashion (at least Ella has), and "alternative lifestyles." One time Ella even suggested to one of the more butchy-looking nurses, who was quite a wild woman with the men, that she might want to try women for a change. Well, I guess that was going a little too far. She's still icing Ella.

Although I am ever grateful to Dr. Azick, the soft-spoken pediatric surgeon from UCSF who saved my baby's life on that operating table, the nurses have been the real healers. We've counted on them to re-member how Rafael looked the day before, to notice when his color has paled or energy waned, to respond to signals in advance when his saturation drops or he's not keeping down his food. They have advo-cated for him when the doctors weren't listening. "Something's not right with this kid, Doc," they insist and insist until somebody pays attention. They are the ones who on a daily level have tended to my son with a mother's love, a woman's love, who have made the difference, fundamentally, in his survival.

3 octubre: ICN

Second day after Rafaelito's surgery. No intestine was lost. "A simple procedure," the doctors told us, simply reconnect the small and large intestine, sew up the stoma. Two days later, Ella holds Rafa in her arms with a respirator down into his lungs, two IVs stuck into the veins in his head, and a tube running down his throat to suck out leakage in his stomach. He has dehydrated, is unable to urinate. And my baby has bloated up to twice his size. His face is a monster's—his eyes, black seeds buried into a mass of fluid. When I put my hand to his cheek to caress him, the imprint remains, deforming him.

We learn later that during his preop prep, the nurses (as instructed by the surgeon) had overcleaned the intestines. I had seen the colon cleanser going through him like Drano. The kid was dehydrating be-fore *the operation and the kidneys eventually stopped functioning.*

I am more worried when the surgeon comes to see him. Dr. Azick wears wide-ribbed corduroy pants. It is the weekend, he doesn't have to be here, so he must be worried, too. And then he admits it, "Frankly, I'm concerned. I don't know what's wrong." I appreciate the admission, but don't like what follows . . . "If his condition doesn't change soon, we'll have to go in again."

That night Ella and I come back for a second visit. After 8:00 p.m. we must enter through the emergency entrance, where a security guard gives us passes after signing us in. The guard laboriously tries to spell out my name, letter by letter. The pen is a stranger to him, and I feel my impatience rise as does my anxiety about Rafaelito. I just want to get in there and see him. But each night, we go through the same interrogation. "Only immediate family," the young man tell us. He is very serious in his fresh-pressed uniform. He is taking his job very seriously. "Yes, we know," I answer for the hundredth time. "She [referring to Ella] is immediate family. Call the ICN; they'll okay us." The same old ritual, the same harassment night after night. Then he can't help himself, a grin begins to crack the professional facade. "You say you're both the moms!" He eyes his buddy co-workers, and the street gang begins to form around us. Oh, they're gonna milk this one for all its worth. They are very bored. "I didn't know two women could have a baby together." But I am primed, too. Thinking of Rafaelito swollen beyond recognition. Don't fuck with me tonight, boys. *We had already filed our complaints, called their supervisor, who always seemed to enjoy the joke as much as they, spoken with the ICN social worker, and in a few days I would write the obligatory letter to the hospital administrator. Pero, para nada. Nobody really gives a damn that two women have their baby in a hospital for over three months, not knowing if he is going to live or die, and they still have to endure insults from testosterone-driven homophobes with no power acting like they got some. (My class and race analysis don't do shit for me when the brothers are standing in the way of my child. The hospital was full of AIDS patients and Ella and I often wondered how their lovers were treated when they came through the same door after hours.)*

That night I can't take anymore. All I can see is Rafael's sweet face buried inside that mask of flesh. "That's right," I say, "you'd be surprised what two women can do together" (or something to that effect). *And I storm through the entrance cursing and screaming at the top of my lungs, hoping Ella's coming up behind me. The guard is shouting after me, but I don't hear anything beyond, "Hey, lady . . ." I am counting in my mind how many times we've gone through this, how many times Ella has had to succumb to questioning when she's called the ICN and a new receptionist answers. "Who are you? What is your relationship to Rafael Moraga?" It's been over three months for chrissakes! My impotence enrages me. I can't protect her from the pain she experiences each time they make her the outlaw. I'm the dyke in the matter, I tell myself. I'm the one who's supposed to be on the outside. But not now. As Rafael's biological mother, I am surrounded by acceptance at the hospital, until Ella walks in and we are again the lesbian couple, the queer moms—exoticized or ostracized. I know this is new for Ella. New and hard. As a femme, she's always passed effortlessly—that is, until she opens her mouth and the lesbian feminist rolls out without restraint.*

If anyone would have stopped me that night at the emergency entrance, I'm sure I would have belted him. Fortunately, no one does, and minutes later, Ella joins me at the elevator. We ride up to the third floor in silence.

4 octubre: 7:00 a.m.

I sit at the edge of a San Francisco fishing pier. It is minutes after dawn. This morning the fog prevents any dramatic sunrise from behind the Oakland hills, but as the ashy light gradually turns the bay waters from still black to green-grey, there is renewed hope. I come to this pier today looking for hope, as I did nine months ago, having just heard the news of my pregnancy. It was a winter night and I carried the seed of whom I did not know then was Rafaelito to the pier's end. And together we floated out into the obsidian waters, harbor lights swimming inside them. We drifted under the Golden Gate and out into the Pacific sea in my dream of the future we would share. There was no doubt then (as there isn't now, learning this morning that Rafa was breathing on his own) that that future would come to pass. But there has been doubt, core doubt, or more closely a deadening fear.

A woman, middle-aged like me, interrupts this writing, asks can she take my picture. She looks familiar to me. "It's a class assignment," she says. I respond, "I don't care." And I don't, for she has a kind smile and is a simple woman like me.

I walk the pier in search of miracles, the daily miracles of which my son's relentless struggle to be here reminds me. Over night, the pier houses the homeless, a stupid term for people, but that's what I call them in my mind as I pass the makeshift tents, the shopping carts pinned against plastic tarp to keep out the wind. Now a tugboat passes by, otro milagro perfectly red-and-white striped, perfectly tugboat, steadily churning its way under the Bay Bridge. The bridge is the same color as the sky, steel grey. The cars travel across it, miniature in the distance, and everything becomes my baby's point of reference: the tugboat story in children's books, Tonka trucks, miniature cars that my other son used to horde and collect by the dozens.

The day has entered fully into itself now, as I hope my son will when I go to visit him this morning under the heat of warming lamps and a web of IVs. On my way back, I pass joggers in sweat pants, thick-waisted Central Americanos in nylon windbreakers, una Latina lifting her knees to her chin military-marching style. Her morning exercises. The gulls continue to hover in anticipation of fisherman. In hours their bellies will be full of fish gut, discarded pieces of bagel. The ferries are in full steam, commuting before my eyes' horizon with ten-minute regularity.

6 octubre: Sueños

In the dream my baby has returned home to us; he is extremely vulnerable. At a theater event, I show him to my friends. He is a small worm, the color of the stoma that used to protrude from the side of his belly, a deep pinkish red. His face is a design of small markings, like brushstrokes. There are no real features. My friend queries, "He will grow, won't he?" I accept his appearance as perfectly normal.

Other dreams follow the same pattern. He is so tiny, so vulnerable. I sometimes forget that I have him, start to leave a place without him. At other times, Ella forgets him. He is always on the verge of disappearing, melting away, dissolving in water. We have lived with that low-grade fear, like a fever, for over three months now.

8 octubre

On the day of what will be my son's arrival, I awake with the sunrise. Its gold passes over the garden, drying up the night fog's moisture and spills briefly into our bedroom window. My baby is coming home. I check the date. He is a Libra baby, of sorts, entering the world about ten days after his original due date. All this time he was to have been growing in my womb. Instead he is rushed into this world and has survived a two-pound, six-ounce birth weight, two major surgeries, and myriad infections.

We have an enormous amount to be grateful for—fundamentally his life. That he was born in 1993, not 1963, and there were surgeons to find and root out his illnesses early on. But more importantly that from the beginning of his life he was surrounded by great love. Yes, love from my familia (blood and all my queer relations), with candles burning across the continent towards his survival. But also love from his caregivers, the nurses who came to feel Rafaelito was a part of them.

Today, this day, may be Rafaelito's return to us after all. Since Friday, it has been an everyday occurrence, the promise of his coming home, followed by the disappointment. Yet, I feel the time closing in, it could surely be today. The grey dawn invites his coming.

Throughout the wee hours of the morning, the U.S. Air Force's "Blue Angels" strip the sky of its necessary quiet. *Ironic,* I think, their name—*my son's name*—his innocence and vulnerability, their steel delight in stripping off the canopy of our heavenly protection. Angels, they are not. It is too early to be awake, and yet I know my baby will have me up at this hour most days. I look forward to those moments of solitude with him. His crib and cradle and changing table are covered with cloths now, as during Lent, awaiting the resurrection. All is in order.

16 octubre

Rafael Angel is discharged from the hospital.

*It is a full week later than expected, always some unexpected "prob-
lem" or "potential problem" cropping up. The nurses kept reassuring,
"It's better this way. The worse thing is to get him home and to have
to bring him back again."* Unfathomable, *I think.*

*Nurse Bobbie, fittingly, is the one to do the honors. We marvel at
how everything comes full circle, her picking him up in Los Angeles,
admitting him in S.F. Now three and half months later, she does the
paperwork for his discharge and we load up to get this kid home. And
I mean "load up": the cards, the stuffed animals, the mobiles, the
little notes Nurse Rose made in her curled calligraphy, the angel-
figures of every shade and shape, the tiny wardrobe of tee shirts and
sleepers, doll-sized knit caps and booties, the handmade blanket from
my tía Eva, the photographs of Rafa at various stages in his hospital
stay (some with his little neighbors held up by moms and nurses grinning in the background), the thumb-sized moccasins Cynthia and Dina
brought from Pine Ridge, Deborah's healing stones and Stacey's ar-
rowheads, the stone angel my sister gave him on her visit to S.F.,
Angelina's tiny Indio doll, and finally, the green-and-white felt-cov-
ered image of la Virgen my mother had given me when I first went
into the hospital over fifteen weeks earlier. I had pasted the scapular
to Rafael's incubator in Hollywood on his birthday. It stayed with
him through the trip up north and throughout his entire time at Kaiser S.F.*

*We pile all of this—what had decorated Rafaelito's "apartment"
(the nurses' name for his crib)—onto a wheelchair, along with a bag
full of medicine, complimentary diapers and formula, and a preemie-
sized bathing tub (Rafa is still only four and one-half pounds). After
last-minute pictures with nurses and docs, Ella carries Rafa's car
seat, I carry Rafa, and Bobbie maneuvers the wheelchair-moving-van
out of the ICN. As the elevator opens onto the lobby floor, Ella and I
spot two dyke moms coming in with their baby. The first and only
lesbian moms we've seen in three and a half months. And this is San
Francisco.*

Later, stuffed into the front seat of my little truck, Ella and
I keep eyeing the sleeping bundle next to us. Free at last, we
keep thinking. No cliché. Free at last.

Notes

1. Original journal entries are in roman type.
2. Tede Matthews, San Francisco-based writer, activist, queer solidarity worker, queen.
3. Pseudonym.
4. My friend and poet Audre Lorde died, after 14 years of battling cancer on November 17, 1992. Cesar Chavez, president of the United Farm Workers, died in his sleep April 23, 1993, twenty miles from his birth town of Yuma, Arizona.
5. Rather than reconnecting the intestine where the removal of the dead matter had taken place, the surgeons give the baby an ileostomy in order to relieve stress on the colon. For the next three months, Rafaelito will be defecating into a small bag attached to his lower right abdomen.
6. The operation involved reopening the first incision from the previous operation, closing up the stoma, and reconnecting the intestine so that Rafael could once again pass stool normally through the rectum.

Los Espíritus Siguen Hablando: Chicana Spiritualities

Lara Medina

The spiritual practices of many Chicanas emerge from a purposeful integration of their creative inner resources and the diverse cultural influences that feed their souls and their psyches. Accepting their estrangement from Christianity, whether Protestant or Catholic (and their wounded souls), many Christians (re)turn to an *indígena*-inspired spirituality, learn to trust their own senses and bodies, recreate traditional cultural practices, and look to non-Western philosophies—all of which offers us a (re)connection to our selves, our spirits, and to the ongoing process of creating *nuestra familia.* As they journey on paths previously prohibited by patriarchal religions, Chicanas define and decide for themselves what images, rituals, myths, and deities nourish and give expression to their deepest values.

Chicanas venturing into often undefined spiritual arenas continue a tradition of religious agency as lived by many of our *antepasados, abuelas, madres, y tías.* Our *consejeras, curanderas, rezadoras, espiritistas,* and even *comadres* practiced and still practice their healing ways in spite of, in lieu of, or in conjunction with the sacraments and teachings offered by the Christian churches. Likewise, contemporary Chicanas, either as self-taught healers or as trained officiates, follow in the footsteps of our foremothers to provide spiritual nourishment for themselves and their communities.

This article provides a glimpse of how twenty-two Chicanas define, live, and express their spirituality as individuals and as members of communities. Through these voices we hear the ways they have learned to supplant patriarchal religion with their own cultural knowledge, sensibilities, and sense of justice. Their experiences differ widely, yet they share a common desire for healthy and creative lives, with their spirits intact and a willingness to teach and share their thoughts and practices with others.

Unknowingly, this article began several years ago, when I actively began to explore my spirituality outside of institutional religion. Like many Chicanas, I grew up in a strict Catholic environment, reciting the prayers that meant little to me, receiving the sacraments, internalizing the infamous Catholic guilt. My rebellious years led me away from the faith and spiritual awareness of life. Little did I think that, years later, I would return to the church with tears on my face, in need of answers to life's crises. I found comfort at the time, ministers both men and women willing to listen to my story and my seeking. My questions led me to study theology, as I wanted to know more of "the truth." Ironically, my three years spent studying church teachings, scripture, ritual, and ministry exposed me to the lies of the religion, and I was delighted! What freedom to learn that patriarchy made Mary a virgin, perhaps the resurrection did not really happen, and that Jesus died not to forgive sins but because of his resistance to the power of the state. Liberation theology and feminist theology enabled me to revisit the religion I inherited from my parents. Although a liberating experience, I groped to find a place for my voice, a Chicana feminist liberationist. A Chicana committed to a religion only if it addressed the economic and political struggles of her people, only if it dealt with its own inherent sexism, homophobia, and racism and that of the society in which it functioned.

After graduating, I became a lay minister, a preacher, counselor, ritual leader, but because of my gender unable to bless the folks or the bread they came to consume on Sundays. Unwilling to accept these limitations, I began meeting with a group of Chicanas/Latinas in a spiritual circle or community outside of the church. They were *mujeres* like me, wanting more than what the church offered them. We wanted to know our own spirits, our own Goddesses, our own ways of blessing and praying.

I eventually left the patriarchal Eurocentrism of the church, as the contradictions were too great to reconcile. However, I continue to identify as a "cultural Catholic," as one who appreciates many of the popular religious expressions of Mexican Catholicism. The next few years introduced me to Chicanas engaged in creating spiritual circles on their own authority. Many of these *mujeres* had been working on their spirituality for years. What struck me was their commitment to inner growth and the building of *nuestra cultura* based on feminine wisdom as a natural evolution of their keen political awareness. These *mujeres* involve themselves in a variety of spiritual practices that reflect not only their diversity but the different arenas they have chosen to "locate their spirituality."[1] Utilizing their intuition, gut, and intellect, they discern the multiplicity of ways they can decolonize their spirits in order to heal and be healed.

The voices who help shape this narrative have committed themselves to develop a spiritual perspective to life and the realization that "we are the generation to teach healing."[2] We have our elders and our *curanderas* in our communities, but often they are not easily accessible as they age or choose to live very private lives. These Chicanas have had to seek out the teachers, traditions, and unlearned knowledge, combined with their own sensibilities, to do "*la tarea, nuestro trabajo*–changing culture and all its oppressive interlocking machinations."[3] Formal interviews, spontaneous dialogues, and my own participation and facilitation of *ceremonias* informed my writing and affirmed my understanding. The *mujeres* quoted throughout the text honored me with their integrity and their power. Representing various educational levels from high school graduate to Ph.D. candidate, and ranging from age 23 to 55, most were born in the United States, are of second and third generation, and reside either in San Francisco or Los Angeles. All are from working-class origins and range in occupations from educator, artist, therapist, and student, to community organizer, writer, and entrepreneur. All of the women concern themselves with political issues facing the Chicano/Latino community. Their levels of political activism vary and occur in a variety of arenas, from the classroom to city hall to the streets. Three of the women identify as lesbian, nineteen as heterosexual. Fourteen of the women participate in spiritual circles on a regular basis. Two of the women own and operate healing spaces for the public, one a *botánica* in San Francisco and the other offering "*alternativas espirituales y prácticas.*"

Spirituality

Spirit and spirituality can be somewhat mysterious words. Western thought separates spirit from body, mind, and woman. "We are taught to find spirit outside of ourselves rather than finding spirit within ourselves."[4] In order to begin to heal, we must first reformulate dichotomous and wounding understandings of spirit or God. Lisa says very accurately how so many of us:

> grew up with the image of God as a white man in a robe on a throne in the clouds. I didn't realize how alienating this was until I understood issues of gender oppression and power relations . . . I give thanks that things change and that I have sisters who collectively resist male oppression . . . The language and images I use to speak of God have changed. Spirit as creator is a power incorporating both female and male power, or at times I want to call to my source of strength as a woman and that is Goddess or Great Mother.[5]

For Maria Elena, God or spirit is defined as "truth, energy, love . . . the impulse or essence of life . . . spirit feels like the energy of life."[6] Toni speaks of God or spirit as a very intimate "source of strength rather than condemnation . . . I have learned to search for that source inside of me."[7] (Re)locating and (re)naming spirit as energy, power, love, mother, or source of strength within us as well as among and beyond us, transcends a dichotomy between spirit and woman, spirit and humanity.

Spirituality then becomes our own individual way of connecting with the spirit within us as well as with those around us. As Antonia states:

> Spirituality is about connection. Connecting to our feelings, emotions, our own bodies, our own integrity, our own sexuality, our own intellect. It is also understanding the connections between each other, whether we like it or not. Realizing our connectedness requires me to be respectful of myself as well as others. The *isms* in our societies, like racism or homophobia, set up others as being different than ourselves, that they are bad. But understanding connections acknowledges we are both human and requires us to examine our *isms* . . . Respect and integrity are the behaviors resulting from these connections. My spirituality informs how I see others . . . It has to do with coming into contact with the sacred in us.[8]

Zosi, who identifies herself as *consejera intuitiva,* believes that spirituality is "life essence." For her it goes beyond our relations with other humans:

> It is not only how you deal with other people every day, but with plants and animals as well. It is your outlook, what keeps you going, where your faith lies. It is knowing that something connects us to each other and to the earth. Sea water is almost the same as placenta liquid. We are of the earth and there are many connections from ourselves to the earth, yet there is something beyond the earth as well.[9]

In an essay by Audre Lorde, "Uses of the Erotic," the spiritual as the erotic is identified in the myriad of human experiences that moves what is "deepest, and strongest and richest within each of us," that which provides a deep sense of satisfaction and connection to our capacity to feel, to create. Naming this creative energy/power as the erotic, Lorde challenges the patriarchal definition of the erotic as a non-spiritual, non-rational aspect of women to be controlled unless utilized in the service of men. In order to control this power in women, and thus its potential to create change, patriarchy separates the erotic from anything other than sex. In (re)claiming the erotic/the spiritual in that which allows us to fully experience the depth of our creative power, we experience its force in activities ranging from delivering a speech we feel passionate about, sharing deeply with a friend, taking a walk, organizing a campaign, as well as "writing a good poem to moving into sunlight against the body of a woman I love."[10] The erotic/the spiritual redefined becomes that which moves us, tantalizes us, that which brings forth our energy, our power, our creativity. Settling for nothing less, our work, our relations, our art become sites holding erotic spiritual power.

Healing the split between the spiritual and the physical also challenges patriarchy's division of spirituality and sexuality:

> Sexuality is not just about our sexual behavior. My sexuality is about my strongest felt feelings. For example, I am an artist, but there are moments when I am not doing my art yet I am still being creative. [Likewise,] my sexuality is not restricted to the moments I am in bed with someone. I think creativity, sexuality,

and spirituality are all connected. They come from the same place in me that acknowledges who I am and celebrates that with someone else. I may do it intellectually, or in political action, or over good conversation with a friend. Western thought says only artists are creative people, sex only belongs in bed. We become disconnected from our own sexuality, our own creativity. Sexuality is about exploring your own intuition, trusting and expressing your knowledge about things . . . Creativity is another way of expressing our sexuality merged with our spirituality.[11]

Antonia speaks of the interconnections between spirituality, sexuality, and creativity and broadening our understanding of how each can be expressed. Tony speaks of how sexual behavior and spirituality can merge as well:

Spirituality and sexual behavior are not in conflict with one another, but it takes a lot of soul searching to bring the two together. When intimacy, trust, respect, and commitment are present in sexual behavior then the sexual act can be a spiritual experience.[12]

Understanding the connections defies the female role models honored as spiritual women within patriarchal religion. As Carolina points out, "The worst thing [patriarchy] can say about a woman is that she is lustful. So they take her sexuality away and create virgin madonnas who are seen as good, powerful women. Powerful, as their sexuality is in control . . . We are taught to venerate the virgin mother but not the woman."[13] Making the connections reinscribes the creative/sexual/spiritual power we carry in our daily lives.

For the lesbians interviewed, making the connections or healing the split takes on a particular urgency, as they have had to battle not only sexism but the threat of eternal damnation. Antonia explains:

When I was eighteen and realized I was lesbian, it horrified me because I thought it literally meant I was going to hell! There was a significant spiritual crisis. Not until I considered trusting my identity, risking the consequences and living with integrity, could I step away from my Catholic upbringing.[14]

(Re)capturing one's own spiritual authority and autonomy for *mujeres* rendered completely invisible by homophobic doctrine becomes not only a creative act but a political act as the systems of domination are circumvented. (Re)defining "where we locate our spirituality"[15] subverts dominant cultural norms which traditionally place spiritual authority in the hands of male mediators who can easily orchestrate a monopoly over the sacred.

(Re)claiming one's spiritual power as an act of self-determination can directly affect our politics. Lisa, a community organizer, comments, "The work I engage in every day is about liberation and resistance. This has great spiritual significance for me. It is very tied into my conception of who I am."[16] Spirituality no longer remains a non-rational aspect of life, but rather the power of energy behind creative, sexual, political activism.

Cultural Influences

The spiritual practices of the women interviewed are informed by a *mestiza* consciousness. Being a product of many cultures—Indian, Spanish, African, European American—the *mestiza* stands at the crossroads where she can choose to balance the multiple and diverse cultures which inform her daily experiences and psyche. The effort to work out a synthesis requires the ability to live in more than one culture, to make sense out of contradictory values, and to create a way of life which transcends opposing dualities.[17]

Since the Chicano civil rights movement beginning in the 1960s, activists began looking to their indigenous ancestral roots to reclaim values and philosophies that would unify and solidify the emerging Chicano consciousness. Alienated from their Christian heritage, their efforts represented a spiritual renaissance rooted in *indigenismo*, a world view and way of life that understands the interconnections among all of life.[18] Artists and community workers assigned themselves the responsibility of recreating Mesoamerican traditional ceremonies that would "nurture and sustain ethnic pride and cultural solidarity as a necessary first step towards the formulation of a new cultural resistance."[19]

Five of the women interviewed were among the originators of some of the first communal ceremonies which not only solidified a Chicano consciousness but offered emotional and psychic healing against the weight of colonization. From 1979 to 1984, Flores de Aztlán, a group of six women under the artistic direction of Josefina Gallardo, a *Mexicana* trained in Maya and Azteca *danza*, met once a week to develop *danza* based on Mesoamerican traditions and values "while incorporating present day spiritual growth and reality."[20] As a collective, they extended traditional concepts with members doing the research and designing their ceremonial garb. Chicano/*indígena* music of the group Kukulkán accompanied the *danza*. Presenting at various community events, these *mujeres* participated in the building of a culture determined to regain a silenced heritage.

At the same time, other spiritual circles had begun in California, circles which developed communal ceremonies such as Fiesta de Maíz, in Los Angeles and San Diego, Fiesta de Colores in Sacramento, and Día de los Muertos, statewide. Calmécac, meaning school of learning in Nahuátl, organized in Los Angeles due to the efforts of Chicana and Chicano mental health workers who understood the need to heal the spirit in their work with the community. As a collaborative effort between Calmécac, Flores de Aztlán, and Kukulkán, the first Fiesta de Maíz was held in Los Angeles on June 5, 1979. This first fiesta included the participation of Esplendor Azteca, the *danzante* troupe of the now-deceased maestro Florencio Yescas, of Tacuba, Mexico. It also brought together artists involved at Self Help Graphics. Similar efforts nationwide served to communicate and implant the spiritual, political, and cultural ideals of the emerging Chicano/a consciousness during this "cultural nationalist phase of the Chicano Movement."[21] According to one of the members of Flores de Aztlán:

> We were developing a Chicano calendar of ceremony . . . Through the ceremonies we acknowledged the different directions and the continuation of the cycle of life. Fiesta de Colores honored spring, Fiesta de Maíz honored summer, and Our Lady of Guadalupe celebrated the new year. We were also learning the full moon ceremony and the sweat lodge ceremony.[22]

Other artistic endeavors also helped to transmit cultural

knowledge. In reflecting on the influence of these early community efforts, Carolina, who was involved in *teatro* groups, says, "We were alive and growing, talking about Tonantzin, learning to drum, being politically active, learning from Native American brothers and sisters, sharing our commonalities."[23] These initial experiences of immersing themselves in ancestral indigenous knowledge provided the stage for further spiritual growth and development. Patricia shares:

> In the 1960s and 1970s I starting grasping my spiritual power. I wanted to go back to who my people really were and what they did before the imposition of Christianity . . . We began to give ourselves the structures and foundations to have our own strength.[24]

Mexicano elders, such as Arnaldo Solís, transmitted knowledge through oral tradition, as did elders and teachers of North American native peoples. The process of forging a spiritual path informed by northern and southern indigenous ways resulted in Chicana/ *mestiza*/ *indígena* ceremonial practices. Becky, one of the founding members of Calmécac in Los Angeles, speaks of this process as "my effort to bring together the various traditions of the *indígena* of the continent to create the ceremony we think needs to continue."[25] Linda Vallejo now facilitates the sweat lodge ceremony for Chicanas and Latinas in Los Angeles. Taught the tradition by her participation in sweats run by Lakota, Navajo, Chicano, and California Indian tribes (Chumash, Gabrieleño, and Tule River people), Linda explains:

> I have not had a hierarchy of teachers. They have all been at the same big table . . . giving me responsibility. The ways I have been taught to pray are *indígena*, the way I play the drum, stand, the language I use is *indígena*. The tools I use are from my experiences in the different fiestas, *danzas*, sweat lodges, sundances. The multiple experiences are specific to the *indígena* of this continent . . . I open and close the sweat ceremony in a Sioux tradition taught to me by Beverly Littlethunder, but I incorporate a mixture of traditions. I sing Chicano, Sioux, Seneca, California Indian, and Navajo songs in the sweat. Each leader follows her spirit. I use my creative intuition and am comfortable with the

rhythm of the lodge.It is understanding the rhythm of things. We
can't get it from a book.[26]

As *mestizas* living between the north and the south, these
women act as bridges between groups. Their concerted efforts to learn from northern native peoples but through their
own lenses and experiences as Chicanas result in specific and
unique ceremonies. This time the bridges lead to their own
power, their own identity as *mestiza* women of the Americas.

Participating in ceremonies not only shares healing knowledge but builds political alliances between Chicanas and northern *indígena* peoples. Analuisa, a founding member of
Calmécac and member of Flores de Aztlán, reflects on her
participation in the Sundance ceremony and what it has taught
her about struggle:

> The Sundance requires great sacrifice and dedication. Dancing
> for four days for the sacred renewal of the Earth and the people
> . . . I learned to make sacrifice on behalf of the people protesting
> at Big Mountain and for Mother Earth. In the ceremony, the
> water we would normally drink we instead give up to the Earth.
> The ritual allows for the concrete as well as the symbolic sacri-
> fice necessary to transcend the secular and become immersed in
> the sacred.[27]

For Lisa, her exposure to Chicana/*indígena* ceremonies "incorporates our visceral understanding of what it means to live
in the U.S. under constant cultural oppression. The sharing is
very liberating politically, psychologically, and emotionally."[28]

Chicanas seeking to reclaim their indigenous ancestry by
learning from and struggling with northern native peoples often receive criticism from purists or those who believe we must
limit ourselves to the traditions of Mesoamerica. While encouraging *mestizas* to return to *indigenismo*, purists often ridicule the efforts of Chicanas to learn from northern *indígena*.
Chicanas refusing to accept such a dichotomous understanding of where they find spiritual strength accept their location
in history. Identifying as *mestiza* women, these Chicanas "learn
from where we are at and what we have access to. The spirit
would laugh if we couldn't have access to our spirituality be-

cause of our experience in multicultural living."[29] The *mestiza's* ability and willingness to draw from her many cultural influences can appear as a uniquely *mestiza* characteristic. But like the *indígena* of the continent, different tribal people historically shared food, shelter, ideas, and culture when the environment or politics necessitated exchange. In reflecting on intertribal relations, Linda shares:

> I don't think drawing from many traditions is specific to Chicanas. It is specific to ceremony. For example, the major ceremonies are intertribal. You will hear songs from different peoples. I have danced at a Sioux Sundance on Navajo land singing songs from different tribes. Tribal people meet people from different areas and share their songs. The mixture becomes indigenous. I have heard Yaqui songs in the middle of a California Luceño Ghostdance. It is not a Chicano urban reality but an indigenous reality . . . Chicanos are becoming indigenous.[30]

While many elders have been brought up in a specific tradition, they share their spirit with those they meet. "Eventually you must go out of your *barrio* and meet people from other places and integrate it into your style of living. Learn to sing other songs; the oral tradition shares knowledge."[31] While it remains important for Chicanas to know their unique indigenous history, "to feel the spirit of her own people as there is strength for her there, to sing her own songs,"[32] they can connect with the multiple realities that resonate with their spirits. Combining these experiences with Chicano and Mesoamerican *indígena* traditions results in a meaningful expression of ritual or ceremony which seeks to heal, strengthen, affirm, and build la cultura Chicana. As one woman says:

> When I began to connect with traditional [indigenous] practices, I felt like I was at home . . . I felt like I went back five hundred years. I could feel the spiritual connection to those original ceremonies, and I never felt like that before. I really felt a spiritual, deep inner connection.[33]

While *indigenismo* provides a source of balance and nourishment for these women, the romanticization of indigenous people and their practices can occur at the popular level, as with the image of the male Aztec warrior. Often depicted in full plumage supporting a dying Aztec woman, the image became a predominant one depicting Chicano ancestry during the 1960s and 1970s. The image still persists in some sectors of Chicano communities on murals or T-shirts or even within the *danza* of many Aztec troupes who "don't present a balance of feminine and masculine powers in their *danza*."[34] The persistence of the warrior, limited to military or domineering power, reinforces a distortion of the values of interconnectedness, balance, equality, and humility that traditionally characterize *indigenismo*. In reflecting upon the warrior image, Linda shares:

> The image of the Aztec warrior has been misused and created misunderstanding about Nahuátl culture. The warrior caste was only part of the culture, but it has received primary attention. It would be as if all humanity perished and the only thing left was the army or the marines. We are not going to pass on the traditions of the military as representing the entire culture. This is what has happened for the Aztecs, which has misguided a lot of people. A lot of Chicanos have glorified the warrior *Azteca*.[35]

What appears as indigenous spirituality through the uncritical appropriation of popular images becomes a way to encourage patriarchy, cultism, and cultural nationalism.[36] Glorifying spiritual power as domination becomes a way to hide from the hard work of creating gender equality and cross-cultural dialogue. *Indigenismo*, as practiced by the Chicanas interviewed, rejects hierarchies of power, redefines a warrior as "a constructor,"[37] and commits to the deconstruction of dualities, all of which lead to "healing the split that originates in the very foundation of our lives, our culture, our languages, our thoughts."[38]

While *indigenismo* plays a vital role in the lives of these women, so do additional cultural influences such as African-inspired spirituality. Petra grew up in Montana and eastern Oregon as a daughter of a Mexican father and Blackfoot Indian mother. She owns and operates a *botánica* called La Sirena. Her great grandmother was a *curandera* and spiritualist, and her grandfather had "his own candle rituals and meditations." The spiritual tradition she resonates most with now is Ifa, one of the oldest religions in the world, originating in Nigeria. Aspects of Ifa include the worship of ancestors and *orishas* or deities who were at once people now offering us lessons. Petra shares:

> Ifa offers a magical ritual that I feel very comfortable with as a result of my childhood experiences . . . It is about learning to trust your mind, stomach, instincts, and spirit guides. Spirituality is a very individual thing. It has to do with how you feel about something and how you choose to use it.[39]

While practicing an African religion, Petra still draws from the spiritual traditions taught to her by her family. "My spirituality comes from both sides of my family and it comes together. For example, doing candle ritual along with using herbs or burning sage and standing over it naked after childbirth for purification."[40]

Zosi, daughter of a Yaqui mother and a Turkish-Iraqi father, but raised Catholic, now practices a combination of these influences; practicing egg cleansings to purify one's energy from her Yaqui grandmother, praying to Our Lady of Guadalupe from her Mexican Catholicism, and reading coffee grinds for direction from her Middle Eastern father. She offers her private clients a specific tradition or combination of traditions most appropriate to their needs and life experiences.[41]

Patricia experienced much of her healing through African-American woman-centered ritual and metaphysical teachings. She integrates these experiences with *indígena* practices and feels strongly that Chicanas should integrate cross-cultural knowledge into their lives.[42]

Eastern thought, through Buddhism, also has influenced some of the women. For Linda Villanueva, her research into Buddhism occurred as a result of an early attraction to India:

> As a child I was fascinated with the life of Christ. I thought he was from India, so I started exploring the history of India . . . I became very interested in Buddhism and how they perceived

the divine. It made sense and related to my American Indian values. I was initiated into Buddhism and lived in India for two years.[43]

Toni, who calls herself a "lapsed Mexican Catholic with Buddhist tendencies," has experienced healing to her spirit through channeling with Tibetan monks, African drumming, Native American healing rituals, and performance art. Dolores also practiced Buddhism for several years and is now "learning how my abuela, a Tarahumara Indian, learned through her dreams . . . how to communicate in silence."[44]

Catholic ritual also continues to resonate with some of the women. While they do not adhere to Catholic doctrine, religious practices of their ancestors continue to have their place at certain times:

> I feel Catholic in a cultural way. I don't follow the rules . . . Seeing members of my family baptized, going to weddings, funerals, and novenas, has kept our family together. In my home I have the image of Our Lady of Guadalupe along with elements that identify me with my indigenous culture. I have a *nicho* of Santo Niño de Atocha because he was important to my grandfather. I want to carry on the tradition even though I don't have a particular relationship with this saint.[45]

Hilda visits Catholic churches "when they are empty, to see the lighted candles and smell the incense in the air. There is something about it that comforts me."[46]

Learning a "radical Catholic vision," for a few of the women, has led to a positive recognition for the role Christianity has played at certain points in their development. "The roots of my politicization are from a Catholic youth group I belonged to in high school. I learned that everyone is equal and that the gospels demand justice. I was taught to see Jesus as an older brother. My political consciousness comes from this."[47] Mona reflected on the impact liberation theology made on her during her travels to El Salvador. "I experienced life and death with the *campesinos* on a daily basis . . . I saw them make a connection to Christ and the land through liberation theology. I was able to make a spiritual connection with Christ. The Mayas are able to integrate their indigenous beliefs and

Christianity. This is a path, a process for me . . . I don't know where I will come out."[48]

Many of the women interviewed participate in spiritual circles of small communities for the purpose of learning healing traditions or creating new ones for the overall goal of healing themselves and the larger Chicano/Latino community. Many of their efforts reflect the evolution of their earlier involvement with communal celebrations during the Chicano Movement. For others, their efforts reflect a more recent exposure to ceremony.

Ceremonia

Many of the women participating in ceremony during the 1970s realized early on "that we must develop for ourselves how to conduct *ceremonias* which will provide us and the *gente* with a sense of purposeful belonging and spiritual connecting."[49] Lacking women teachers among the elders coming from Mexico, these women combined knowledge of traditional ways learned through oral history and archival research with their own intuition, experience, values, and objectives. Their creation of *ceremonia* exemplifies the process *mestizas* engage in as they participate in the making of meaning and the production of knowledge. Inés Hernández captures this experience when she says:

> *O sea, hemos tenido que recobrar y revalorizar lo que es nuestra cultura no sólo por medio de investigaciones formales sino también y en gran parte según nuestra intuición y los mandatos del corazón.*[50]

The work of creating ritual articulates not only a spirituality but an identity, and the ritual itself becomes a political act. The creation of ceremony by the Chicanas interviewed is not merely for personal pleasure. Unlike the individualism within New Age spirituality and ritual, Chicanas develop ceremonies as tools for daily survival within a society that seeks to silence us. As tools or strategies of resistance for personal and communal healing, they challenge the norms of the dominant culture. Much like generations of Mexicanos living a synthesized Christian/indigenous faith, *mestizas* creating their own religious spaces, implementing their own language and gestures to name what has deepest meaning to them, express "a language of defiance and ultimate resistance."[51]

Ritual as an act of resistance lies within the ceremony of Fiesta de Maíz in Los Angeles. Seven of the women interviewed participate in this annual ceremony. Under the direction of Calmécac, women and men join together to honor the importance of *maíz* in Chicano culture and the importance of adolescents in the life cycle. The process of growing up is likened to the process of harvesting *maíz.* Attention and honor given to our youth supplants Western norms, which fail to provide young people with rites of passage acknowledging their importance for the future of the community. According to Calmécac:

> Today's youth, especially, is in need of acknowledgment and spiritual integration into the fabric of our community. They need our individual and collective nurturance, teaching, comfort, guidance, protection, and examples of living in balance and harmony. This year's Fiesta de Maíz is dedicated to the spiritual healing and strengthening of the youth and their families, and the commitment by all to walk together in Flor y Canto.[52]

The ceremony consists of the community gathering to build altars in honor of the four directions of the universe and then forming a large circle around the young boy and girl chosen to represent all of the youth of the community. Participants ask permission of the spirits to perform the ceremony, followed by an honoring of the four directions of the universe and elders offering a blessing for the ceremony. The youth sit in the south, the direction of children and innocence. Representatives from the various directions offer *consejos*, or advice, to the youth. The youth become visually transformed through the donning of ceremonial garb which symbolizes their maturity and affirms the native dress of their ancestor. They then sit in the west, the direction of growth and stability. They receive gifts from the community emphasizing their particular strengths and how they might be used for self-empowerment and the empowerment of the community. For example, a talking stick is given to the young woman to encourage her to publicly voice her ideas. A sketch book is given to the young man to encourage his artistic abilities for the benefit of the community. The youth then address the community with their own *consejos* and lessons. Prayers of thanks are directed to the community and the ancestors.

Calmécac's focus on healing tradition seeks to fill the spiritual vacuum existing for many Chicanos who no longer practice any type of spiritual tradition. A member of Calmécac states:

> Even though many parents are Catholic or Protestant, they no longer practice it, so the children are not being taught to have a spiritual sense of themselves. If something as socially acceptable as Christianity is not being taught or practiced, much less *indigenismo* . . . there exists a real vacuum.[53]

While efforts to fill this spiritual vacuum take on a very public nature for Calmécac, more private yet communal endeavors are undertaken by several of the women interviewed. Meeting monthly, these women purposefully gathered to share ritual, beliefs, and knowledge. In discussing her participation in a spiritual circle named Corazón, Carolina shares:

> Women find that there is power as they come together to discuss and share what they believe . . . to talk about magic, mystery, our bodies and how we relate to the universe. This grows into something political . . . We gather to discuss our ways.[54]

Corazón also meets on a monthly basis to participate in a sweat lodge ceremony. Over the past five years they have built and managed the lodge on land owned by one of the members, gathering the wood, rocks, sage, and other resources needed for the ceremony. While some of the members are more knowledgeable in the tradition than others, the style of leadership empowers each member to assume more responsibility when she feels ready. Considering themselves a leadership circle, their purpose is to "pass on knowledge to lead. We must walk away from our ego as we do not want only one leader."[55] Before each sweat, the women take time to talk about themselves and particular challenges they face. During the sweat, the women pray together, purify themselves, and build endurance to face life's challenges. For Patricia the sweat lodge "helps me be aware of my weaknesses but also harness power."[56] For Raquel, a fire keeper, "The fire has taught me about myself . . . that I am a strong woman but my strength does not have to be a physical strength."[57]   Carolina notes, "The more we do the ceremony, our bonds grow tighter, we grow together. As leaders in our jobs, our communities, we gain strength from sharing in the experience."[58]

Four of the women interviewed participate in another spiritual circle that has been meeting for the past four years. Four to six mujeres meet monthly to create ritual around the events taking place in their lives. Pregnancies, engagements, deaths, and the variety of life's transitions are ritualized. Much of what they do comes from the desire to create expressions for their spirituality rooted in a quest for self-determination and the liberation of their communities. Most of the women received Catholic formation. All have rejected its constraints and contradictions, with some maintaining a Catholic identity in a cultural way. All of the women are activists, whether in the community or in the academy. They consider themselves warriors. As one member states, "A warrior fights for her people. War is waged in many ways . . . from resistance against oppression to organizing or promoting a vision of what should be. A warrior is a constructor."[59]

Filling a spiritual vacuum, creating community, and empowering ritual comprised the goals of the group at their initial gathering. One member expressed her desire for meditations so that "she can do political organizing with love."[60] Other women wanted to reconcile their traditional religious formations that no longer made sense to them. Space to express doubts, fears, hopes and to discover ways to pray created a common bond. A general consensus arose that they would be embarking on a journey. After four years, the women express enthusiasm and commitment to the circle. One woman shares:

> It is an amazing experience . . . As a scholar I can move away from the academy and have a spiritual connection to my life, to my work. I sometimes get caught up in intellectualizing, so it [en-

ables me] to feel things on a different level . . . It is cultural production. It is the mixing of different influences. I see people doing
that in their research and I see us doing that with spirituality.[61]

Soon after forming the circle, the women acknowledged
that growing up in a patriarchal society does not provide essential affirmation to young women at the time of puberty.
Their decision to create a puberty rite for themselves, with
the assistance of a member of Calmécac, served to regain a
sense of the power they hold as women, particularly at the
time of menstruation. As one member comments:

> For those of us who have had a miserable time with our periods
> . . . never able to claim it as something powerful, we gave it new
> meaning. Every month now when I go through tremendous PMS,
> I remember what we did and that the cramps are the way of the
> goddesses telling us we need to be alone, to reflect. At times this
> isn't easy to do, but I try and find the space to light my candles,
> pull out my journal, and write about what I am feeling. I am able
> to take what we do in the group and do it in a private setting.[62]

The spiritual work these women engage in enables them
to take control over their lives. By reclaiming traditions that
have their well-being in mind, such as puberty rites, women
gain a sense of balance and power. The lack of such ritual in
patriarchal societies results in females often having to struggle
to gain the confidence to take positions of leadership. If women
experienced rituals focusing on their abilities throughout their
development, they would be prepared to assume positions of
authority quite naturally. Inés Talamantez affirms this in her
discussion of the ceremonies for young females among the
Mescalero Apache people, "Any post-patriarchal tradition must
incorporate ceremony that specifically links girls and women
to the knowledge and use of power that will be required of
them when they assume responsible roles of leadership and
authority."[63]

Chicanas purposefully gathering to plan and carry out rituals in honor of transition and transformation points in their
lives exemplify what Gloria Anzaldúa describes as "cultivating our ability to affirm our knowing. Jauntily we step into new
terrains where we make up the guidelines as we go."[64] Never

taught ways to honor a woman's life cycle, her sexuality, or her intellectual and emotional decisions, these Chicanas decide to shape and form their own healing and self-empowerment. The rituals that take place can serve as models for other Chicanas in their search for their own healing, "New ways, feminist ways, *mestiza* ways" are injected into our culture.[65]

A woman from the wider community of activists requested a blessing ritual for her journey to the East Coast, where she would live for two years to finish her dissertation. At a gathering of supporters, women from the circle ritualized this significant point in her life. After invoking the goddesses Coyolxauhqui and Tonantzin through poetry, we encircled her with ground *maíz* as a symbol of nourishment blessing the space. The circle provided protection from structures such as hierarchies intending to disempower her. We then offered her gifts of candles: a red one in honor of her female power, a blue one symbolizing balance, a white requesting guidance, and a purple one honoring her *mestizaje*. Prayers said in her honor accompanied water which blessed her forehead in praise of her intellect, her heart for her love and creativity, her hands for the labor she would engage in and the new people she would touch, her feet for the walking of new paths. *Maíz* marked her path as she left the circle and began her journey.[66]

The public acknowledgment of the task ahead of this woman validated her intellect and her emotions. She received the affirmation of the community. Though a very simple ritual, it served to position the woman in the center of the community, as an agent of her intellectual pursuits. Using cultural symbols such as the *maíz* and colored *velas* we drew from the sensibilities of home practices. Combining intellect, intuition, and gut, we inscribed the ritual space with the language and actions that would highlight the resourcefulness and inner strength this woman exemplified.

As the healing work this spiritual circle engages in becomes known to the wider Chicano/Latino community, they receive requests to honor the variety of life's turning points, such as births, adoptions, house blessings, and deaths. In responding to a request to honor the passing of a young man, members of the circle facilitated the building of a community altar in his honor. The ritual involved an honoring of the four directions and invoking the spirits of the ancestors. A close friend of the soul who had passed read a letter addressed to him. Others shared their feelings or explained the symbol they brought to the altar. Music carried our thoughts and prayers. A sharing of *pan* and his favorite drink, tequila, was shared by everyone gathered. The ritual closed with a prayer of thanks to the spirits. Many folks expressed their gratitude to those who facilitated the ritual, as they "would not have known what to do. It gave us the opportunity to grieve together and say good-bye to our friend."[67] The work of these women fills the spiritual vacuum experienced by men and women and represents the significance that empowering ritual plays for the entire culture. As new ways to renew ourselves are discovered, a culture regenerates itself.

Not all of the women interviewed participate in spiritual circles, yet they have found ways to nourish their spirituality. The decision to identify and practice what strengthens them speaks to their self-determination and what Cherríe Moraga calls "a deeper inquiry into ourselves."[68] For Antonia:

> working with a healer who has the ability to read energy in my body and adjust it, increase it or balance it . . . attending a poetry reading or walking down the street breathing and being aware of the divine all around me nourishes my spirituality. On a good day, all my waking moments are sacred.[69]

Maryann finds nourishment for her spirituality inside of herself as well as through the faith she sees in others:

> I have learned to trust what is inside of me. I've been able to find my spirituality in the little miracles that happen every day. The good things but also the negative things that I walk through with someone or that someone walks through with me . . . My spirituality is very much linked to my grandmother, who has a tremendous amount of faith. I used to limit her faith to what the Catholic Church teaches, but now I understand it is her faith and she merely uses the building of the church to meditate and be alone.[70]

As Chicanas act individually or within groups to discover and create their regenerative powers, they consciously produce culture. Our multiple ways of connecting with self, spirit, and others results not in a singular spirituality but in spirituali-ties emanating from the ability to "navigate across cultural boundaries."[71] Living on borders, living in the centers of our own spaces, Chicanas "pick, borrow, retain, and create dis-tinctive cultural forms."[72] Perceiving the world in ways which include rather than exclude differences serves our need to in-tegrate the multiple realities we emerge from and the cross-cultural alliances we must build.

When asked what *consejos* could be given to Chicanas and *mestizas* embarking on a spiritual journey, several of the women stressed the need to gravitate towards other women also on the same search, women wanting to question, seek, grow, and read. Linda emphasized the importance of finding people "who will allow you to think and learn according to your own soul, personality, psyche, and spirit . . . Look for people who will say, 'I will be happy to share with you, but you will have to find your own road eventually.' This is how your songs will come to you."[73] Another woman shared the importance of not being afraid to question and not relying on others for all the answers. "If you find a person whose ideas you feel com-fortable with, continue to seek them out and go forward, but don't put all your faith in one person. We all have spirituality within us. Talk with others—reading helps along the path—but it comes from within. It is a process of getting to know your-self."[74] Petra emphasized the need to nurture oneself and above all use one's power. "Women must believe they have power within themselves and find ways to access it. Nurture your-self, listen to stories, call on your ancestors, listen to your dreams . . . sit down and figure out the rituals . . . Just know you have power within you."[75]

The process of creating alternative spaces for expressing a mestiza-inspired spirituality demands that we ask "ourselves questions about what types of images subvert, pose critical alternatives, transform our worldviews and move us away from dualistic thinking about good and bad."[76] Retaining the *santos* revered by our *abuelos*, renewing hidden relationships with indigenous goddesses such as Coyolxauhqui, Tonantzin, Ixchel, Yemaya, or Corn Mother, lighting candles as well as sage or copal, meditating, chanting or making prayer ties removes the limitations placed upon us by Western thought which teaches religious practices should not be mixed. As *mestizas,* our very nature calls us to cross borders, to make sense out of contradictory values, to "pick up the fragments of our dismembered womanhood and reconstitute ourselves."[77] We must be able to shift our perspectives so that new knowledge can be created. This knowledge must serve the purpose of making strategic change, not only in our thinking but in the ways *la cultura* Chicana expresses its deepest values. In the process of developing our own strategies, Chicanas bring to life centuries of strong and spirit filled women . . . *y los espíritus siguen hablando.*

Notes

1. Antonia Villaseñor, interview, February 1995.
2. Patricia Parra, group discussion, March 1995.
3. Gloria Anzaldúa, *Making Face, Making Soul* (San Francisco: Aunt Lute Foundation, 1990), xviii.
4. Bert Saavedra, group discussion, March 1995.
5. Lisa Durán, interview, March 1994.
6. María Elena Fernández, interview, March 1995.
7. Toni García, interview, March 1995.
8. Antonia Villaseñor, interview, February 1995.
9. Zosi, interview, February 1995.
10. Audre Lorde, "Uses of the Erotic: The Erotic as Power," in *Weaving the Visions: New Patterns in Feminist Spirituality,* eds. Judith Plaskow and Carol Christ (San Francisco: Harper, 1989), 208-213.
11. Antonia Villaseñor, interview, February 21, 1995.
12. Toni García, interview, March 1995.
13. Carolina Saucedo, group discussion, February 11, 1995.
14. Antonia Villaseñor, interview, March 1995.
15. Ibid.
16. Lisa Durán, interview, March 1994.
17. Gloria Anzaldúa, *Borderlands: La Frontera* (San Francisco: Aunt Lute, 1987).
18. Elizabeth Martínez, "Seeds of a New Movimento," *Z Magazine* (September 1993), 55.
19. Tomás Ybarra-Frausto, "Arte Chicano: Images of a Community," in *Signs From the Heart: California Chicano Murals,* ed. Barnet-Sánchez, (Albuquerque: University of New Mexico Press, 1993), 64.
20. Analuisa Espinoza, written correspondence, March 1995.
21. Tomás Ybarra-Frausto, "Arte Chicano," 64.

22. Linda Vallejo, interview, March 1995.
23. Carolina Saucedo, interview, January 1995.
24. Patricia Parra, group discussion, February 1995.
25. Calmécac and Becky Bejar, group discussion, August 1994.
26. Linda Vallejo, interview, March 1995.
27. Analuisa Espinoza, interview, May 1994.
28. Lisa Durán, interview, March 1994.
29. Linda Vallejo, interview, March 1995.
30. Ibid.
31. Ibid.
32. Ibid.
33. Virginia Espino, interview, March 1994.
34. Analuisa Espinoza, interview, March 1994.
35. Linda Villanueva, interview, May 1994.
36. Elizabeth Martínez, "Seeds of a New Movimento," 56.
37. Lisa Durán, interview, February 1992.
38. Gloria Anzaldúa, *Borderlands*, 80.
39. Petra Martínez, interview, August, 1994.
40. Ibid.
41. Zosi, interview, January 1995.
42. Patricia Parra, conversation, March 1995.
43. Linda Villanueva, interview, May 1994.
44. Dolores Chávez, group discussion, March 1995.
45. Monica Russel Rodríquez, interview, August 1994.
46. Hilda Escalante, group discussion, March 1995.
47. María Elena Fernández, group discussion, March 1995.
48. Mona Devich-Navarro, group discussion, March 1995.
49. Analuisa Espinoza, interview, May 1994.
50. Inés Hernández, "Cascadas de estrellas," in *Esta Puente, Mi Espalda*, eds. Cherríe Moraga and Ana Castillo (San Franicsco: Ism Press, 1988), 263.
51. Virgilio Elizondo, "Popular Religion As the Core of Cultural Identity in the Mexican American Experience," in *An Enduring Flame: Studies on Latino Popular Religiosity*, eds. Anthony M. Stevens-Arroya and Ana María Díaz-Stevens, (New York: Bildner Center, 1994) 116.
52. "Fiesta de Maíz," program booklet, (July 18, 1993), 1.
53. Linda Vallejo, interview, May 1994.
54. Carolina Saucedo, interview, January 1995.
55. Patricia Parra, group discussion, March 1995.
56. Ibid.
57. Raquel Salinas, group discussion, March 1995.
58. Carolina Saucedo, group discussion, January 1995.
59. Lisa Durán, interview, March 1994.
60. Lisa Durán, group discussion, February 1992.

61. Teri Gómez, interview, March 1994.

62. Ibid.

63. Inés Talamantez, "Images of the Feminine in Apache Religious Tradition," in *After Patriarchy*, eds. Paula M. Cooey, William R. Eakin, and Jay B. McDaniel (Maryknoll, N.Y.: Orbis, 1993), 132.

64. Gloria Anzaldúa, *Making Face, Making Soul*, xxvii.

65. Ibid., xxvii.

66. Ritual for Naomi Quiñónez (September 12, 1993).

67. Ritual for César Torres (May 1994).

68. Cherríe Moraga, "En busca de la Fuerza femenina," in *The Last Generation* (Boston: South End Press), 71.

69. Antonia Villaseñor, interview, March 1995.

70. Maryann Villareal, interview, March 1995.

71. Vicki Ruiz, "Dead Ends or Gold Mines? Using Missionary Records in Mexican American Women's History," in *Unequal Sisters*, eds. Vicki L. Ruiz and Ellen Carol DuBois (New York: Routledge), 311.

72. Ibid, 311.

73. Linda Vallejo, interview, March 1995.

74. Carolina Saucedo, interview, March 1995.

75. Petra Martínez, interview, August 1994.

76. bell hooks, *Black Looks: Race and Representation* (Boston: South End Press, 1992), 4.

77. Cherríe Moraga, "En busca de la Fuerza femenina," 74.

La Virgen de Guadalupe and Her Reconstruction in Chicana Lesbian Desire

Carla Trujillo

The Virgin Mary miraculously appeared to a poor Indian man, Juan Diego,[1] on the morning of December 9, 1531. She appeared at the site where once a temple stood in tribute to the Aztec goddess, Tonantzin, "Our Lady Mother" (Anzaldúa 1987, 28). She identified herself in Nahuatl as "Te Coatlaxopeuh," which means "the one who will crush the serpent god" (Kennis 1993). She is called La Virgen de Guadalupe since her name is homophonous to the Spanish "Guadalupe" (Anzaldúa 1987), and she identified herself to Juan Diego as "the ever Virgin St. Mary, Mother of the true God" (Valeriano, translated by F. Velázquez, 1931).

Many indigenous people believed that this appearance of a Mexican Virgin Mary who identified herself by her Nahuatl name was a reincarnation of the Aztec goddess Tonantzin. In any case, the Virgin Mary's miraculous appearance came at a good time for the Catholic church, since nine million Indians were reportedly baptized after this appearance in the subsequent eight years (Lafaye, translated by I. Vitale, 1983). Though initially some priests viewed "Guadalupism," as the cult of the Virgin Mary was called, as a dangerous pagan idolatry, others saw her widespread popularity as a means to further conversion to the Catholic faith. Thus, in 1754, two hundred years after her appearance to Juan Diego, a papal bull declared her to be the Patroness and Protectress of New Spain (Campbell 1982, 8).

The Virgin Mary's popularity grew. During the Spanish conquest of Mexico, various images of the Virgin were used by the Conquerors against the indigenous people. The Virgins received military honors and were given rank as generals, since they led armies to victory (Campbell 1982, 8). Later, the Virgin Mary was used in the Mexican Revolution for Independence by Father Miguel Hidalgo, Emiliano Zapata, and others as the rallying cry for liberation. The Virgin's image was used as a means to motivate the people toward freedom (Campbell 1982, 8; Anzaldúa 1987, 28). Later, her image was used by striking grape workers in the 1965 Delano strike and in subsequent strikes and protests as a unifying symbol alongside the black eagle of the United Farm Workers.

Today La Virgen de Guadalupe remains one of the most venerated images in Mexicano/Chicano culture. The omnipresence of her image is replicated in many differing places and fashions: churches, chapels, schools, houses, home altars, earrings, scarves, refrigerator magnets, even on liquor bottles. Commonly, one also sees La Virgen de Guadalupe tattooed on the backs, arms, and chests of Chicano/Mexicano men. My brother, who never went to church in his life, had a six-inch representation of the Virgin Mary tattooed on his back.

The Virgen de Guadalupe continues to be, as Gloria Anzaldúa states, "the single most potent religious, political, and cultural image of the Chicano/Mexicano . . . As a symbol of hope and faith, she sustains and insures our survival." Eric R. Wolf (1958, 38) indicates that "Mother, food, hope, health, life; supernatural salvation from oppression; chosen people and national independence–all find expression in a single symbol."

The Virgen de Guadalupe has also served as an "alternate Eve." The good woman who symbolically steps on the serpent, turning down temptation and living in a virtuous service to God.[2] In this light, her image brings forth the link between Catholic teachings and Mexican history and cultura. The Catholic Church, in particular the teachings of Marianismos, venerate the Virgin Mary/Virgen de Guadalupe in the following manner:

> The powerful example of Mary . . . impels the faithful to become like the Mother . . . to treasure the Word of God . . . praise God, serve God and neighbor faithfully and offer themselves generously; to act in all things with mercy and humility. (Marian Sacramentry, General Introduction, 17. Reprinted in *The Chil-*

dren of Mary Center for Peace Newsletter, January 1994, vol. 4, no. 1, Mossyrock, Wash.)

The Marian devotion "checklist" also looks to Mary as the

perfect model of the disciple of the Lord . . . who works for that justice which sets free the oppressed and for that charity which assists the needy; but above all, the disciple who is the active witness of that love which builds up Christ in people's hearts. (Ford 1994, 6, 7 (newsletter))

Here we see the representation of the Virgin Mary on many levels. She represents salvation. The poor, destitute, and powerless seek salvation in her when no one else (namely Jesus or God) is able to listen. When I was a child attending catechism in first grade, I distinctly recall the nun telling us that if "we prayed to God and felt he wasn't answering our prayers, then pray to the Virgin Mary. She has a direct line in getting our messages to God."

In addition, the Virgin Mary also symbolizes motherhood. In this representation she connects the family to culture and country. Part of her speech to Juan Diego that day consisted of "Am I not here, your mother? Are you not under my shadow and protection? Am I not your fountain of life? Are you not in the folds of my mantle, in the crossing of my arms?" (Kennis 1993). Mary, as the divine Mother, birthed the man whom many of us were/are taught to believe will save us, having conceived her child without the aid of a man. The Virgin Mary, the all-loving, all-accepting Mother, possesses the power of divine sanction. God is on her side, as she is on his. Those who embrace her are so too embraced.

Yvonne Yarbro-Bejarano indicates that "La Virgen can also be used as a role model for a feminine ideal which includes the virtures of passivity, obedience, unswerving love, and an endless capacity to endure suffering and pain" (1993b).

With the aforementioned background, it is easy to see the Virgen de Guadalupe's appearance on the cover of *Chicana Lesbians: The Girls Our Mothers Warned Us About* (Third Woman Press, 1991), represented from a seriograph entitled *La Ofrenda* (1990) by Ester Hernández, as also miraculous. The seriograph depicts a woman with "La Virgen" either painted or tattooed on her back. The woman is looking over her shoulder at the hand of another woman who is making an offering of a rose to the Virgen, or to the woman who has the Virgin painted on her back. (Roses spilling out of Juan Diego's cloak were reputedly the only way that Guadalupe could convince the dubious bishop that she had indeed appeared.) This hand in Hernández's seriograph is offering a rose back to the Virgin. This might be indicative of Hernández's effort to bring greater validation and credence to the lives of women, Chicanas, and lesbians by this counteroffer.

The Virgin in Hernández's painting closely resembles the pictures of Virgin Marys (or Guadalupes) I saw in churches, books, and on family altars throughout my childhood. This image of La Virgen de Guadalupe as a cultural and religious icon continues to exist in its present form, but has been altered by various artists, such as Yolanda López, who replaced La Virgen with different representations, including transposing her grandmother, mother, and herself into La Virgen's image (see *Guadalupe Out for a Walk*, 1978, *The Guadalupe Triptych*, 1978, and *Guadalupe series: Tableau Vivant*, 1978), or Ester Hernández, who (also) replaced La Virgen with a woman karate kicking herself out of the fiery glow of the divine apparition (see *La Virgen de Guadalupe Defendiendo los Derechos de los Chicanos*, 1976), and lately in *Freedom*, 1994, by Lilly M. Rodríguez, who places La Virgen on top of the head of a woman stripper on stage with comic-strip characters around as audience.

These alterations of La Virgen de Guadalupe occurred during the last twenty years and have been met with differing reactions from various groups in the Chicano community and in other communities as well. The reaction by some people to Ester Hernández's *La Ofrenda* on the cover of *Chicana Lesbians* has been, as one might surmise, anything but positive. Hernández indicated to Norma Alarcón, publisher of Third Woman Press, that for subsequent reprintings she could no longer use *La Ofrenda* as the cover of the book. She stated that she had been harassed and threatened so intensely by certain people in the community that she felt it was in her best interest to remove the piece from the book's cover for any future printings. Needless to say, as editor of the book I was saddened by Ester's decision but understood her predicament and was respectful of her wishes and needs. We found a new cover, a painting by Yan María Castro, entitled *MIS KA'AN Ú* and have carried out the third printing.

When I mentioned the above proceedings to students in a class at San Francisco State University, a Chicana lesbian in the class spoke up and said, "Why do you have to remove the Virgin from your cover? After all, she's our Virgin too." Indeed she is. What she represents for us, however, might be something different than what's commonly ascribed.

If La Virgen de Guadalupe represents all of the things mentioned earlier, why would I want to claim her as mine, much less put her on the cover of a book on Chicana lesbians? It seems that a more appropriate cover would be to find a powerful Aztec goddess or some other mythical character. A careful examination of Hernández's *La Ofrenda,* however, explains why I thought it suitable.

Having *La Ofrenda* on the cover of *Chicana Lesbians* creates several possible cultural and religious reconstructions of La Virgen de Guadalupe. First, Hernández, in the act of painting La Virgen, is also claiming her. Simply by creating the image, the artist possesses what it represents as her own. The woman depicted in the seriograph also claims La Virgen as her own by bearing the image on her back. In this light, Hernández is laying claim to both La Virgen and the woman in the painting. Its significance is not immediately obvious, until one remembers that La Virgen possesses the power of divine sanction. God is on her side. Those who possess her also receive that sanction.

Secondly, La Virgen is a cultural and religious icon. She carries such symbolic weight that people like to keep her close by. As stated, she is commonly seen in the Chicano community in various personifications and, as indicated, is very often seen tattooed on the backs and arms of men. To have her tattooed on the back of a woman is not considered "womanly." The transpositional placement of La Virgen on the back of a woman could be regarded as transgressive. Hernández is claiming La Virgen as hers in a fashion similar to men.

Yvonne Yarbro-Bejarano comments about *La Ofrenda* further, stating that:

the female body [in the seriograph] merely replaces the male's as the normative site of the venerating tattoo. Together the image of the Virgin and the sheer size of the image construct the lesbian body-as-altar, while the lesbian context presses the religious icon transgressively into the representation of lesbian desire. (1995, 184)

Yarbro-Bejarano continues by stating that the offering of the rose is extended in desire of both the Virgin and the woman in the seriograph. Further, I commented to Yarbro-Bejarano that an examination of the seriograph from a distance, with its combination of halo, Virgin, and rose, form what looks like a vagina, complete with clitoris. If *La Ofrenda* is read this way, Yarbro-Bejarano contends that this is a "reconstruct[ion of] one lesbian body out of two . . . refiguring the organs of lesbian sex through the intensity of religious iconography and devotion" (1995, 185).

The placement of the Virgin on a woman's back on a Chicana lesbian book interrupts and redefines previously configured historical and religious uses and views of the icon. *La Ofrenda* transfigures the icon and places her into the daily lives and existence of the Chicana lesbian, much like other Chicana artists have re-constructed her in the image of strong women, women we admire, or women who are simply part of our daily existence. Here we see not rejection of the Virgin Mary but, in recognition of her power and cultural significance, a reclamation and reconstruction of La Virgen in our own way and not as historically ascribed.

The Church created the image of the Virgin Mary into "a role model for feminine ideal." The men of the church support this image and teach their brethren to desire it in their women, while also teaching women to emulate and personify it. Margaret Miles attests to the omnipresence of a male point of view in the production of fourteenth-century religious images:

Not a single image of any woman—saint, Mary, scriptural, or apocryphal figure—was designed or created by a woman. The images we must deal with are images provided for women by men. They formulate and reflect a culture designed by men for the benefit of men. Images of women are men's images of women. (1985, 64)

Enforced emulation of La Virgen in the classic manner
obviously is a means of repression. If we as lesbians claim La
Virgen as our own, we take part of this creation of La Virgen
and redefine her to suit our own needs, much like the artists
previously described. It is also no mystery that heterosexual
Mexicanas/Chicanas have also redefined La Virgen to suit
their needs. Kay Turner cites from interviews of over a decade of Mexicanas in South Texas who create their altars dedicated to the Virgin Mary. Turner remarks that:

> the Virgin holds a central place and she plays a central role in
> the lives of the women who venerate her there . . . [the] women
> forge an alliance with the Virgin Mother that serves their own
> needs, desires, and moral interests as women, wives, daughters,
> and as mothers . . . [these] women . . . modify and subvert re-
> ceived canonical views on the Virgin. (1990, 1-2)

Turner goes on to state that the Virgin is seen by the women
in her study as an aid and source of support of one mother to
another. Here, the women in Turner's study attest to the fact
that the Virgin Mary is reconstructed into a symbol/source of
power, a sympathizer and *not* necessarily as a *model* of purity
and self-sacrifice (ibid., 14). Turner suggests that these women
of South Texas rework a male-defined, male-controlled image
to their own advantage (ibid., 28).

Turner continues by suggesting that "the significance of
Mexican American women's self-determined relationship with
the Virgin" is a form of "entrustment":

> In the home altar tradition, this kind of entrustment is both sym-
> bolized and actualized in the passing down of the tradition be-
> tween women–the entrustment of the tradition from mother to
> daughter–and in the entrusting relationship between the heav-
> enly Mother and the earthly mother. The dynamic . . . creates
> two points of reference for the woman, two sources of guidance,
> and two sources of mediation and empowerment: her own mother
> and the divine Mother. (ibid., 28)

Turner concludes by indicating that the veneration of the
Virgin Mary in altar tradition legitimates female difference as
defined in the practices of female relationships in everyday

life (ibid. 29). Here, women not only acknowledge their difference through the Virgin Mary as a resource of a symbolic mother, but affirm themselves as "subjects in a female-gendered frame of reference" (de Lauretis 1989, 24).

In the Irish Catholic community, the aspect of Marian devotion has been examined by Angela Martin (1993), who conducted interviews of the local parish priests, nuns, lay women, and groups of young girls, and had informed discussions with other inhabitants of a community in western Ireland in 1992. Here, she found discordant views of the Virgin Mary by the priests versus everyone else. The priests contended that the Virgin Mary is "defined exclusively through her Son" and "has no divine power to bestow anything" (Martin 1993, 26, 27). Interview data indicated, however, that among other inhabitants of the town, power indeed *was* attributed to Mary. Informants in Martin's study freely admit to praying *directly to* Mary, "[they] turn to her for answers to their prayers, for the bestowal of graces, and sometimes even for the miracle of physical healing" (ibid., 30). She is regarded as "a friend, a mother; she cares, suffers with, and feels for everyone." Martin concludes by stating that the women in this part of Ireland "transform [the] formal definition of Mary and strip away the limitations that the church as institution places on Mary's power. They give her a divinity of her own" (ibid., 31).

La Virgen de Guadalupe, as stated earlier, has been retained by the Chicano community as one of the most significant icons in Mexican and Chicano culture. To view La Virgen de Guadalupe solely as a model for femininity or as a means for Catholic conversion is far too limited. La Virgen de Guadalupe possesses *power* in the viewpoints of many. She was used as a symbol for *liberation,* for the rights of the oppressed. The Virgin Mary symbolizes *hope* for a better present and tomorrow; *motherhood,* due to the positionality of her placement by the Catholic church; *divine sanction,* because of proximity to the divinity of God, the holy spirit, and her son. It also seems apparent that the Virgin Mary is often regarded differently by men versus women. The men of the clergy, and my observations of men I've undertaken in some Chicano communities, seem to place the Virgin Mary's importance into that of a relationship to a man. Here, the emphasis is placed on her power through God, and via her son. When she's used as a symbol of liberation by men, it's usually because she's transformed to represent the country, which has also been feminized.

Women seem to define La Virgen de Guadalupe more in relationship with themselves. Here, their role as mothers plays important significance, due to their connection with their own motherhood and the divine Mother. Women seem to give the Virgin Mary more direct power, rather than merely representational or relational power. This is significant to the transformation of the Virgin's power into their own as women. What seems implicit is that many women hold La Virgen de Guadalupe at a higher level than men because they feel the male-reified order giving sanction to men and a male God by the church gives them, in turn, little regard. Here, at least, is one person who gives them more.

I interviewed several Chicana lesbians and/or feministas and observed how they display the Virgin Mary in their homes. I have also researched current periodicals focusing on Chicana lesbians for commentary on La Virgen. Additionally, I have attended dramatic performances and have observed a film made by Chicana lesbians which addresses the transformative complexity of the Virgin Mary in their lives.

The Chicana lesbians I observed seem to possess a multiplicitous view of the Virgin Mary. In particular, those who choose to retain her in some manner in their lives accept certain aspects of her cultural and historical iconography yet also reject certain aspects of her cultural and religious representation, for example, her function as a model for "feminine prescribed behavior." It is usually difficult to ignore the presence of the Virgin Mary in one's life if one is Chicana/ Mexicana, particularly if one grows up Catholic. Chicana lesbians, by their very definition, disrupt culturally prescribed behavior and the classically defined heterosexist-gendered programs (Trujillo 1991, 186-194).

Chicana lesbians who embrace La Virgen de Guadalupe— to whatever degree—also seem to retain some part of La Virgen's various representational iconographies. The representation of motherhood and family are found in belief systems of some Chicana lesbians, since La Virgen, in her state as "mother," reinforces the centrality of family in the Chicana lesbian community.

Loyalty to family retains primary importance to many in the Chicano community. One of the main concerns I noted among young gay and lesbian Chicanas/os who were torn between coming out and not coming out to their families was that they would be rejected or disowned. Indeed, many were. Many others, however, were initially rejected by their families, then slowly taken back as time progressed. Cherríe Moraga stated that Chicano gay men and lesbians must "make familia from scratch" when they are rejected or not fully accepted by family for being queer (Moraga 1986, 58). Moraga states that family must be reconstructed from those around you who will love and support you in the entirety of your being. This includes sexuality. This new familia can consist of any who are willing and capable of doing this—"blood relatives" or those whom we choose.

In this light, the preservation—or in the case of many, the re-creation—of family has much to do with the retention of our "Chicanismo," our cultura. La Virgen de Guadalupe represents the simulation of family in the modern nation not only because her image ties together motherhood, country, and culture, but because some of us may need her as part of our redefinition of family. In this manner, she is retained because of her connections to our history, or her representation as the all-accepting mother who replaces the church's eyes of judgment and scorn with those of acceptance and love. We can actively embrace her in this redefinition, and in doing so give sanction to ourselves. The redefined Virgen can represent the validation of us in our culture without the benediction of men, the pope, or any of his supporters. She is retained as a symbol of our personal salvation.

In this way she represents our own familial acceptance and the continuation of our, albeit unique, form of family. A connection to her is a connection to our history. She loves unconditionally, accepting us in our differing sexualities. To embrace the Virgin Mary is to receive that which we wish cherished: ourselves.

The Virgen de Guadalupe's role as a model for "proper" behavior as women was commonly rejected by the Chicana

lesbianas and feministas I interviewed, for it was often acknowledged as a purposeful attempt by the church and some members of the Chicano community to subvert the voice and, ironically, what seem to be the very souls of Chicanas in an effort
to construct a model of service to God and the men who serve
him. Chicana lesbians usually see that the passive, obedient
male-identified view of La Virgen de Guadalupe can't be applied to them (even if they want it to), so rejection of the
gendered role model is automatically performed.

Chicana feministas and lesbianas interviewed[3] on their conceptions and beliefs concerning La Virgen indicate a strong
identification to La Virgen's indigenous heritage and her connection to familia:

> As a kid she represented the honesty and truth inside of me.
> When I think of La Virgen, I think of Tonantzin.—*Osa Hidalgo de
> la Riva, August 14, 1994*

> My acceptance of her represents that which is all of me. My
> indigena heritage is represented. I connect La Virgen de
> Guadalupe and Malintzin.—*Laura Jiménez, August 14, 1994*

> I used to be resentful of her representation at first because of
> what she traditionally symbolized, but knowing her in her power
> as an Indian goddess, she represented a nurturer, a life giver. I
> have a statue of her that belonged to my mother. This also repre-
> sents a connection to my mother.—*Gabriela Sandoval, August 15,
> 1994*

> I mix her with Tonantzin.—*Yolanda James-Venegas, August 15, 1994*

> It reminds me of family . . . of my parents. I have a framed pic-
> ture of La Virgen that my mom got for me.—*Paula Espinoza, Au-
> gust 14, 1994*

This interruption and redefinition of La Virgen de
Guadalupe is what Anzaldúa refers to as a call to Latinas to
unlearn "the puta/virgen dichotomy." Here, she attests to the
importance of reincorporating Tonantzin into La Virgen's religious iconography (Anzaldúa 1987, 84).

Aside from the aforementioned uses of La Virgen de
Guadalupe, Chicana lesbians have also been recreating the
Virgen de Guadalupe in sexualized likeness to themselves.

Victoria de los Santos Mycue published (1993) and later performed the same piece at an erotic reading in San Francisco (April 3, 1994, at Red Dora's Bearded Lady) where she took the iconic, visual representation of La Virgen de Guadalupe and transformed her into her own vagina:

> I could understand and love you better once I understood you in relation to my love for other women, once I understood you in relation to myself . . . The Virgen de Guadalupe is my pussy, my cunt, my own dear muff . . . Your gently tilting face, your beautiful visage, is my clitoris. Our sensors of head and pleasure are one. Your flowing garment and folded arms are the wings of my vagina, the labia. Your belly, framed by your hands held in prayer is your womb, like the precious entrance to me . . . Once I began to see you as my vagina, I began to see you as the symbol for all women, as a deity advocating our empowerment on earth, and not as a repressive silencing force . . . I begin to understand you as advocating "Pussy Power" and thus advocating for both my sex and sexuality. (1993, 1)

This is much like the visual effect of Ester Hernández's *La Ofrenda*, where the fold of La Virgen's robe, the glowing aura around her, and the placement of the hands and face appear to transform La Virgen into a large, powerful vagina. De los Santos Mycue, in turn, also transposes the iconographic representation of La Virgen into a sensual, powerful, beautiful vagina. The transpositionality places de los Santos Mycue in charge of her own vagina while also dismissing the church's view of it. By using La Virgen de Guadalupe, she radically resanctifies the representation of the body, specifically her sexuality within it. The representational Virgen as vagina and de los Santos Mycue's own vagina are intertwined as one. Instead of suppressing her sexuality, the icon of the Virgen de Guadalupe is liberated and in turn is used as a means for de los Santos Mycue to free herself as a sexual person and as a lesbian.

Susana Renaud created a film (1994) entitled *Todo lo que vienen en jardín dar flores y todas las flores son buenas* (Everything that comes from the garden gives flowers and all the flowers are beautiful). This film depicts a woman (Cathy Arellano) making love with "La Virgen de Guadalupe." In the film,

Renaud focused on a full-size statue of La Virgen and brought her to life, by transposing this image with her own. Renaud becomes La Virgen de Guadalupe and proceeds to embrace, then "make love" to Arellano, who heretofore was lying on her bed after she had lit a candle and prayed in front of the statue of La Virgen. Renaud and Arellano make a powerful statement by the reconstruction of La Virgen into a representation of desire, the redemption of the previously defined image of La Virgen as asexual, and the simultaneous embracing and sanctification of Arellano's own lesbian sexuality. Arellano remarked that bringing La Virgen de Guadalupe to life and portraying her in a lesbian-identified, sexualized state makes "[La Virgen] a lesbian. She's transformed from what I grew up with. She's more at my level, more like me."

Both Renaud and de los Santos Mycue re-constructed La Virgen de Guadalupe into a corporeal, sexual rendering of their own images. This is a grand departure from the desexualized (after all, she is a virgin) image of La Virgin used by the church and Chicano community (among others) to render submission of sexual desire into non-sexual activities (such as child care, caretaking of men, and support of the church). Where she was regarded as an ethereal bridge between Earth and God, she is now redefined, at least partially, into a bodily representation of desire. Renaud, de los Santos Mycue, and Hernández create a broad reconfiguration of La Virgen de Guadalupe completely outside of church-defined parameters. A new symbolic representation of La Virgen is generated which liberates the iconographic image and validates the sexuality and the existence of Chicana lesbian desire. López's work (*Guadalupe Out for a Walk*, 1978, *The Guadalupe Triptych*, 1978, and *Guadalupe series: Tableau Vivant*, 1978), and Hernández' early work (*La Virgen de Guadalupe Defendiendo los Derechos de los Chicanos*, 1976), reportray La Virgen de Guadalupe as an "ordinary woman" or as a "powerful woman," breaking out of the passive, male-defined mold as well as "reclaiming and validat[ing] the Indian component of identity" (Yarbro-Bejarano 1993b). In all cases, La Virgen is released from previously confined constructs. This serves not only to liberate those who emulate her but to validate lesbianas and other women who claim her as part of a representation of themselves.

The notion that the Virgen de Guadalupe is being reconstructed from a traditional, Catholic point of view is obviously
not a new phenomenon. As indicated by Turner and Martin,
women have reconstructed the Virgin Mary to fit desired needs
and emphases, which subverts the misogynistic, male-centered
presence common in all biblical and Catholic teachings. The
corepresentation of La Virgen de Guadalupe with Tonantzin
was embraced by indigenous Nahuatl Indians and probably
abetted their conquest by the Spanish (López 1993). Assur-
edly, there are probably countless other reconstructions of the
Virgin Mary in other cultures and countries where the Catholic church has laid its groundwork. Never before, however,
has the Virgen de Guadalupe been reconstructed in sexualized terms as Chicana lesbianas have done/are doing. Mesa-
Baines defines this kind of reconstruction as "the transfigurative
liberation of the icon" (1991, 137).

Empowering the Virgin Mary, imposing her images in conjunction with another, entrusting her with divine representation—are all reconfigurations, but sexualizing her in the
coportrayal of Chicana lesbian identity and the body serves
to empower Chicana lesbians as women, and as lesbians. While
some Chicana lesbians still retain the Virgen de Guadalupe in
the image of the culturally significant, most reverent, all-accepting Mother, others have taken her further in reconstruction by imposing their own images and desires. In doing so,
we claim La Virgen as our own and shatter predefined images. We disengage, in our possession, the aura of passivity
her image brings forth, and create the possibility of sexual
agency. Thus, the Virgen de Guadalupe is retained and functions as a means of validation for a sexualized Chicana lesbian body and an altered belief system.

La Virgen de Guadalupe is as much ours, as Chicana lesbians, as anyone else's. We can reconstruct all that we wish in
order to live our lives as Chicanas and lesbianas in as healthy
and fulfilling a manner as possible. In this effort, the quest for
redefinition of identity, sexuality, and familia generate new
ideologies which simultaneously draw and incorporate motifs
from the wealth of attributes long associated with La Virgen
de Guadalupe. La Virgen de Guadalupe, whom we identify
and transform, doesn't become our Virgen. She remains it.

Writer's Note

If La Virgen de Guadalupe, or "Lupe," as I would affection-
ately call her, decided to spend some time with me as my
woman, I would make sure that life would be different and
much more fulfilling for her. I am certain that I would not
make the same kinds of demands that, say, my monsignor—or
even my father—might make. Let me elaborate: First, we'd
have to have sex. (She must also be a "bottom," though not
the passive kind. I really hate having to do all the work.) This
whole standpoint she's got about chastity would dissipate once
she made love with me. She would remark about the pleasure
she receives and would become an avid spokesperson for equity in sexual pleasure for all women. Second, it would be
important for her to know how much she means to me. Therefore, I would do lots of little things (like dry-clean her robe) to
make her happy. Third, I would be very kind to her and provide for her well-being. Although I'm sure she would make a
lot more money than I would (since she gets all those dona-
tions and offerings from people), I would still make sure that
we always had reservations so that she only slept in the finest
hotels and never again in mangers. Fourth, I would obviously
have no objection to her desire to use her superpowers to do
those things that are meaningful to her. She must be happy
and fulfilled in her own career. I just hope she doesn't have to
travel too much. Fifth, when she does go to work, I would
help her find the best lawyers on this planet as part of my
personal commitment to help her obtain equal partnership in
a quartet with Jesus, God, and the Holy Spirit. Sixth, I would
do my best to get the pope demoted to her executive assistant. (He constantly seems to be doing his best to vie for the
fourth position in the aforementioned relationship.) Seventh,
I would not require her to have children, but if she wanted, I
would want some say regarding whose biological material she
chooses to use. After all, look what happened with her first
son. Eighth, since she's a career woman, I would not expect
her to have our house cleaned and meals prepared when I
come home from work. We would share responsibilities in
cooking and cleaning and, of course, probably eat out more
often.

Now anyone can see that Lupe would end up getting a much better deal if she hung out with me. I think once she got a taste of the benefits of associating with lesbians, she'd probably never go back. Fact is, people probably flipped out in the community over her being placed on the cover of *Chicana Lesbians* because they feared she would like it a little too much. I suppose they might be on to something. Don't you?

Notes

1. Named originally Cuautlaohuac ("he who speaks like an eagle"), born in 1474 of the tribe of Chichimeca Indians, he was baptized by the Franciscans at Tlaltelolco with the name of Juan Diego. Cited from Valeriano, translated by F. Velázquez and E. Hoyt, 1931.
2. Moreover, she's also regarded as a direct contrast to Malinche, whose active, speaking subjectivity was viewed as traitorous in her translator's work with Cortés. See Norma Alarcón's "Traddutora, Traditora: a Paradigmatic Figure of Chicana Feminism," *Cultural Critique*, 1990, pp. 57-87, for an excellent analysis of this subject.
3. I wish to thank Osa Hidalgo de la Riva, Laura Jiménez, Gabriela Sandoval, Yolanda James-Venegas, Cathy Arellano, and Paula Espinoza for their willingness to be interviewed on their personal representations of la Virgen de Guadalupe.

Works Cited

Anzaldúa, Gloria. 1987. *Borderlands: The New Mestiza.* San Francisco: Aunt Lute Foundation Books.
Campbell, Ena. 1982. "The Virgen de Guadalupe and the Female Self-Image: A Mexican Case History." In *Mother Worship*, edited by James J. Preston, 5-24. Chapel Hill: University of North Carolina Press.
de Lauretis, Teresa. 1989. "The Essence of the Triangle or, Taking the Risk of Essentialism Seriously: Feminist Theory in Italy, the U.S. and Britain." *differences* 1, no. 2: 3-37.
de los Santos Mycue, Victoria. 1993. "A Little Prayer." *Sacred River* 3, no. 3 (May/June): 1, 9.
Ford, Paul. 1994. "Marian Spirituality: A Personal Checklist." *Newsletter of the Children of Mary Center for Peace* 4, no. 1 (January) [Fr.

Milan Mikulich, spiritual advisor, Mossyrock, Wash.]

Kennis, Terry. 1993. "Protectress of the Unborn." Reprinted in a pamphlet entitled *Patroness of the Unborn.* Jackson, Calif.: Gloria Dei Press.

Lafaye, Jacques. 1983. *Quetzalcóatl y Guadalupe: La Formación de la Conciencia en México (1531-1813).* Translated by Ida Vitale. México: Fondo de Cultura Económica.

López, Yolanda. 1993. "Artist Provocateur." Interview with Yolanda López. *CrossRoads* 31 (May): 18.

Martin, Angela K. 1993. "Gender and Religious Symbolism: The Virgin Mary and Ritual Space in the Republic of Ireland." *Southern Anthropologist* 20, no. 3: 23-33.

Mesa-Baines, Amalia. 1991. "El Mundo Femenino: Chicana Artists of the Movement–A Commentary on Development and Production." *Chicano Art: Resistance and Affirmation*, 131-140. Los Angeles: University of California, Wright Art Gallery.

Miles, Margaret, R. 1985. *Image as Insight: Visual Understanding in Western Christianity and Secular Culture,* 64. Boston: Beacon Press.

Moraga, Cherríe. 1986. *Giving Up the Ghost,* 58. Los Angeles: West End Press.

Trujillo, Carla, ed. 1991. *Chicana Lesbians: The Girls Our Mothers Warned Us About.* Berkeley: Third Woman Press.

_____. 1991. "Chicana Lesbians: Fear and Loathing in the Chicano Community." In *Chicana Lesbians: The Girls Our Mothers Warned Us About,* edited by Carla Trujillo. Berkeley: Third Woman Press.

Turner, Kay, F. 1990. "Subversive Views of the Virgin: Mexican-American Women Altering the Canon." Paper presented at the American Religions Symposium 1990: The Experiences of the People, October 4-6. Under the auspices of the Department of History and the Humanities Center, University of Utah, Salt Lake City, Utah. Supported by the Quinney Foundation.

Valeriano, Don Antonio. 1931. *The Chronicle of Don Antonio Valeriano Nican Mopohua.* Translated into Spanish from original Nahuatl by Primo Felicano Velázquez: *La Aparición de Santa María de Guadalupe, México.* Archives of the Basílica de Guadalupe. Library of the Cathedral of Mexico. Annuals in Nahuatl: Biblioteque Nationale, Paris: Collection Aubin-Groupil-317.

Wolf, Eric, R. 1958. "The Virgen de Guadalupe: A Mexican National Symbol." *Journal of American Folklore* 71, no. 279 (Jan-Mar.): 38.

Yarbro-Bejarano, Yvonne. 1993a. "Turning It Around," *CrossRoads* 31, no. 17 (May).

_____. 1993b. "La Virgen de Guadalupe." Speech given in Seattle, Wash., December 1993, for El Día de la Virgen.

___. 1995. "The Lesbian Body in Latina Cultural Production." In
¿Entiendes?, edited by Emilie L. Bergmann and Paul Julian Smith,
181-187. Durham: Duke University Press.

Border Perspectives desde las Fronteras: A Reading on Rosario Sanmiguel's "El reflejo de la luna"[1]

María-Socorro Tabuenca C.

Para Norma Alarcón, por su claridad, y para Rosario,
por sus textos y sus fronteras

> The critic does not . . . escape the influences of the specific context in which s/he operates.
> —Angie Chabram

> [T]he Chicana critic has not taken account of her insider/outsider/insider status with respect to multiple discourse structures, some of which cannot easily translate into each other.
> —Norma Alarcón

The People

Angie Chabram's epigraph serves as a departure point for me, given the context in which I have lived almost my entire life: that of the México-United States border and, to be more specific, the Ciudad Juárez-El Paso area. This context has definitely influenced my study preference, since my main projects focus on the so-called literature of the border. Of this literature, I have privileged that which has been written by women, as well as that of their Chicana colleagues.

I take Norma Alarcón's words to call attention to the different discourses on "the border/la frontera" which have been produced recently and how, without noticing it, we have turned into insiders/outsiders/insiders of these discursive structures of "the border/la frontera." Yet the same discourse, north-south, south-north geographic cultural term, cannot, in many instances, be reconciled.

Norma Alarcón's reflection emerges precisely after the last

Encuentro de escritoras Mexicanas y Chicanas, which took place in Tijuana, México, in 1989. According to Alarcón, during this conference Chicana writers and critics found themselves in the middle of a discussion between an Anglo-American and a European scholar over the interpretation of a text by Elena Poniatowska. Because there was no agreement on the interpretations of both critics, "two bands formed," dividing the audience. The Mexicanas identified with the analysis of the European, while the Chicanas leaned toward that of the Anglo-American—who was presenting a sociopolitical approach. This event led to the "increasing gap between Mexicanas and Chicanas, which resulted in our marginalization and silence. We became spectators to a textual performative that claimed to incorporate us" (Alarcón 1995, 73).

The previous incident represents a discursive structure that persists as much at both the academic and the popular level. At the academic level, on the one hand, symposia are created to establish links between Chicana/o and Mexicana/o intellectuals. However, on the other hand, an abyss is created because some of the parties seem to be inflexible in their points of view, and the conversation breaks down. Inflexibility is seen on both the Mexican and Chicana/o sides of the discussion. On the part of Mexican writers and critics, prejudices sometimes interfere with the dialogue in several ways. One, as Alarcón explains, is that

> [B]ourgeois Mexicanas[os] in general tend to find distasteful an identification with their "prole" kin, who are not "gente decente," the "customary" epithet through which race-class positions are segregated in Hispanic societies. (Alarcón 1995, 74)

Due to this prejudice, Chicana/o writers are sometimes seen as inferior by Mexicanas/os. This bias tends to manifest itself in the traditionalist proclivity for Eurocentric universals such as "art," "beauty," and "literature." Many Mexican writers and academics still hold these universals sacred and reject Chicana/o literature, which questions the canon.

The apparent willingness of understanding the Chicana/o Movement and therefore (y como consecuencia, de la expresión chicana) Chicana/o expression, is clear in Ana Rosa

Domenella's lecture[2] regarding the different activities and workshops they were having in el Programa Interdisciplinario de
Estudios de la Mujer at El Colegio de México. In her talk, she
mentions that women from el Taller del PIEM presented papers at the three "Encuentros de literatura mexicana y chicana
escrita por mujeres," taking into account what they called "lo
chicano y [el] análisis literario de algunos cuentos de escritoras
chicanas." Nevertheless, Chicana/o writings were not considered within the literary realm, as Domenella elaborates:

> El título elegido también tuvo una gestación grupal y es
> descriptivo . . . al mismo tiempo: "Las chilangas[3] leen a las
> chicanas." En su escritura y edición final participamos once
> compañeras, pero incluía un número mayor de talleristas y
> entrevistados. De más está decir de que la ponencia molestó la
> hipersensibilidad política y afectiva de las chicanas y adláteres;
> el tono no era laudatorio y se nos recriminó una tradicional
> incomprensión centralista. Recibimos, sin embargo, algunos
> elogios y reconocimientos por los análisis literarios. (6)[4]

Domenella's last phrase suggests that some people from the
audience—composed of writers and scholars—strongly agreed
with el Taller literary analysis and conclusion: Chicana texts,
according to a "traditional and centralist analysis" *Chilangas*
did, fail literary relevance. Even though the previous conclusion comes from a literary analysis, it brings our attention to
another point of departure that Alarcón does not mention in
her text. Domenella implies that in the encuentro the Chicanas
felt offended by the critique advanced by the Mexicanas to the
Chicano texts. However, we can read between the lines that
the point of departure between Mexicans and Chicanas goes
beyond mere differences on textual analysis.

The estrangement and inflexibility do not come only from
the Mexicans. At the same time, Chicana/o writers and scholars have maintained a certain distance from the Mexicanas/
os. Being aware of the race-class differences, some Chicana/o
writers and critics are also reluctant to alter their position. Several Mexican writers and critics I have interviewed—most of
them from the north of México—manifested that many
Chicanas/os they know do not accept any critique to their works

because they feel threatened beforehand. To Mexicanas/os, Chicanas/os do not want to accept that not necessarily all they consider literature is a literary text, since most Mexicanas/os do not believe in marginal literature. Yet these Mexican writers I have interviewed do not allude to the code switch within the writings as a "failure" or "impurity." They talk about a necessity in the mastering of techniques, forms, use of the language(es), images, creativity, and so on in certain writings published by Chicanas/os. On the topic of marginal literature, Mexicanas have especially declared that even women's voices are marginal voices, and that women need to find their own voices; literature is, and has always been, Literature.

Part of the obstacle in this discussion is also the interpretation of literature, and marginal literature by some novice Chicana/o writers. On this matter, Mary Helen Ponce and myself had a very long conversation during the tenth anniversary of Mujeres Activas en Letras y Cambio Social (MALCS). In our dialogue, both of us agreed that marginal voices should speak and ought to be heard. But we also agreed that the writing process, as well as writing itself, requires rigorous work, dedication, and a critical approach by the writer her/himself.

Apparently, we have at hand a problem without a solution, because we find ruptures between Mexicans and Chicanas/os not only in the textual analysis but also in the extratextual. Beyond the textual analysis we can find race and class issues that act as barriers—maybe not as strong as the ones seen in the Tijuana encuentro, but still latent. These issues could be addressed, however, in the realm of textual analysis; Mexicans follow literary canons that have been in place for centuries. To this day, these canons still guide, in large part, texts and textual analysis by Mexicans. In contrast, Chicana/o literature has grown outside of U.S. canons. It has emerged as an alternative voice that claims its alterity, its own voice—a unique voice which emanated from/and was written by the subaltern her/himself. This is a very different articulation from the voices that emerged in Mexican literature claiming alterity from some marginal sectors.

How can we then reconcile these diametrically opposed visions? How can we observe las fronteras/the borders not as "one side and the other" (Bruce-Novoa 1992) but as a space in which one side and the other fit? How to accept at yet an even more difficult level the *other* when there is a series of discursive structures and cultural texts that exclude them? How can we Chicanas accept our colegas Mexicanas—their race, class, gender, cultural-identity prejudices, and their writing—in our discourses? What capacity do we Mexicanas have to include the Chicanas—their race, class, gender, cultural-identity prejudices, and their writing—in our discourses? What role do we fronterizas play in all this—with our race, class, gender, cultural-identity prejudices, our writing, and our discourses? What bridges do we build, burn, or cross in our texts, in our discursive structures, and in our daily lives?

I do not know if these questions have an answer at this time. Furthermore, I do not know if we can find a single answer for each one. I believe that they can have many answers simultaneously. Moreover, the answers cannot be definitive. At each moment my perception of the past changes. At each moment teachers, friends, books, and my own thoughts are part of the process. The questions outlined in the previous paragraph have been with me for a long time. For some time I did not have a clue about them; however, now I can see some light. I started to catch a glimpse of the answers when I discovered the Mexican otherness, my Mexicana otherness; when I discovered the Chicana otherness, my Chicana otherness; when I became aware that neither my parents, my siblings, nor even my best friend are fronterizas/os like me. In other words, when I became aware of the large variety of fronteriza/o identities within myself and the others. Identities that emerge from a large variety of variables, such as geopolitical space, gender, sexual preference, class, political orientation, education, and the epoch. And among these differences there is the positioning of the subject which make our identities even more dynamic, more performative.

At different times and with a variety of researchers, such as Norma Alarcón, Norma Cantú, María Herrera-Sobek, Claire Joysmith, Juanita Quiñones-Goergen, Juan Bruce-Novoa, Ricardo Aguilar, Rolando Romero, Antonio Vera-León, and Axel Ramírez, I have discussed the problematic nature of "lo mexicano," "lo chicano," and "lo fronterizo." We talked long and hard; though we could not arrive at conclusions. We all agree that we develop an identity as writers or critics on the foundation of an identity based on cultural traits associated with a region, a nation, a social class, an ethnicity/race, and/ or a gender. I see that this foundation permeates our discourse and shapes our choices. Also, I see that this master identity generates monolithic structures of discourse that interfere with the dialogue among us as common people. Since we all come from different perspectives, we live in a constant tension. However, there is a common foundation for Mexicanas/os, Fronterizas/os, and Chicanas/os: the border. This border brings us together and tears us apart. It brings us together when we see it as place of transit, as an empty space, as a transitory state where we all fit together—a place we can establish a dialogue in spite of our prejudices, our discourses, our writings. It tears us apart when we want to own it; when we assume that it is "our" territory, geographically, and textually; when we do not accept the voices and expressions of *the other* nor the articulations from our own *otherness*; when we assume our master identity and not our multiple subjectivities.

This essay attempts to address the question of how can we observe the borders not as one side and the other but as a space in which one side and the other fit. It presents several borders that I observe and experience as an inhabitant, as a historical subject of the borders where I live. Also, in the second part, I include a brief summary of some discourses about the borders and the literatures on both sides of the Río Bravo/ Río Grande, since the borders and their literatures are becoming more and more important every day. Finally, in the third part of the essay, I analyze "El reflejo de la luna," by Rosario Sanmiguel, a Mexicana border writer, which presents a view of Ciudad Juárez-El Paso as a set of borders. Sanmiguel's boundaries are shaped by geography, nationality, race, class, and gender, which illustrate, at a textual level, various issues in our discussion.

The Geographic-Textual Border

The idea of "the border" has been very prominent in a number of academic disciplines since the mid-eighties. In the United States, a popular topic of discussion has been the breakdown of monolithic structures. Border studies have attempted to "dismantle the patriarchal and Anglo-centric confinements of the term 'American,' specifically as it relates to 'American literature'" (Anderson, n.d.). South of the border, the disjunction of "Mexican literature has become more evident, largely due to greater recognition given to the border region's literary output" (Anderson, n.d.). Nevertheless, the latter has not yet reached adequate dissemination, due in large part to its marginal geographic position within the country and to the rising trend of Chicana/o theory in the United States.

When one examines studies of border literature, two very distinct perspectives come into view: the Mexican perspective, which focuses on the literature produced within the region, and the U.S. perspective, which focuses on Chicano/a and Latin American literature, which does not necessarily address geographical border issues.

The Chicana/o critique has rearticulated the border space, and Aztlán has retraced its edges in an attempt to capture a global perspective. This is with a desire to "remap the borderlands of theory and theorists" (7), as Héctor Calderón and José David Saldívar propose in *Criticism in the Borderlands.* This work proposes "La Frontera" (the borderlands) as the new metaphor of the Chicana/o *habitat.* Thus, la frontera "becomes a Chicano Eden, the original paradise" (Romero 1993a, 230). Chicanas and Chicanos in their texts visit and revisit the border in a "longing for unity and cohesion" (Romero 1993b, 56), in search of an identity.

The aforementioned idea can be noted in Gloria Anzaldúa's search for a mythological space in *Borderlands/La Frontera* (1987). In Anzaldúa's work, the border is also a metaphor in which the border space as a geopolitical region converges with discourses of ethnicity, class, gender/sex, and sexual preference. Her book posits the emergence of a new border conscience and identity which allows a multiple and fragmentary subject.

In *The Dialects of Our America,* José David Saldívar seems to traverse a space impregnated with the Latinity which Latin American writers promoted during the nineteenth century in their effort to reach that utopian site in which geopolitical borders would be erased. Saldívar sets out to articulate "a new transgeographical conception of American culture—one more responsive to the hemisphere's geographical ties and political crosscurrents than to the narrow national ideologies" (xi). However, Saldívar's border continues to be one of academia, in which attempts at inquiry are often still seen through the luminaries of canonical literary discourse, such as the nineteenth century authors.

Saldívar's conclusions, as far as this essay is concerned, are both useful and important. He proposes that it is difficult to theorize in general at present because current theory is not written from a critical "distance" but from "a place of hybridity and *betweenness* in a global border composed of historically connected post-colonial spaces" (152). Saldívar's words are very useful to me because, in addition to his reflections on being in a hybrid space of interpolation, the global borders he identifies seem very real. They are perceived from my own position of articulation—the Juárez-El Paso border area. After all, the U.S.-Mexican border is indeed a place in which (post)colonial spaces are historically connected.

As can be observed in this brief review, the border as perceived from the United States is more of a textual–theoretical–border than a geographical one. U.S./Chicana/o scholars use the border metaphor to create a multicultural space in the United States in order to erase geographical boundaries. This is done throughout the works of such authors as Emily Hicks, José David Saldívar, and Gómez-Peña. Others, like the Chicano/a writers and intellectuals anthologized by Héctor Calderón and José Saldívar, have transformed the space of Aztlán of the sixties and seventies into "the border." This has been done in response to the numerous geographic, cultural, ideological, and linguistic boundaries which have been crossed in the last twenty-five years. Gloria Anzaldúa and Harry Polkinhorn use the real border to construct an alternative Chicano/a discourse and to denounce centralist hegemony in both Mexico and the United States. Their border is "an open wound," as mentioned by Anzaldúa, but it is also a place in which one searches for her or his roots. These border discourses all have something in common. For Chicanos/as, the border is a place sought through memory and the written word. It is the promised land, the encounter with Latin American and Mexican traditions. It is the locus of a desired identity.

In México, on the contrary, the few critiques written about the border are devoted to demystifying the concept of "el Norte bárbaro y vendido/the barbarian and sold north." As of the eighties, this critique has also shifted the border cities–long ago centers of prostitution and contraband–into producers, promoters, and consumers of regional and local literature. La literatura de la frontera/the literature of the border in Mexico is related, then, more to a trope or a *locus amoenus* than to a sociocultural movement.

The study of what is referred to as the literature of the northern border began in the mid-eighties. The emergence of this literary form, as well as its analysis, was due to a number of factors. Rosina Conde and Francisco Luna, among others, agree that interest in border culture and its literature came to the forefront at that time because of the obsession on the part of Mexico City authorities "to reinforce the romantic ties of national identity" (Luna 1994, 79), to "cultivate and nationalize the border states by revealing the essence of what it was to be Mexican" (Conde 1992, 52), and to "give jobs to their buddies on the border" (M. Villarreal, interview, February 20, 1995) through the Border Cultural Program (*Programa Cultural de las Fronteras*).

Although official patronage through government programs was largely designed to put a "chastity belt on Mexican nationality in order to protect us from foreign influence" (Luna, 80), border residents were forced "to adopt a role dictated to them which was based on a false premise" (Luna, 52). There were social factors which enabled literature to develop more in northern Mexico than had been done in the past. Humberto Félix Berumen (1994) discusses other factors which rapidly opened new avenues in the development of literature in the northern border states: a burgeoning middle class, the demand for educational and cultural services, the association of writers who decided to produce and publish their work in their places of origin, the presence of a market of readers, and the increased diversity of local publications. In general, the consensus is that the literature of the northern border states experienced dynamic and significant growth during the eighties. The emergence of regional literary forms was clearly indicative of a tendency to reject the federal government in Mexico City and to affirm regional interests, as paradoxical as this may seem in light of support programs subsidized by the federal government.

The centralist policy of *domesticating the barbarians of the North and teaching them what culture is* demonstrates a total unawareness and lack of respect for the *Other* while ostensibly favoring the region by promoting forums *on* northern border literature.[5] Similarly, the Mexican government's promotion of decentralization and the promise of NAFTA during the 1980s, although presented as panaceas, have resulted in consequences such as the population boom along Mexico's border with the United States. This is all closely related to the processes mentioned by Berumen, which are also reflected in the perspectives of Conde, Luna, and Villarreal, to mention a few. Nevertheless, considering the lack of autonomy of Mexican states, it would be naive to think that any artistic-cultural phenomena could be promoted without the previous blessing (or malediction) of the Mexican government. That is to say, one can hardly discuss the manifestation of artistic production in the northern states without acknowledging the fact that the matter first passed from one desk to another within the federal government's bureaucracy in Mexico City.

This problematic becomes a vicious circle, since, at present, there are numerous small presses, independent journals, and cultural magazines in the northern states that have problems surviving because of the central cultural politics. These politics deal with publication, distribution, and promotion. For example, a large chain of bookstores such as Cristal or Sanborns, will not "endanger" their business by accepting a contract with these presses, even though the small presses commit themselves with the bookstores' management not to be a burden. Small-press editors are willing to promote and distribute their books and/or journals, but they also want to have a small space in the large bookstores. Consequently, for writers and cultural promoters outside Mexico City, or those without the blessing of "someone" in México, the endeavor becomes difficult. In México someone can be a very good writer, but if s/he does not have the benediction of the center, her/his chances of being known or acknowledged are arduous.

The previous paragraph illustrates also another point in the discrepancy among Mexicanas/os and Chicanas/os. For Mexican authors from the margins–the northern border in the case of my study–this socioeconomic situation presents an important issue. Most of my interviewees have declared that the greater disadvantage they have is not only with the Mexicans from the center but also with the Chicanas/os. A general observation is that it is not the same being in the margins within the first world, as the Chicanas/os are, as living in the margins of the third world, as we are. At present, Chicana writers have many more opportunities than we have, and are promoted more in México than we are. We do not know if that is good or bad, but we think we should be granted, at least, the same opportunities. Therefore, for Mexican border writers, aside from the literary discussion I presented in the first section, there is a of lack of recognition on both the central México and the Chicana/o sides.

I believe it is important to take these socioeconomic and cultural issues into account, not as chisme, nor a complaint, but as something that is present and sometimes so enmeshed in our discursive structures that the conversation is obstructed between Mexicanas, Chicanas, and Fronterizas.

In order to round out my review of proposals for the delimitation of northern Mexico's border literature, I have grouped Sergio Gómez Montero, Humberto Félix Berumen, Gabriel Trujillo Muñoz, and Francisco Luna all together because the four essayists agree on most points of discussion. These authors have done more to comment on the literature of Mexico's northern border region regarding surveys. However, it is necessary to point out that the study of this literature is in its first stage, since very few critics have done research work on this subject and most of the work written is descriptive.

In order to study the literature of northern Mexico, one must not view either its literature or geography as a massive whole. The region is made up of diverse topographies, natural resources, and climates. Urban development differs significantly from one state to the next. Consequently, contrary to the concept of "border literature" in the United States, *la literatura de la frontera norte* is a phenomenon set into motion differentially by the unique cultural factors existing in different places of the geographical border.

The literature of Mexico's northern border emerged and coalesced during the 1970s. This holds particularly true for the more important urban centers of the border states. Literary production and, on innumerable occasions, publication takes place in cities located on the border or in other major cities in Mexico's northern states. Novels, short stories, and poetry stand out as the most widely employed literary forms. Among the diverse themes of both genres, the border's geographic realities (mountains, the sea, the desert, the border, cities, etc.) are fundamental. The colloquial and vernacular quality of the language permits the portrayal of the region's typical linguistic characteristics, thus bilingualism is a not uncommon peculiarity. The re-creation of everyday life is given priority, and the representation of urban space is one of its unique traits, without falling prey to the provincial *costumbrismo* of the past.

The authors producing this literature were born, for the most part, in the 1950s, and their work began to be published in the 1980s. They can be placed into three different groups: those who have produced a body of well-established work which is recognized both in Mexico City and internationally; those authors who have managed to establish solid reputations within the national literary scene; and writers who participate in creative endeavors which are not widely recognized outside of their local communities. It is important to note that not all border writers write about their regional contexts or experiences; a number place their writings at a distance from the region's temporality and sociological conflict.

Two of the most recognized women writers that have produced and written from the U.S.-México border and from the boundaries of race, class, and gender are Rosina Conde, from Tijuana, and Rosario Sanmiguel, from Ciudad Juárez. Conde has declared that, before the geographical border, the first border she was aware of was the border of gender. Sanmiguel claims that she does not remember living in a world without borders:

> La frontera es un espacio muy violento. Te agrede por todas partes. No es sólo el hecho que tengamos a los Estados Unidos pegados a nosotros y a los agentes de migración vigilándonos la entrada o el tránsito. Es la forma en que ocupamos los espacios. Aquí caminamos todos los espacios. Todos pululan por el aire. Se cruzan la pobreza y la riqueza, los mexicanos y los chicanos, los cholos y los chorchos, los hombres y las mujeres, los heterosexuales y los homosexuales. El primer mundo y el tercer mundo. Sin embargo, es fascinante; violenta pero fascinante. Cuando descubres todos sus espacios y todos sus rincones, no la puedes dejar.[6]

A trait in common with Chicana writings is that Conde and Sanmiguel elaborate on topics of gender consciousness or female issues. Sanmiguel's and Conde's daily life spaces are subverted and their characters rearticulate the house, the office, the streets, the h(m)otels, the whorehouses, and even their own bodies (because, in México, the state still regulates women's bodies). The traditional *chronotopes* of the patriarchal literature are transgressed by *el sujeto-que-escribe*, which in both cases, as character or narrator and writer, is a female subject (Díaz-Diocaretz 91). Therefore, as Iris Zavala (1993) has said, "[E]l cambio de sujeto de enunciación implica un cambio de episteme o de óptica y de ética" (69). In other words, spaces such as the whorehouse or the bar are seen from a different perspective by Sanmiguel or by Conde as compared to male writers. The previous situation is manifested in a variety of ways in Chicana literature, where the world vision of Chicana writing is in constant tension with Chicano writing.

Note, for example, Rosina Conde's work compared to Sanmiguel's. On the one hand, as those of many Chicana writers, Conde's texts are well known for their overt insurrection against male-dominated society. She also uses direct, aggressive language, especially when dealing with the topic of sexuality. Orality is an important characteristic of her style, and she privileges colloquial language in her texts. In general, the point of view of her narrative is first person. The main character is always a woman who is constantly linked to an oppressive system; however, the writer always offers her a way out. Her themes challenge traditional familial and marital structures. A questioning of power is continually seen in relations between father and daughter, brother and sister, husband and wife, mother and daughter, and women. Her texts paint an environment of distrust and a lack of communication with the other in all sorts of relationships between heterosexual or lesbian partners. Also, we find exploitation of workers, dancers, and whores in the few texts that address the border life, since Conde rarely describes the scenario where the action takes place.

On the other hand, in Sanmiguel's texts we find a recreation of the environment of Ciudad Juárez-El Paso, where the author creates stories of death, loneliness, solitude, adultery, puberty, personal introspection, and social problems from the area. Her narrative style is subtle but powerful. For example, in her book, *Callejón Sucre,* the central characters are primarily autonomous women who possess clear minds to make decisions. This characteristic applies to all of Sanmiguel's female main characters. There is no distinction, regardless of age or social class. One observes in Sanmiguel's stories the development of relationships between women, particularly the relationship between mother and daughter. Mothers are portrayed with a variety of characteristics: warm, distant, dedicated, tireless, and even as blackmailer. But regardless of the mother's character form, we find the daughter maintaining enough of a distance to allow her to reaffirm her individuality.

Sanmiguel's women express their feelings without inhibitions and have intimate relationships with their bodies that transgress the established order. Her language mixes reflexion and description as she discusses lesbianism, masturbation, and abortion. Though the tone of the language is not aggressive, should the dialogue or description require a particular word, Sanmiguel goes straight to the point without euphemisms.

We also find the social conflicts characteristic of the area, but always through the eyes of inhabitants of the El Paso-Juárez border. Here we see issues such as Border Patrol abuse, illegal migration, and employer abuse of non-documented female workers.

For the third part of this essay I will present a detailed analysis of Rosario Sanmiguel's story "El reflejo de la luna." I have selected this text because it allows us to see several characteristics of the geographical border as well as attributes of border literature. We will see through her writing how many hybrid spaces emerge out of the background provided by the geographic space.

The Literary Text

The short stories of Rosario Sanmiguel included in her book *Callejón Sucre y otros relatos* (1994), are indicative of the characteristics mentioned in the previous section. The story that ends the book, "El reflejo de la luna," could be considered as the most "fronterizo"[7] of all her texts. As opposed to her other stories, in this one the city described is not the Mexican one, given that the characters live and move about in El Paso, Texas. This results in several boundaries being crossed in the narration that have nothing to do with geographic territory per se, but grasp less visually noticeable edges, like those of gender, class, race, and cultural identity.

The selection of this story by Rosario Sanmiguel for this anthology answers, to a certain degree, the last two questions posed in the first section: What role do we fronterizas play in all this, with our prejudices, our writing, and our discourses? And what bridges do we build, burn, or cross in our texts? In my studies of the discourses produced *en/sobre/y desde la frontera: in/about/and from* the border, I consider it necessary to encompass the vision of both sides of the discourses and observe in them, as in the case of Sanmiguel in "El reflejo de la luna," the way *la otredad,* the otherness, is registered, and how Sanmiguel establishes a dialogue with different border identities in her writing.

This essay focuses on the possible borders that are presented in "El reflejo de la luna" using a sociocritical approach. This perspective "is guided toward the examination of those ways in which the text is handled by the different discourses co-existing in a given society, viceversa" (Malcuzinski 1991). Moreover, given that social discourse is vital for sociocritique, I will outline the form in which Rosario Sanmiguel utilizes different levels of language and illustrate how she proposes a reading that points into different dimensions.

As indicated, the urban space of "El reflejo de la luna" is

not situated in the boisterous Ciudad Juárez, but is located on the other side of the border, El Paso, Texas. In this account, the central area of the city is described in detail while a part of its history is also told. In this story, *el sujeto-que-escribe* is devoted to exploring, among other things, the relationship between the main characters, Nicole and Arturo, who have been raised in different cultures.

Because of its structural characteristics and especially because of its extension, "El Reflejo de la luna" could be considered a short novel or noveleta.[8] This noveleta is divided into seven sections or chapters. Of these, five carry the title in English, one in Spanish and the first, "Cooper y Luna," in a mixture of both languages, in which Spanish prevails. The last chapter and those which are in English indicate the sites where the action of the segment that precedes them develops and permits us to imagine the interior and exterior world of the characters. The polyphonic nature of the titles evokes the Bakhtinian *enunciado vivo*/live utterance. Such utterance touches thousands of dialogical threads which actively participate in the social dialogue (Bakhtin 1989, 94).

As an example of this social dialogue, we have the chapter entitled "Cotton Fields," which touches several of these dialogical threads. One is that which refers to the place where Nicole spent her childhood and where her maternal family was forced to live, migrating from one cotton field to another. Yet another thread indicates the exploitation of the main character's family which, set in the social text, is tied with that of all the migrant families that have found themselves in the same situation. The *cotton fields* of the Latino or Mexican migrants confer with those of the south of the United States, where African-Americans were enslaved during the last century. The semantic weight of the English enunciation carries with it negative connotations that evoke domination and poverty.

In contrast, the title "Vientos del sur" does not apply to a specific place, and compared with "Cotton Fields," has a very different referential load. If the previous one offers an image of domination, migration, and lack of economic resources, "Vientos del sur" suggests a poetic vision of celebration and greatness. It transports us to an open space in which the ideology tacitly includes tradition and wealth.[9]

In this chapter, the history of Arturo and his migrant family is discussed. But opposite to Nicole's, Arturo's is a rich family who moved to El Paso from the city of Chihuahua. The threads that this title touches, like those of "Cotton Fields," are equally varied. The first is related to the author's position of articulation, the México-United States border, in which the geographical south is México in general and in particular the city capital. When Rosario Sanmiguel turns to Chihuahua city, she appeals to the concepts of aristocracy, wealth, and tradition, which reinforce the history of Arturo's family.

Furthermore, the title refers not only to Arturo's family or to the aristocracy of Chihuahua and/or of México but it evokes the remote Mexican splendor: For a Mexican of the north, a reading of the "south" speaks of the source of the cultural and national identity. It represents the symbol of their roots and the mythical space of México's greatness.

Another possible dialogical thread that this title touches upon is the notion of the south in the United States. This idea denotes conservatism, lineage, economic abundance, and separatism. Its residents were large landowners (as in Chihuahua) who cultivated cotton and advocated slavery. This last perception of the south is linked with that of the *cotton fields* mentioned before.

It is interesting to note the form in which Sanmiguel chooses the language that moves more dialogical strings in the two names of the sections of "El Reflejo de la luna." On the one hand, "Cotton Fields" shapes a part of Nicole's life and presents a fragment of the American history, which is characterized by its infamy. On the other, "Vientos del sur" indicates Arturo's genealogy and, with it, the greatness of a lost country. The use of the two languages serves to present the social context in which the main characters of this story have grown up–thus the contrast between them.

As we have seen, the polyphony and the plural-lingualism of the noveleta are given at the subtitle level as well as in the development of the story. The narration indicates the multiculturalism of the Texas city. In this way, Sanmiguel introduces a good representation of the ethnicities that live in El Paso. Through its pages travel a Chicana lawyer and a Mexican-El Pasoan entrepreneur. A white American of the well-todo class, an undocumented Mazahua Indian, a Hindu doctor, a Turkish traveler, and two German women are also introduced. The noveleta posits the tensions between the different characters due to their gender, class, and ethnic origin, presenting part of the problems of this border zone.

In spite of mentioning the ethnicity of some characters, the narrative voice does not abound in details of the culture of each one of them. However, the text elaborates on the cultural heritage of the leading characters. The noveleta opens with the presentation of the main characters, Nicole Campillo and her husband Arturo Alcántar. Nicole is a lawyer who specializes in undocumented and migrant workers. At the time she is preparing a lawsuit against a white American who has attempted to rape a Mazahua Indian.

The chronology of the noveleta is reduced to a full day. It begins early in the morning, when Nicole prepares to review the papers for the case Maza vs. Thompson. It ends the following dawn, once the lawyer leaves the matrimonial bed and is poised "frente a la luna del armario" (149) in front of the dresser mirror. Yet the time is not linear, since there are several flashbacks throughout, where we get to know the families of Nicole and Arturo, in addition to their first encounter. The retrospective also exposes aspects of the offense against Guadalupe Maza.

The tension between Nicole and Arturo is evident from the beginning. This tension reinforces the desire of the protagonist to delineate her autonomy:

En esta ocasión el caso sería aún más difícil. Había motivos para desconfiar del resultado. Dick Thompson era hijo del director de la Cámara de Comercio, un viejo rico, amigo de la familia de Arturo y a quien ellos le debían algunos favores. (106)

[On this occasion the case would be yet more difficult. There were reasons to distrust the outcome. Dick Thompson was the son of a director of the Chamber of Commerce, a rich old man, friend of Arturo's family, to whom they owed many favors.]

The italics in the text emphasize that Nicole does not feel part of Arturo's family, including her husband. In this commentary one infers the feasible injustice of the American system upon presenting Thompson as a member of a powerful family, since he and his family can influence an outcome favorable to Thompson. The racial-ethnicity/social class and gender element permeates the story from the very beginning.

The first argument Nicole and her husband have is due to Arturo's reluctance to approve his wife working with this case. The excuse is her pregnancy. From that moment, the cultural differences become clarified and *el sujeto-que-escribe* gives an account of the social context and the plural-lingualism of the region:

> *Para una Mujer que buena parte de los veranos de su infancia había pizcado . . . en los* cotton fields *del sur de Texas, las preocupaciones de Arturo resultaban infundadas. Presentarse en la corte, enfrentar al abogado blanco, o varios, no sería más duro que tener siete años, ir tras la madre—que también cargaba un costal de algodón—y llevar la yema de los dedos inflamada y sangrante.* (108)

> [For a woman who had spent a good part of the summers of her childhood picking . . . cotton in the fields of the south of Texas, Arturo's preoccupations seemed groundless. To go before the court, or face one or several white attorneys, would be no harder than being seven years old, going after her mother—who was also carrying a bag full of cotton—and having the fingertips inflamed and bloody.]

Nicole belongs, on her mother's side, to a migrant peasant family who remained on the U.S. side because of the Treaty of Guadalupe Hidalgo. Of her father's history she only knows that he died before she was born and that he was an undocumented worker who, together with her mother, followed "la ruta del wes" [the western route] (148). The lawyer belonged to the punished generations ("si acaso la atrapaban hablando español" [if she was caught speaking Spanish] (117)) in class, and was of those who were embarrassed during adolescence for being poor. Her experiences, though, caused her to specialize in immigration matters and gave her a strong consciousness of class and race.

Arturo, on the other hand, is the grandson of a rich migrant who arrived in El Paso from Chihuahua during the Revolution of 1910. He was raised "in Spanish and in the Mexican way," but educated in private El Paso schools. "Su lengua materna era el español" [His mother tongue was Spanish] says the narrative voice, "pero la mayor parte de las veces se comunicaba en inglés" [but the majority of the time he communicated in English] (130). In a social context, Arturo is a very particular border person:

> Se creía mexicano pero no lo era en su totalidad; había nacido y se había criado en los Estados Unidos. Eso no significaba que comprendía a fondo la manera de percibir el mundo de los chicanos . . . Nunca se había sentido discriminado . . . Tampoco se identificaba plenamente con los mexicanos. Nada tenía en común con los hijos de trabajadores agrícolas que llegaban . . . Entre él y esos mexicanos había diferencias insalvables. Era como si Arturo viviera siempre en la frontera. A un paso de pertenecer, pero al mismo tiempo separado por una línea imperceptible trazada por la historia. (130)

> [He believed he was a Mexican but was not in totality; he had been born and had been raised in the United States. This did not mean that he understood in depth the way Chicanos perceived the world . . . He has never felt discriminated against . . . Neither did he identify fully with the Mexicans. He had nothing in common with the children of agricultural workers who were arriving . . . Between him and those Mexicans there were insurmountable differences. It was as if Arturo always lived on the border. A step from belonging, but at the same time separated by an imperceptible line traced by history.]

The contrast between *cotton fields* and *Vientos del sur* elaborated previously acquires more sense as the story develops. Arturo's aristocratic blood and his life experiences do not permit him to relate to the experiences of his wife, nor to those of his fellow Mexican paisanos. The social gap prevents him from understanding even Nicole and/or to identify himself with those who by a closer cultural heritage–the "true" Mexicans– would be his own.

Arturo reminds the reader, in this segment, of the "Mexican bourgeois" from Norma Alarcón's citation from section I, who could not identify with *"la prole"* because they were not *"gente decente."* Here, Arturo is, without even perceiving it, an insider within the so-called Hispanics in the United States, who have enjoyed the privileges of the system, but at the same time is an outsider in relation to his own people, because of his prejudices. Nicole is an insider, since she finds herself playing an important role within the legal system. But is an outsider since the same legal system presents obstacles, leaving her, as well as Guadalupe Maza, the Mazahua Indian, outside the game, given her ethnicity, class, and gender.

It is in this way that the characters are going to be in opposition on numerous occasions, "sobre todo cuando se trataba de situaciones que ella asociaba con el racismo" [particularly in situations that she associated with racism] (134). Nicole herself comments that upon meeting him, those cultural differences were the ones which most attracted her to him, but that after two years of marriage this posed a distance between them. Nicole feels her husband does not know her yet.

The details about Arturo's identity are that he can relate to those, like him, who have had the opportunity of growing up in the two countries, knowing two cultures, and speaking two different languages. Furthermore, because of their social position, these kind of fronterizos have been able to enjoy the best of both worlds. Yet they have lived totally distant from the social reality which Nicole embodies.

For a border person such as Arturo, it is difficult to be seen as a Chicano, since the term to him is associated with the poor or with gang members. There are a great many Mexican-Americans who do not know the political connotation of the word, and ignore that there once existed a social movement of great social and political importance which continues to be relevant in the United States.

Arturo is also unable to understand that his wife's interest in the case of the raped Indian woman goes beyond Guadalupe Maza herself. Nicole's proclivity is a matter of principle. Her commitment is due to what she experienced in her daily life in the *cotton fields*. The interest of the protagonist is based on her knowledge of the society in which she has grown up. A colonizing society where the white man, represented by Thompson, feels he has the right to abuse Guadalupe because she is triply marginal: She is indigenous, a woman, and undocumented. Thompson embodies the hegemonic system which feels it is within his full right to abuse any person who is not from his group. In this case the victim is an undocumented indígena, which puts her at a greater disadvantage before the repressive system. The criticism by Sanmiguel in this text acquires a relevance with political undertones. On the one hand, the system "forbids" the entry of undocumented persons, and, on the other, it is able to contract and to abuse them by denying them the most basic rights. The case of Guadalupe Maza is even more pathetic, since her position of disadvantage is greater. The white system exploits her by paying her a smaller wage than would be paid to someone "legal" or "white" and also abuses her sexually.

Nicole sees in Guadalupe all the raped women, all the undocumented people, and all the indígenas exploited by a race that believes itself to be superior. She knows the law and is prepared to fight to achieve justice. The attorney is conscious of the fact that "ni Guadalupe era una indígena desamparada, ni ella era una chicana indefensa. Las dos eran mujeres sin privilegios, acostumbradas a la lucha diaria; hijas de trabajadores migrantes." [Guadalupe was neither a relinquished indígena, nor was she a defenseless Chicana. The two were women without privileges, accustomed to the daily struggle, daughters of migrant workers.] (122) Protected by the law, she is not going to allow discrimination against Guadalupe either for gender, ethnicity, or for legal status in the United States.

The solidarity of Nicole with Guadalupe Maza and other raped women goes beyond the differences of class and gender. The latter establishes a link between two marginalized ethnicities, both in México as well as in the United States. Rosario Sanmiguel transcends the story, and on the sly, offers a critique of two cultural systems that oppress ethnic minority groups.

The history that molds the character of Nicole could very well be related to the words of Barbara Harlow (1991) who, upon speaking of the development of the feminist/Chicana movement of the last decade indicates that

[N]ot only has it become necessary . . . to "identify with" other struggles on an individual or personal level or even on the basis of "roots"–but furthermore to participate actively in identifying those struggles according to political and historical exigencies. (149-150)

Within the cultural text, Nicole's reality, as compared to Arturo's, is not limited to that of the residents of the U.S.-México borderlands. The experience of the protagonist establishes a dialogue with the thousands of migrant families living in the United States. Nicole, unlike many members of these families, has internalized the spirit of the Chicana/o movement and carries it with her. The attorney answers to the prototype of what Norma Alarcón (1991) calls the generation of the "intellectual revolutionary miracle" (210).[10] Her history corresponds to that of many girls and boys whose parents needed to leave them with some relative so that they could become professionals and stop the pattern of becoming migrant workers.

The protagonist suffered the involuntary abandonment of her mother, who decided to leave her with her grandmother so that she could go to school. This incident made Nicole resentful towards her mother for a long time, but her mother's and grandmother's strength made her be more conscious of her ethnicity, class, and gender.

This text by Sanmiguel is enriching from many angles. It outlines the geographical situation of the border, but its exposition is not limited to geography. In addition, there is also a search of women through the body. For example, in a visit that Nicole makes to her gynecologist to have a checkup, she details the following:

> *El estetoscopio en su espalda desnuda le provocó un ligero estremecimiento que aumentó la tensión que sentía . . . el tacto vaginal vendría enseguida y ella era demasiado suceptible a todo lo relacionado con el cuerpo, sus órganos, sus palpitaciones, sus líquidos, la sangre . . . Unos dedos fuertes y seguros entraron en ella. El útero es un camino, pensó Nicole estremecida.*(110)

[The stethoscope on her naked back provoked in her a light shake that increased the tension she was feeling . . . The vaginal exam would be next and she was too susceptible to all that was related with the body, its organs, its palpitations, its liquids, its blood . . . Some sure and strong fingers entered her. The uterus is a road, thought Nicole, shaken.]

The exploration of the body of a woman indicates, in addition to a thematic unity in the narrative of Sanmiguel, an important point of identification with the feminine gender. Maternity in this statement is seen as another characteristic of the daily life of a woman, in the same way that in other stories she speaks of early menopause and of menstruation. By describing the uterus as *"el camino que conduce al centro de mí misma"* [the road that drives to the center of myself] (110), she disarticulates the idea of the lack of penis/phallus and rearticulates the recognition of a completed and autonomous self, not of a deficient and subordinate self. Nicole makes it possible for a woman to examine her intellectual as well as corporal interior and define herself.

Not only does "El reflejo de la luna" subvert the established order by Nicole's conduct but also with her attitude. She constantly challenges her husband and questions the U.S. hegemonic system. The attorney is an independent woman, an autonomous "owner of herself" (137). Her autonomy, however, is outlined in a different way than that of the other feminine characters of Rosario Sanmiguel.

One characteristic that calls the most attention from the subversive narrative of Sanmiguel is the way she readdresses "feminine passivity." With the exception of Nicole, all of her characters are calm and silent. In this narration, the lawyer is openly combative. This makes one think about the possibility that the text implies in those differences of character a cultural discrepancy between Chicanas and Mexicanas.[11]

Another discrepancy in the social order that is projected in the noveleta is Arturo's nature. The character is described as "impulsivo y melancólico" [impulsive and melancholic] (129). In addition, the narrative voice mentions that his father thought he was inferior, given his docility. Arturo is a conciliating and gentle man. He is the one who is always prepared to negotiate when arguing with Nicole. The characteristics that Sanmiguel imparts to her masculine character offer a different vision of what is supposed to "be a real man," though finally Arturo is not free from acting within the cultural standards of tradition:

Nicole se le escapaba en las fisuras de la noche. Su único recurso en la batalla era el amor . . . La sabía más allá del tacto y de las palabras, como si encontrara un patio interior donde sola habitaba. La penetró con rabia, largamente; empujó . . . hasta arrancarla de sí misma. (148)

[[For Arturo] Nicole escaped in the fissures of the night. His only recourse in that battle was love . . . He knew she was beyond touch and words, as if she found an interior courtyard where only she existed. He penetrated her with a long rage, pushing until she was torn from herself.]

The masculine character reacts opposite to what is expected, from what is described in the course of the text. Arturo's passivity becomes fury upon feeling that he can lose his wife. His only weapon is love, and his only form of attack is through penetration. This action rearticulates the already given text, "the man." To recover his wife, Arturo uses the main weapon that throughout history has been used to subdue women: the penis.

The previous scene is the next to the last of the noveleta and belongs to the section titled "Memorial Park." The title will acquire, like the others studied, a special meaning. On the one hand, it places the characters in the old park where Nicole and Arturo's house is located. On the other hand, it establishes a game with what happens in this final chapter. "Memorial" does not express a tribute to the heroes of the wars, as is the case of the park in El Paso. The word connotes an appeal to memory.

Nicole and Arturo make a tour to the park and, through it, Nicole searches her memory until she finds the figure of her dead father. Nicole's unfinished family history, which was offered in "Cotton Fields," comes to a close in this chapter. As opposed to Arturo's history, which was outlined completely in "Vientos del sur," the history of Nicole's father was given in almost imperceptible fragments.

The memories generated in "Memorial Park" make clear the lawyer's interest in defending the undocumented: Her father was one of them and he had died under unclear circumstances. The title, then, touches another dialogic thread: that of yielding tribute, together with the heroes of the wars, to the heroes in the daily struggle of the *cotton fields.* The park "of memories" is another reiterative element of the unjust and oppressive system that, as was seen in the case of Thompson, first "forbids" the crossing of the undocumented but then "permits" them to work at low wages to end up being abused by the system. In this section, it is implied that the foreman or the agent of the border patrol (or both) are responsible for Nicole's father's death.

The noveleta ends with the presence of Nicole *frente a la luna del armario* [in front of the dresser mirror] once Arturo has possessed her. In this final scene we realize that her husband has only been able "to rip her from herself" for a moment. Nicole will not succumb to the petitions and recommendations of her husband to abandon the Thompson vs. Maza case. Nicole's loyalty towards her father and to those who, like her progenitor, are exploited, weighs heavily on her. The attorney is an individual, independent of her mate and with her own conscience. Arturo does not know nor understand her. Their cultural and social principles are diametrically opposed.

For Nicole, her husband stops being a concern. She is busy in her ponderings. All through the final chapter and especially in the last scene, we take note of this. She appears posing nude before the dresser mirror, and instead of seeing her image reflected, she finds the calm look of her mother. The description makes it known to us that Nicole has finally reconciled with her mother.

The figure of the mother in this end is a key element that emphasizes not only reconciliation with the mother but with the woman reflected in the mirror. The foregoing points towards the search for her own identity by way of the feminine body. Here self-affirmation as a woman is shown by way of reflection of the other woman, also showing loyalty to the mother.

With this ending, what is emphasized is the idea that Nicole herself outlined in her statement, "The uterus is a road that carries me to the center of myself." The uterus takes her to be in touch with her own maternity and to establish a link with her mother, her grandmother, and with the mothers and grandmothers who have existed; that is to say, with women. It is to establish again that union with Guadalupe Maza and with all raped women, undocumented or indigenous women. It is women bonding, which has also been suggested by Norma Alarcón (1990) within Chicana literature.

Alarcón explains that Chicana writers such as Cherríe Moraga, Sandra Cisneros, Ana Castillo, Alma Villanueva, Lucha Corpi, and Gloria Anzaldúa, among others, have used their own body to illustrate the various social and ideological orders. In a search of their genealogy, Chicana writers have developed an ambivalent attitude towards the mother. On the one hand, the mother is seen as a working woman who has sacrificed herself in the fields or factories in order to support her family. But on the other hand, it is the mother who is in charge of transmitting the traditional cultural paradigms which betray the interests of the daughter. However, they generate a solidarity with the mother by recreating and rearticulating her image. After this reinterpretation, a new bonding is created. A bonding that allows Chicana writers to be in touch with and rearticulate other female characters such as grandmothers, soldaderas, campesinas, or indígenas like Malinche. Contemporary Chicana writers have rearticulated women who have been abused by sexism or racism and have been granted a voice. The same way that Rosario Sanmiguel articulates Guadalupe Maza, Nicole's mother, or Nicole herself.

The reflection in the dresser mirror in this story by Rosario Sanmiguel projects the image of a woman that is constructed through all her stories: a calm woman, a complete woman. A woman that before "she came to life" is reconciled with her mother to break with the mold of the past. Liberated from her inheritance, the woman emerges with a new image, alive, and dynamic. A feminine fragmented subject that proposes a new ethic and a vision of a different world.

The narrative of Rosario Sanmiguel is a place in which the geography of the Juárez-El Paso border has a relevant position. Without a doubt, the subjects that circulate in her pages are identified with the city(ies) they inhabit. However, the urban space in Rosario Sanmiguel's writing is a mere narrative artifice. The situations in which she involves the reader exceed the geographic-temporal limits that outline for us the various problems I discussed at the beginning. Problems of race, gender, class, and culture are present in "El reflejo de la luna." This is one of the ways which Rosario Sanmiguel as *fronteriza* and *escritora de la frontera mexicana* builds and crosses the bridges between cultures and writings. Standing on her own bridge,

Sanmiguel pauses, observes, and articulates *la otredad de las fronteras* into an heterogeneous and multiple text that confers with the social context that surrounds her and her writings.

Through a glance in the mirror, Rosario Sanmiguel gives the reader a glimpse of the multiple realities in Nicole's life. The light of the moon allows her to see beyond her mere reflection on the mirror. In the same way, the reader can observe the different dimensions of the border through Rosario Sanmiguel's literature.

Notes

1. This essay was translated from its original Spanish version by my friends Lourdes Villalva-Muguerza and Roland Chanove. My deepest thanks to them.
2. PIEM–Segundo encuentro de talleres–enero 1990. Un espacio para pensar y trabajar en libertad (II Parte). Presented at *II Encuentro de talleres y seminarios del PIEM: Los espacios para la mujer*. El Colegio de México, Mexico City. January 24-26, 1990. (Photocopy from PIEM library.)
3. People from Mexico City are called chilangos/as.
4. The title was also picked as a group discussion and at the same time is descriptive (of the situation): "Las chilangas leen a las chicanas" [Chilangas reading Chicanas]. In writing the paper and editing the final version, only eleven of us participated, even though the participants during the workshop and the interviews were many more. It would be an understatement to say that the paper bothered the political and affective hypersensibility of the Chicanas and other people in the room: The tone was not laudatory, and we were recriminated with traditional and centralist incomprehension. However, we were praised and acknowledged by some people because of our literary analysis.
5. I underlined *de* in the Spanish original of this paper (*de* la frontera) because a conference takes place every two years on the northern border. Its participants are mainly writers from south-central Mexico and those writers whose careers had been made in Mexico City. Well-known Chicano literary critics and authors are also invited to participate.
6. Personal interview, April 8, 1994.
"The border is a very violent space whose inhabitants are always subjected to aggression. It is not only that we have the United States next to us and the Border Patrol and Immigration agents keeping an eye on us every time we cross, or sometimes even when we drive. It

is the way we occupy the spaces. Over here we walk through all the spaces; they pullulate in the air. In here richness and poverty blend together, as well as Mexicanas/os and Chicanas/os, cholos and highfalutin, women and men, homosexuals and heterosexuals. The first and the third world. Nevertheless, [the border] is fascinating; violent but fascinating. When you discover all its spaces and its nooks, you cannot leave."

7. Here the border is not only territorial but also spans all that is outside the personal context, like the limits established by Mikhail Bakhtin in *Teoría y estética de la novela,* translated by Helena Kirukova and Vincente Cazcarra (Madrid: Taurus, 1989); as well as in "Toward a Reworking of Dostoevsky's Book" (1961), Appendix II, *Problems of Dostoevski's Poetics,* translated by Carl Emerson (Minneapolis: University of Minnesota Press, 1984), 283-302. I am also taking into account the concept of border elaborated by Homi Bhabha (1994), which includes influences of one culture or more which express a culturally hybrid culture, a subjective conscience of the dominant position of the subject, tension between the sides that feed the border space. For Bhabha there is no such thing as an exact reality; rather, there are reflexes where subject loses a position of dominance and becomes dominated by the object.

8. See the definition by Oscar Mata that appears in *Fuentes Humanísticas* 6, year 3, (First semester 1993): 71-73.

9. An interesting elaboration of the subject of the north/south relationship on the American continent is that of Marco Antonio Jerez in "Ontología y expresión en la frontera septentrional de la Nueva España," which appeared in *Literatura fronteriza de acá y de allá,* edited by Guadalupe Beatriz Aldaco (Hermosillo, Sonora: Instituto Sonorense de Cultura; México: Consejo Nacional para la Cultura y las Artes, 1994), 33-41.

10. Alarcón does this as she explains Chicano/a literature and its male and female writers. Alarcón goes deeper in the vision of the writers. For the female writer she explains, "unfolds towards the working class, the peasant class and intellectual middle class. Her own body, then, serves as a prism through which various social and ideological orders can be illuminated." See Alarcón, 1990. "La literatura chicana: un reto sexual y racial del proletariado."

11. The cultural discrepancy which one thinks of is, basically, that of the degree of social activism characteristic of this new generation of Chicana academics and writers vis-à-vis the supposed "bourgeois passivity" of the Mexicanas, or the "moscas muertas" that they are according to Norma Alarcón quoting Elena Poniatowska. See Alarcón, 1995. "Cognitive Desires: An Allegory of/for Chicana Critics."

Works Cited

Alarcón, Norma. 1990. "La literatura chicana: un reto sexual y racial del proletariado." *Mujer y literatura mexicana y chicana. Culturas en contacto* 2, coords. Aralia López González, Amelia Malagamba, y Elena Urrutia, 207-212. México: El Colegio de México; Tijuana: El Colegio de la Frontera Norte.

___. 1995. "Cognitive Desires: An Allegory of/for Chicana Critics." In *Las formas de nuestras voces: Chicana and Mexicana Writers in Mexico,* edited by Claire Joysmith, 65-86. México: Universidad Autónoma de México/Centro de Investigaciones sobre América del Norte; Berkeley: Third Woman Press.

Anderson, Danny. Forthcoming. "La frontera norte y el discurso de la identidad en la narrativa mexicana del siglo XX." *puentelibre. Revista de cultura* 7.

Anzaldúa, Gloria. 1987. *Borderlands/La Frontera: The New Mestiza.* San Francisco: Aunt Lute.

Bakhtin, Mikhail. 1989. *Teoría y estética de la novela.* Translated by Helena Kirukova and Vincente Cazcarra. Madrid: Taurus.

Berumen, Humberto Félix. 1994. "El cuento entre los bárbaros del norte (1980-1992)" In *Hacerle al cuento (La ficción en México),* edited by Alfredo Pavón, 201-224. Tlaxcala, México: Universidad Autónoma de Tlaxcala.

Bhabha, Homi K. 1994. *The Location of Culture.* London and New York: Routledge.

Bruce-Novoa, Juan. 1992. "Metas monológicas, estrategias dialógicas: la literatura chicana." *Palabras de allá y de acá. Memoria del 6to. Encuentro Nacional de Escritores en la Frontera Norte de México 1991,* 11-17. Ciudad Juárez, Chihuahua: Universidad Autónoma de Ciudad Juárez.

Calderón, Héctor, and José David Saldívar, eds. 1991. *Criticism in the Borderlands: Studies in Chicano Literature, Culture, and Ideology.* Durham: Duke University Press.

Chabram, Angie. 1991. "Conceptualizing Chicano Critical Discourse." In *Criticism in the Borderlands: Studies in Chicano Literature, Culture, and Ideology,* edited by Héctor Calderón and José David Saldívar, 127-148. Durham: Duke University Press.

Conde, Rosina. 1992. "¿Dónde está la frontera?" *El Acordeón. Revista de Cultura* 7: 50-52. México: Universidad Pedagógica Nacional.

Díaz-Diocaretz, Myriam. 1993. "La palabra no olvida de donde vino: Para una poética dialógica de la diferencia." *Breve historia feminista de la literature (en lengua Castellano).* I Teoría feminista: discurso y diferencia. Coords. Myriam Díaz-Diocaretz e Iris M. Zavala.

262 *María-Socorro Tabuenca C.*

262 *María-Socorro Tabuenca C.*

Pensamiento Crítico/Pensamiento Utópico 80, 77-124. Barcelona: Anthropos-Comunidad de Madrid.

Díaz-Diocaretz, Myriam, and Iris M. Zavala. 1993. *Breve historia feminista de la literatura española (en lengua Castellano)*. Barcelona: Anthropos-Comunidad de Madrid.

Harlow, Barbara. 1991. "Sites of Struggle: Immigration, Deportation, Prison and Exile." In *Criticism in the Borderlands: Studies in Chicano Literature, Culture, and Ideology,* edited by Héctor Calderón and José David Saldívar, 149-166. Durham: Duke University Press.

Luna, Francisco. 1994. "Visiones fronterizas." *Literatura fronteriza de acá y de allá. Memoria del Encuentro Binacional "Ensayo sobre la literatura de las fronteras."* Comp. Guadalupe Beatriz Aldaco, 79-84. Hermosillo: Instituto Sonorense de Cultura; México: CONACULTA.

Malcuzinski, Pierrette. 1991. *Sociocríticas: Prácticas textuales/ Cultura de fronteras.* Teoría literaria: Texto y teoría 7 Amsterdam and Atlanta, Ga.

Romero, Rolando J. 1993a. "Postdeconstructive Spaces." *Siglo XX/ 20th Century* 11: 225-33.

____. 1993b. "Border of Fear, Border of Desire." *Borderlines Studies in American Culture* vol. 1, no. 1 (Sept.): 36-70.

Saldívar, José David. 1991. *The Dialetics of Our America: Genealogy, Cultural Critique, and Literary History.* Durham: Duke University Press.

Sanmiguel, Rosario. 1994. *Callejón Sucre y otros relatos.* Infinita Colección 1. Chihuahua: Ediciones del Azar.

Villarreal, Minerva Margarita. Personal interview conducted through the Border Cultural Program (Programa Cultural de las Fronteras), El Paso, Texas, February 20, 1995.

Zavala, Iris M. 1993. "Las formas y las funciones de una teoría crítica feminista. Feminismo dialógico." *Breve historia feminista de la literature (en lengua Castellano).* I Teoría feminista: discurso y diferencia. Coords. Myriam Díaz-Diocaretz e Iris M. Zavala. Pensamiento Crítico/Pensamiento Utópico 80, 77-124. Barcelona: Anthropos-Comunidad de Madrid.

To(o) Queer the Writer–
Loca, escritora y chicana

Gloria Anzaldúa

Queer Labels and Debates

I believe that while there are lesbian perspectives, sensibilities, experiences and topics, *there are no "lesbian writers."*

For me the term lesbian *es problemón.* As a working-class Chicana, mestiza[1]--a composite being, *amalgama de culturas y de lenguas*--a woman who loves women, "lesbian" is a cerebral word, white and middle-class, representing an English-only dominant culture, derived from the Greek word *lesbos.* I think of lesbians as predominantly white and middle-class women and a segment of women of color who acquired the term through osmosis, much the same as Chicanas and Latinas as-similated the word "Hispanic." When a "lesbian" names me the same as her, she subsumes me under her category. I am of her group but not as an equal, not as a whole person--my color erased, my class ignored. *Soy una puta mala,* a phrase coined by Ariban, a *tejana tortillera.* "Lesbian" doesn't name anything in my homeland. Unlike the word "queer," "lesbian" came late into some of our lives. Call me *de las otras.* Call me *loquita, jotita, marimacha, pajuelona, lambiscona, culera*--these are words I grew up hearing. I can identify with being *"una de las otras"* or a *"marimacha,"* or even a *jota* or a *loca porque*--these are the terms my home community uses. I identify most closely with the Nahuatl term *patlache.* These terms situate me in South Texas Chicano/*mexicano* culture and in my experiences and *recuerdos.* These Spanish/Chicano words resonate in my head and evoke gut feelings and meanings.

I want to be able to choose what to name myself. But if I have to pick an identity label in the English language I pick "dyke" or "queer," though these working-class words (formerly having "sick" connotations) have been taken over by white middle-class lesbian theorists in the academy. Queer is used as a false unifying umbrella which all "queers" of all races, ethnicities, and classes are shoved under. At times we need this umbrella to solidify our ranks against outsiders. But even when we seek shelter under it we must not forget that it homogenizes, erases our difference. Yes, we may all love members of the same sex, but we are not the same. Our ethnic communities deal differently with us. I must constantly assert my differentness, must say, This is what I think of loving women. I must stress, the difference is in my relationship to my culture; white culture may allow its lesbians to leave--mine doesn't. This is one way I avoid getting sucked into the vortex of homogenization, of getting pulled into the shelter of the queer umbrella.

What is a lesbian writer? The label in front of a writer positions her. It implies that identity is socially constructed. But only for the cultural "other." Oblivious to privilege and wrapped in arrogance, most writers from the dominant culture never specify their identity; I seldom hear them say, I am a white writer. If the writer is middle-class, white, and heterosexual s/he is crowned with the "writer" hat--no mitigating adjectives in front of it. They consider me a *Chicana* writer, or a lesbian Chicana writer. Adjectives are a way of constraining and controlling. "The more adjectives you have the tighter the box."[2] The adjective before writer marks, for us, the "inferior" writer, that is, the writer who doesn't write like them. Marking is always "marking down." While I advocate putting Chicana, *tejana*, working-class, dyke-feminist poet, writer-theorist in front of my name, I do so for reasons different than those of the dominant culture. Their reasons are to marginalize, confine, and contain. My labeling of myself is so that the Chicana and lesbian and all the other persons in me don't get erased, omitted, or killed. Naming is how I make my presence known, how I assert who and what I am and want to be known as. Naming myself is a survival tactic.

I have the same kinds of problems with the label "lesbian writer" that I do with the label "Chicana writer." *Si, soy Chicana*, and therefore a Chicana writer. But when critics label me thus, they're looking not at the person but at the writing, as though the writing is Chicana writing instead of the writer being Chicana. By forcing the label on the writing they marginalize it.

I've had the legitimacy issue thrown at me by another Chicana lesbian, Cherríe Moraga. In a book review of *Border-lands/La Frontera*, she implied that I was not a real lesbian because I did not stress my lesbian identity nor did I write about sexuality. I gathered that she wanted me to focus on lesbian sexuality. Her criticism implies that there is such a thing as a lesbian writer and that a lesbian writer should only write about lesbian issues and that lesbian issues are about sexuality.[3] It is ironic that some straight Chicanas/os, seeing only sexual difference because to them it is a glaring difference, also stress lesbian and gay aspects of my identity and leave out the culture and the class aspects. Always the labeling impacts expectations. In this double bind, one reader may view the label as a positive attribute, another as a way to marginalize.

This anthology's[4] topic, "lesbian writers writing about their own writing," assumes the existence of a "lesbian" writer. It follows the tradition in which white middle-class lesbians and gay men frame the terms of the debate. It is they who have produced queer theory and for the most part their theories make abstractions of us colored queers. They control the production of queer knowledge in the academy and in the activist communities. Higher up in the hierarchy of gay politics and gay aesthetics, they most readily get their work published and disseminated. They enter the territories of queer racial ethnic/Others and re-inscribe and recolonize. They appropriate our experiences and even our lives and "write" us up. They occupy theorizing space, and though their theories aim to enable and emancipate, they often disempower and neo-colonize. They police the queer person of color with theory. They theorize, that is, perceive, organize, classify, and name specific chunks of reality by using approaches, styles, and methodologies that are Anglo-American or European. Their theories limit the ways we think about being queer.

Position is point of view. And whatever positions we may occupy, we are getting only one point of view: white middle-class. Theory serves those that create it. White middle-class lesbians and gays are certainly not speaking for me. Inevitably, we colored dykes fall into a reactive mode, counter their terms and theories--as I am doing, as I have to do before I can even begin to write this essay. We focus on the cultural abuse of colored by white and thus fall into the trap of the colonized reader and writer forever reacting against the dominant. I feel pushed into trying to "correct" the record, to speak out against it while all the time realizing that colored queers are not responsible for educating white lesbians and gays.

What I object to about the words "lesbian" and "homosexual" is that they are terms with iron-cast molds. There are assumptions made, by both insiders and outsiders, when one identifies with these terms. The words "lesbian" and "homosexual" conjure up stereotypes of differences that are different from those evoked by the word "queer." "Queer" also provokes different assumptions and expectations. In the 1960s and 1970s it meant that one was from a working-class background, that one was not from genteel society. Even though today the term means other things, for me there is still more flexibility in the "queer" mold, more room to maneuver. "Lesbian" comes from a Euro-Anglo American mold and "homosexual" from a deviant, diseased mold shaped by certain psychological theories. We non-Euro-Anglo Americans are supposed to live by and up to those theories. A mestiza colored queer person is bodily shoved by both the heterosexual world and by white gays into the "lesbian" or "homosexual" mold whether s/he fits or not. *La persona está situada dentro de la idea en vez del revés.*

I struggle with naming without fragmenting, without excluding. Containing and closing off the naming is the central issue of this piece of writing. The core question is, What is the power and what is the danger of writing and reading like a "lesbian" or a queer? Can the power and danger be named and can queer writing be named? How does one give queer writing labels while holding the totality of the group and the person in one's mind? How do we maintain the balance between solidarity and separate space, between the *gueras/os* and the *morenas/os*? "Where are our alliances, with our culture or our crotch?"[5] *En vez de dejar cada parte en su región y mantener entre ellos la distancia de un silencio, mejor mantener la tensión entre nuestras cuatro o seis partes/personas.*

Identity is not a bunch of little cubbyholes stuffed respec-
tively with intellect, race, sex, class, vocation, gender. Identity
flows between over, aspects of a person. Identity is a river--a
process. Contained within the river is its identity, and it needs
to flow, to change, to stay a river--if it stopped it would be a
contained body of water such as a lake or a pond. The changes
in the river are external (changes in environment--river bed,
weather, animal life) and internal (within the waters). A river's
contents flow within its boundaries. Changes in identity likewise are external (how others perceive one and how one perceives others and the world) and internal (how one perceives
oneself, self-image). People in different regions name the parts
of the river/person which they see.

La busqueda de identidad--How Queer is Queer?

Often I am asked, "What is your primary identity, being lesbian or working-class or Chicana?" In defining or separating
the "lesbian" identity from other aspects of identity, I am asked
to separate and distinguish all aspects from one another. I am
asked to bracket each, to make boundaries around each so as
to articulate one particular facet of identity only. But to put
each in a separate compartment is to put them in contradiction or in isolation, when in actuality they are all constantly in
a shifting dialogue/relationship--the ethnic is in conversation
with the academic, and so on. The lesbian is part of the writer,
is part of a social class, is part of a gender, is part of whatever
identities one has of oneself. There is no way that I can put
myselves through this sieve and say okay, I'm only going to let
the "lesbian" part out and everything else will stay in the sieve.
All the multiple aspects of identities (as well as the sieve) are
part of the "lesbian."

I can understand that impulse to nail things down, to have
a checklist which says that for you to be a dyke, a radical lesbian, or an S/M lesbian, you must pass certain criteria. But
when those criteria are applied to people who fall outside the
characterizations defined by white, middle-class lesbians and
gays, (such as racial ethnic/Others) it feels very totalitarian. It

feels more totalitarian for dykes of color than for lesbians because the checklist and criteria come from gay white ideology,
whether its proponents are white or colored.

Different lesbians and gays scrutinize the cultural/Other to
see if we're correct--they police us out of fear of instability
within a community, fear of not appearing united and fear of
attack by non-gay outsiders. But I fear a unity that leaves out
parts of me, that colonizes me, that violates my integrity, my
wholeness, and chips away at my autonomy. We police ourselves out of fear as well. Because of our *mestizaje*, colored queers
have more communities to deal with (ethnic, class, white lesbians, etc.) that analyze us to determine if we "pass."

The same thing is true of the dyke community: it wants to
pinpoint the dykes who are in the closet, the lesbians who are
out, the queers who are activists, gays who are writers. You are
privileged differently if you are out there being a model of
"the good lesbian." And if you're not, if you happen to be a
lesbian and you write a story in which the protagonist is male
or a straight woman, then you're criticized for supporting the
patriarchy by writing traditionally, for writing about concerns
that are not seen as "lesbian concerns." But yet, what these
lesbian readers fail to see is that a lot of times, in presenting
traditional content or characters that the gay community thinks
support the patriarchy, they may not be "seeing" that the queer
colored writers are doing something radical or critical via the
form and/or style. The story may depict violence of men against
women. The white lesbian "reads" this as a text perpetuating
the oppression of women. Often, in showing "how it really is,"
colored dykes actually effect changes in the psyches of their
readers. Often the lesbian reader misses the subtle subversive
elements and hidden messages. Her binocular vision, focusing
on the trees, misses the forest.

Reading Them Reading Me

A strange thing happens when I attend poetry or prose readings where two or three lesbian feminists read. Often nothing
they say moves me because it is too predictable, too "white"
and racist in its ignorance of colored gay experiences. I have

done a number of readings within the white lesbian community and almost always have received a very generous reception. They may squirm when I bring up racism and class oppression, but they seem to swallow what I say. I've also read in
the Latino/Chicano Mission community (where I have drawn
smaller crowds), and have felt they would rather I had checked
my queerness at the door. On the other hand, poems and stories dealing with race and class are received with much fervor.

Once in the Haight district, I read to an audience of white
and colored hippies, straight beats, and non-literary people.
Later in a poem, I tried to express the feelings of "at-home-
ness" I experienced with them. I realized that they had been
open and receptive to my work and that class had something
to do with it. When I read poems dealing with colored queer
or Chicana issues, the audience didn't have any preconcep-
tions. I felt accepted, respected, and valued in a more total
way than I had experienced in the "lesbian" or the Mission
communities in San Francisco. These feelings are central to
the interaction between writer, reader, and text. Class *y el
conflicto de clases* is at the core of this paper, perhaps more than
dealing with being "queer of color."

In the past the reader was a minor character in the triangle
of author-text-reader. More and more today the reader is becoming as important if not more important than the author.
Making meaning is a collaborative affair. Similar class, ethnic,
and sexual identity is a strong component of a bond between
writer and reader. This intimate interactive relationship I have
with readers has to do with a colored queer feminist mestiza
identity. Not all writers experience this interaction. This interaction comes with the realization that writing is a collaborative, communal activity not done in a room of one's own. It is
an act informed and supported by the books the author reads,
the people s/he interacts with, and the centuries of cultural
history that seethe under her skin. The idea of shared writing
is not yet part of the consensual reality of most writers.

A lot of my poems, stories, and essays (what I call
autohistorias) are about reading--not just reading as in the act
of reading words on a page but also "reading" reality and reflecting on that process and the process of writing in general.
The Haight poem is about me reading, about other people

reading me, and me reading them reading me. Most of these people at the Haight reading were straight, and a lot of them were men--what you would consider chauvinist and anti-feminist--yet they were there for me in a way that the other groups such as the politically correct or the politically aware groups weren't. What was it about them that was open and receptive? They would call out encouragement, would rock and hum to my words--they were listening with their bodies and not just their intellects. They weren't "reading" me the usual way. They were "reading" my readings in front of me. Their faces were not blank nor passive. They saw me as vulnerable, a flesh-and-blood person and not as a symbol of representation, not as a "Chicana" writer. They saw me as I wanted to be seen then-- as an embodied symbol.

Reading Like a Lesbian

Reading like a queer feminist, which includes listening like one, may be how one would distinguish dyke-feminist or feminist from non-dyke/feminist. Queer readers want to interact, to repeat back or reflect or mirror, but also do more than just reflect back and mirror--to add to the dialogue. White lesbians feel that colored dykes have important things to communicate, or perhaps they want to really "listen to" and "read" us better in order to mitigate and correct their ethnocentrism. And that might be why dykes of color have such a low patience with texts and public events that don't allow us to participate fully. When I attend white women's music concerts there's so little part of me that gets to interact that there's nothing there for me. When I read Emma Pérez or Terri de la Peña, or watch comedians Mónica Palacios and Marga Gómez perform, and when I study the art of Ester Hernández, I realize what is missing from white lesbian texts--colored queer rites of passage.[6]

Though the Haight-Ashbury audience responded best (back then in 1980-81), in 1991, lesbian and gay readers and audiences (who have learned to "read" me in their classrooms) not only are beginning to reflect back my ideas but to also actively engage with me and my theories.

Queering the Writer and Reading With a Queer
Facultad

We queers also label ourselves. It is we as well as white, middle-class heterosexuals who say, "S/he's a gay writer." The gay community wants so badly to have pride in its artists and writers; it wants to shout it from the rooftops. There is a hunger for legitimacy in queers who are always trying to "discover" gay movie stars and great writers.

Can a straight woman or a man write a lesbian story? The questions are, Are you a dyke writer because you're a dyke, or are you a lesbian writer because the concerns that you write about are lesbian concerns? In other words, Is there such a thing as a lesbian language, dyke style, lesbian terminology, dyke aesthetics, or is it all up to the individual who's writing, regardless of whether she's a dyke or a straight woman, or a man? This is the same question that theorists asked in earlier debates--can a man write as a straight woman, can a man read as a woman? *We all know that women read as men and women write as men, because that's how we were taught.* We were trained to read as men. Little girls read the books that boys read, but the boys never read the books with little girl heroines, and so women are taught to read westerns and spy novels and mysteries, and the "serious" literature,[7] but we also read "women's literature," watch soap operas, read romances, read women's mysteries. But men aren't taught to read women. How and why do we break with this gender socialization? Isn't the departure as significant as establishing the criteria? Reading affects the development of female and male identity. I, for one, define my life and construct my identities through the process of reading and writing--dyke detective novels, cultural theory, Latin American fiction. Can we apply this in the same way to the lesbian readers and lesbian writers?

A straight woman reader of dyke writings would likely not catch a lot of the undercurrents having to do with dyke sexualities or sexual experiences (unless, of course, she has a lot of lesbian friends). Queers (including cultural Others) can fill in the gaps in a lesbian text and reconstruct it, where a straight woman might not. I am arguing for a lesbian sensibility, not a lesbian aesthetic.

Reading is one way of constructing identity. When one reads something that one is familiar with, one attaches to that familiarity, and the rest of the text, what remains hidden, is not perceived. Even if one notices things that are very different from oneself, that difference is used to form identity by negation—"I'm not that; I'm different from that character. This is me; that's you." Yet readers have an attraction to the unfamiliar, a curiosity. Which is why straight readers read gay literature. When a straight writer writes about us, perhaps also out of curiosity—or latent queerness or to capitalize on a trendy forbidden lifestyle—s/he often ends up appropriating our lives, paying them token attention, and focusing on sex instead of the full complexity of our lives. So while we do write for straight readers, they don't write for us.

Identity formation is a component in reading and writing, whether through empathy and identification or disidentification. If it's a lesbian who's reading, she will have more incentive to keep reading when she reaches a dyke-concern-laden passage in my writing. There will be more doors and windows through which she can access the text than if she's a non-lesbian. If she's a working-class dyke of color, however, there are even more *entradas*, more identity-making opportunities. If she's a Chicana lesbian she's got the greatest possibility of finding herself represented in my writing. But some Chicana dykes, such as urban dwellers or younger ones, may be excluded from my writing, while others bearing other kinds of "otherness" may plug into my writing. Just as we speak in different ways, we read in different ways, write in different ways. Educational and lived experiences change the way we speak, hear, read, and write.

However, there are straight, white, academic women who sometimes "see into" and "see through" unconscious falsifying disguises by penetrating the surface and reading underneath the words and between the lines. As outsiders, they may see through what I'm trying to say better than an insider. For me then it is a question of whether the individual reader is in possession of a mode of reading that can read the subtext, and can introject her experiences into the gaps. Some conventionally trained readers do not have the flexibility (in identity) nor the patience in deciphering a "strange," that is, different, text. Reading skills may result from certain ethnic, class, or sexual experiences which allow her to read in non-white ways. She looks at a piece of writing and reads it differently.

I'm also a reader of my own work. And as a reader, I usually have more in common with the Chicana dyke than I do with the white, middle-class feminist. I am in possession of both ways of reading--Chicana working-class dyke ways of reading, and white middle-class heterosexual and male ways of reading. I have had more training in reading as a white middle-class academic than I do reading as a Chicana. Just like we have more training reading as men.

Reading With One's Foot In One's Mouth

Learning to read is not synonymous with academic learning. Working-class and street people may go into an experience--for example an incident taking place on the street--and "read" what is taking place in a way that an academic couldn't. One always writes and reads from the place one's feet are planted, the ground one stands on, one's particular position, point of view.

When I write about different ideas, I try to flesh out and embody them rather than abstract them. But I don't always spell things out. I want the reader to deduce my conclusions or at least come up with her own. Often the working-class person or the colored dyke will automatically identify with that experience and say, "Oh, yeah, I've lived it, or my friend has told me she's lived that," or whatever. The white, middle-class academic woman might see it in terms of where the author positions herself; whether she is "rereading" (reinterpreting) or reinscribing certain patriarchal signs, whether s/he locates herself in a specific historical period, whether she is self-reflective about her writing. These are approaches and moves she has learned to make as a feminist critic, and they are different from the moves that the streetwise person utilizes. The street reader looks at an experience as something that's alive and moving or about to move, whereas the academic looks at the flattened out, abstract theory on these pages that is not connected to the actual experience. Being queer, being of color, I consider myself standing in the Borderlands (the actual crossroads or bridge) of these two "readings." I may be able to read the situation in the street from the point of view of a streetwise person, and I can look at these abstract theoretical writings and be able to read them academically because of the schooling that I've had.

One of the things that I've discovered about people critiquing my writing is that they want me to flesh out more of the gaps, provide more transition. I suppose this is so they don't have to do as much work. "In my instruction in tutoring writing," commented Vicki Alcoset, my writing intern, who is Chicana and Jewish, "this is the main hidden agenda that defines 'good' writing in the U.S. The point is to assume the reader is lazy, wants everything spelled out for her/him. If the reader has to work to get meaning, the writing is no 'good.'" Another reason that people sometimes want me to elaborate is because they want to know my meaning as well as their own. Roz Spafford, a college composition writing instructor at University of California at Santa Cruz,[8] suggests that perhaps the reader is looking for fullness and complexity, and a desire not to project their experience/thinking onto mine, a desire to listen fully. But for me, what's fun about reading is those gaps where I can bring my experience into the piece of the writing and use concrete images to go off into my own experience. It makes the writing richer because I can bring more into it. But we haven't been taught to read in that manner. We have, in fact, been taught not to trust it. I think that I can "read" that way because I'm in my inner world, my psychic and imaginary worlds, so much that I've developed the *facultad* to navigate such texts. The more I interact with the text the better. The more entrances, the more access for all of us.

White Lesbian Formula Writing

One of the things that I find very boring about some lesbian writing--fiction and non-fiction--is an almost formulaic impression or imposition on the writing of what lesbians should think about--a kind of politically correct way of writing that feels very sterile, very flat. One formula leads to the underlying belief that to be a lesbian writer you have to write about sexuality, and that the predominant concern of our work should be sexual relationships or sexuality. It's a given. This ideological imprint makes us view our sexuality in a preconstructed way. It tells us dykes how to think and feel about our bodies. Perhaps if we weren't supposed to write about sex so much, the writing would be more vital and vibrant. Besides, not all dykes want to write about sex or sexuality. Which brings us back to an earlier point: Is lesbian writing called such when it's not about lesbianism/sexuality but is by a lesbian?

Certain tropes that are considered lesbian properties--the coming-out story, the lesbian couple relationship, the breakup--have become formulaic. The formula is very white and mostly middle class and so prevalent that it is almost a genre. A coming-out story is different if it is written from the perspective of some "Other,"--racial, cultural, class, ethnic, or for whatever reason a lesbian has been "othered." A lot of cultural Others take the white lesbian patterns as models, so that whatever freshness of perspective, of presentation, of self-confrontation, encountering oneself as a lesbian and confronting one's community as a lesbian—instead of having that fresh, unique presentation of it, what we do is we copy this other model that's white middle-class. It kills our writing. If it's not possible to entirely change the formula, I'd at least like to see it be more representative of the diverse realities of queers, to read it and write it through other cultural lenses. I think that dykes have breached an opening in the dialogue about women connecting with our bodies. Dykes bridged some of the political, theoretical, cultural, critical concepts/beliefs with concrete experience--external/internal, sexual, and corporeal. And that was really good.

A rainbow is a bridge. The word is used politically by Native Americans--it derives from Native American people symbolizing the way different people communicate and relate with each other. It's the vision that the Native Americans have of the red and the white and the black and the yellow being able to communicate and make alliances. According to the Native Americans, they were the keepers of the Earth and they were the ones that would facilitate this rich, multi-alliance, multi-bridging. A bridge excludes racial separatism. So the concept has taken a beating recently because of the reactionary times we're going through and the upsurge in racism and white supremacy. But I can see that in the 1990s a rainbow *serpent* composed of new mestizas/os, bi- and multi-racial queer people who are mixed and politicized will rise up and become important voices in our gay, ethnic, and other communities.

Writer's Note

This essay is in progress and is excerpted from a longer piece. It started as a takeoff on the transcription of my part in an interview/dialogue with Jeffner Allen. *Gracias a mis* interns Dianna Williamson, Vicki Alcoset, Audrey Berlowitz, and Michelle Ueland, and also to Betsy Warland and Roz Spafford, who made comments: grammatical, stylistic, and conceptual.

Notes

1. The new mestiza queers have the ability, the flexibility, the malleability, the amorphous quality of being able to stretch this way and that way. We can add new labels, names, and identities as we mix with others.

2. Personal communication with Dianna Williamson regarding her commentary on this text, April 1991.

3. Moraga, Cherríe. "*Algo secretamente amado*: A Review of Gloria Anzaldúa's Borderlands/La Frontera: The New Mestiza." In *The Sexuality of Latinas,* edited by Norma Alarcón, Ana Castillo, and Cherríe Moraga. Berkeley: Third Woman Press, 1989.

4. "This anthology" refers to the book in which this essay previously appeared. See *Inversions: Writing by Dykes, Queers and Lesbians,* edited by Warland (Vancouver, B.C.: Press Gang Books, 1994).

5. Dianna Williamson in her commentary on this text, April 1991.

6. *Chicana Lesbians: The Girls Our Mothers Warned Us About,* edited by Carla Trujillo. Berkeley: Third Woman Press, 1991.

7. The debate is not settled as to what's "serious" literature as opposed to woman-centered literature. The terms are suspicious ones to embrace. Does this imply that what women read is not "serious," i.e. not important? This piece is not the place to take on that discussion.

8. The book Spafford uses for Lit 203 at the University of California at Santa Cruz, *Facts, Artifacts and Counterfacts: Theory and Method for a Reading and Writing Course,* by David Bartholomae and Anthony Petrosky (Portsmouth, New Hampshire: Boynton Cook, 1986) suggests reading is misreading.

Laying It Bare:
The Queer/Colored Body in
Photography by Laura Aguilar[1]

Yvonne Yarbro-Bejarano

The portraits of Los Angeles photographer Laura Aguilar, in tandem with the texts she incorporates in many prints, construct the individual and collective self while breaking silences imposed by the sexism, homophobia, and racism of the art world. In the field of Chicana/o Studies, Aguilar's work interrogates certain cultural nationalist discourses of identity and community. Chicana artists and cultural critics have shown how such nationalist representations critique the ideal white body of "American" identity by positing a quintessential Chicano body that is conceived as male, working-class, heterosexual, and racially marked as Indian/mestizo.[2] Aguilar's work invites us to rethink/re-vision "Chicano" and its bodies. Through her photography, she puts other bodies into circulation that contest the ideal body of Chicano identity in cultural representation, problematizing the singular "community" and exploring multilayered identities. In this, she joins other artists and writers in theorizing and representing the queer colored body as part of the "we" that calls itself "Chicana/o."

Like writer Cherríe Moraga, Aguilar talks about her assumption of a Chicana identity as a conscious choice with political ramifications.[3] The artist's public identification as both Chicana and lesbian prompts me to locate her work in the context of current debates on lesbian/gay esthetics, visibility, and appropriation, in dialogue with recent exhibitions of queer art, especially *In A Different Light* (Berkeley's University Art Museum). Recently I was asked to participate in a public radio panel to discuss the question "Is there a lesbian/gay esthetic?" I assumed that the formulation of the question itself was to provoke discussion, for one thing the diverse panelists agreed upon is that there is no single esthetic, just as there is no one lesbian or gay identity. Our radio panel discussion also touched on the use of the terms "lesbian" and "gay" or "queer" when speaking of esthetics. For example, those who now call themselves queer tend to be wary of the identity politics that characterize the earlier lesbian and gay movements. We were also quick to note that the question of a lesbian or gay esthetic elides other differences, notably gender and race.

As Jackie Goldsby points out, race is not absent from these formulations at all, rather such discourses "take race as their referential starting point—only they position whiteness as . . . the normative center of political and theoretical discussions about sexuality and identity" (238, 239). For example, when some white gay artists react to their public's demand for "gay content" by claiming their right to simply represent "humanity," they ignore the parameters that determine who gets to count as "merely human" in cultural representation in the first place. For Jewelle Gomez, much of the energy of Harlem Renaissance writers was spent proving "we, too, are human" (225).[4] Our task as cultural critics is to complement the analysis of racism with accounts of *how* race works, how it can empower as well as constrain as it interacts with other components of experience and individual artistic practices (Goldsby, 249). Even within the highly circumscribed category of "Chicana lesbian artist," we find vastly differing esthetics and deployments of race. For example, in its coding of a lesbian love story through a Native American tale in which Coyote takes a female form to seduce a woman, Celia Rodríguez's watercolor *Tapándole el ojo a la macha* (from the *Changas* series) contrasts with Aguilar's bluntly frontal approach in her photographic portraiture.

For Lawrence Rinder, co-curator of *In a Different Light,* the "extraordinary creativity" in gay and lesbian art today "may be happening not because of a solidifying of gay and lesbian identity but precisely because of a crisis in that identity" (7). Nearly a decade ago, Stuart Hall (1988) addressed the generalization of a postmodern sense of identity as fragmented, open-ended, and internally diverse, and reminded us of the concrete histories of material displacement fueling such insights for people of color. While some of us may continue to be annoyed by the cavalier ignorance or appropriation of the contributions of theorists of color to this sense of identity, what interests me in the context of the present essay is the concrete effect of the general diffusion of this perspective on the practices of queer artists of color, including the exhibition and reception of their work. By examining the components of Aguilar's individual esthetic, I hope to contribute to a critical context for the discussion of the artwork of other Latina lesbians and to an awareness of the common thematic concerns that unite Latina lesbian artists and writers across their disciplines and media.

Some contributors to the catalogue of *In a Different Light* take a stab at defining a "gay" or "queer" sensibility,[5] while recognizing that the boundaries between mainstream and lesbian/gay cultural practices are extremely porous (Rinder, 12, 43). This reciprocity accounts for the well-known representational practice of appropriating or "queering" the signs of straight culture, recoding or rewriting them, as Aguilar does with the tradition of the fine art nude. Other evidence of a "queer sensibility" may be glimpsed in her work, such as the female nude with the text "Fuck Your Gender" on her crotch (from the *Clothed/Unclothed* series).

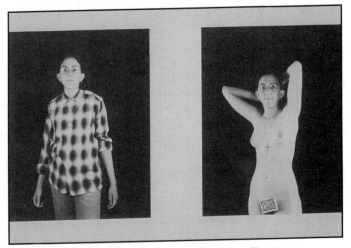

Untitled, from the "Clothed/Unclothed" series
(1990-1994, silver prints, 20 x 32)

At the same time, Aguilar's portraiture–in the self-portraits and the *Latina Lesbian* and *Plush Pony* series–destabilizes individually and collectively claimed *lesbian* identity by considerations of the subjects' race, reminding the viewer that no one becomes who they are in relation to only one set of oppositions[6] but rather to a number of different positions, each of which "has its own point of subjective identification" (Chua, 259).

Rinder comments that *In a Different Light* marks a shift of focus from who people are to what people do. For the critical analysis of a lesbian artist's esthetic, this means focusing on how the artist practices her art rather than assuming (or expecting) that her identity determines both content and esthetic. Rinder's insistence that *In a Different Light* had "less to do with representing gay and lesbian lives than with conveying gay and lesbian views of the world" (2) remits us to a history of lesbian and gay exhibitions. This history began in 1978 with *A Lesbian Show*, in response to invisibility in the realm of cultural representation and exclusion in the notoriously straight-white-male art world.[7] Commenting on the radical nature of *A Lesbian Show*, Harmony Hammond recalls the women for whom the risks involved were too great: "As one's personal life was made public, artists risked everything from family and community disapproval to job discrimination or artistic stereotyping" (46). As the same barriers persist throughout the eighties to the nineties, a tension vibrates between the continued organization of exhibitions under the rubric of sexual identity, sustaining public expectations of sameness, and the move away from monolithic or essentialist notions of identity. Pam Gregg characterizes the *All But the Obvious* exhibition (1990) as a "sampling of old and new," from "paintings and photographs of women together to works that defied an essentialist reading of lesbian identity" (65). In contrast to *A Lesbian Show*, which originally included no work by women of color, more than half the women in *Situation* (1991) were artists of color.[8] In spite of this diversity, "Some viewers were disappointed that many lesbian artists had not 'progressed' past straightforward portraiture" (Gregg, 65). Similarly, Roberta Smith in *The New York Times* chose to focus on those works in the 1993 Whitney Biennial exhibition that projected a particular sense of identity, in order to condemn them: "The unfortunate impression created is that to succeed, the art of minority artists and women must be closely tied to their personal situation, preferably to their sense of victimization" (quoted in Chua, 258). Even as we applaud the move away from fixed or absolute notions of identity, we must understand the politics behind sweeping judgments that see identity and esthetics as parallel lines "that never converge" (Chua, 258) and dismiss as valueless portraiture and work that is "content-driven" in its representation of lesbian lives and experiences.[9]

The historical trajectory of lesbian visibility in the arts is drastically reduced within a Chicana/o context. Given the racism and elitism of the art world, it is not surprising that a major retrospective of Chicano movement art, *Chicano Art: Resistance and Affirmation*, happened only in the last decade of this century.[10] The scarcity of lesbian images in Chicana/o art history is compensated in part by a rich and influential body of writing by Chicana lesbians, especially Cherríe Moraga and Gloria Anzaldúa. An important milestone that marked a welcome polyphony of voices was the publication of *Chicana Lesbians: The Girls Our Mothers Warned Us About* (1991), edited by Carla Trujillo, with Ester Hernández' seriograph *La Ofrenda* on its front cover: a female nude in profile with a full back tattoo of the Virgin of Guadalupe offered a thorny rose. That the artist withdrew this image from the anthology's second printing is an eloquent testimony to the discomfort and outright hostility with which representations specifically marked as lesbian are met in the Chicana/o community. More recently, the Galería de la Raza in San Francisco's Mission District presented *Queer Raza: El Corazón Me Dio un Salto* (1995) as part of its (Re)Generation Project. In spite of the cross-generational emphasis of this project, the show focused exclusively on the "new" generation of gay, lesbian, or queer artists, glossing over the fact that the "old" generation never had an exhibition, and losing the opportunity for discussion of the forces that kept certain highly influential lesbian artists of the Chicano art movement so tightly closeted. Given the constraints queer raza artists face both in the dominant culture and within their own communities, it seems more important than ever to undertake a public analysis of their work, including the "Queer Raza" exhibition.[11]

Lesbian and gay artists have enjoyed increased opportunities in mainstream galleries, museums, and publications since 1991 (Gregg) and in Los Angeles, especially since April 1992, following the civil disturbances in the wake of the Rodney King verdict. Yet greater visibility in mainstream venues has not translated into greater accessibility or power in the art world, nor, as Aguilar knows too well, into even modest economic success, although she has had numerous shows, curating invitations, and reviews. Aguilar's economic marginalization owes as much to the racism, sexism, and homophobia of the art world as to her auditory dyslexia, which has had and continues to have a profound impact on her. Photography has been a primary means of self-expression, given her severe dyslexia, as well as a necessary outlet for the rage and frustration at her multiple exclusions. In addition to the pressures and stress of chronic under- and unemployment, extreme economic restrictrions have alarming ramifications for the practice of her art as well as her emotional well-being.

Although some would say the window of visibility of gay and especially lesbian images in advertising has already closed, nothing could be more bitterly ironic than this new fashionability at a time when artists of Aguilar's caliber are sometimes too poor to work and homophobic legislation and gay bashing of all kinds are on the rise. Caffyn Kelley, the editor of the anthology *Forbidden Subjects: Self-Portraits by Lesbian Artists,* addresses the need for different kinds of lesbian images in a punitive social context:

> Explicit lesbian images are crucially important. Yet I believe what is most "forbidden" about lesbian identity is not the sexual activity which delineates it. The challenge we pose to a patriarchal and heterosexist order comes clear when we integrate our pleasure in women with our self-knowledge and our stance within the body politic. (6)

The lesbian-identified political stance for many artists of color includes not only a critique of patriarchy and heterosexism, but also of racism, imperialism, and colonialism.

Speaking from my own position as a Chicana lesbian academic, I am hungry for images, including the erotic, of lesbians of color, especially Chicanas, and of queerboys of color as well. The absence of these representations in my life impover-ishes me and defrauds my experience. This absence also drives my overall intellectual project of analyzing queer texts in a variety of media in my teaching and writing. It is not always easy, possible, or useful to distinguish between my desire for these images as a spectator and as a critic, in part because I am also starving for a representation of Chicana lesbian desire in all its range and complexity. This is why I respond so strongly to Aguilar's portfolio, for the desire that flows through it does not limit itself to the sexual: It is for social justice, community, and representation in all its meanings.

Before concentrating on Aguilar's nineties work, I would like to touch on several earlier pieces as they relate to the representation of lesbian self-identification and prefigure some of the concerns of the later work. In addition to thematic con-tinuity, I am particularly interested in the incorporation of family snapshots in the early photo collages, providing a bridge between "fine art" photography and the historical role of the photography in the self-representation of people of color. As

Eddie Melts, from the "Plush Pony" series
(1992, silver print, 11 x 14)

Jewelle Gomez points out, "We projected the image we held of ourselves privately, and the camera couldn't avoid it" (231). In addition to the specific role they play in the photo collages, the conventions of the snapshot combine with those of the fine art photograph in Aguilar's esthetic as a whole.

In a collage from 1985, *Self-Portrait: Cowgirl* (photo Xerox, 8 x 11 inches), a large cartoonish figure of a "tomboy" in cowboy clothes and three snapshots of Aguilar as a young girl and as a young woman are superimposed over erotic images of two women together. In another collage from the same year, *Self-Portrait: Lesbian Woman* (photo Xerox, 8 1/2 x 11 inches), the snapshots placed over a similar background are of Aguilar as a young adult, in line with the redundantly emphatic text "lesbian woman." What the background images in the two collages have in common is the women's whiteness and "beauty" in fulfillment of the feminine ideal in mainstream U.S. culture. Aguilar's skin appears relatively pale in the later black and white portraits, but in the racialized erotic context of the photo collages the darker skin tone of the color snapshots contrasts with the whiteness of the background women. By placing her snapshots over such images, Aguilar seems to be exploring where her body and her identity fit in. This gesture characterizes her later nude self-portraits as well as the attitudes of other subjects of her portraiture, while the diffidence and relaxed intimacy of many of her "professional" photographs recall the familiar air of the snapshot.

The photo collages already display the ambivalence characteristic of some of her later work: By juxtaposing her snapshots and the images, the artist seems to be saying, "I am this"; by placing her images on top of and partially obliterating the background erotic scenes racially marked as white, she distances herself ("I am not that"). While this ambivalent positioning harmonizes with what Amy Scholder defines as a permeable queer sensibility ("We're there and not there and almost anything can be read on a number of different levels" 177-178), Aguilar's deployment of it here in the context of racial difference and sexual sameness demonstrates its remarkable flexibility to describe an "insider/outsider" position determined by multiple factors and shifting according to context.[12]

Two self-portraits from 1985-86, showing the artist in a kiddy pool, playfully juxtapose female adulthood and girlhood, as in the first photo collage, while hiding most of the adult body (*Playing Around*, 8 x 10 inches). This eclipse of the body is more pronounced in the print in which she is wearing a comic disguise (*Clowning Around*, 8 x 10 inches). These pieces announce concerns with hiding/exposing the body and the mask-like nature of social roles, and at the same time contrast sharply with a frontal, full-body self-portrait from 1987, the year Sybil Venegas cites as her public coming out.

In this relatively small print (*Guadalupe and Pee Wee*, 8 x 10 inches), the artist uses her clothed body spatially to interrogate Chicana identity. The subject of the photograph appears between two groupings of popular Mexican icons: a doll and rasquache ceramics on the left, and the Virgin of Guadalupe, the Mexican flag, and a rosary on the right. In a humorous gesture towards the commercialization of the clichéd images, the Mexican flag adorns a cigarette lighter. Casually positioned among the objects on the right is a Pee Wee Herman doll, denoting U.S. popular culture and queer camp. The subject's expression is elusive, between dejected and defiant.

The image just discussed (*Guadalupe and Pee Wee*) is a precursor of one of Aguilar's most reviewed photographs. In *Three Eagles Flying* (1990, three silver gelatin prints, 24 x 60 inches, each panel 20 x 24 inches), two formal elements appear that play a major role in her (self-)portraiture: the nude and the large size of the prints. *Three Eagles Flying* positions Aguilar's

Three Eagles Flying (1990, silver prints, 24 x 60)

body between the two flags that symbolize her bicultural experience, making explicit the dynamic between Mexican and Anglo culture hinted at by the Pee Wee Herman doll in the previous piece and visually capturing the tensions and constraints inherent in living "in-between" (Anzaldúa's "borderlands").[13] The placement of the subject between the two flags suggests no home in either, while the rope around her neck and hands and the equally binding flags around her body convey the punitive and psychic aspects of failing to "fit in." *Three Eagles Flying* is a signature piece in Aguilar's portfolio that illuminates her portraiture, or the configuration of what she refers to as "the people around her" (Alfaro), as both a search for and interrogation of "community" or "nation."

The bottom half of her body is less hidden than bound by the U.S. flag, while her head is covered by the Mexican flag as in a hostage situation. Critics have commented on the visual/verbal pun of the print's title, playing off the "águila" of Mexican identity, the eagle of U.S. imperialism, and the surname Aguilar. Ironically, none of the three eagles is flying (Hulick): One is imprinted on the flag, another is wrapped around her head, and the woman named Aguilar is trapped by the constructs of national identity and culture symbolized by the two nations' flags. The U.S. flag binds the subject below the waist, suggesting a critique of the exclusionary constructions of lesbianism as white. On the other hand, her face is hidden from the spectator by a symbol of Mexican national identity, referencing the ideal mestizo body of Mexican/Chicano nationalism. Aguilar is too dark for white America; but perhaps also too light/white (with her half-Irish mother) in a Chicano or Mexican context. Again, a possible answer to the question that drives her art—where do I/we fit in—seems to be nowhere.

At the same time, the imposing size of the subject's body interrupts the binary *U.S./Mexico* to create the focal point of the composition as something more than either pole (I am the product of this conflict, but more than this). Her breasts are free, as if suggesting the impossibility of completely imprisoning or constructing her body through monolithic definitions of race or nation. The representation of the female body as both constrained by and escaping rigid constructs of identity in *Three Eagles Flying* recalls Moraga's writing of flesh that is specifically female, lesbian, and mestiza as the site of a desire that can overflow and destabilize binary categories of "us" and "them."

In Sandy's Room (1990), a nude self-portrait reclining in a chair in front of a fan, conveys a wonderful sense of openness: the window, the body given over to the wind from the fan, its vulnerability to the camera. The generous margins around the subject contribute to the sense of spaciousness. This print is from a series in which the artist photographed herself nude for the first time. Another piece from this series (*Nikki's Poem on My Mind*, triptych, 8 x 10 inches each) shows the subject standing in front of the window featured so prominently in *In Sandy's Room*. In a recent presentation of her work at Stanford University (November 2, 1995), the artist spoke of her desire to challenge herself by posing nude and how she overcame her nervousness by repeating a fragment from Nikki Giovanni's poem "Mirrors" over and over in her mind, until by the time she posed for *In Sandy's Room* she felt quite comfortable and relaxed:

> The face in the window . . . is not the face in the mirror . . . Mirrors aren't for windows . . . they would block the light . . . Mirrors are for bedroom walls . . . or closet doors . . . Windows show who we hope to be . . . Mirrors reflect who we are . . . Mirrors . . . like religious fervors . . . are private . . . and actually uninteresting to those not involved . . . Windows open up . . . bring a fresh view . . . windows make us vulnerable. (22)

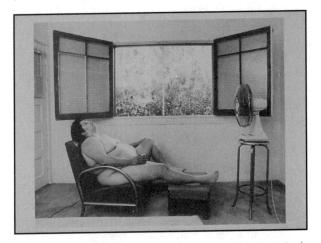

In Sandy's Room (1990, silver print, 16 x 20; 1993, 3 x 5 feet)

This text captures many of the key aspects of Aguilar's esthetic project (looking at the self, questions of identity, the (blurred) boundary between the private and the public, the relationship between the subject and the viewer, the vulnerability of "opening up") and highlights the important relationship between verbal and visual languages in her work. Here, the text stands in a significant yet invisible relationship to the finished self-portrait, while in other pieces, the written text or title is incorporated into the finished print.[14] Played against the relaxed airiness of the print's ambiance the subject's expression is emotionally ambivalent. Is she depressed? Is she just hot?[15]

The original print of *In Sandy's Room* was already relatively large at 16 by 20 inches; the remake, in 1993, achieves mural proportions (3 by 5 feet). The magnitude of this and other self-portraits is an integral part of their impact on the viewer, correlating with the size of the subject's body and writing large the issues of gender, race, and sexuality that Aguilar's art addresses. As in the esthetics of muralism, seeing a familiar object on a larger than expected scale changes our perception of it as well as our perception of the issues addressed by the image (Baca in Neumaier 259, 263).

In addition to single-image portraits, many of Aguilar's pieces group as few as two and as many as twelve images under a single title. The images of the early photo collages relate internally, while dual images structure some nude portraiture and the *Clothed/Unclothed* series. Even in the *Latina Lesbian* series, the text placed below the subject decenters the single image and invites the spectator to make connections between image and text. There are also groupings of three, four and five within a single print.[16] The multiple self-portraits are of particular interest: *Five Lauras* (1991, five panels, 3 x 5 feet each), and *Twelve Lauras* (1993), which combines twelve individual prints to form a self-portrait mural measuring 6 feet 4 inches by 6 feet 4 inches.[17] Multiple imagery and monumental size magnify a certain way of thinking about identity and the self: I am not only one thing; I am this and also this; together we look like this. Aguilar's portraits convey a sense of shifting and layered individual and collective identities that contests an ideal subject or body of cultural or national identity. The images are heterogeneous, yet they communicate comfortably with themselves and with one another.[18]

The *Clothed/Unclothed* series, begun in 1990, is composed of untitled pendant diptychs (20 x 32 inches, 16 by 20 inches each), in which the subject or subjects pose in clothes on the left and without clothes on the right. The juxtaposition invites

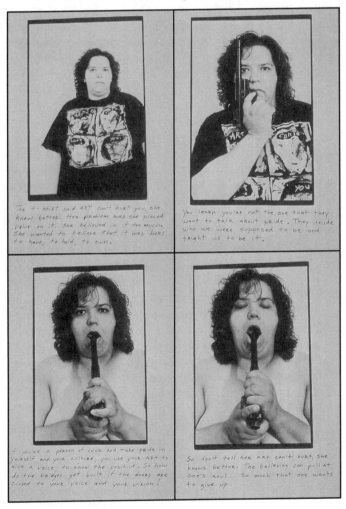

Don't Tell Her Art Can't Hurt (1993, siver prints, 50 x 160)

the viewer to think about the associations of nudity with vulnerability and sexuality and about clothing as a "socializing technology" (Veneciano) in the construction of gender or sexual identity (as in a "feminine," "gay," "butch," or "queer" look). The clothed/unclothed dynamic is an important one in the portfolio as a whole, not just in the series of that name. In *Don't Tell Her Art Can't Hurt* (1993, 50 x 160 inches, four silver gelatin prints, 3 feet by 5 feet each), the contrast between clothed and unclothed heightens the tension between the self-targeted violence and an undercurrent of potentially outward-turned threat, rejection, or violence. In the two nude images with the gun in her mouth, Aguilar channels her rage and frustration at an exclusionary art establishment in an image of suicidal depression. But in the two clothed images on the left there is an indeterminate moment in which it is not altogether clear what she will do with the gun. In *Three Eagles Flying* the crossover treatment of the flags as clothing illuminates the nude portraiture by revealing the conflict between the assertion of the non-ideal body and clothing that visually signals gender, sexual, and cultural identities. The nude portraits strip away these particular public personas and roles and oblige the subjects to reveal themselves through their bodies alone. This is not to imply that bodies are "real" or "true" as opposed to social constructions such as gender or race. Rather, the nudity highlights both subjects' and viewers' culturally conditioned attitudes and feelings about bodies, race, and sexuality. Aguilar's nude portraiture engages exclusionary ideals of beauty and sexuality and how these ideals are internalized and contested by their "Others."

The categories of confrontation and vulnerability Diana Emery Hulick perceives as "the twin poles of Aguilar's work" (53)[19] are at play in the construction of spectator positions as well. For some, these bodies pose a challenge; for others they are familiar, ordinary, empowering. and beautiful. Latino performance artist Luis Alfaro comments that:

> When a critic praises Aguilar for making visible the "outcasts" and "marginalized" of our society, Aguilar knows that the critic is caught up in the isms that she is trying to expose in her work. What we see as queers in our community are people like ourselves. (17)

Aguilar confronts "the myths surrounding the body" (Alfaro) by simply photographing herself and the people she knows: "I photograph the people around me—women, people of color, gays and lesbians. I wouldn't know what to do with the perfect body. Can we get comfortable with the imperfections?" (Alfaro). The contrast between Hulick's emphasis on confrontation and Alfaro's and Aguilar's dwelling on familiarity indicates that Aguilar's photographs are doing different things for different viewers. While Aguilar does not reveal the name of the sitters, ostensibly to protect their privacy, many are readily identifiable by spectators in some way connected to these communities, throwing yet another spin on the shifting viewer positionality in the reception of Aguilar's art.

It would be easy to assume that those spectators who do not share the subject positions of the sitter(s) would read the work as confrontational, but it is not a question of binary "outsider" and "insider" viewing positions. The same dynamic may be played out within a single viewer. Even spectators sharing all the sitters' subject positions may oscillate among a range of possible responses, including rejection and identification, repulsion and seduction, pride and shame. As a viewer of Aguilar's nudes, I contextualize my own complex response in relation to multiple histories of representation that repress certain bodies or place them on the "outside." Within Chicana/o art, for example, the marginalization of work that openly identifies as Chicana *and* lesbian points both to a conflicted history of racial and sexual representations as well as an attachment to *certain* embodiments of the identity "Chicana/o." These histories shape my response, in both the residue of shame they leave behind as well as in the exhilirating sense of resistance Aguilar's nudes evoke in me. The multiplicity of possible responses to Aguilar's work underlines the protean nature of desire, which refuses to be constrained within any one "correct" response, as well as the absence of any one community within whose boundaries these images are "at home."[20]

Like Robert Mapplethorpe's, Aguilar's nude portraiture interrupts the Western fine-art nude tradition, with its Euro- and andro-centric constructions of the perfect or desirable body, by photographing the "Other," both racial and sexual.[21] But she uses a very different strategy from Mapplethorpe's subversive blurring of the boundaries between fine art and pornography, which is where images of the naked bodies of people of color are to be found in abundance. Gay male porn stages racialized desire as well as racist stereotypes of Asians (Fung), blacks (Mercer), and Latinos (Ortiz). The lesbian radical sex zine *On Our Backs* has featured white lesbians adopting the cholo image on its cover, and offensive Mammy greeting cards sell briskly in white gay culture. Faced with a representational history in which the bodies of people of color are "always already pornographic,"[22] Aguilar photographs her sitters as both objects and subjects.

They are writing subjects who author their own texts, as in the *Latina Lesbian* series or the *Clothed/Unclothed* print with the "Fuck Your Gender" text, projecting a sense of agency and political consciousness while mitigating the degree of the sitter's exposure. The written text—the writing internal to the prints as well as the series titles (*Latina Lesbians, Plush Pony*)—calls attention to the self-construction of Latina lesbians, and provides a

Carla, from the "Latina Lesbians" series
(1987-1994, silver print, 11 x 14)

rich source for studying their identity politics. In other pieces, Aguilar cultivates this esthetic, combining both visual and verbal languages to critique her exclusion as a woman of color from the art world. In *Will Work for Axcess* (1993, five 16 x 20 inch silver gelatin prints) the artist stands outside a mainstream art establishment with the words of the title written on a sign covering her body, combining the bold genre of the political protest placard with the resonant pathos of the homeless and unemployed, which in Aguilar's case is not entirely metaphorical or ironic. The spelling of "Axcess" is perhaps a straitforward mistake, but it also evokes axes hacking open the closed doors of the art world through force. *Don't Tell Her Art Can't Hurt* positions four images of the artist above four texts, authored by Aguilar yet referring to herself in the third person:

> The t-shirt said ART can't hurt you, she knew better. Her problem was she placed value on it. She believed in it too much. She wanted to believe that it was hers to have, to own.
> You learn you're not the one that they want to talk about pride. They decide who we were supposed to be and taught us to be it.
> If you're a person of color and take pride in yourself and your culture, you use your art to give a voice, to show the positive. So how do the bridges get built if the doors are closed to your voice and your vision?
> So don't tell her art can't hurt, she knows better. The believing can pull at one's soul. So much that one wants to give up.

The fact that Aguilar chooses to privilege the printed text in this way, in spite of her conflicted personal history with the word due to her auditory dyslexia, acknowledges and exploits the power of verbal language in naming and self-representation.

Aguilar's sitters are not only subjects of the written word; they are also photographed as both objects and subjects of the gaze. Jeffrey Hoone comments that *Twelve Lauras* (1993) has the effect of being photographed from behind a bathroom mirror. In the large multiple self-portraits of 1991 and 1993, Aguilar displays an easy intimacy with her body, touching herself in a tender inventory of parts that she shares with the spectator but that does not seem to be primarily *for* the viewer. Her shifting expressions, which critics describe as ranging from "neutral" to "questioning" and "defensive,"[23] contribute to this sense of elusiveness in the moment of maximum exposure. The gaze of the subject in the self-portraits seems less engaged with the spectator than with the kind of self-appraisal already noted in the photo collages. This dual dynamic (looking at the viewer, looking at themselves) also seems to be at work in some of the prints in the *Clothed/Unclothed* series in which the subjects return the gaze of the camera. In these images, the subjects' expression differs clothed and unclothed. In the multiple nude portraits the subjects negate or decenter the gaze of the spectator in a different way: in their inwardness they seem oblivious of the viewer, or even of one another. One self-portrait consists of a shot of Aguilar's torso from behind, offered to spectators to accept or reject; but her back is turned on the viewer's response.

Aguilar works with, but also diffuses, the power relationship implicit in the "gaze of the camera/object of the gaze" dynamic in photography. Some sitters comment on how Aguilar changes in a photo session as she assumes the authority of the one behind the camera. Yet they also say that Aguilar doesn't "take" photographs but makes the photo session a col-

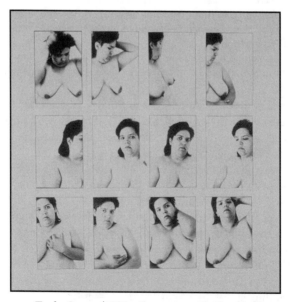

Twelve Lauras (1993, silver prints, 6′ 4″ x 6′ 4″)

laboration in which subject(s) and photographer not only jointly select the best photos (Lazzari) but actually produce the images together: what shots and poses to use, how much of the body and the self to reveal (Alfaro).[24] In Mapplethorpe's work the power dynamic between photographer and sitter is overdetermined by race (the gaze is white, the object of the gaze is black). In her self-portraits Aguilar inhabits the hyphen of the subject-object dynamic as both the subject of the gaze and the object of her own mestiza desire. As a lesbian of color photographer, Aguilar erases the difference of race while retaining her power over the image in relationship to lesbian and gay subjects/sitters of color.

In the *Latina Lesbian* series (1987-1990, 11 x 14 inch silver gelatin prints) and the *Plush Pony* series (1992, 11 x 14 inch silver gelatin prints), sitters and photographer share sexual, racial, and gender identities. In both these series, the subjects are clothed and Aguilar chooses to focus on other aspects of their identities/relationships than the erotic or the sexual, or to foreground other investments of erotic energy and desire.[25] While the *Latina Lesbian* series presents a range of women, from college educated to skilled laborers (Hulick, 54), the *Plush Pony* prints focus on a particular group of working-class women, including butch-femme individuals and couples, from the cultural milieu of the bar of the same name in East L.A. Hulick contrasts the "quiet and sometimes tender gazes" of some of the *Clothed/Unclothed* subjects with the proud, defiant stance of the *Plush Pony* subjects (54). (As a femme-identified spectator, I would add that their expressions are also very tender and downright cute!) These prints make a statement about who these women are and should also be read in the context of a particular history and a particular culture. In lesbian history, the bar culture of the fifties with its butch-femme roles was a battlefield. Bars were routinely raided by police and butch women were routinely beaten and raped. *The Persistent Desire*, an anthology edited by Joan Nestle, recuperates the experiences of these precursors of radical lesbian-feminist militancy and activism, who took the punishments the dominant society metes out for making an erotic/sexual practice a public, visible identity. The lesbian feminist movement's embarrassment at and censure of butch-femme self-styling has much to do with anxiety over social acceptance of homosexuality but also with race and class, as butch-femme culture was/ is largely practiced by women of color and working-class women.[26] Aguilar's *Plush Pony* series works against the silences imposed within lesbian (and Chicano) history, creating a visual record of their faces and their lives.

Just as she is both subject and object of her own desiring gaze in her self-portraits, and photographs her sitters as both subjects and objects, her insider/outsider position is clear in these juxtapositions of Chicana/o communities, some of which she places herself within, as in the inclusion of her own portrait in the *Latina Lesbian* series, and some of which she photographs more from the "outside," as in the *Plush Pony* series. The *Plush Pony* series represents but one of the communities that construct "Chicana/o" in Aguilar's portfolio, forming constellations of different social groupings, loosely interconnected through Aguilar's photography and insider/outsider position.

Aguilar's esthetic goes beyond merely presenting an alternative vision of what is good, true, and beautiful to interrogating the very binary divisions on which the philosophy of esthetics has traditionally been based. For example, her images are not asexual or non-erotic, but the sexual/erotic energy in Aguilar's portraiture is unconventionally routed and more dispersed. The knowledge that the three subjects of one of the *Clothed/Unclothed* prints are siblings is a case in point, as nudity

Untitled, from the "Clothed/Unclothed" series
(1990-1994, silver prints, 20 x 32)

among adult siblings is uncommon.[27] Images of nude couples or groups, rather than the single object of desire, further re-route the desire invested in the "subject/object of the gaze" dynamic. In the *Clothed/Unclothed* print of an African-American couple, both subjects are looking at the camera/viewer, but have an aura of selfhood about them and loving intimacy between them that interacts with spectators' voyeuristic desire to objectify them. The peculiar charge of these portraits derives in part from the incorporation of nudity, with its potential shock value, in an esthetic of the ordinary that quotes the casual informality of the family snapshot. Precisely because of the subjects' ordinariness and relaxed familiarity, the viewer remains excruciatingly aware of their nudity, while finding it difficult to reduce them entirely to estheticized or sexualized objects. (This dynamic does not necessarily cancel out the pleasure of objectification; it merely offers a different kind of pleasure.) The path of desire in Aguilar's photographs is certainly complex, tracing a pattern more like a web or an internal circulatory system, rather than the subject/object linearity.

Another dimension of the sensual experience of viewing these portraits of course lies in the beauty of Aguilar's printing itself, for example in the print of the African-American couple. Besides the gleaming sharpness of the prints themselves, much of the esthetic pleasure for the spectator derives from Aguilar's treatment of the bodies as sculptural forms unanchored in any particular environment (Hulick), together with the sheer size of many of the images.

As many writers in the catalogue of *In a Different Light* point out, the individual esthetic of any lesbian, gay, or queer artist does not arise in a void but in relationship to other artistic practices, both mainstream and alternative. Aguilar's representation of the "non-ideal" body is read in the context of Western art's marginalization of racial and sexual "Others," while the size of many of her subjects resonates within other cultural histories in which massive bodies carry different connotations. For example, while she comes to it along very different paths and would not identify herself with radical feminism, Aguilar's prints echo radical lesbian-feminism's incisive critique of the sexist Western ideal of feminine beauty and its negative consequences for women's self-image and the female body, including the rampant social diseases of anorexia and bulimia. Aguilar is not the first Chicana to take on issues of body size and self-image in her work; Josefina López put Chicanas on stage in their underwear comparing "llantas," and acknowledged her debt to the "fat is a feminist issue" analysis in a prepublication version of her play *Real Women Have Curves*. Radical lesbian-feminism also created a matriarchal iconography featuring the Earth Mother in the shape she has taken in numerous cultures for thousands of years: an abundance of female flesh and attributes. Margaret Lazzari points out how the size of Aguilar's nude self-portraits accentuates the fleshiness of her body. In other words, there are erotic as well as political investments in these images for some viewers. We find a similar confluence of the erotic and the political around issues of body size in *Fat Girl: A Zine for Fat Dykes and the Women Who Want Them*, which features images of diverse racial identities and sexual practices as well as guidelines for fat activism, for example, demanding that other lesbian erotic publications expand their standards of desirability in the images they publish.

From a spectator position of confrontation, it is perhaps difficult to see the encounters among sitter, photographer, and viewer in Aguilar's work as erotic or loving exchanges. For Marita Gootee in *Forbidden Subjects*, the direct frontal view of the female torso symbolizes love (51). In this sense, Aguilar's lesbian portraiture runs parallel to writing by Chicana lesbians that addresses internalized oppression and the need to foster self-love as lesbians and mestizas. Work that presents frontal nudity *does* seek a direct encounter with the viewer (Gootee), but it is not only confrontational. For Jean Weisinger, in the same anthology, "Photographing the self" (and, I would add in Aguilar's case, "the people around you") "is an act of love and a gift to others" (16). In exposing themselves, by making public what is most private, Aguilar and her sitters make themselves vulnerable, not just in showing their naked bodies to the world, but also in sharing something of themselves (Alfaro). It is the gift of this openness that ultimately makes both sitter and spectator vulnerable, as the artist acknowledges: "I'm trying to allow the softness of myself to be

out and be represented in these photographs. I believe that
the viewer is as vulnerable as the nude person in the clothed/
unclothed series because as they view the images they are
hopefully seeing images of themselves" (Alfaro).

This gesture of giving in Aguilar's nude portraiture, cap-
tured succinctly in the print of the male nude extending his
hands toward the spectator (*Heart*, 1993-94, 11 x 14 inches and
8 x 10 inches), recalls the male cross-dresser in Lourdes Portillo's
film *La Ofrenda*, who explains the meaning of the "ofrendas"
for the Days of the Dead and offers an apple to the camera.
Although I remain skeptical of our ability to isolate a lesbian
or queer esthetic, I am intrigued by the recurrence of certain
themes in the cultural production of Latina lesbians, particularly this notion of the gift or offering in Aguilar's nude portraiture and a cluster of representations that share the same
title, "La Ofrenda": Hernández's image on the first edition of
Chicana Lesbians, Moraga's short story in *The Last Generation*,
and the photographic triptych and poem by Marcia Ochoa
(*The Lesbian Body*). We expect a Latina lesbian "view of the

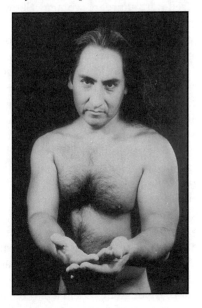

Heart, from the "Nude Portraits" series
(1993-94, silver print, 11 x 14)

world" to encompass themes that stem from experiences of marginalization and exclusion; these "offerings" explore the risky yet potentially empowering gift of opening in multifaceted desire to the other. Taking the risk to offer something of themselves to the camera contributes to the much-noted presence and strength of the subjects in Aguilar's photographs.[28]

The belief in art voiced in *Don't Tell Her Art Can't Hurt* confirms this sense of photography as empowerment of individuals and a lens for interrogating and possibly building community that cuts across race, class, gender, and sexual lines. In spite of, or perhaps because of, the less-than-utopian relations among all the groups Aguilar photographs, her prints construct an alternative "imagined community" (Anderson) composed of sitters and photographers, subjects and viewers. Her artistic practice also includes donating her images of male nude couples and groups for HIV educational brochures and offering free workshops in photography as artist-in-residence at the Gay and Lesbian Services Center: Exposing Ourselves (photo as documentary), Time Out Let's Play (for HIV-affected people), Women's Eye (self-portraiture for women), Show and Tell for and by Women.[29] For Aguilar, the discovery of photography in her teens represented a tremendous channel for self-expression after many frustrating years in L.A. schools that misdiagnosed her auditory dyslexia. Now, even as she struggles on a daily basis to survive, she offers this language for other people to learn, express themselves in, and communicate with.

In conclusion, Aguilar's photography activates older discursive and representational traditions of Chicana/o nation, community, and identity in queer ways. Her portraits deconstruct various social disguises, yet Aguilar's esthetic eludes the representation of the "real" or "authentic" face under the mask through her signature treatment of frontal nudity; large, even monumental formats; multiple rather than single images; and by eliciting different responses from different viewers or from the same viewer. Fostering communication through photography, Aguilar gives us images of diverse urban groups, queer raza, and other people of color. Working from a Chicana lesbian standpoint, Aguilar engages in a participatory process with sitters and spectators of deciding what bodies matter[30] in "Chicana/o" and "American" identity.

Notes

1. This essay was first developed in the Stanford Center for Chicano Research Colloquium Series in winter 1993. I presented it in an earlier version at the NACCS conference in Spokane, Washington, in spring 1994. My thanks to all who contributed comments and suggestions for improvement, especially Luz Calvo for her insightful reading of the last draft.

2. See, for example, Chabram-Dernersesian's *I Throw Punches*.

3. "I am a direct descendent of the Chicano movement of the 1960s. Someone once said to me you are what you identify yourself to be. We all have choices and make them. I chose to be, amongst other things, a Chicana" (Blaszkiewicz).

4. For a discussion of this issue in the context of Audre Lorde's writing, see Holland's "Humanity Is Not a Luxury."

5. For example, "a way to overwhelm reality . . . whose practice hinges . . . on decisively choosing as if over is" (Harris 187), or a "queer feeling of being constantly displaced, a perception that experience is elsewhere, encoded rather than defined . . . Queer sensibility depends on a sense of irony or camp or stretch of imagination as engaged with the dominant culture" (Scholder 177-78).

6. See Alarcón's "The Theoretical Subject(s)."

7. See Blake's essay in the *In a Different Light* catalogue for a useful history of art that is similar in "intention, organization and tactics" (14) to queer artistic practices, including Fluxus, the women's art movement, and punk.

8. Gregg ascribes this difference in part to the show's "embracing a diverse lesbian sensibility and refusing prescribed notions of identity" (65).

9. For Gregg, "Because much community activity must still focus on basic rights, and since identities are constantly evolving, portraiture remains valid and important" (65). See Lippard's *Mixed Blessings* for an analysis of the forces that determine whose work has value and whose does not in the art world.

10. See Gaspar de Alba's University of New Mexico dissertation for an analysis of this groundbreaking exhibition, as well as for a critique of its gender politics.

11. For my first steps toward a critical analysis of Latina lesbian art, see "The Lesbian Body in Latina Cultural Production."

12. See Trinh for a very useful discussion of the insider/outsider, especially pages 74-75 of the chapter "Outside In Inside Out."

13. Luz Calvo's work in progress on this piece, "Oh Say, Can You See (me)?" offers a brilliant analysis of its representation of "the multiple and ambivalent subject positions of those living in the

(post)colonial diaspora," as well as of how "it stages ambivalent points of identification and desire" for the spectator.

14. Aguilar's *How Mexican Is Mexican* installation (1991) incorporated texts and images in a way similar to the *Latina Lesbian* series.

15. Blake reads this image as exhibiting a kind of powerfully self-contained sexuality, arousing straight anxiety at a queer sexuality that is "somehow self-pleasuring and self-sufficient" (30-31). I agree with Blake's assessment that the image does not need or make a place for the viewer, and suggest that its unsettling self-sufficiency is a quality shared by many of Aguilar's portraits.

16. *Guadalupe and Pee Wee* and *Three Eagles Flying* place the artist's body in dialogue with two images or groups of images of national or cultural identity, while one of her nude portraits includes four men, and a print from the *Plush Pony* series features four women and one man.

17. Compare Marcia Ochoa's *(sometimes it's the little things that give you away),* composed of thirteen images measuring 30 x 40 inches, in "The Lesbian Body in Latina Cultural Production."

18. In an interview with Blaszkiewicz on the television program *Woman to Woman,* Aguilar stated that the "key" to her portraits is that "they are people who are comfortable with who they are."

19. Hulick details the formal and technical aspects of the confrontational dimension: "The confrontation is accomplished through the frontal positioning of her subjects, the direct eye contact with the viewer, and the relatively large (14 x 18 inch and 20 x 32 inch) size of her black and white silver prints. Her printing increases this sense of encounter. Although her prints are full-scale photographs, they convey a hard brilliance and a sense of high contrast. Her subjects generally crowd the frame, filling it to the edges." (53) Hulick goes on to link the dimension of vulnerability to Aguilar's integration of art and life.

20. The concept of identification is notoriously undertheorized in explanations of spectatorship. I hope to contribute more to this discussion in my future study of Chicana cultural production.

21. For Mercer, Mapplethorpe subverts "the narcissistic self-image of the West" by dint of "a strategy of promiscuous intertextuality, whereby the over-valued genre of the fine-art nude is 'contaminated'" by fantasies of black men's sexuality (356).

22. "If by pornography I mean the writing or technological representation and mass marketing of the body as explicitly sexual." (Goldsby 244).

23. Alfaro comments on Aguilar's "ability to coax the viewer into studying the range of emotions within a subject."

24. For Hulick, the use of Polaroid film strengthens this collabora-

tive relationship, providing time spent together waiting for the image to develop and instant feedback.

25. Hammond explains the dearth of sexual or erotic imagery in the early lesbian exhibitions: "because lesbianism at that time was gender-based, and lesbians did not want to be solely identified on the basis of their sexual activity; and because artists were leery of the ever-present objectifying male gaze" (46).

26. See Lorde's *Zami* for a description of this milieu in this time period.

27. Quoted in Hulick, from personal communication with Aguilar (54).

28. Aguilar's use of a 4 x 5 camera and Polaroid film, as in the *Clothed/ Unclothed* series, contributes to her subjects' great presence and the clarity and control of her prints (Hulick).

29. Many of the writers in the catalogue of *In a Different Light* stress the interaction of queer artists with different kinds of communities as part of their artistic practice. Blake places as much importance on "making community" as on "making art" (17), while for Scholder "What seems particular to '90s lesbian and gay cultural productions is that . . . they are linked by a sense of community; not one single community, but to any of myriad social groups that include people who are queer" (178).

30. The phrase is Judith Butler's.

Works Cited

Alarcón, Norma. "The Theoretical Subject(s) of *This Bridge Called My Back* and Anglo-American Feminism." *Making Face, Making Soul: Haciendo Caras.* Ed. Gloria Anzaldúa. San Francisco: Aunt Lute, 1990. 356-369.

Alfaro, Luis. "Queer Culture: 'Exposing Ourselves': Photography Expression Workshops by Laura Aguilar." *Vanguard* (August 7, 1992): 17.

Anderson, Benedict. *Imagined Communities: Reflections on the Origin and Spread of Nationalism.* London: Verso, 1983.

Blake, Nayland, Lawrence Rinder, and Amy Scholder, eds. *In a Different Light: Visual Culture, Sexual Identity, Queer Practice.* San Francisco: City Lights Books, 1995.

Blake, Nayland. "Curating *In a Different Light.*" Blake, Rinder, and Scholder. 9-43.

Blaszkiewicz, Laura. "Laura Aguilar." *Woman to Woman.* Los Angeles (Century Cable Television, The Rock, Calif.): Kick Up Your Heels Productions, 1992.

Butler, Judith. *Bodies That Matter: On the Discursive Limits of "Sex."* New York: Routledge, 1993.

Chabram-Dernersesian, Angie. "I Throw Punches for My Race, but I Don't Want to Be a Man: Writing Us–Chica-nos (Girl, Us)/Chica*nas*–into the Movement Script." *Cultural Studies.* Eds. Lawrence Grossberg, Cary Nelson, and Paula Treichler. New York: Routledge, 1992. 81-95.

Chua, Lawrence. "The Postmodern Ethnic Brunch: Devouring Difference." Blake, Rinder, and Scholder. 253-262.

Fat Girl: A Zine for Fat Dykes and the Women Who Want Them 3 (1995).

Fung, Richard. "Looking for My Penis: The Eroticized Asian in Gay Video Porn." *How Do I Look: Queer Film and Video.* Ed. Bad Object-Choices. Seattle: Bay Press, 1991. 145-160.

Gaspar de Alba, Alicia. "*Mi casa [no] es su casa*: The Cultural Politics of the CARA Exhibition." University of New Mexico Dissertation, 1994.

Giovanni, Nikki. *Those Who Ride the Night Winds. Poems.* New York: Morrow, 1983.

Goldsby, Jackie. "Queen for 307 Days: Looking B(l)ack at Vanessa Williams and the Sex Wars." Blake, Rinder, and Scholder. 233-252.

Gomez, Jewelle. "Showing Our Faces: A Century of Black Women Photographed." Blake, Rinder, and Scholder. 223-232.

Gootee, Marita. "Looking In." Kelley. 51.

Gregg, Pam. "All But the Obvious and Situation." Blake, Rinder, and Scholder. 64-66.

Hall, Stuart. "New Ethnicities." *Black Film British Cinema. ICA Documents 7.* London: Institute of Contemporary Arts, 1988. 27-31.

Hammond, Harmony. "A Lesbian Show." Blake, Rinder, and Scholder. 45-49.

Harris, Bertha. "An Introduction to *Lover.*" Blake, Rinder, and Scholder. 183-197.

Holland, Sharon P. "Humanity Is Not a Luxury: Some Thoughts on a Recent Passing." *Tilting the Tower.* Ed. Linda Garber. New York: Routledge, 1994. 168-176.

Hoone, Jeffrey. "Laura Aguilar." *Contact Sheet 78.* Syracuse, N.Y.: Light Work, n.d.

Hulick, Diana Emery. "Profile: Laura Aguilar." *Latin American Art 5,* 3 (1993): 52-54.

Kelley, Caffyn, ed. *Forbidden Subjects: Self-Portraits by Lesbian Artists.* Vancouver, B.C.: Gallerie, 1992.

Lazzari, Margaret. "Curriculum Viva: An Art of Persona by Latinos of Los Angeles." *Visions Art Quarterly* (Spring 1992): 18-19.

Lippard, Lucy A. *Mixed Blessings: New Art in a Multicultural America.* New York: Pantheon, 1990.

Lorde, Audre. *Zami: A New Spelling of My Name.* Trumansburg, N.Y.: The Crossing Press, 1982.

Mercer, Kobena. "Looking for Trouble." *The Lesbian and Gay Studies Reader.* Eds. Henry Abelove, Michele Aina Barale, and David M. Halperin. New York: Routledge, 1993. 350-359.

Nestle, Joan, ed. *The Persistent Desire: A Femme-Butch Reader.* Boston: Alyson Publications, 1992.

Neumaier, Diane. "Judy Baca: Our People Are the Internal Exiles." *Making Face, Making Soul: Haciendo Caras.* Ed. Gloria Anzaldúa. San Francisco: Aunt Lute, 1990. 256-270.

Ortiz, Christopher. "Hot and Spicy: Representation of Chicano/Latino Men in Gay Pornography." *Jump Cut* 39 (1994): 83-90.

Rinder, Lawrence. "An Introduction to *In a Different Light.*" Blake, Rinder, and Scholder. 1-8.

Scholder, Amy. "Writing *In a Different Light.*" Blake, Rinder, and Scholder. 177-82.

Trinh, T. Minh-Ha. *When the Moon Waxes Red: Representation, Gender and Cultural Politics.* New York: Routledge, 1991.

Trujillo, Carla, ed. *Chicana Lesbians: The Girls Our Mothers Warned Us About.* Berkeley: Third Woman Press, 1991.

Veneciano, G. Daniel. "Overturning Expectations: *L.A. Iluminado:* Eight Los Angeles Photographers at Otis/Parsons Gallery." *Artweek* 22, 29 (September 12, 1991): 20.

Venegas, Sybil. *Identity and Identity: Recent Chicana Art from "La Reina del Pueblo de Los Angeles de la Porcíncula."* Los Angeles: Laband Art Gallery, 1990.

Weisinger, Jean. "So the World Can See." Kelley. 11-16.

Yarbro-Bejarano, Yvonne. "The Lesbian Body in Latina Cultural Production." *¿Entiendes? Queer Readings, Hispanic Writings.* Eds. Emilie L. Bergmann, and Paul Julian Smith. Durham: Duke University Press, 1995. 181-197.

Tomboy

Mónica Palacios

This piece is taken from the show *Deep in the Crotch of My Latino Psyche.*

When I was four, five, and six, I was extremely shy and I had
a pixie hair cut.
Adults would stick their faces in my space and ask,
"Are you a boy or a girl?"
"Girl!"
Shouting up into their adult world.
Wishing they hadn't asked me that.
Wondering if I looked like a freak or something.
I just didn't feel like a little girl.
Sugar and spice and everything nice.
I don't think so.

It was raining really hard but my mom, dad, and little brother
Greg, went to the toy store anyway. It was Sunday and we
respected our obligations.
Greg got this totally cool machine gun and I–I don't know
what possessed me, perhaps societal pressure–I got this doll.
During our drive home I knew I made the wrong choice. By
the time I got inside, I was bawling my head off because I
wanted a machine gun too. I cried so much, my dad went back
to the toy store and returned home with a
brand new machine gun.
I was really happy then.

I was always the Dad, the Soldier, or the Sheriff.

The Christmas that I was five was the year I got my cowboy
drag.
"Getty up, Miss Kitty."

I was just getting over the chicken pox, so my week had been hellish.

But waking up Christmas morning to a cowboy hat, shirt, leather vest with fringe, chaps, Levi's, 2-tone boots, and a holster with 2 guns—I was spent.

The land of little boys was ADVENTURE–DANGER–BUDDIES!

And really cool toys.

Don't get me wrong, I never wanted to physically be a boy.

Although I did try peeing standing up a couple of times—and I did pretend to shave with dad.

I liked my girl body. I just wanted what they had—POWER!

I soon reached the age where I was supposed to like boys and they were supposed to like me back.

They liked me back alright—too much!

They were so annoying and I was just in the 4th grade!

This is when I started feeling that MALE SEXUAL POWER!

They didn't attack me or anything, but they would really tease me.

"Hey, Mónica, he says he loves you."

"Mónica meet José behind the school yard because he wants to kiss you."

"Hey, Mónica, come out of your house because we want to FUCK YOU!"

Fuck me?! Jeeez, I'm just in the 4th grade and I'm still begging my mother for an Easy Bake Oven!

Because I, like many of you, wanted to bake a cake with a light bulb.

This Male Sexual Power thing—when I didn't ask for it—made me crazy! And it continued through elementary school, jr. high, high school, and college.

Who told them it was OK to invade
my space—
my body—
my soul—
on their terms?

Who told them it was OK to grab my tits and laugh as I walk
down the corridor to my science class?
Who told them it was OK to verbally, sexually harass me until
I'm in tears as I wash my car in front of my house?
Who told them it was OK to
FUCK ME even though I said NO????!!!!!!

In high school. I didn't have many boyfriends which was OK
with me but not in my circle of friends. Because I hung out
with boy-crazy girls and all they could talk about were their
boyfriends.
"Mónica, you know my boyfriend who I love very much and I
would stick a fork in my eye to prove my love?"
"Yeah."
"Well, we can't have sex unless he can come twice so we have
sex all the time. I can't wait to see him again and his sperm."

Oh god and the sperm. And there was always so much of it.
Where did it come from? Sperm on tap!
I couldn't handle it.
Or their tongues down my throat.
Hands up my shirt.
Dicks inside—get that hose away from me!
There were moments when I thought I was enjoying myself—
but no, not really.

And, folks, please note, I don't hate men. I don't want to read
somewhere: *funny but hates men.*
I have close male friends. I do shows with men.
It's just that Male Sexual Power—I allowed it because
I was taught to accept it.

You're thinking, "OK, Mónica, you were having fantasies of
women all this time."
No, I wasn't, because the institutions that were telling me to
have sex with men were also telling me not to have sex with
women because that is like really really gross!
And during these confusing stressful heterosexual years, I had
men—MEN—tell me: "I think you're going to become a lesbian. I'll go put on my clothes now."

I wished they would have told me sooner. I wished someone would have taken me aside–preferably an angel–and said: "The reason you felt like an outsider when you were growing up, the reason you couldn't handle all that Male Sexual Power, the reason you've had these unexplainable weird feelings for women–is because you were born a lesbian and NOBODY TOLD YOU!"

But now I know. Because I have reached
DEEP IN THE CROTCH OF MY QUEER LATINA PSYCHE.
And it told me to kiss that woman.
And she tasted like honey.
And I kissed her entire body until I passed out!
When I came to–I realized I
was a lesbian!
lesbian–Lesbian–LESBIAN!
"How about an orgasm, lesbian woman?"
And I didn't have horns or fangs or this uncontrollable desire to chase Girl Scouts: "Hey little lady, can I bite your cookies?"

I was ready to embrace myself.
I was ready to embrace other women.
And feel safe.
And feel a sense of equality.
And feel myself gripping her sensual waist.
Massaging her inviting curves.
Kissing her chocolate nipples.
And sliding my face down
Lick
Down
Lick
Down
Lick
Wanting all of her inside my mouth
And knowing I was never going back
Because honey is
too sweet
To give up.

History and the Politics of Violence Against Women

Antonia I. Castañeda

This speech was given during International Women's Day rally and march, San Antonio, Texas, March 5, 1995.

I dedicate this talk to the soul of the Mayan woman who was thrown alive to the dogs because she refused to have sex with her captor.

Statistics: Local and National

Rape is the fastest growing violent crime in the nation.
In San Antonio, reports of sexual assault rose by more than 16 percent in 1995–from 565 cases to 658–while the number of other major crimes, including murders and burglaries, plummeted.
One in three women will raped in her lifetime.
Ninety percent of all rapes are intraracial; the assailant and the victim are of the same "race."
Only one in ten rapes are reported to law enforcement.
Two hundred women per hour are physically abused by spouses or live-in partners.
Of all women killed in Texas, 38 percent were murdered by their intimate male partners. The national average is 30 percent.
Battering is the number one crime and cause of injury to women in the United States.
Seventy percent of men who batter their wives also batter their children.
In 95 percent of all domestic violence assaults, the assaults are committed by men against women.
Two hundred million dollars, or five hours of military spending, could pay for the annual support of 1,600 rape crisis centers and battered women's shelters.

We are here in the name of twenty-year-old Ada Powell—shot and killed on her way to work by two men in a car who first honked and waved at her and her sister, then followed them onto the San Diego Freeway, and shot to kill on an early spring day in 1992.

We are here in the name of fifty-one-year-old Shirley Lowery, who was stabbed nineteen times by her live-in partner in a Milwaukee courthouse, where she had gone to get a two-year injunction against him because he repeatedly raped her and threatened to kill her if she left him. He succeeded.

We are here in the name of Joanne Little and Inés García, who in the 1970s killed the jailers who raped them in their cells after they had been arrested and were in police custody.

We are here in the name of Anna Mae Ashquash, the Cree woman who was murdered for her political activities in the Indian Rights Movement.

We are here in the name of Anita Hill, who broke the silence about sexual harassment at the highest levels of government and made it impossible for the nation to ignore the reality of sexual harassment, sexual threat, and sexual assault that women face daily in the workplace.

We are here in the name of all women, so that every woman—whatever her race, sexual orientation, culture, class, age, or physical condition can be in the streets, at school, at work, at play, or any other place by herself, can be with anybody of her own choosing, in a manner of her own desire, wearing whatever she pleases, and can do so freely—without the abiding threat and actuality of rape and all of the other forms of sexual and other violence that constantly assault our bodies, our psyches, our spirits, our emotions, our souls. We see ourselves daily displayed, violated, dismembered, abused, objectified, and discarded—on TV, in music, books, rape jokes, sexual harassment at work, in the classroom, on the street, grocery store porn magazines, billboards, record jackets, soap operas, films.

Let us be clear at the very outset that rape and other violence against women are acts of domination—acts of power—the direct expression of sexual politics, and thus are violent political acts of sexual and other aggression against women. Rape and other forms of sexual violence are primary instruments of terrorism used against women to maintain heterosexual male supremacy, to sustain the patriarchy and all its structures, and to preserve the gender status quo. Violence against women is a logical extension of sexism and the politics of male domination.

Let us be equally clear about the relationship of sexism/ violence to other forms of domination, and the importance of rape in maintaining those other forms of domination. I am speaking here specifically about the relationship between sexism and racism, classism, and homophobism. While sexism affects women most directly, the latter three affect both women and men and thus cut across gender. Yet all these forms of domination originate in a sexism/male domination which is itself rooted in a normative heterosexuality that conceptualizes and defines male sexuality as aggressive and female sexuality as submissive.

Thus, it is imperative that we understand that in the United States, in the Americas, rape and sexual violence are inextricably tied to a pervasive racism with its attendant, vicious violence against people of color—against African Americans, Asian Americans, Chicanos/Latinos, and Native Americans; it is tied to a pervasive homophobism with its attendant violence against lesbians and gays; and to pervasive classism with its attendant violence against the economically poor, "lower classes," now called "the urban underclass."

All of these forms of power, of domination, of oppression are interrelated. They derive from, feed upon, and sustain one another; they are rooted in the invasion of the Americas, in a colonialist domination that began over 500 years ago with Columbus, and which today is the common legacy we live with daily—albeit from different positions of power and privilege depending on our gender, our race, our sexual orientation, our class, and our physical condition.

That legacy is rooted in sexual and other violence against women. The first political acts of domination were acts of rape and sexual aggression against women—first against Native American women, then against their mestiza daughters, and then against black women torn from their African homelands, enslaved and raped to labor themselves and to produce laborers to feed the colonial economies of Spain, England, and subsequently, the United States.

Michele de Cuneo, a nobleman from Savona who came with Columbus on the second journey in 1493-1496, left us an account of the first documented rape in the Americas. He was the perpetrator and, in 1493, he wrote boastfully to a friend:

> While I was in the boat, I captured a very beautiful Carib woman, whom the aforesaid Lord Admiral (Columbus) gave to me, and with whom, having brought her into my cabin, and she being naked as is their custom, I conceived the desire to take my pleasure. I wanted to put my desire to execution, but she was unwilling for me to do so, and treated me with her nails in such wise that I would have preferred never to have begun. But seeing this (in order to tell you the whole event to the end), I took a rope-end and thrashed her well, following which she produced such screaming and wailing as would cause you not to believe your ears. Finally we reached an agreement such that, I can tell you, she seemed to have been raised in a veritable school of harlots.

This narrative written by the rapist himself 503 years ago, establishes the interpretation of rape upon which this country's rape laws were based until less than twenty years ago. This interpretation, upheld and sanctioned by the courts, by the judicial system, by society and culture, is one in which a woman may first resist, but then succumbs to what "she wanted all along." The mentality and underlying assumptions this interpretation conveys is:

1. That Women ask for it because of the way they are dressed.
2. That "no" really means "yes."
3. That women enjoy being raped.
4. That historically women of color could be raped, beaten, worked to death or killed with impunity precisely because they are of color.

Racism intersects with sexism to pit women of color and white women against each other. Women of color are sexualized and racialized. White women are reified as the incarnation of both sexual and racial purity. That reification is bought at the price of the devaluation of women of color.

It is important that we reflect upon the origins and on the contemporary effects of these interrelated multiple oppressions and violences on all of us. For Native American women this means that they and their people have been under siege and in a state of war for over 500 years. If even briefly, let us examine these interlocking oppressions and the resistance to them from the beginning of the invasion of the Americas to the present.

In 1547, the Aristotelian scholar Juan Ginés de Sepúlveda argued that the Spaniards had a perfect right to "rule over these barbarians of the New World and the adjacent lands, who in wisdom, intelligence, virtue and humanitas are as inferior to the Spaniards as infants to adults and women to men."

While Sepúlveda, writing in Spain, justified conquest and determined that Indians, like women, were inferior beings, Spaniards colonized the American landbase on the basis of sexual and other violence towards both women and men. The practice of raping the women of a conquered group has remained a feature of war and conquest from the second millennium to the present. Its most recent manifestations were in Vietnam, in the Gulf War, in Bosnia, and now in Chiapas.

Under conditions of war or conquest rape is a form of national terrorism, subjugation, and humiliation wherein the sexual violation of women represents both the physical domination of the women and the symbolic castration of the men of the conquered group.

In the Spanish invasion of California initiated in 1769, the Franciscan missionaries described how:

> in the morning, six or seven soldiers would set out together . . . and go to the distant rancherías (villages) even many leagues away. When both men and women at the sight of them would take off running . . . the soldiers, adept as they are at lassoing cows and mules, would lasso Indian women, who then became prey for their unbridled lust.

Almost two hundred years after Junípero Serra's description of the violence against Indian women in the founding of California, an account from the Vietnam war in 1966 relates that an American patrol held a nineteen-year-old Vietnamese girl captive for several days, taking turns raping her and finally murdering her. The sergeant planned the crime in advance, telling the soldiers during the mission's briefing that the girl would "improve their morale." American soldiers "bonded" with each other on the basis of gang-raping a Vietnamese girl. Still more recently, the wholesale rapes of Muslim women in Bosnia and of women in Chiapas once again brutally reveal the historical truth that women's bodies are the battlefields of men's wars with each other.

The politics of gender, sexuality, race, and conquest included corporal punishment and violence to exact labor from Indian women in the mission system. Of the use of force against women, one priest wrote that women in the California missions were whipped, placed in the stocks, or shackled only because they deserved it. But their right to privacy was always respected–they were whipped inside the women's dormitory. Whipping women in private, he stated, was part of the civilizing process because it "instilled in them the modesty, delicacy, and virtue belonging to their sex."

Similarly, slavery in the English colonies relied as much on routine sexual abuse and the virtual institutionalization of rape as it relied on the whip and the lash to keep the enslaved workers in line. In the words of Angela Davis, "One of racism's salient historical features has always been the assumption that white men–especially those that wield economic power–possess an incontestable right of access to black women's bodies." Thus, sexual coercion was an essential element of the social relations between slavemaster and slaves. The right claimed by slave owners and their agents over the bodies of female slaves was a direct expression of their presumptive property rights over black people.

The politics of racism, labor exploitation, and of institutionalized sexual abuse of black women and the vicious stereotype of the black man as a rapist of white women continued after the abolition of slavery. The post-Civil War period saw group rapes of black women by the Ku Klux Klan and the lynching and mutilation of black men for allegedly raping or threatening to rape white women.

In the Euro-American war against Mexico and the conquest of California and the now U.S. Southwest, both Indian women and men took the brunt of wholesale violence. Indian women in particular experienced wholesale rape.

When California entered the nation as a free state in 1850, meaning slavery was outlawed, it simultaneously passed a law to allow apprenticeship or indenture of Indian males under eighteen, and females under fifteen years old–a euphemism for enslavement. Under the cover of the apprenticeship provisions of the laws of 1850 and 1860, the abduction and sale of Indians–especially young women and children–were carried on as a regular business enterprise in California. The price depended on age, sex, and usefulness, and ranged from $30 to $200. A common feature of the trade was the seizure of Indian girls and women who were held by their captors as sexual partners or sold to other whites for sexual purposes. Dealers in Indian women in the early 1850s classified their "merchandise," as "fair, middling, inferior, refuse," and set their prices accordingly.

Mexican women, whose country lost the war, were now among the conquered. Rosalia Vallejo de Leese, who was pregnant during the Bear Flag Revolt in June 1846, described how John C. Fremont and his band of outlaws held her captive and threatened to torch her home, with her female relatives in it, unless she complied with their demands.

The commonly held notion that women, due to their scarcity during the California gold rush, were afforded moral, emotional, and physical protection and respect by Anglo miners, does not hold for either Indian or Mexican women. Mexicanas, as part of the nation that lost the war and part of the group of more knowledgeable, experienced, and initially successful miners competing with Anglos in the gold fields, became one object of the violence and lawlessness directed against Mexicanos/Latinos. It is significant that Juanita of Downieville and Cheptia of San Patricio, the only women hanged in California and in Texas, were Mexican. Both had killed white men who tried to assault them.

Similarly, Asian American historian Sucheng Chan finds the intersection of gender, race, sexuality, and labor to be key to the legislation on Chinese exclusion and immigration from the 1870s to 1943. Contrary to the common belief that Chinese laborers were the target of the first exclusion act, the effort to bar another group of Chinese–prostitutes–preceded the prohibition against male workers who had been brought in to work as unskilled laborers in the racially segmented labor force that kept them mobile, transient, exploitable, and expendable.

Chinese women, like men, were brought to the United States as contract workers—as another source of mobile, exploitable, expendable, and cheap labor. Unlike men, however, Chinese women were brought for the purposes of sexual labor—to "provide sexual services to the Chinese male workers," at the moment that the miscegenation laws prohibiting interracial marriage were extended to include Asians. Most often, Chinese women were brought under false pretenses, including abduction and enslavement. Once in California, their sexuality was impugned. Chinese women's sexuality was a pivotal issue in legislative hearings, committee meetings, and statutes, in municipal ordinances, and in the Chinese-exclusion laws. The laws barred all Chinese women who sought admission into the United States. The government's targeted exclusion of Chinese women effectively prevented Chinese families, and thus a full-fledged Chinese society (societies), from establishing themselves in the United States during the 19th century. And no Chinese woman in California, regardless of her social standing, was safe from harassment.

For women of color, the inseparable, interlocking oppressions have produced a conceptualization of our sexuality as promiscuous women who offered their favors to white men. Thus these stereotypes, which abound in the historical and popular literature as well as in all aspects of nineteenth- and twentieth-century popular culture in the United States, include the placed Indian "squaw" who readily gives her sexual favors, the passionate Black or mulatto woman who is always ready and sexually insatiable, the volatile Mexican woman who is fiery eyed and hot blooded, and the languid, opium-drowsed Asian woman whose only occupation is sex.

Let me underscore the relationship between the past and the present. The legacy of the Americas is violence and exploitation based on sex, gender, race, sexuality, class, culture, and physical condition—based on the power and privilege to exploit and oppress others that each of those elements confer on us. We all share the historical legacy—it is our common heritage. Today, it is evident in Propositions 187 and 209 in

California; in the recent violent beating of undocumented workers Alicia Sotero and Enrique Flores in El Monte, California; in the anti-gay ordinance in Colorado; in the dismantling of affirmative action, such as the Hopwood decision in Texas; in the attacks against welfare mothers; and in environmental racism, Nafta, and multiple forms of attacks against working peoples.

Where do each of us stand on each of these interlocking elements? And what will each of us do with this historical legacy? I would ask each of us to interrogate ourselves, our organizations, our workplaces, our families—to examine our individual gender, sexual, racial, and class politics, and our power and privilege in each realm.

We cannot change the last 500 years, but we can change the next 500. We must take personal responsibility to act against rape, sexual violence, racism, sexism, homophobism, classism. Every time we remain silent and do not take a stand against these interlocking evils wherever we encounter them, we become complicitous with them and we reproduce them. In brief, we become perpetrators of the sexual and other violence that is being committed.

I challenge each of us individually and all of us collectively to recognize the privilege and power that we have—to examine our gender, racial, sexual, and class politics. We must challenge ourselves and each other to define a politic where we use every ounce of our power and privilege to stop rape, to stop sexual and all other forms of violence against women specifically, and to stop all of the multiple violences of sexism, racism, homophobism, and classism in our lives and society, beginning right here today in San Antonio.

What can you do? You can resist. Whoever you are, you can say *No—it stops here—it stops with me.* And we can find ways to take individual and collective political action.

Women

1. Break the silence if you have been raped, molested, sexually assaulted, sexually harassed. Register and file complaints and grievances, bring charges against the perpetrator or perpetrators.

2. Work with organizations such as rape crisis centers to help other women and victims of sexual crimes.

3. March, rally, protest, and take back the night.

4. Work with and vote for politicians who support women's sexual, reproductive, and civil rights.

5. Take a personal stand—no matter how unpopular. Challenge and speak out clearly and directly to friends, family, teachers, co-workers, and so on against any form of sexism, racism, homophobism, ableism, or any other kind of violence that is occurring in your presence.

6. Take self-defense classes and teach what you have learned to other women.

Men

1. Learn about your unearned male privilege and power and about how you use that male power and privilege to perpetuate sexism and other violences against women.

2. Recognize and do not participate, do not perpetuate any form of sexism and its attendant violences against women under any circumstances.

3. Break the silence and the protection that men have historically afforded each other: Do not protect other perpetrators. Stand up to your peers—take the heat of their disapproval.

4. Work to politicize and educate other men about their sexism and its attendant violences.

5. Work with and vote for politicians who support women's sexual, reproductive, and civil rights.

6. Determine the multiple ways in which you perpetuate the structures of power and domination and work against those structures, to tear them down—to change them.

Note

An abridged version of this speech appeared in essay form in *La Voz de Esperanza: The Voice of Peace & Justice in San Antonio*, April, 1995. The Esperanza Peace & Justice Center, San Antonio, Texas. Gracias.

The Silence of the Obejas: Evolution of Voice in Alma Villanueva's "Mother, May I" and Sandra Cisneros's "Woman Hollering Creek"

Verónica A. Guerra

> Silenciosa: adj. quiet: person, house, object: noiseless.
> Silenciar: v. to muffle, hush up, to cast into oblivion.

So defines and translates the dictionary *La Petit Larousse* (García, Pelayo y Gross, et al., eds. 1980) the difference between the verb and adjective forms of this word. A derivative of this, "Silenciada" (silenced) forms the past participle form of the verb and can be used both as a participial adjective and as the passive form of the verb in what Noam Chomsky calls the Active/Passive Transformation.

Usually, both English and Spanish speakers use the word "silenciosa" (silent) as well as "silenciada" (silenced) to refer to women and children, as in "The children were silenced" or "The girl was silenced." While the word "silencioso" (silent) is often applied to men, as in "the strong silent type," seldom do we hear the word "silenciado" (silenced) applied to men except as a pejorative.

Is it mere coincidence, then, that the adjective form more often than the passive participle form is usually applied to men, whereas the passive form is more often than not applied to women and children? The passive form "silenciada" can often be applied to women and children with no pejorative connotation. However, when one speaks of a "silenced" male, he, in a sense, becomes more effeminate. Yet, when one speaks of the "quiet, silent, strong male," images of virility and potency are elicited.

These connotations take on even more powerful undertones when one sees them used in the context of literature, especially in the description of men and women characters in fiction as well as poetry. Whether men and women are portrayed as "silent" or "silenced" bears deep implications for the creation of character, point of view, poetic tone, and the concept of voice both as theme and technique in literature. Since much of contemporary Chicana fiction and poetry exploits the concepts of voice and silence both as theme and literary technique, it would be well to explore this gender paradox of "silenciosa/o" and "silenciada/o." Such an exploration might shed light on how contemporary Chicana literature explodes the myth of the stereotypically "strong silent macho" and the "silent and/or silenced passive female."

In this essay, explorations of the use of the silence/silenced paradox in Alma Villanueva's poem "Mother, May I" and Sandra Cisneros's story "Woman Hollering Creek" will serve to illustrate the evolution of voice in Chicana literature. First, both works indicate that both authors skillfully employ the concepts of voice and silence (with its ramifications of being silenced) to strengthen narrative point of view and poetic tone and thereby create realistic characters. Second, both literary selections illustrate the theme of voice, especially in the character development of the protagonist.

The Paradoxical Theme of Voice and Silence

The theme of voice or the development of voice from a state of virtual silence and non-entity to a state of recognition, self-worth, and identity currently is a topic that interests both literary writers as well as psychologists. A political element that has furthered interest in this psychological construct, of course, has been the development of the women's movement and consciousness raising of women as oppressed minorities. Such an event has indeed been a fortuitous one. Not only has it served to focus on gender inequality, but it has served to fuse a collaboration between the fields of psychology and literature in an effort to create literary characters that are more realistic and that mirror the social dilemma of contemporary women. Whether intentionally or by mere coincidence, both fields now focus interest on this construct, and one even aids the other in either artistic creation and interpretation or in scientific exploration. It is not unknown for psychologists to receive inspiration from fictional characters, and at the same time it is not uncustomary for literary critics to apply the discoveries and theories of psychology to literary analysis and interpretation. Hence, in this essay, reference to a psychological study of women's cognitive styles, *Women's Ways of Knowing*, by Mary Belensky and her team of psychologists (1986) will frame the interpretation of the theme of these two literary pieces by Alma Villanueva and Sandra Cisneros as well guide the analysis of their technique of narrative point of view, poetic tone, and poetic voice.

A Paradigm for the Theme of Voice and Silence

The text *Women's Ways of Knowing* by Mary Belensky et al. (1986) resulted from a large cross-sectional study of women from socially and ethnically diverse backgrounds in the United States. Belensky and her associates interviewed hundreds of women in an effort to discover the epistemology and learning style of women. Their study, a pioneer in the field of learning theory and feminine learning styles had many implications for pedagogy and teaching and was one of the more influential pieces in helping to create gender equity in the classroom. Crucial to this exploration, as well as a side benefit of it, was Belensky's discovery of the importance of both inner and outer voice in the development of female cognition.

According to Belensky and her associates, the acquisition of voice evolves in five stages: (1) the initial stage of "the silent woman," (2) the stage of "listening and received knowledge," (3) the stage of inner voice and subjective knowledge, (4) the stage of rational voice and procedural knowledge, and finally (5) the stage of connected knowledge or integrated voices (Belensky et al. 1986, 134). Belensky claims that though these stages are hierarchical, they are not exactly linear or sequential and there can exist overlap as there exists overlap in the studies of moral development that were done by Kohlberg back in the 1970s. She does say that the stage of received knowledge correlates sharply with and prepares the learner for the stage of procedural or rational knowledge. The stage of subjective knowing and reliance on intuition, however, is a prerequisite for and coincides with the final stage of integrated voices and knowledge. Whereas the silent listening, and procedural or rational stages appear to correlate more with male cognitive style and a reliance on male linear thinking, subjective knowledge, intuition (inner voice), and integrated voice or knowledge appear to correlate more with a female or androgynous cognitive style. At this final stage, there is simultaneous reliance on both intuition and reason, on both analysis and synthesis, on both right brain and left brain, resulting eventually in what is called constructed knowledge.

The Silent/Silenced Woman Dichotomy

An exploration of Belensky et al.'s (1986) analysis of the first three stages (the silent stage, the listening stage, and the inner voice stage) proves very enlightening when used as a means to explore theme and character interpretation as well as in analysis of literary technique in modern feminist literature. Especially is this application appropriate for Alma Villanueva's "Mother, May I" and Sandra Cisneros's "Woman Hollering Creek," because both encapsulate within their concentrated narratives the entire evolution of voice in oppressed minority women from the initial stages of silence and being silenced to the intermediate, but climactic stage of subjective knowledge and inner voice. Both works demonstrate movement towards a moment of epiphany, when the main character (Cleofilas in "Woman Hollering Creek") and the Poetic Persona (the "I" in "Mother, May I") experience that moment of enlightenment, epiphany, or manifestation and move on to the acquisition of voice.

Like the characters in both Cisneros's and Villanueva's selections, the women sampled in Mary Belensky's study also appear as "silenced" women with little awareness of their "intellectual capabilities." The silent women, Belensky claims, "live—selfless and voiceless—at the behest of those around them. These women are passive, subdued, and subordinate." (Belensky et al. 1986, 30)

Belensky delineates two stages of silence: the completely silent stage and the listening stage or the stage of received knowledge. At both the silent and listening stage, the silent woman sees life in terms of polarities: good or evil, black or white, right or wrong. There is, however, an important difference: whereas the silent or silenced woman moves in a world totally isolated and incommunicative, the listening woman turns to and worships others in authority, especially those who rule the patriarchal system. The isolated silent woman sees herself as "deaf and dumb" (Belensky et al. 1986, 30). She feels passive, reactive, and dependent, at times, even on the very source of oppression. The listening woman, nevertheless, goes beyond isolation, engages in communication and identifies with the oppressor or those in authority or institutions. She seeks even to imitate them and learn from them as experts and sources of knowledge and authority. This step, though interrupted later by the stage of inner voice and subjective knowledge, is the first step in women's programming into a male patriarchy with male values and a male, more linear rational mode of thinking.

During the initial stage, however, an important distinction exists between the silent woman and the silenced woman. The silenced woman, as the passive participle form of the adjective indicates, connotes a woman totally subjugated by male power. The silent woman, as the descriptive adjective suggests, connotes a woman that may or may not be silenced internally. Many states of consciousness exist that can explain what appears externally as a woman silent by choice. Usually, many of these altered conscious states are the result of brainwashing and stereotyping and represent the internalization of a very male-oriented consumerism that mesmerizes women through advertising into accepting these degrading images. For example, one stereotype could be the mysterious sexual silence of the "femme fatale." Or it could be the silence of naiveté, the "dumb blond" stereotype content with "pleasing her man." On the other hand, the silence could be a ploy to "tune out" the world, to escape the drudgery of male patriarchy or to maintain power. If this is the case, then the silence represents a much more advanced stage of "inner voice," wherein the woman has learned to tune out male programming and listen to her intuition. Whatever the reason, the big difference between being silent and being silenced is the idea of agency and passivity. The woman silent by choice connotes more agency. The silent woman, brainwashed by the "femme fatale," or "dumb blond" stereotype, however, connotes painless passivity. The silenced woman, aware of her passivity, however, is in a state of very painfully aware submission. This is the woman that appears as the protagonist in both Alma Villanueva's poem and Sandra Cisneros's short story. It is only when the protagonist is in this intermediate stage of painful awareness of being silenced that she can grow from the stage of complete silence to the stage of inner voice and received knowledge. Similarly, in Chicana literature, Norma Alarcón (1988) claims that it is when the protagonist has reached this stage, when they "become women who are brave enough to face their own subjectivity" (150), that they are thrown into a crisis of meaning that enables them to make the break from being silenced and being engendered only as women to accepting their own voice.

The Silent/Silenced Stage in Villanueva's "Mother, May I"

The curious interplay between the silent woman and the silenced woman shows itself dramatically in what Marta Ester Sánchez refers to as the "Birthing of the Poetic 'I' in Alma Villanueva's 'Mother, May I'" (Sánchez 1985, 24). In this autobiographical poem, the silence and the silencing are more symbolic and multidimensional in meaning than literal. The concept of voice applies not only to the development of the poetic persona's voice but to voice as poetic technique. The thematic oppositions characterizing the relationships among the three central identities of the protagonist in this poem generate, according to Sánchez, different kinds of poetic modes or poetic voices:

> I use the term "mode" to identify and describe the different strategies of address used by Chicana poets to communicate with their audiences. These strategies fall into two main categories:

narrative, discursive modes and lyrical, imagistic modes. These modes are not mutually exclusive. In some poems they interact and interrelate with each other.

In "Mother, May I," Villanueva's most interesting and dynamic work, the poet relates the private and intimate details of her life. By doing so she suggests that her own private world is as meaningful and as important as any public one. Villanueva's personal confession, inspired by Sylvia Plath and Anne Sexton, reveals her use of variants of the two main modes mentioned earlier: a documentary, narrative mode and a mythic cosmic mode. (Sánchez 1985, 10)

In my analysis of Villanueva, I discovered that both these modes correlate highly with the theme of the silent/silenced woman in juxtaposition to the theme of voice. Villanueva relies on the first mode, the documentary/narrative mode, to express the protagonist's social, concrete reality. In doing so, she focuses on the heroine as the silenced woman, subjugated and oppressed by a dominant white Anglo-Saxon patriarchy. In these scenes, the poetic "I" is passive, acquiescent, and at the mercy of external forces. But then, Villanueva also relies on the poetic, more lyrical and imagistic mode. This she does to express the poetic persona's universal vision of liberation and acquisition of the poetic voice, as well as to describe the altered states of consciousness of the interior silent world of the protagonist, a world of magical realism and poetic images that is her escape from the cruel reality of her social and concrete life. In sum, Alma Villanueva juxtaposes, rather than integrates, the poetic voice and the narrative voice. The poet's narrative style and poetic style fluctuate to show the difference between the moments of silent reverie and the traumas of being silenced. Through this alternating style, the protagonist moves in her journey of initiation into that moment of epiphany when she acquires her intuitive voice and enters the realm of subjective knowledge that Mary Belensky points out in her study.

Summary of the Poem

Divided into three parts and spanning about forty pages,

"Mother, May I" recounts the joys and innocence of childhood as the protagonist grows up in a San Francisco working-
class neighborhood with a Mexican grandmother and aunt
who speak primarily Spanish. Because of the mother's absence
(she returns only once or twice), the girl grows up attached to
her grandmother, a wise old crone, her mentor and educator.
At the age of six or seven the child is traumatized through a
rape experience, but tells no one about it. Shortly after that,
the mother reappears and has the child committed to an or-
phanage and the grandmother to a retirement home. Eventually the girl goes to a foster home, and the first part ends in
another climactic trauma with the death of the grandmother,
when the girl secretly and symbolically drops a red rose into
the grave at the funeral.

Part II begins when the young protagonist, now an adolescent, escapes from her foster home, goes and lives with her
aunt, and gets herself pregnant with a boy whom she dearly
loves. Unfortunately, her dreams of marriage and living "happily ever after" are dashed when the boy's family do not allow
them to marry, and she is forced to have the child alone. After
a few years, though, a reunion with her childhood sweetheart
and father of her child does result in marriage. His service in
Vietnam, however, cuts short her happiness, and the husband,
returning with many traumas, brutalizes her, and he is in turn
"locked away." As part II ends, the poetic persona is looking
for her grandmother's gravesite. Upon finding it, she experiences a climactic epiphany in which she begins to find her
identity as a person and poet.

To illustrate the heroine's transformation, part III breaks
the narrative mode of the poetic voice and shifts to a more
metaphoric and imagistic lyrical point of view to represent
her shift from a voiceless silent and inarticulate woman to a
highly articulate poet who has found her inner voice.

Analysis of the Theme of Voice and Silence

Villanueva accomplishes the task of communicating the bulk
of the theme of silence and voice in this poem through the
motif and imagery of what Sánchez (1985) calls the action of

"taking in and holding in" versus the action of "giving out," "expressing" or "expelling." (42). The metaphor of holding in and repressing are negative in connotation and suggest being silenced by others. The metaphor of taking in, on the contrary, implies ingestion either of food, ideas, or images through listening or silent meditation and is positive (Sánchez l985).

Conversely, the action of expelling, like expelling excrement or repressed feelings, has negative connotations, since it implies a previous silencing, gagging, or repressing, whereas the action of expressing, like voicing opinion or expressing self, is positive (Sánchez 1985).

For example, the physical act of ingesting food is seen as pleasurable when the poet, as an infant, notwithstanding the opinion of her elders, ingests her "little rubber doll" because she hopes it will produce a "baby in her poop." Being at the oral and anal Freudian stages, the infant girl is spontaneous and has not yet been socialized into "holding in" her bodily impulses. This physical act of ingesting, pleasurable to her, is at odds with society, and though this socialization forms the infant girl's sense of the appropriate use of voice and silence, "From the poem's onset," claims Sánchez (1985, 44), "the child's creative impulses are in conflict with society's rules. The child expresses her anal and oral impulses but quickly learns to control them" (1985, 44) in the same way that later she is socialized to keep quiet through the silencing efforts of a patriarchal order that defines women's roles as inferior.

Whereas the first experience of holding in, repressing, and silencing occurs in a home where two Mexican women were in turn dominated by machismo, the second experience, notes Sánchez (1985), is related to the experience of male-female sexuality and, traumatically, occurs in the very public setting of the external, social world. The specific incident is the protagonist's rape by an adult male, an aberration from the reproductive sexual act in which the woman takes in—eats, so to speak—the male sperm and releases or creates a baby. Hence a potentially positive and creative experience turns negative as the rapist forces the girl to put his penis into her mouth. The positive action of swallowing in the first example and likewise, figuratively speaking, the positive act of ingesting ideas acquired by listening, is replaced in this second instance by the negative action of gagging, and by the same token, repressing feelings spiritually and subconsciously. The gagging also serves a metaphorical function: It represents the repression of the girl's power of speech to tell about her experience. In the first example, the child expresses her biological functions physically and verbally and quickly learns she is not supposed to express them. In the rape scene, she is forced to experience the rape and is then also intimidated into repressing it (Sánchez 1985).

This theme of the silent voiceless victim who is afraid to denounce her attacker is also reiterated in Cisneros's story, "Red Clowns," as it is in "Mother, May I." Esperanza's experience of rape in "Red Clowns" serves, as Herrera-Sobek (1988) says, not only "as a political signifier of women's inferior status," but also as a painful epiphany, a sobering up or awakening of her situation. Like Esperanza's, the protagonist's response in Villanueva's poem is to block out the rape and to become silent and withdrawn, a reaction common to victims of sexual assault. Both personas (in "Red Clowns" and "Mother, May I") "become silent entities dominated by ingrained patriarchal vectors where the name of the Father is law, and years of socialization to obey the Father's law transforms the female subject into a willing accomplice in her own rape" (Herrera-Sobek 1988, 173).

The Silent/Silenced Stage in Cisneros's "Woman Hollering Creek"

The tense interplay between silence and being silenced also forms the backdrop for Sandra Cisneros's "Woman Hollering Creek." Cisneros skillfully manipulates time, place, and narrative point of view within the context of a short story with virtually no dialogue and pure narration. Through a stream of consciousness, third-person, limited-omniscience narrative, the reader catches glimpses and impressionistic views in a disjointed time sequence of flashbacks of Cleofilas's rocky marriage and abusive husband.

Summary of "Woman Hollering Creek"

The story begins in the context of a wedding day reverie, when Cleofilas remembers her father saying, "I am your father, I will never abandon you." It then flashes forward to the present, where she is sitting by the creek's edge with her little boy, Juan Pedrito, recalling "how when a man and a woman love each other, sometimes that love sours." This flashback fore-shadows an impending doom that the reader fears will even-tually occur: Cleofilas's disintegration of her "dream" mar-riage and her eventual return to her father's home. She then, unexpectedly, flashes back again to her girlhood, a time be-fore the marriage when what she "had been waiting for, has been whispering and sighing and giggling for, has been antici-pating since she was old enough to lean against the window displays of gauze and butterflies and lace, is passion . . . the kind the books and songs and telenovelas describe when one finds the great love of one's life." (Cisneros 1991, 43).

Her silent reverie then takes her to the time right before and after the wedding, in Seguín, Texas. Cleofilas's reverie then flashes to another short recollection of La Gritona, the creek that runs behind the house, and then recalls musing on the strangeness of the name and asking her two neighbors, Dolores and Soledad, about the origin of the name. This scene ends with Cleofilas's tender remembrance of herself cross-ing the bridge over La Gritona as a newlywed with Juan Pedro, "full of happily ever after," which is abruptly inter-rupted by a painful remembrance of the first time he struck her.

From there, four more short, painful flashbacks follow, pointing to the inevitable truth: her own spousal abuse by Juan Pedro and the deteriorating state of her marriage. The flash-back and reveries she recalls when sitting by the creek abruptly end, and the scene is now back to a later present where she, pregnant with his second child, is begging Juan Pedro for money and permission to see the doctor. From then on, the movement from moments of silent escape into fantasy to mo-ments of being brutally silenced gain speed, until the moment of transformation at the end, when, while crossing the bridge, she erupts for the first time into laughter.

Analysis of Voice and Silence in "Woman Hollering Creek"

It is through this stream of consciousness narrative mode that the reader becomes intimately familiar with the "inner voice" of the protagonist, Cleofilas. Several symbols, images, and events throughout the flashbacks serve to expose Cleofilas's inner voice. Her ruminations reveal her as the silenced, long-suffering woman who never speaks her mind except in her reveries. From the outset, she is disposed to rearranging her life around her husband's, and even the details of her wedding day are all arranged for her:

> And yes, they will drive all the way to Laredo to get her wedding dress. That's what they say. Because Juan Pedro wants to get married right away, without a long engagement since he can't take off too much time from work. (Cisneros 1991, 45)

As in many other short narrative selections by Chicanas, Cleofilas here is typical of what Norma Alarcón says characterizes the "female speaking subject many Chicana writers employ" (Alarcón 1988, 148). Cleofilas, through Cisneros's skillful exploration of Cleofilas's subjectivity, embodies the woman who has to abide by the "symbolic social contract" that says women "may have a voice on the condition that they speak only as wives and mothers" (1988, 148). Hence, Cleofilas, according to this "social contract," does not question the union, especially if it is approved by her parents. This is revealed in Cleofilas's naiveté about her husband's occupation and her fantasy about what she has been socialized to believe about marriage:

> He [Juan Pedro] has a very important position in Seguín, with, with . . . a beer company, I think, Or was it tires? Yes, he has to be back. So they will get married in the spring when he can take off work, and then they will drive off in his new pickup–did you see it?–to their new home in Seguín. Well, not exactly new, but they're going to paint the house. You know newlyweds. New paint and new furniture. Why not? He can afford it. And later on add maybe a room or two for the children. May they be blessed with many. (Cisneros 1991, 45)

The narrative point of view of this interior dialogue is am-
biguous. For one, it reveals Cleofilas's thoughts, her fantasies,
but also behind that, the reader can sense the tone of her
family's and neighbor's voices, especially in the lines "May
they be blessed with many." Thus, Cleofilas's inner voice is
not just hers but the voice of her society's expectations about
marriage, which she has internalized in the process of being
socialized by the patriarchal microcosm of her family.

Cleofilas's interior dialogue further serves to accentuate
the tension between the fantasy, especially symbolized by the
telenovelas, and the reality of her life. The fantasy is the lie
the patriarchal world has "fed" her about married life. She
constantly returns after episodes of abuse to this fantasy world
of her inner voice. But yet even her inner voice, which weaves
stories of romantic heroines such as "Topazio" or "Cristal" to
assuage the pain of her abuse and neglect, is a voice that she
has internalized from what the society, the commercial world
of telenovelas, and the materialistic world of patriarchal values have fed her. The voices from the past heard in the flashbacks remind Cleofilas that women speak only as wives and
mothers, and that if they are very good, someday "their prince
will come," as he does in the telenovelas. Nonetheless, the
voices alternate between the dream promised by the voices in
the flashbacks and the present reality:

> Cleofilas thought her life would have to be like that, like a
> telenovela, only now the episodes got sadder and sadder. And
> there were no commercials in between for comic relief. (Cisneros
> 1991, 53)

Thus, slowly but irrevocably, society's internal voices and
expectations of happiness and fantasy are replaced by her own
real voice, disillusioned yet liberated from the lies that shaped
her world. This realization does not come suddenly, and even
as the inevitable truth begins to erode her dreams, her recol-
lections of abuse, of the starkness of her married life, are at
first glossed over in her efforts at denial and at the false hope
that things will change:

> Or at times, when he is simply across from her at the table put-

ting pieces of food into his mouth and chewing. Cleofilas thinks, "this is the man I have waited my whole life for?"

Not that he isn't a good man. She has to remind herself why she loves him when she changes the baby's Pampers, or when she mops the kitchen floor, or tries to make the curtains for the doorways without doors, or whiten the linen. Or wonders a little when he kicks the refrigerator and says he hates this shitty house and is going out where he won't be bothered with the baby's howling and her suspicious questions. (Cisneros 1991, 49)

Besides the internal dialogue between the split voices representing fantasy and reality, certain fictional elements and characters in the setting serve as symbols that further intensify the struggle between Cleofilas's refuge to her silent sanctuary and the reality of being brutally silenced. The two neighbors, Soledad and Dolores, by their very names represent the solitude and pain that surround her:

On the other hand there were the neighbor ladies, one on either side of the house they rented near the arroyo. The Woman Soledad on the left, the Woman Dolores on the right . . . The neighbor ladies, Soledad, Dolores, they might have known once the name of the arroyo before it turned English but they did not know now. They were too busy remembering the men who had left through either choice or circumstance and would never come back. (Cisneros 1991, 47)

The creek La Gritona (Woman Hollering) also constantly acts as a cruel mockery to Cleofilas's lack of voice. Her heightened curiosity over what the "grito" (holler) means further accentuates the pain and rage Cleofilas has to constantly repress:

La Gritona. Such a funny name for such a lovely arroyo. But that's what they called the creek that ran behind the house. Though no one could say whether the woman had hollered from anger or pain . . . Pain or rage, Cleofilas wondered when she drove over the bridge. (Cisneros 1991, 47)

It is as if Cleofilas becomes the creek itself. She is La Gritona, surrounded by solitude (Soledad) on the left and pain

(Dolores) on the right. The two neighbors (Pain and Solitude) serve as foils that further accentuate Cleofilas's situation as an alienated and helpless woman silenced by an abusive husband as well as by loneliness and pain. Soledad, on the one hand, is a constant reminder of her aloneness, since Juan Pedro is hardly ever around and he has already given her reason to suspect infidelity when she was in the hospital delivering their first child:

> A doubt. Slender as a hair. A washed cup set back on the shelf wrong side-up. Her lipstick, and body talc, and hairbrush all arranged in the bathroom a different way. (Cisneros 1991, 50)

Dolores, on the other hand, is a perfect portrait of the Catholic Stabat Mater statue, whose garden of "red red cockscombs fringed and blushing a thick menstrual blood" (Cisneros 1991, 47) remind the reader of the seven-sword-pierced heart of "La Dolorosa" so often found in small Catholic home altars. Dolores here plays the same role the iconography of the Catholic Family plays in Viramontes's "Snapshots." Alarcón (1988) says that "within the Mexican/Chicano culture, the authoritative model, however unconscious, to which fathers (masculine values) have recourse is the Catholic Family and its assumed social authority" (150). Viramontes, Alarcón says, uses religious Catholic iconography to allude to religious expectation and dogma that Catholic male hierarchy imposes on women. Alarcón feels that in order to cope, many women of letters (and probably by the same token also protagonists in fiction) in their quest for subjectivity turn to mysticism and "opt for the convent" rather than accept the social symbolic contract engendering them as women.

In Cisneros's short story, both Soledad and Dolores mirror these Hispanic Women of Letters by opting for their own self-inflicted cloistered lives. They prefer isolation and chose their sexually frustrated spinsterhoods, "vistiendo santos" (dressing saints). To look back in retrospect, regretfully, is not an option. Otherwise, they may come face to face with that "crisis of meaning" and risk psychosis, like Olga Ruiz in "Snapshots," and this would be unbearable. Taken together, both women also serve as constant role models and reminders to

Cleofilas of what is expected of her by this symbolic contract as Hispanic wife and mother. Both are also omens warning her of the distasteful destiny that awaits her.

In sum, Cisneros juggles and juxtaposes flashbacks and present time to create a musical, rhythmic style of point and counterpoint that accentuates fantasy and reality. What surrounds Cleofilas appears as dull, discordant, black and white, a mockery of her harmonious and technicolored fantasies. Her drab life of silence and repression always come as staccato points that cut short her silent, inner world of telenovelas and beautiful women with handsome men. Cleofilas is truly a woman caught between the fantasy of silence to which she retreats and the reality of being silenced by an abusive husband.

Received Knowledge and the Listening Stage

Mary Belensky and her colleagues (1986) conclude, based on their study, that at the positions of received knowledge and procedural knowledge, other voices and external truths prevail. This stage of received knowledge coincides with listening and begins simultaneously with the silent stage. For the listener, a sense of self is embedded in external definitions and roles or in identification with external institutions, disciplines and methods. For women in our society, this typically means adherence to sex role stereotypes or second rung status for women dictated not only by a White Male Patriarchy, but also by the women themselves. This stage is characterized by a programming of women by what Martha Ester Sánchez (1985) calls "female enforcers of male values" (60). Belensky (1986) feels that these women seek gratification in pleasing others, in measuring up to external standards, in being "the good woman" or "good wife" or "good student." A sense of authority arises primarily through identification with a power group and its agreed upon ways of knowing.

These characteristics of the listening woman at the received knowledge stage clearly surface in the protagonists both in Villanueva's poem and Cisneros' short story.

The Listening Stage in "Mother, May I"

The listening stage and the stage of received knowledge, as in Belensky's case studies, begin in the life of Villanueva's poetic persona simultaneously with the silent and the silenced stage. It, however, continues on afterwards, or as we shall see later, in the third and final stage, the stage of subjective knowledge and inner voice. Ironically, it is this very act of listening which figuratively acts as the Achilles heel in ending the stage of listening and beginning the stage of adherence to intuition and inner voice. Nonetheless, as in the case studies analyzed by Belensky and her associates, listening initially is the skill that men exploit in women to keep them ignorant and submissive (Belensky et al. 1986).

In Villanueva's "Bloodroot," as in "Mother, May I," the protagonist's listening stage runs simultaneously with the silent stage. It is evident from the very beginning and forms the backdrop against which the poetic persona is socialized, brainwashed, and programmed into a male-dominated culture. Listening to and identifying with authority can be seen again in Villanueva's use of the metaphors of "taking in" and "holding in" as opposed to "giving out" and "expressing" or "expelling" (Sánchez 1985, 42). The first action which molds the young girl into a "listening entity" is again, as in the silent state, the biological ingestion of food. The physical acts of nourishment described in the poem parallel symbolically the more abstract acts of social nourishment obtained through listening. Unfortunately, her action of swallowing a tiny rubber doll to mimic a creative act incurs humorous disapproval from her aunt:

> My aunt came in and I peed and pooped and I said–I just made a salad–she didn't look too happy. (Villanueva in Sánchez 1985, 305)

as well as from her grandmother:

> I used to swallow my tiny rubber dolly and have a baby in my poop. I loved to find it. My grandma found me doing it. She wasn't mad. She smiled a little. She said–it'll get stuck and grow as big as you and you won't have any room left–so I stopped. (Ibid, 306)

To reinforce the previous claim about the poetic persona's oral and anal stages, again here the child's spontaneous urges to take in literally and listen, figuratively, are in conflict with society's rules. She listens to the family's patriarchal values as embodied in her aunt and grandmother. Just as she is socialized into controlling her physical impulses, the child is also programmed by these same patriarchal values to curb her speech (putting out) and to listen (hold in). She quickly learns not to "express" or "expel" all her words and opinions, but to "hold in" or repress, so that others who are her elders can teach and guide her.

The second instance that reinforces the patriarchal values of listening in women is likewise associated with ingesting or taking in, but takes on a more sinister tone, at the traumatic rape scene when she is forced first to listen to the rapist's instructions. In much the same way, the protagonist in Villanueva's poem finds a parallel in the protagonist in Cherríe Moraga's play *Giving Up the Ghost*. Corky, the main character in this play, is forced to listen to her rapist whose commands to "Open her legs more" remind her of her father's words. Likewise, the young girl in "Mother, May I," narrates only the results of the commands the rapist issues her when she says that:

> he put me down.
> he took off my dress.
> he took off my T-shirt.
> he took off my panties.
> and then he said
> —do you want to suck something
> good?—
> (Villanueva, in Sánchez 1985, 312)

The young girl hopes that if she complies, she will be set free by the rapist. Unfortunately, the humiliation of having to listen to a stranger's commands while suffering the indignity of being stripped only leads to the young girl's ultimate traumatic moment: having to swallow his penis and gag on his sperm:

> he'll let me go. so I said

>   –OK–
>   he put it in my mouth
>   and it didn't taste like anything.
>   it hurt my mouth but I
>   wouldn't cry and then
>   he made me lie down
>   and the stickers hurt
>   and I was getting all dirty
>   and I knew if I cried
>   he'd kill me.
>   (Ibid, 312)

According to Sánchez (1985) the positive action of swallowing or taking in, in the first example, is replaced in this second example by the negative action of gagging or holding in. I agree with Sánchez that the gagging serves as a metaphor with multidimensional meanings, referring not only to the physical act of holding in but also the more symbolic acts of repression and silencing. It serves to represent the repression of the girl's powers of speech to tell about her experience. She is forced to experience a very negative "holding in" and then is intimidated into repressing it emotionally and verbally. The rape also represents the initial phase of disillusionment in what Belensky (1986) believes triggers the stage of received knowledge into giving way to the stage of subjective knowledge. The young girl in this poem, like the women in Belensky's study, begins to suspect that listening is not always going to obtain her favors from the male elders that she has been taught to respect, emulate, and worship. She has been betrayed.

The young girl's tomboy stage, which follows immediately after the rape as a way to cope, also is part of Belensky's paradigm of the listening stage. According to Belensky, it is the listening woman's last-ditch effort to identify with the oppressor. It represents not just a coping mechanism but a hope that imitation will bring a sense of control plus the male competitive potential and rational thinking that has made him so successful:

>   it was then I decided to become a boy,
>   I've found the rooftops.

> I've found the fences.
> I've found the highest rock
> and I've sat on it.
> I've found the secret places
> in Golden Gate Park
> and listened to voices.
> I've found the ocean
> and reached it, riding
> my own bike.
>   (Villanueva, in Sánchez 1985, 313)

As in Cherríe Moraga's play *Giving Up the Ghost*, the young protagonist seeks both identification with and revenge against the social order that puts women at a disadvantage in the social symbolic contract. Their imitation of men is both an identification with the oppressor and, ironically, a rebellion against the expectation of men that women act and dress as women. This identification with and rebellion against male norms finds its parallel in Lorna Dee Cervantes's "Bird Ave." "The representation of tough, teen-age Chicanas," says Herrera-Sobek, walking down the streets on hot summer days, challenging the world with their street talk and street cunning strikes another blow to the image of the passive, timid Chicana." (1988, 11) The bright red T-shirt that the poetic "I" in Villanueva's poem wears to her grandmother's funeral is just as loud a scream of rebellion as the shocking, attention-getting costumes, teased hair, and tight skirts of the pachucas in "Bird Ave." Both the poetic persona in "Mother, May I," as well as Cat eyes, Mousie, and Flaca Flea in "Bird Ave," "refuse to capitulate, to fade, disintegrate into nothingness" as a result of their rapes, and "not wishing to display any vulnerability, they hide their wounds in macho body language and a rough exterior" (Herrera-Sobek 1988, 12) as a way to cope with their dissociated feelings and split subjectivities.

The Listening Stage in Cisneros's "Woman Hollering Creek"

Whereas the poetic persona in Villanueva's "Mother, May I,"

seeks refuge in the coping mechanism of tomboyish behavior, Cleofilas's arrival at the listening stage expresses itself in a coping mechanism more similar to that of the main character, Arlene, in Helena María Viramontes's "Miss Clairol" (Viramontes 1985). Both women (Cleofilas and Arlene) seek to please their men and "stand by their men." They listen to and show acceptance of male patriarchal values by fantasizing about the materialistic and commercial world of beauty and sex symbols which the capitalistic male mentality holds up as a mirror for women to imitate. They are the typical "silent" women in Belensky's study, for whom male consumerist values have become so subconsciously embedded that they are blissfully unaware of them. They have internalized the stereotypes of the "femme fatale" or the "dumb blond" of the telenovelas.

Cleofilas's way of knowing in "Woman Hollering Creek" is like that of many of Belensky's subjects at the received knowledge or listening stage. Cleofilas's listening and adherence to these values can be seen during her quiet moments of silent reverie when she fantasizes about the telenovelas:

> But what Cleofilas had been waiting for, had been whispering and sighing and giggling for, had been anticipating since she was old enough to lean against the window displays of gauze and butterflies and lace, is passion. Not the kind on the cover of the "¡Alarma!" magazines, mind you, where the lover is photographed with the bloody fork she used to salvage her good name. But passion in its purest crystalline essence. The kind the books and songs and telenovelas describe when one finally finds the great love of one's life, and does whatever one can, one must do at whatever cost. (Cisneros 1991, 44)

Again here, as before, Cisneros's subtle use of the stream of consciousness, third-person omniscient narrator lets us be privy to Cleofilas's thoughts, which in turn reveal the patriarchal programming about women's status that she has been brainwashed into accepting.

Likewise, in Viramontes's "Miss Clairol" (Viramontes 1985) the author calls the reader's attention to the fact that Arlene, the mother, has already been completely brainwashed into the "if you have one life to live, live it as a blonde," syndrome.

Her feeble attempts at living the American Dream through blond hair contrast with the reality of her drab, alienated empty life. Herrera-Sobek, in *Chicana Creativity and Criticism: Charting New Frontiers in American Literature* (1988) further supports this view: "This short story is a harsh indictment of a consumer oriented capitalist society that values superficialities such as hair color, nail polish, false eye lashes and trivialities" (32). Like Cleofilas, Arlene is completely alienated from her true harsh reality of poverty because she has "bought into" the Anglo male dream of the sexy, sensuous, and mysterious female whose only occupation is to please the man.

As in the Belensky case studies (1986), the act of listening is also the seed implanted in Cleofilas's mind that eventually destroys her false illusions and tells her that these dreams are not to be trusted. This begins for her the initiation, through painful disillusionment, into the freedom of subjective knowledge and reliance on inner voice as sources of truth. From pages 43 to 53 of her book, *Woman Hollering Creek and Other Stories*, Cisneros again structures the fantasy flashbacks in a manner reminiscent of the point-counterpoint musical structure previously cited. As the crescendo of Cleofilas's fantasy decreases, her moments of disillusionment increase. The inevitable denouement is foreshadowed and hinted slightly at the beginning when she recalls that her father had said before her wedding, "I am your father, I will never abandon you."

The inevitable disillusionment becomes more insistent on page 47, with the first shocking realization that the husband had struck her. The flashback culminates on page 53, and comes to a close dramatically when, as previously noted, she realizes that "there are no commercials in between for comic relief. And no happy ending in sight" (Cisneros 1991, 53).

> She thought this when she sat with the baby out by the creek behind the house. Cleofilas de . . . ? But somehow she would have to change her name to Topazio, or Yesenia, Cristal, Adriana, Stefania, Andrea, something more poetic than Cleofilas. Everything happened to women with names like jewels. But what happened to a Cleofilas? Nothing. But a crack in the face. (Ibid)

After that, Cisneros shifts narrative point of view from the omniscient stream of consciousness to the third-person, external-objective observer. By so doing, she increases suspense by keeping the reader ignorant of what is on Cleofilas's mind. Simultaneously, she also signals Cleofilas's final disillusionment with her interior world of silent fantasy and her rite of passage to reliance on inner voice and subjective knowing.

Stage of Subjective Knowledge and Inner Voice

At the stage of subjective knowing, Mary Belensky and her associates (1986) say that women focus on a "quest for self" and "at least, a protection of a space for growth of self" (58) which they see as primary. This means a turning away from listening to external patriarchal values and a turning inward to intuition and that "still small voice" within them. What Belensky and her team of psychologists discovered is that the women who had reached this stage had come there via some trauma or experience of failed male authority. Many subjective knowers in Belensky's study had had fathers who belittled them or squelched their curiosity or chastised them for questioning. "What comes through most strongly in all these stories from women is the picture they paint of failed male authority. Their sense of outrage and disappointment is pervasive" (57-58).

In Chicana literature, images of these women abound also. For example, in her article, "Making Familia From Scratch: Split Subjectivities in the Work of Helena María Viramontes and Cherríe Moraga," Norma Alarcón's (1988) interpretation of Cherríe Moraga's protagonist Corky and Viramontes's main characters Olga Ruiz and Noemi show that Chicana writing reflects a preoccupation with women's subjectivity and with the patriarchal society "engendering them as women" (35). Likewise, the "trinity" of Pachucas portrayed by Lorna Dee Cervantez in "Bird Ave." are definitely women whom male authority has failed and who now seek refuge in their inner voice and the subjectivity of their individual selves as well as their sisterhood (Herrera-Sobek 1988, 11).

They flaunt their independence from the world of telenovelas and Clairol commercials as they did towards the culmination of the listening stage by "their visual shocking attention getting costumes of the Pachuca–teased tough hair, and teased tough skirts" (Cervantes in Herrera-Sobek 1988, 11).

As both Alarcón (1988) and Yarbro-Bejarano (1988) indicate, women concerned with their own subjectivity abound in Chicana literature, and the Chicana writers' employment of these female subjects represents not only an innovative literary technique but an act of literary rebellion. Alarcón, for one, claims that Chicanas are increasingly making use of "female-speaking subjects who hark back to explore the subjectivity of women" (1988, 148). Yarbro-Bejarano also reinforces Alarcón's claim when she says that "the fact that Chicanas may tell stories about themselves and other Chicanas challenges the dominant male concept of cultural ownership and literary authority" (1988 141). Yarbro-Bejarano agrees with Gloria Anzaldúa that, "By delving into this deep core, the Chicana writer finds that the self she seeks to define and love is not merely an individual self, but a collective one" (141).

Subjective Knowledge and Inner Voice in "Mother, May I"

As in Cherríe Moraga's play, *Giving Up the Ghost* (Moraga 1986), the rape scene in Alma Villanueva's "Mother, May I" serves as the turning point that starts the protagonist's initiation into reliance on inner voice and subjective knowledge. Through the rape, the young girl begins her initiation into disillusionment and awareness that culminates when she returns to visit her grandmother's graveyard for the second time.

Both Villanueva's and Moraga's rape scenes share many similarities. In both, the violent act is visited upon the young women, transforming them into silent, invisible, non-existent entities. Both protagonists find sanctuary in the world of tomboys as a coping mechanism. In both, the act of having to "take in" or "hold in" either the screwdriver or the penis produces a "hole" not only physically but metaphorically: a sense of nothingness spiritually and symbolically. In both, the act of "holding in" produces a long silence and repression of feel-

ings. In Moraga's play, Corky yields fearfully to the command-
ing voice of someone who reminds her of her father. In
Villanueva's poem, the poetic persona is likewise intimidated
by a father figure who commands her to "suck something good"
and thereafter represses her voice.

In both, the themes of dissociation and the disembodied
feeling after sexual assault are reiterated. Corky is transformed
into a shapeless entity robbed of feeling and sensations; she
becomes a "hole." Likewise, the poetic persona in Villanueva's
poem, Sánchez indicates, "feels more intensely the dissociation between an inner unembodied self and an outer embodied self" (1985, 50). Both Protagonists (Corky and the poetic
"I") "lose their identities as human beings and are transformed
into formless entities devoid of feelings and bodily sensations"
(Herrera-Sobek 1988, 152).

Whereas the rape scene signals the disintegration and dissociation of personality for both protagonists, for Alma
Villanueva's poetic "I" the final graveyard scene initiates her
journey into integration and acquisition of voice. Her moment
of epiphany is simultaneously a moment of illumination,
birthing, and resurrection. Previously at the funeral, the young
girl, symbolically and defiantly dressed in red, drops a red
rose into her grandmother's grave and hears it squish, just as
her voice is squished. As Sánchez says, "The rose is the metaphoric containment of the girl's self" (1985, 49). Her inner
voice, which for the time being is repressed, seeks expression
in the loud brilliance of "red." At the second graveyard scene,
this action is karmically reversed. The girl's return to her
grandmother's grave mirrors also the graveyard scene in
Katherine Anne Porter's "The Grave." In this short story, the
main character Miranda and her older brother stumble upon
their grandmother's partially exhumed grave and find two trea-
sures: a ring with a dove, and a gargoyle. They reluctantly
exchange gifts that are more gender appropriate: the ring for
Miranda, the gargoyle for her brother. Shortly afterwards, they
come upon a mother rabbit that her brother has killed. They
find inside the little fetuses, and whereas the boy is elated by
his victory, the girl is horrified by the memory of "crushed
life" in a womb that has become a tomb. To cope, she buries
the thought in her subconscious until she is in her late twen-

ties. The moment of epiphany comes when she sees some sugared rabbit candies in a marketplace in Mexico, and the entire unpleasant memory of life/death, womb and tomb are resurrected in her subconscious. It is this moment of epiphany that provides her an opportunity to reverse the unpleasant-ness of the earlier experience and transform it into a release and rebirthing. The grandmother's tomb, the ring Miranda resurrects from it, and the dead fetuses buried in the dead mother's womb/tomb symbolize and foreshadow Miranda's return to the tomb of her buried subconscious and the previously mentioned opportunity to resurrect those long repressed feelings and give them voice.

A parallel symbolic scene occurs when Villanueva's protagonist arrives also at her grandmother's tomb. Her interior as well as vocal dialogue with her grandmother initiates this process:

> We look for you, my
> husband and I.
> We look for you till
> I'm dizzy. Are you
> here, mamacita. Are you
> here? he says—here
> it is—he's found
> you, a "13"
> in the ground. They said
> —Jesus Villanueva
> is "13"—
> I touch the one, the
> three.
> I begin to cry
> and no one stops
> me. I didn't
> know it, but
> a seed spilled out
> and my mouth ate it. I think
> that's when the rose took root.
> (Villanueva in Sánchez 1985, 325)

Like the ring, the dead fetuses, and the sugared candy rabbits in Porter's "The Grave," the seed spilling out of the protagonist's mouth in "Mother, May I," is also a symbol that triggers her voice and resurrects her repressed feelings from the womb/tomb of her subconscious. The rose (her voice) that was squished takes root. The girl, Sánchez (1985) remarks, figuratively swallows her grandmother's "seed" and in so doing undoes the gagging experience of choking on the semen at the rape scene. The grandmother's tomb, a metaphor for the girl's buried subconscious, becomes now a figurative womb that provides hope of resurrection and the seed of a new life. Sánchez interprets the seed as representing restoration. It is a metaphor for the nurturing grandmother and a restoration of the phallus. But more important than that, it represents the restoration of her personal voice and the birthing of her new, poetic voice.

> and she heard a voice, distant
> and small, but
> she heard it,
> and her mouth opened slightly
> and a word spilled out. The word
> was "I."
> (Villanueva in Sánchez 1985, 325)

The birthing of the poetic "I" that the poetic persona experiences is both a rebirth and a resurrection, and because it takes root from the grandmother's seed, it is a kind of parthenogenesis. Like Jesus' birth, it is virginal, unaided by male intervention. The poet reinvents herself through a matrilineal line going from mother to daughter, purely and asexually.

Psychologically, something very similar happens, claims Mary Belensky (1986), to women who are "subjectivist knowers." "Looking back on their childhood many of these women . . . no longer are willing to rely on higher status, powerful authorities . . . but instead they consider turning to . . . . female peers, mothers, sisters, and grandmothers" (60).

This psychological behavior pattern is echoed metaphorically in Villanueva's poem. The grandmother, literally buried in the earth, figuratively in the girl's subconscious becomes a womb that provides the heroine with a new source of life. This primordial connection between women is echoed also in Villanueva's "Bloodroot" and, as previously mentioned, in Katherine Anne Porter's "The Grave." This tomb/womb, death/resurrection archetype reiterates the Demeter/ Persephone myth: an archetypal violent separation and eventual reunion between mother and daughter that signals the circular death and rebirth cycle of the seasons in a very pure and chaste parthenogenic manner without the intervention of male agency. Sánchez also repeats this fact when she says that Villanueva dramatically rejects the genital model of birthing in favor of a more magical, non-genital one. "The seed," she says, "is absorbed by the mouth. The interaction is between woman and woman in this metaphoric virgin birth" (1985, 54). The woman who has rediscovered her inner voice and subjective knowledge gives birth to herself, reinvents herself. The grandmother's name, María de Jesus, suggests Sánchez, implies an androgyny of gender inherent in the name of Jesus. In Catholic mythology, she says, it also suggests a non-genital birth as Christ is conceived by Mary without "knowing man."

As Sánchez states, Villanueva shares with many women poets a preoccupation with giving birth to themselves and their poetic voices by becoming, so to speak, their mothers.

Subjective Knowledge and Inner Voice in "Woman Hollering Creek"

Cleofilas's moment of awareness when she realizes she has no other alternative but to rely on her inner voice for guidance happens less dramatically than the birthing of the poetic "I" in Villanueva's poem, "Mother, May I." Cleofilas's journey of transformation literally and figuratively begins when she begs Juan Pedro for permission and money to go see the doctor, and culminates in her journey with Felice, the nurse, as they make their escape across La Gritona, Woman Hollering creek. Again, as in Villanueva's poem, Cleofilas's pregnancy foreshadows her own imminent birth, for she carries not just Juan Pedro's seed but also the seeds of repressed silence gestating in her subconscious and eager to be allowed to birth in a new voice.

It is by no accident that the two nurses who plan her escape are each named Felice and Graciela, symbolically, "happiness" and "grace." Both have come along at a rare moment of "grace" to bring her happiness and serve as midwives in the birthing of her new self. As in Villanueva's poem, this metaphorical birthing of the inner voice is also a parthenogenesis, a virgin birth resulting from a trinity or sisterhood of women without the intervention of a male.

Cleofilas's escape in the truck with Felice is truly a moment of grace, when the door of opportunity opens and she must pass through or never be freed. The moment of epiphany arrives when both she and Felice cross over the creek, and Felice lets out a yell "like a mariachi." The bridge and the creek symbolically become a birth canal and Felice's scream as well as Cleofilas's "ribbon of laughter" are simultaneously the primal scream and birth pangs of both mother and first born. Cleofilas's crossing of the bridge physically also signals her transition from a stage of repression and silencing to a stage of inner voice and subjective knowledge. Cisneros's portrayal of Cleofilas's reaction as a "long ribbon of laughter like water" (56) is a very aesthetic and fitting conclusion, since nowhere before then does the reader even catch a glimmer of Cleofilas's smile or giggle. "Her laughter, gurgling like water," (56) becomes for Cleofilas the first explosive attempt to resurrect from the tomb/womb of the subconscious her repressed and long buried feelings.

Cisneros now allows us to see Cleofilas from the narrative point of view of the third-person camera angle, from the outside. There is no longer any need to probe her subconscious thoughts, for Cleofilas has released her silent fantasy world in exchange for freedom and voice. Cisneros's skillful portrayal of the dialogue between Felice and Cleofilas suggests openness. Felice's comment, "Nothing around here is named after a woman? Really unless she's the Virgin" (55), suggests to Cleofilas this woman's awareness and ultimate triumph over the male-dominated society that surrounds them. Felice owns a power that she, Cleofilas, did not have up to now and which she admires:

Everything about this woman, this Felice, amazed Cleofilas. The fact that she drove a pickup, a pickup, mind you, but when Cleofilas asked if it belonged to her husband, she said she didn't have a husband. The pickup was hers. She had chosen it. She herself was paying for it. (55)

Felice's spontaneous behavior is a totally pleasant surprise to Cleofilas:

What kind of talk was that coming from a woman?" Cleofilas thought. But then again, Felice was like no other woman she had ever met. (55)

Hence, Cleofilas and the poetic persona in "Mother, May I" illustrate in their respective epiphanies the power of women to evolve from a passive state of being silent and silenced, through a stage of listening, to a more blissful stage of inner voice and subjective knowledge. These protagonists illustrate not only the theme of the evolution of voice but also illustrate a fresh innovation as well as rebellion in literary technique that, according to some Latina writers, has resulted in "Hispanic women taking the literary world by storm." Like the main characters, for example, in Viramontes's "Snapshots" and Cherríe Moraga's *Giving Up the Ghost*, both Cleofilas and the poetic persona in "Mother, May I" are women who are brave enough to explore their own subjectivity. The action in both narratives now comes full circle, and as mentioned previously, in the introduction, both protagonists are thrown into what Alarcón claims is a "crisis of meaning that begins with their own gendered personal identity and its relational position with others" (1988, 152). This crisis of meaning, as portrayed by both the poetic persona and Cleofilas, culminates in an awakened state of awareness that is the beginning of subjective knowing and acquisition of an inner voice.

It is also by no coincidence that in both these stories both protagonists engage in a regretful looking back at the past before they achieve their own identity and voice. Again here, an analogy is appropriate: Norma Alarcón says that "in looking back (and so many Chicana writers have their speaking subjects look back . . .) both Corky in Cherríe Moraga's *Giving up the Ghost* and Olga Ruiz in Viramontes's 'Snapshots' enact, as Irigaray asserts, an analysis 'after the fact' of the treacherous route on the way to becoming a 'woman' or not becoming a 'woman'" (Alarcón 1988, 150). Like Olga and Corky, Cleofilas in particular also looks back with both pleasure initially, and later with increasing regret and disenchantment and likewise arrives at that "crisis of meaning" when she must choose between remaining as a silenced victim or becoming an articulate human being.

In conclusion, both Villanueva's "Mother, I," and Cisneros's "Woman Hollering Creek" mirror and encapsulate in concentrated narrative form the mythic journey a woman takes in her rite of passage from a subjugated underworld of silence to a liberated stage of discovering an inner voice, a subjective fountain of knowledge and an intuitive wellspring from which she draws strength. The story of Persephone's rescue from the underworld and her eventual return to her mother, Demeter, forms the archetype that underlies the rescue of both Cleofilas and the poetic "I" in "Mother, May I" from the dark underworld of their subconsciously repressed voices. Both works, though brief, are powerful and dramatic and relevant not just because they find validity in the psychological reality of voice documented by Belensky and other psychologists, but because they point to the eternal, mythic archetype of death/resurrection, the tomb/womb paradox. Both literary selections affirm the power of women to provide a world hungry for meaning a modicum of faith in the regenerative powers of Earth as Gaia, the fecund female principle.

Works Cited

Alarcón, Norma. 1988. "Making Familia from Scratch: Split Subjectivities in the work of Helena María Viramontes and Cherríe Moraga," in María Herrera-Sobek & Helena María Viramontes, *Chicana Creativity and Criticism: Charting New Frontiers in American Literature.* Houston: Arte Público Press.

Belensky, Mary F., Blythe Clinchy, Nancy Goldberger, and Jill Tarule. 1986. *Women's Ways of Knowing.* New York: Basic Books.

Cisneros, Sandra. 1991. *Woman Hollering Creek and Other Stories.* New York. Vintage Books.

Herrera-Sobek, María. 1988. "The Politics of Rape," in María Herrera-Sobek and Helena María Viramontes, *Chicana Creativity and Criticism: Charting New Frontiers in American Literature.* Houston: Arte Público Press.

Herrera-Sobek, María, and Helena María Viramontes. 1988. *Chicana Creativity and Criticism: Charting New Frontiers in American Literature.* Houston: Arte Público Press.

Moraga, Cherríe. 1986. *Giving Up the Ghost.* Los Angeles: West End Press.

Sánchez, Marta Ester. 1985. *Contemporary Chicana Poetry: A Critical Approach to an Emerging Literature.* Berkeley: University of California Press.

Villanueva, Alma. 1978. *Mother, May I?* Pittsburg: Motheroot Publications.

Viramontes, Helena María. 1985. *The Moths and Other Stories.* Houston: Arte Público Press.

Yarbro-Bejarano, Yvonne. 1988. "Chicana Literature from a Chicana Feminist Perspective," in María Herrera-Sobek and Helena María Viramontes, *Chicana Creativity and Crticism: Charting New Frontiers in American Literature.* Houston: Arte Público Press.

Mestizaje as Method: Feminists-of-Color Challenge the Canon[1]

Chéla Sandoval

> For the Chicana feminist it is through our affiliation with the struggles of other Third World people that we find our theories and our methods.
> —Sonia Saldívar-Hull (1991)

The Chicana feminisms that spanned the late twentieth century were deployed in five different modes. Sociologists Denise Segura and Beatriz Pesquera typify three of these as "Chicana liberalism," "Chicana insurgency," and "Cultural nationalism"–to these we can add Chicana separatism.[2] None of these Xicanismas,[3] these Chicana deployments of feminism, however, have been as broadly recognized, exchanged, or appropriated as has the fifth, *"Chicana Mestizaje,"* mode, defined in 1987 by Gloria Anzaldúa in her foundational book *Borderlands/La Frontera: The New Mestiza*.[4] This "borderlands" feminism, many argue, calls up a syncretic form of consciousness made up of transversions and crossings; its recognition makes possible another kind of critical apparatus and political operation in which *mestiza* feminism comes to function as a working chiasmus (a mobile crossing) between races, genders, sexes, cultures, languages, and nations. Thus conceived, *La conciencia de la mestiza* makes visible the operation of another *metaform* of consciousness that insists upon polymodal forms of poetics, ethics, identities, and politics not only for Chicanas/os but for any constituency resisting the old and new hierarchies of the coming millennium.[5] Much has already been written about this borderlands consciousness, investigated as it is across disciplines and seemingly from within every academic and theoretical location. Whether citing the pivotal contributions of scholars from the domain of Chicano/a Studies, particularly those of R. Saldívar, Alarcón, Rechy, Castañeda, J. Saldívar, Anzaldúa, Saldívar-Hull, or Paredes, or whether citing such writers as Giroux, Butler, Deleuze, Barthes, Harding, Hayles, Lorde, or Gibson, borderlands theorizing is the contemporary imaginary that is reforming disciplinary canons.[6] This essay makes obvious the links that tie the *mestiza* form of Chicana feminism to what is named "U.S. third world feminist criticism" in an effort to demonstrate how both have inspired and engendered an emerging cross-disciplinary and transnational politics of resistance that is increasingly theorized as "border," "diasporic," "hybrid," or *"mestiza/o"* in nature. Both U.S. third world feminism and Chicana *mestizaje* have developed similarly a specific methodology, one for which scholars across disciplines are seeking in the attempt to identify techniques capable of advancing cross-disciplinary study.

Scholars are trained to look to the OED, the *Oxford English Dictionary,* in order to find some originary point for meanings that reverberate outward and away from our words. When I was asked by the editors of *The Oxford Companion to Women's Writing in the United States* to devise the historical and conceptual definition for a social, literary, intellectual, and methodological movement that had never before been similarly canonized, I felt bear down the weight of history and meaning.[7] Yet to write this definition one need only recapitulate the long (if unrecognized) trajectory of struggle by Chicanas and other feminists of color to write into history this very movement.[8] I agreed to the project on the condition that I could take up this trajectory, to make explicit that which seems to have slipped through and escaped contemporary academic canonization and official histories: "U.S. third world feminism" understood as critical apparatus, theory, and method.

Reasons for this academic disappearance (even truancy)[9] have to do with the 1970s form of social movement called U.S. third world feminism itself: It was polymodal, composed of differing and mobile structures of consciousness difficult to express in traditional linear narrative. Moreover, this particular social movement was generated out of the juxtaposition of anticolonial and antisexist U.S. histories that are often underestimated or misunderstood. Further, to understand a form of criticism as "U.S. third world feminist" without also naming and describing the practices that comprise its *methodology* tends to confuse and conflate its specificity with other forms of feminism devised by U.S. women of color since the 1950s. The definition devised to describe the methodological, theoretical, historical, and social practice of "U.S. third world feminism" would need to account for these problematics.[10] During the course of my investigation, I became increasingly intrigued and moved as I traced the so-called third world liberation exchanged within the boundaries of the United States during the late twentieth century as it became extended, translated, and transformed into U.S. third world feminism, *mestiza* feminism, and now "borderlands" theory and "diaspora" studies by the century's end. In what follows the Oxford encyclopedic entry that defines "U.S. third world feminist criticism" is resituated in order to emphasize the similarities of its apparatus with varying theoretical, methodological, and historical apparatuses that are being worked out across disciplines, though under the auspices of differing terminologies, rubrics, and rhetorics.[11] The Oxford definition of U.S. third world feminist criticism insists upon a singular site, however, and from this location rises a critical apparatus for the analysis of language, politics, and historical narrative that was devised, enacted, and developed by U.S. women of color during the post–World War II period. The mystery is the disappearing act: how this theoretical and methodological formulation, including the more technical aspects of what we now call *mestiza* feminism, *mestizaje* as critical apparatus, womanism, diaspora, and/or border studies, continues to slip away from disciplinary understanding and recognition.

Mapping the Site

This mystery is at least partially explained when examining the name for this late 1960s social movement, which links two apparently contradictory geographies in the phrase "U.S. third world feminism," as if the "U.S." and the "third world" could together represent a single political locality. In this sense, simply voicing the name enacts an untried revolution: a geopolitical upheaval of nation-state and its social imaginaries, and an innovative pulling together again of what U.S. feminists of color hoped could be a trans-national, -gendered, -sexed, -cultural, -racial, and coalitional political site.[12] Between 1969 and 1991 this site became the terrain of a thriving artistic, literary, academic, and political movement. Practitioners of U.S. third world feminism identified and developed what they believed to be a theory, method, and praxis permitting entry to an unexplored mode of historical consciousness: a form of oppositional, antisexist, and antiracist consciousness that had developed evasively in the very maw of the postmodern first world. The women of color participants in this U.S. social movement believed themselves both inheritors and creators of this unexplored decolonizing and feminist subjectivity, their hope was to invite and link together citizen-subjects who had previously been separated by gender, sex, race, culture, nation, and/or class into a new alliance, countrypeople of an unprecedented psychic terrain.

*

This form of U.S. third world feminism—understood as an aesthetic, intellectual, and political social movement—arose in recent times, though there are long histories of alliance between women of color in the United States. Examples range from the councils held by Seminole, Yamassee, and African women during times of territorial colonialism and slavery to the coalitions made among Chinese, Chicana, and African women in protective leagues and labor movement struggles during the 1920s, 1930s, and 1940s.[13] The contemporary formulation of the "U.S. third world feminism" described here, however, is based in the great global struggles for decolonization of the nineteenth and twentieth centuries. These geopolitical struggles generated a new form of alliance among peoples of color both outside of and within the United States as expressed in the 1960s transnational slogan and demand for "Third World liberation." This term signified solidarity among new masses of peoples differentiated by nation, ethnicity, language, race, class, culture, sex, and gender demarcations but who were allied nevertheless by virtue of their similar sociohistorical, racial, and colonial relationships to dominant powers. This fresh sense of alliance influenced the transforming identities of U.S. peoples of color, especially those participants of the great social movements of the 1960s and 1970s. Activists of color involved in the civil rights, antiwar, Black, Chicano, Asian, Native American, student, women's, and gay liberation movements saw themselves as bonded, despite distinct and sometimes contrary aims and goals, in a coalitional form of consciousness opposed to dominating powers and oppressive racial and social hierarchies. To be a citizen/subject of the United States who was also a "third world liberationist" during this period, then, did not mean being committed solely to racial, decolonial, and class liberation. For U.S. peoples of color the term increasingly meant to ally with what semiologists now identify as the "third" and repressed force that nevertheless constantly rises up through dominant meaning systems, breaking apart two-term or binary divisions of human thought.

By 1971, grassroots organizations of "U.S. third world feminists" began to form across the United States, bringing together women of color who, in spite of severe differences in historical relations to power, color, culture, language, gender, and sexual orientation, were surprised to recognize in one another profound similarities. A great number of their newsletters, pamphlets, and books were produced by underground publishers from 1971 to 1974, including separate works by Janice Mirikitani (1973) and Francis Beale (1971), both entitled *Third World Women*, which were meant to affirm and develop the revolutionary kind of shared sisterhood/citizenship insistently emerging in the corridors and backrooms where U.S. feminists of color congregated. The burgeoning women's liberation movement, however, was not yet able to imagine, recognize, or contain this other kind of female alliance. As early as 1970, for example, Black feminist Francis Beale had already published an essay in the groundbreaking collection *The Black Woman: An Anthology* (reprinted one year later in the famous *Sisterhood Is Powerful*), which prophesied that U.S. women's liberation would fast become a "white women's movement" if it insisted on organizing along the gender demarcation male/female alone, when, as Sojourner Truth had so eloquently elaborated in 1851, U.S. peoples of color are denied easy or comfortable access to *either* of these socially constructed categories.[14] Again, in 1970, Chicana feminist Velia Hancock wrote in the *Chicano Studies Newsletter* that "white women focus on the maleness of our present social system" as if "a female dominated white America" will take a more reasonable course for U.S. peoples of color of *either* gender. In *Sula* (1973) Toni Morrison suggested that women of color must understand they are "neither white nor male, and that all freedom and triumph was forbidden to them," so "they had to set about creating something else to be." That "something else to be" was explored throughout the seventies by a growing number of U.S. third world feminist artists, writers, critics, theorists, and activists, including Wendy Rose, Leslie Marmon Silko, Antonia Castañeda, Bea Medicine, Barbara Smith, Pat Parker, Rosaura Sánchez, Maxine Hong Kingston, Audre Lorde, Lorna Dee Cervantes, Judy Baca, Teresa Hak Kyung Cha, Azizah Al-Hibri, and Margaret Walker. As Barbara Noda (*Bridge,* 1981) put it, U.S. feminists of color were "lowriding through the women's movement"; that is, they were developing the imagery, methods and theories necessary for cruising through any dominant meaning system on behalf of this "something else"– this other "third" force that would become distinctive of U.S. third world feminist critical theory.

By the 1980s, U.S. third world feminism became an influential intellectual presence. In 1981 the National Women's Studies Association held the first U.S. conference on the troubled relations between white women and women of color entitled "Women Respond to Racism." Three hundred women of color attended to establish the first official "National Alliance of U.S. Third World Feminists." Their statement of purpose argued that U.S. third world feminism is organized according to a "*fundamentally different structure*" from that of other feminisms, as well as from other U.S. social movements for racial justice. That same month, *This Bridge Called My Back, A Collection of Writings by Radical Women of Color* (1981), edited by Cherríe Moraga and Gloria Anzaldúa, was released. Here, as Toni Cade Bambara (1981) put it, a growing number of U.S. third world feminists are "putting in telecalls to each other. And we're all on the line." *Bridge* was quickly followed by the founding of Kitchen Table: Women of Color Press, the journal *Third Woman*, and the publication of a plethora of writings by U.S. feminists of color. These writings included Bernice Reagon's "Coalition Politics, Turning the Century" (1983), an explication of hegemonic white consciousness trapped in a prison-house of identity that makes alliance across difference impossible; and Audre Lorde's 1982 *Zami,* in which women of color realize "that our place was the very house of difference rather than the security of any one particular difference." This U.S. third world feminism, understood as a "third" space, a bridging "house of difference" engaged the imaginations and commitments of diverse artists throughout the 1980s, including Angela Davis, Shirley Geok-lin Lim, bell hooks, Maxine Baca Zinn, Aída Hurtado, Kitty Tsui, Gayatri Spivak, Beth Brant, Janice Gould, June Jorden, Cherríe Moraga, and Barbara Christian, whose works reflect only the surface of a sea of contributions produced by U.S. feminist/womanist activists of color during the 1980s.

A Sleight-of-Consciousness: La Conciencia de la Mestiza as Differential Consciousness

East Indian feminist theorist Chandra Mohanty has written that "simply being a woman, or being poor or Black or Latino," is not "sufficient ground to assume a politicized oppositional identity" (1991). What is required, as Fredric Jameson points out,[15] is a specific methodology that can be used as compass for self-consciously organizing resistance, identity, praxis, and coalition under contemporary first world, late-capitalist cultural conditions. Examination of U.S. third world feminist works developed between 1965 and 1991 reveals their combined insistence upon a structured theory and method of consciousness-in-opposition to U.S. social hierarchy that is capable, when all actors agree to its methods, of aligning a variety of oppositional social movements with one another across differing gender, sex, race, culture, class, or national commitments. This theoretical and methodological compass was represented, developed, and utilized by U.S. feminists of color during 1968-1988 because, as Native American theorist Paula

Gunn Allen put it in 1981, so much has been taken away that "the place we live now is an idea"—and in this place new forms of identity, theory, practice, and community have become imaginable. In 1987, Gloria Anzaldúa redefined and specified that the practice of U.S. third world feminism required *"la conciencia de la mestiza,"* the consciousness of the "mixed blood." *La conciencia de la mestiza* is born of life lived in the "crossroads" between races, nations, languages, genders, sexualities, and cultures: It is a developed subjectivity capable of transformation and relocation, movement guided by the learned capacity to read, renovate, and make signs on behalf of the dispossessed in a skill that Anzaldúa calls "la facultad" (1987). So too does the philosopher Maria Lugones claim that the theory and method of U.S. third world feminism requires of its practitioners nomadic and determined "travel" across "worlds of meaning." Black feminist theorist Patricia Hill Collins describes the skills developed by U.S. women of color who, through exclusion from male-controlled race liberation movements and from white-controlled female liberation movements, were forced to internalize an "outsider/within" identity that guides movement-of-being *according to an ethical commitment* to equalize power between social constituencies. And Gayatri Spivak suggests "shuttling" between meaning systems in order to enact the "strategic essentialism" necessary for intervening in power on behalf of the marginalized—this, in order to practice the political method Alice Walker names "Womanism": the political hermeneutic for constructing "love" in the postmodern world.[16] These examples direct our attention not only to the features of a specific "U.S. third world feminist" critical paradigm. This paradigm is the compass sought by Jameson that can enable "cognitive mapping" under first world, postmodern cultural conditions. Indeed this paradigm can be recognized as a theory and method for mobilizing oppositional forms of consciousness in the postmodern first world.

This theory and method understands oppositional forms of consciousness, aesthetics, and politics as organized around the following five points of resistance to U.S. social hierarchy: (1) the "assimilationist" (or "liberal") mode; (2) the "revolutionary" (or "insurgent") mode; (3) the "supremacist" (or "cultural-nationalist") mode; (4) the "separatist" mode; and (5) the "differential" *"mestiza"* (or "womanist," "*Sister Outsider*," "third force" it has generated many names) mode of "U.S. third world feminist praxis." It was this last, differential mode that enabled U.S. feminists-of-color to understand and utilize the previous four, not as overriding strategies, but as *tactics* for intervening in and transforming social relations.[17] Viewed under the auspices of U.S. third world feminism understood as the differential practice of *mestizaje,* the first four modes are performed, however seriously, only as forms of "tactical essentialism." The differential oppositional praxis wields and deploys each mode of resistant ideology as a potential *technology of power.* The cruising mobilities required in this effort demand of the differential practitioner commitment to the process of metamorphosis itself: This is the activity of the trickster who practices subjectivity-as-masquerade, the oppositional agent who accesses differing identity, ideological, aesthetic, and political positions.[18] Such nomadic "morphing" is not performed only for survival's sake, as in earlier, modernist times. It is a set of principled conversions, informed by the skill of "*la facultad,*" that requires differential movement through, over, and within any dominant system of resistance, identity, race, gender, sex, class, or national meanings: The differential strategy is directed, but it is also a "diasporic/immigration" in consciousness and politics enacted to ensure that ethical commitment to egalitarian social relations enter into the everyday, political sphere of culture. Indeed, it is important to understand that it is this ethical principle that guides the deployment of all the technologies of power utilized by the differential practitioner of this theory and method of oppositional consciousness. The differential theory and method of oppositional consciousness has been developed in many forms across disciplines, but this ethical principle most clearly drives the critical apparatus of Chicana feminist *mestizaje* and its *conciencia de la mestiza.*

*

The field here defined as "U.S. third world feminist criticism" is not an easy terrain. Debates continue among U.S. women of color over which forms of resistance comprise the most effective U.S. third world feminist practices and how such resistances should be valued, distinguished, translated, or named. Today, alternative contending names range from "transnational" or "transcultural" feminisms, where issues of race and ethnicity become sublimated, to more technical terminologies—such as "the differential," *"la conciencia de la mestiza"* (which specifies the techniques of *la facultad, Coatlique,* and *nepantla* forms of conseciousness), "womanism," or "third space feminism—which together signify the activities of the "U.S. third world feminism" identified here,[19] to "U.S. women-of-color feminism," which emphasizes the exclusion of its population from legitimate state powers by virtue of color and/or physiognomy. U.S. women-of-color-feminism tends to commit to one or more of the five technologies of power outlined earlier as a means of increasing and reinforcing racial and tribal loyalties and self-determination. This focus is more specific than that of third space, or U.S. "third world feminism" however, which when understood as a technical and critical term is focused, above all else, on the differential, *mestiza,* and poetic deployment of each technology of power. As such, U.S. third world feminism is not inexorably gender, nation, race, sex, or class linked. It is, rather, *a theory and method of oppositional consciousness* that rose out of a specific deployment, that is, out of a particular *tactical* expression of U.S. third world feminist politics that more and more became its overriding strategy. The tactic that became this overriding, differential strategy is guided, above all else, by the imperatives of social justice that can engage a hermeneutics of love in the postmodern world.

The differential strategy both generates and depends upon *la conciencia de la mestiza* in order to function. This *conciencia* recognizes and identifies all technologies of power as consensual illusions. When resistance is organized as either assimilationist, integrationist, revolutionary, supremacist, or separatist in function, the differential U.S. third world feminist criticism reads and interprets these technologies of power as transformable social narratives designed to intervene in reality for the sake of social justice. The differential maneuvering required here is a sleight-of-consciousness which activates a new space: a *cyberspace* where the transcultural, transgendered, transnational leaps necessary to the play of effective stratagems of oppositional praxis can begin, a process Judith Butler theorizes as "the performative." Aesthetic works, identified, read, and interpreted with the analytic tools of differential criticism, are marked with both disruption *and* continuity; as well as by immigrations, diasporas, border crossings, and by politics, poetics, and procedures. Also, they are marked by tactics, strategies, movement, position and styles of travel. These are all produced, however, with the aim of equalizing power on behalf of the colonized, the nation-, class-, race-, gender-, and sexually subordinated, as stated by U.S. third world feminist Merle Woo in *Bridge* (1981).

The so-called "flexibility of identity" once required for survival under conquest, colonialism, and domination is being required today of every first world citizen living under transforming postmodern global economies. This mobility of identity is only one requirement of the neocolonial forces that marshal postmodernity in the first world. Yet this same challenge to subjectivity, singularity, and traditional citizenship also clears the way towards a utopian and coalitional postcolonial state. Oppositional *mestizaje* occurs when the unexplored *affinities inside of difference* attract, combine, and relate new constituencies into a coalition of resistance. Any such generalized and politicized coalitional consciousness, however, can only occur on the site of a social movement that was once overlooked because it was perceived as limited, restricted by gender, sex, or race identity: U.S. third world feminism; a feminism developed by U.S. women of color and by Chicana feminists under the sign of "la conciencia de la mestiza." That is, coalition can only take place through the recognition and practice of a "U.S. third world feminist" form of resistance that is capable of re-negotiating technologies of power through an ethically guided, skilled, and differential deployment—a methodology of the oppressed that is only made possible through *la conciencia de la mestiza.* The remaining questions are these: If subjectivity is "masquerade," as Anzaldúa argues in *Haciendo Caras*,[20] can men and women of any race, nation, class, sex, or gender identification inhabit the subject positions required by U.S. third world feminist criticism, Chicana *mestizaje* as critical apparatus, and differential social movement? In what ways would doing so slide the rule of canon?

Notes

1. This essay is dedicated to Angela Davis and the Women-of-Color Cluster in the History of Consciousness Program at the University of California at Santa Cruz, whose work has renewed my faith.
2. Denise Segura and Beatriz Pesquera, "Beyond Indifference and Antipathy: The Chicana Movement and Chicana Feminist Discourse," *Aztlán: A Journal of Chicano Studies*, 19, no. 2 (1992): 69-93. For the most up-to-date historical and critical analysis of Chicana feminist writings, see Teresa Córdova's brilliant chapter "The Emergent Writings of Twenty Years of Chicana Feminist Struggle: Roots and Resistance." Córdova's contribution situates and interprets some of the most influential work to date, including that of Angie Chabram, Cynthia Orozco, Deena González, Yvonne Yarbro-Bejarano, Norma Alarcón, Aída Hurtado, Alma García, Norma Cantú, María Herrera-Sobek, Rosa Linda Fregoso, and Emma Pérez, to name only a few. This chapter can be found in *The Handbook of Hispanic Cultures in the United States*, edited by Felix Padilla (Houston: Arte Público Press, 1994), 175-202. Deena González's recent essay "Chicana Identity Matters," engages Chicana lesbian feminist theory, in *Culture and Difference: Critical Perspectives on the Bicultural Experience in the United States*, edited by Antonia Darder (New York: Bergen and Garvey, 1995). For the method through which these theoretical approaches to Chicana feminism and other social movements are classified, see Chéla Sandoval, "U.S. Third World Feminism: The Theory and Method of Oppositional Consciousness in the Postmodern World" in *Genders* 10 (Spring 1991): 1-24.
3. "Xicanisma" as a term for describing Chicana feminisms, was formally introduced into U.S. academic vocabulary by Ana Castillo only recently. See *Massacre of the Dreamers: Essays on Xicanisma* (New York: Penguin Books, 1995).
4. Gloria Anzaldúa, *Borderlands/La Frontera: The New Mestiza* (San Francisco: Spinsters/Aunt Lute, 1987). Also see Sonia Saldívar-Hull's excellent proposal for Chicana mestizaje, "Feminism on the Border: From Gender Politics to Geopolitics," in *Criticism in the Borderlands: Studies in Chicano Literature, Culture, and Ideology*, edited by Héctor Calderón and José David Saldívar (Durham: Duke University Press, 1991), 203-221.
5. For excellent discussions of mestizaje as a methodological apparatus, see Rafael Pérez-Torres, *Movements in Chicano Poetry: Against Myths, Against Margins* (Boston: Cambridge University Press, 1995); Sonia Saldívar-Hull, "Feminism on the Border"; Alicia Gaspar de Alba, "The Alter-Native Grain: Theorizing Chicano/a Popular Culture," in *Culture and Difference*; Daniel Alarcón, "The Aztec Palimp-

sest: Toward a New Understanding of Aztlán," in *Aztlán: A Journal of Chicano Studies* 19, no. 2 (1992): 33-68; and note 4 above. Also see Chéla Sandoval, "New Sciences: Cyborg Feminism and the Methodology of the Oppressed," in *The Cyborg Handbook*, edited by Chris Gray (New York: Routledge, 1995).

6. For recent and succinct overviews of "diasporic" and borderlands theorizing, see Carl Gutiérrez-Jones, "Desiring B/orders," *Diacritics* (Spring 1995); and James Clifford, "Diasporas," *Cultural Anthropology* 9, no. 3 (1994): 302-339. Also see Ramón Saldívar's essay "The Borderlands of Culture: Americo Paredes's *George Washington Gómez* and Chicano Literature at the End of the Twentieth Century," in *American Literary History* 5, no. 2 (1993); José Saldívar's forthcoming *Border Matters: The Multiple Routes of Cultural Studies* (Berkeley: University of California Press); Antonia Castañeda's excellent *Native Women in California* (Durham: Duke University Press, forthcoming); Americo Paredes, With His Pistol in His Hand: A Border Ballad and Its Hero (Austin: University of Texas Press, 1958); Héctor Calderón and José Saldívar, *Criticism in the Borderlands: Studies in Chicano Literature, Culture and Ideology* (Durham: Duke University Press, 1991); John Rechy, *The Miraculous Day of Amalia Gómez* (New York: Arcade, 1991); Norma Alarcón, "Chicana Feminism: In the Tracks of 'the' Native Woman," *Cultural Studies* 4 (1990), and "The Theoretical Subjects of *This Bridge Called My Back* and Anglo American Feminism," in *Borderlands: Studies in Chicano Literature, Culture and Ideology*, edited by Héctor Calderón and José Saldívar (Durham: Duke University Press, 1991); Antonia Casteñeda, "Women of Color and the Rewriting of Western History: The Discourse Politics and Decolonization of History," in *Pacific Historical Review* 61, 1992; Mary Louise Pratt, *Imperial Eyes: Travel Writing and Transculturation* (London: Routledge, 1992); Audre Lorde, *Zami, A New Spelling of My Name* (Trumansburg, N.Y.: Crossing Press, 1982); Aiwah Ong, "On the Edge of Empires: Flexible Citizenship Among Chinese in Diaspora," *Positions # 1* (1993); Homi K. Bhabha, "DissemiNation: Time, Narrative, and the Margins of the Modern Nation," in *Nation and Narration* (London: Routledge, 1990); Giles Deleuze and Felix Guattari, *Anti-Oedipus: Capitalism and Schizophrenia* (New York: Viking, 1983); Roland Barthes, *Image/Music/Text*, translated by Richard Miller (New York: Hill and Wang, 1977); Donna Haraway, "Situated Knowledges: The Science Question and the Privilege of Partial Perspective," in *Simians, Cyborgs, and Women: The Reinvention of Nature* (New York: Routledge, 1991).

7. This definition appears as "U.S. Third World Feminism" in the *Oxford Companion to Women's Writing in the United States*, edited by

Cathy Davidson and Linda Wagner-Martin (New York: Oxford University Press, 1995), 880-882. For an excellent discussion and analysis of this definition, see Katie King, *Theory in its Feminist Travels: Conversations in U.S. Women's Movements* (Bloomington: Indiana University Press, 1994).

8. The most cited examples of U.S. feminists of color arguing for a specific method called "U.S. third world feminism" can be found in Cherríe Moraga and Gloria Anzaldúa's collection *This Bridge Called My Back: Writings by Radical Women of Color* (New York: Kitchen Table/ Women of Color Press, 1981). See also Chandra Talpade Mohanty's reknowned collection and her essay "Cartographies of Struggle: Third World Women and the Politics of Feminism," in *Third World Women and the Politics of Feminism*, edited by Chandra Talpade Mohanty, Anne Russo, and Lourdes Torres (Bloomington: Indiana University Press, 1991). Also Chéla Sandoval's spring 1983 "Comment on Susan Krieger's 'Lesbian Identity and Community'" in *Signs*.

9. The mystery of the academic erasure of U.S. third world feminism is a disappearing trick. Its exemption from the academic canon short-circuits knowledge but secures the acquittal of a "third," feminist "force" about which Derrida said, "it should not be named." Not named, he hoped, in order that what is performative and mobile never be set into any place: freedom resides, thus, everywhere. It is out of this terrain that U.S. third world feminism calls up new kinds of people, those with skills to rise out of citizenship to agency: countrypeople of a new territory. For these countrypeople, who are no longer "U.S. third world feminist," the game is beginning again: new names, new players.

10. See Donna Haraway's, "'Gender' for a Marxist Dictionary: The Sexual Politics of a Word" in *Simians, Cyborgs, and Women: The Reinvention of Nature* (New York: Routledge, 1991), which deals with a similar set of problematics in defining the term "gender."

11. Forms of this methodological apparatus are being developed in academic terrains as diverse as sociology and physics, from new historicism to cultural studies, from semiotics to "situated knowledges," and even within immigration and diaspora studies.

12. See the 1981 report on the National Women's Studies Association Conference, which details how U.S. feminists of color decided to name their alliance "U.S. Third World Feminism" in order to emphasize their affinities with women of color living outside the boundaries of the U.S. This emphasis has since shifted, and the preferred name for this U.S. alliance had become "feminist" or "womanist" women of color. See Chéla Sandoval, "The Struggle Within: A Report on the 1981 N.W.S.A. Conference" (Oakland,

Calif.: Center for Third World Organizing, 1981), reprinted as "Feminism and Racism" in *Haciendo Caras: Making Face, Making Soul,* edited by Gloria Anzaldúa (San Francisco: Spinsters/Aunt Lute, 1991). 13. For histories of U.S. women of color see Antonia Castañeda, "Women of Color and the Rewriting of Western History: The Discourse, Politics, and Decolonization of History," *Pacific Historical Review* 61, 1992; Asian American Women United of California, eds., *Making Waves: An Anthology of Writings by and About Asian Women* (Boston: Beacon Press, 1989); Paula Giddings, *When and Where I Enter: The Impact of Black Women on Race and Sex in America* (New York: William Morrow, 1984); Ellen Dubois and Vicki Ruiz, eds., *Unequal Sisters: A Multicultural Reader in U.S. Women's History* (New York: Routledge, 1990); Gretchen Bataille and Kathleen Mullen Sands, eds., *American Indian Women: Telling Their Lives* (Lincoln: University of Nebraska Press, 1984); Rayna Green, ed., *Native American Women* (Wichita Falls, Tex.: Ohoyo Resource Center, 1981); Paula Gunn Allen, ed., *Spider Woman's Granddaughters* (Boston: Beacon Press, 1989); Albert Hurtado, *Indian Survival on the California Frontier* (New Haven: Yale University Press, 1988); Nobuya Tsuchida, ed., *Asian and Pacific American Experiences* (Minneapolis: University of Minnesota Press, 1987); Toni Cade Bambara, "Preface," in *This Bridge Called My Back: Writings by Radical Women of Color,* edited by Cherríe Moraga and Gloria Anzaldúa (New York: Kitchen Table/Women of Color Press, 1981).

14. Note the implication of another "third space" gender already implied here, which today is being theorized as the category of the decolonizing "queer" as conceived by scholars of color such as Emma Pérez, Cherríe Moraga, Gloria Anzaldúa, Audre Lorde, Kitty Tsui, Makeda Silvera, or Paula Gunn Allen. See Moraga, *The Last Generation* (Boston: South End Press, 1995); Pérez, "Sexuality and Discourse: Notes from a Chicana Survivor," in *Chicana Lesbians: The Girls Our Mothers Warned Us About,* edited by Carla Trujillo (Berkeley: Third Woman Press, 1991); Lorde, *Sister, Outsider* (New York: Beacon, 1981); Tsui, Wong, and Noda, "Coming Out, We Are Here in the Asian Community: A Dialogue with Three Asian Women," *Bridge* (Spring 1979); Asian Women United of California, eds., *Making Waves: An Anthology of Writings By and About Asian American Women* (Boston: Beacon Press, 1989); Allen, "Beloved Women: The Lesbian in American Indian Culture," *Conditions* 7 (1981); Makeda Silvera, ed., A Lesbian of Color Anthology: Piece of My Heart (Ontario: Sister Vision Press, 1991); Deena González, "Identity Matters," in Antonia Darder, ed., *Culture and Difference: Critical Perspectives on the Bicultural Experience* (New York: Bergen and Garvey, 1995); Sandoval,

"Comment on Susan Krieger's Lesbian Identity," *Signs* (1983).
15. See Fredric Jameson's *Postmodernism, or the Cultural Logic of Late Capitalism* (Durham: Duke University Press, 1991), especially the sections on cognitive mapping.
16. Paula Gunn Allen, "Some Like Indians Endure," in *Living the Spirit* (New York: St. Martin's Press, 1987); Gloria Anzaldúa, *Borderlands* (1987); María Lugones, "Playfulness, 'World'-Traveling, and Loving Perception," *Hypatia* 2 (1987); Patricia Hill-Collins, *Black Feminist Thought: Knowledge, Consciousness, and the Politics of Empowerment* (New York: Routledge, 1990); Gayatri Spivak, "Criticism, Feminism and the Institution," *Thesis Eleven* 10/11 (1984-85), and "Explanations of Culture," in *The Post-Colonial Critic* (New York: Routledge, 1990), 156; and Alice Walker, *In Search of Our Mother's Gardens: Womanist Prose* (New York: Harcourt Brace Jovanovich, 1983).
17. These strategies were understood and utilized as tactics for intervention by U.S. women of color in 1960s and 1970s ethnic liberation movements as well as in women's liberation movements. For explication of these usages see Adaljiza Sosa Riddell, "Chicanas en el Movimiento," *Aztlán* V (1974); Cherríe Moraga and Gloria Anzaldúa, eds., *This Bridge Called My Back* (1981); Barbara Smith, "Racism in Women's Studies," in Gloria Hull, Patricia Bell Scott, and Barbara Smith, eds., *All the Blacks Are Men, All the Women Are White, But Some of Us Are Brave* (New York: Feminist Press, 1982); Bonnie Thorton Dill, "Race, Class and Gender: Perspectives for an All-Inclusive Sisterhood," *Feminist Studies* 9 (1983); Mujeres en Marcha, eds., "Chicanas in the '80s: Unsettled Issues" (Berkeley: Chicano Newsletter, 1983); bell hooks, *Feminist Theory: From Margin to Center* (Boston: South End Press, 1984); Alice Chai, "Toward a Holistic Paradigm for Asian American Women's Studies: A Synthesis of Feminist Scholarship and Women of Colors' Feminist Politics," *Women's Studies International Forum* VIII (1985); Cynthia Orozco, "Sexism in Chicano Studies and the Community," in Teresa Córdova, Norma Cantú, Gilberto Cárdenas, Juan García, and Christine Sierra, eds., *Chicana Voices: Intersections of Class, Race, and Gender* (Austin: University of Texas Press, 1986); Chéla Sandoval, "Feminist Agency and U.S. Third World Feminism," in Judith Kegan Gardiner, ed., *Provoking Agents: Theorizing Gender and Agency* (Bloomington: Indiana University Press, 1995); and "U.S. Third World Feminism: The Theory and Method of Oppositional Consciousness in the Postmodern World" *Genders* 10 (1991): 1-36.
18. Judith Butler has recently theorized the method of U.S. third world feminist practice as "the performative," aligning this most interesting contribution from the domain of "queer theory" with what

is theorized here as the "methodology of the oppressed." See *Gender Trouble: Feminism and the Subversion of Identity* (New York: Routledge, 1990).

19. For excellent work on third space feminism see Emma Pérez, "Feminism-in-Nationalism: Third Space Feminsim at the Yucatan Feminist Congresses of 1916," in Norma Alarcón, Caren Kaplan, and Minoo Moallen, eds., *Between Women and Nation: Transnational Feminisms and the State* (Durham: Duke University Press, forthcoming). On transnational feminisms see *Scattered Hegemonies: Postmodernity and Transnational Feminist Practices*, ed. Inderpal Grewal and Caren Kaplan (Minneapolis: University of Minnesota Press, 1994). The work on *la conciencia de la mestiza, la facultad, coatlique*, and *nepantla* is by Gloria Anzaldúa in *Borderlands*. See also Pat Mora, *Nepantla: Essays from the Land in the Middle* (Albuquerque: University of New Mexico Press, 1993). For the relationship of the differential and *la conciencia de la mestiza* to "cyberspace," see Chéla Sandoval, "Re-Entering Cyberspace: New Sciences of Resistance" in the journal *Dispositio: Subaltern Studies*, XIX, 75-93, eds., José Rabassa, et al., 1996.

20. Gloria Anzaldúa, "Introduction: Haciendo Caras, Una Entrada," in *Making Face, Making Soul, Haciendo Caras: Creative and Critical Perspectives by Feminists of Color*, ed., Gloria Anzaldúa (San Francisco: Aunt Lute, 1990).

General References on U.S. Third World Feminism

Allen, Paula Gunn. "Beloved Women: The Lesbian in American Indian Culture." *Conditions* 7 (1981): 37-49.

Anzaldúa, Gloria. *Borderlands, The New Mestiza*. San Francisco: Aunt Lute, 1987.

____, ed. *Haciendo Caras, Making Face, Making Soul: Writings by Feminists of Color*. San Francisco: Aunt Lute, 1990.

Bambara, Toni Cade, ed. *The Black Woman, An Anthology*. New York: New American Library, 1970.

Beale, Francis. *Third World Women*. New York: Third World Newsletter, 1971.

Brant, Beth, ed. *A Gathering of Spirit: A Collection by North American Indian Women*. Ithaca: Firebrand Books, 1988.

Fisher, Dexter, ed. *The Third Woman: Minority Women Writers of the United States*. Boston: Houghton Mifflin, 1980.

Hancock, Velia. *Chicano Studies Newsletter*. Berkeley: Chicano Studies Collective, 1970.

hooks, bell. *Ain't I A Woman: Black Women and Feminism.* Boston: South End Press, 1981.

Hull, Gloria, Patricia Bell Scott, and Barbara Smith, eds. *All the Blacks Are Men, All the Women Are White, But Some of Us Are Brave.* New York: Feminist Press, 1982.

Hurtado, Aída. "Reflections on White Feminism: A Perspective From a Woman of Color." Circulating unpublished manuscript, 1988.

Katz, Jane. *I Am the Fire of Time–Voices of Native American Women.* New York: Dutton, 1977.

Lorde, Audre. *Sister, Outsider.* New York: Crossing Press, 1984.

___. *Zami: A New Spelling of My Name.* Boston: Persephone Press, 1982.

Mirikitani, Janice, ed. *Third World Women.* San Francisco: Glide Publications, 1973.

___. *Time to Greez! Incantations from the Third World.* San Francisco: Glide Publications, 1975.

Mohanty, Chandra Talpado. "Cartographies of Struggle: Third World Women and the Politics of Feminism," in *Third World Women and the Politics of Feminism.* Edited by Chandra Talpado Mohanty, Anne Russo, and Lourdes Torres. Bloomington: Indiana University Press, 1991.

Moraga, Cherríe. *Loving in the War Years.* Boston: South End Press, 1983.

Moraga, Cherríe, and Gloria Anzaldúa, eds. *This Bridge Called My Back: Writings by Radical Women of Color.* New York: Kitchen Table/ Women of Color Press, 1981.

Moraga, Cherríe, and Amber Hollibaugh. "What We're Rolling Around in Bed With." *Heresies* (1981): 26-38.

Morrison, Toni. *Sula.* New York: Knopf, 1973.

Nieto-Gomez, Anna. "Sexism in the Movimento." *La Gente* 6, no.4 (1976): 8-12.

Noda, Barbara. "Lowriding Through the Women's Movement." In *This Bridge Called My Back: Writings by Radical Women of Color,* edited by Cherríe Moraga, and Gloria Anzaldúa, 138-139. New York: Kitchen Table/Women of Color Press, 1981.

Reagon, Bernice. "Coalition Politics: Turning the Century." In *Home Girls,* edited by Barbara Smith. New York: Kitchen Table/Women of Color Press, 1983.

Sandoval, Chéla. "U.S. Third World Feminism: The Theory and Method of Oppositional Consciousness in the Postmodern World." *Genders* 10 (1991): 1-36.

Trinh Minh Ha. *Woman Native Other.* Bloomington: Indiana University Press, 1989.

Torres, Lourdes, Chandra Mohanty, and Anne Russo, eds. *Third*

World Women and the Politics of Feminism. Bloomington: Indiana University Press, 1991.

Witt, Shirley Hill. "Native Women Today: Sexism and the Indian Woman." *Civil Rights Digest* 6 (Spring 1974): 8-16.

Woo, Merle. "Letters to Ma." In *This Bridge Called My Back: Writings by Radical Women of Color,* edited by Cherríe Moraga, and Gloria Anzaldúa, 140-147. New York: Kitchen Table/Women of Color Press, 1981.

Chicana Feminism: In the Tracks of "The" Native Woman

Norma Alarcón

As Spain prepared to celebrate the quincentenary of "the dis-covery," in 1992, contemporary Chicanas had been deliber-ating on the force of significations of that event. It took almost 400 years for the territory that today we call Mexico to ac-quire a cohesive national identity and sovereignty. Centuries passed before the majority of the inhabitants were able to call themselves Mexican citizens. As a result, on the Mexican side of the hyphen in the designation Mexican-American, Chicanas rethink their involvement in Mexico's turbulent colonial and postcolonial history, while also reconsidering, on the Ameri-can side, their involvement in the capitalist neocolonization of the population of Mexican descent in the United States (Barrera et al. 1972).

In the 1960s, armed with a post-Mexican-American criti-cal consciousness, some people of Mexican descent in the United States recuperated, appropriated, and recodified the term Chicano to form a new political class (Acuña 1972; Muñoz 1989). Initially, the new appellation left the entrenched (middle-class) intellectuals mute, because it emerged from the oral usage in working-class communities. In effect, the new name measured the distance between the excluded and the few who had found a place for themselves in Anglo-America. The new Chicano political class began to work on the hy-phen, eager to redefine the economic, racial, cultural, and po-litical position of the people. The appropriation and recodifi-cation of the term Chicano from oral culture was a stroke of insight precisely because it unsettled all of the identities con-ferred by previous historical accounts. The apparently well-documented terrains of the dyad Mexico/United States were repositioned and reconfigured through the inclusion of the excluded in the very interiority of culture, knowledge, and the political economy. Thus, the demand for a Chicano/a history became a call for the recovery and rearticulation of the record to include the stories of race/class relations of the silenced against whom the very notions of being Mexican or not-Mexican, being American or not-American, and being a citizen or not a citizen had been constructed. In brief, the call for a story of Chicanas/os has not turned out to be a "definitive" culture as some dreamed. Rather the term itself, in body and mind, has become a critical site of political, ideological, and discursive struggle through which the notion of "definitiveness" and hegemonic tendencies are placed in question.

Though the formation of the new political Chicano class was dominated by men, Chicana feminists have intervened from the beginning. The early Chicana intervention is available in the serials and journals that mushroomed in tandem with the alternative press in the United States in the 1960s and 1970s. Unfortunately, much of that early work by Chicanas often goes unrecognized, which is indicative of the process of erasure and exclusion of raced ethnic women within a patriarchal cultural and political economy. In the 1980s, however, there has been a reemergence of Chicana writers and scholars, who have not only repositioned the Chicano political class through a feminist register but who have joined forces with an emergent women-of-color political class that has national and international implications (McLaughlin 1990).

In the United States, the 1980s were, according to the Ronald Reagan administration, the decade of the Hispanic—a neoconservative move assisted by the U.S. Census Bureau (Giménez 1989) and the mass media to homogenize all people of Latin American descent and occlude their heterogeneous histories of resistance to domination, in other words, the counter-histories to invasions and conquests. At the same time, in the 1980s, a more visible Chicana feminist intervention has given new life to a stalled Chicano movement (Rojas 1989). In fact, in the United States, this appears to be the case among most raced ethnic minorities. By including feminist and gender analysis into the emergent political class, Chicanas are reconfiguring the meaning of cultural and political resistance and redefining the hyphen in the name Mexican-American (Anzaldúa and Moraga 1983; Alarcón 1989, 1990).

To date, most writers and scholars of Mexican descent refuse to give up the term Chicana. Despite the social reaccommodation of many as Hispanics or Mexican-Americans, it is the consideration of the excluded evoked by the name Chicana that provides the position for multiple cultural critiques–between and within, inside and outside, centers and margins. Working-class and peasant women–perhaps the "last colony," as a recent book announces (Mies et al. 1989)–are most keenly aware of this. As a result, when many a writer of such racialized cultural history explores her identity, a reflectory and refractory position is depicted. In the words of Gloria Anzaldúa:

> She has this fear
> that she has no names
> that she has many names
> that she doesn't know her names
> She has this fear
> that she's an image
> that comes and goes
> clearing and darkening
> the fear that she's the dreamwork inside
>   someone else's skull . . .
> She has this fear that if she digs into herself
> she won't find anyone
> that when she gets "there"
> she won't find her notches on the trees . . .
> She has this fear that she won't find the way
>   back (1987, 43)

The quest for a true self and identity, which was the initial desire of many writers involved in the Chicano movement of the late 1960s and early 1970s, has given way to the realization that there is no fixed identity. "I" or "She," as observed by Anzaldúa, is composed of multiple layers without necessarily yielding an uncontested "origin." In the words of Trinh T. Minh-ha, "Things may be said to be what they are, not exclusively in relation to what was and what will be (they should not solely be seen as clusters chained together by the temporal sequence of cause and effect), but also in relation to each other's immediate presences and to themselves as non/ presences" (1989, 94). Thus, the name Chicana, in the present, is the name of resistance that enables cultural and political points of departure and thinking through the multiple migrations and dislocations of women of "Mexican" descent. The name Chicana is not a name that women (or men) are born to or with, as is often the case with "Mexican," but rather it is consciously and critically assumed and serves as point of redeparture for dismantling historical conjunctures of crisis, confusion, political and ideological conflict, and contradictions of the simultaneous effects of having "no names," having "many names," not "know[ing] her names," and being someone else's "dreamwork." Digging into the historically despised dark (*prieto*) body in strictly psychological terms may get her to the bare bones and marrow, but she may not "find the way back," to writing her embodied histories. The idea of plural historicized bodies is proposed with respect to the multiple racial constructions of the body since "the discovery." To name a few, indigenous (evoking the extant as well as extinct tribes), *criolla, morisca, loba, cambuja, barcina, coyota, samba, mulatta, china, chola.* The contemporary assumption of *mestizaje* (hybridism) in the Mexican nation-making process was intended to racially colligate a heterogeneous population that was not European. On the American side of the hyphen, *mestizas* are non-white, thus further reducing the cultural and historical experience of Chicanas. However, the *mestiza* concept is always already bursting its boundaries. While some have "forgotten" the *mestiza* genealogy, others claim an indigenous, black or Asian one as well. In short, the body, certainly for the past 500 years in the Américas, has been always already racialized. As tribal "ethnicities" are broken down by conquest and colonizations, bodies are often multiply racialized and dislocated as if they had no other contents. The effort to recontextualize the processes recovers, speaks for, or gives voice to, women on the bottom of a historically hierarchical economic and political structure (Spivak 1988).

It is not coincidental that as Chicana writers reconstruct the multiple names of *mestiza* and Indian, social scientists and historians find them in the segmented labor force or in the grip of armed struggles. In fact, most of these women have been (and continue to be) the surplus sources of cheap labor in the field, the canneries, the maquiladora border industries, and domestic service. The effort to pluralize the racialized body by redefining part of their experience through the reappropriation of "the" native woman on Chicana feminist terms marked one of the first assaults on male-centered cultural nationalism on the one hand (Alarcón 1989), and patriarchal political economy on the other (Melville 1980; Mora et al. 1980; Córdova et al. 1986; Ruiz and Tiano 1987; Zavella 1987).

The native woman has many names also—Coatlicue, Cihuacoátl, Ixtacihuátl, and so on. In fact, one has only to consult the dictionary of *Mitología Nahuátl*, for example, to discover many more that have not been invoked. For many writers, the point is not so much to recover a lost "utopia" nor the "true" essence of our being; although, of course, there are those who long for the "lost origins," as well as those who feel a profound spiritual kinship with the "lost"—a spirituality whose resistant political implications must not be underestimated, but refocused for feminist change (Allen 1988). The most relevant point in the present is to understand how a pivotal indigenous portion of the *mestiza* past may represent a collective female experience as well as "the mark of the Beast" within us—the maligned and abused indigenous woman (Anzaldúa 1987, 43). By invoking the "dark Beast" within and without, which many have forced us to deny, the cultural and psychic dismemberment that is linked to imperialist racist and sexist practices are brought into focus. These practices are not a thing of the past either. One has only to recall the contemporary massacres of the Indian population of Guatemala, for example, or the continuous "democratic" interventionist tactics in Central and South America, which often result in the violent repression of the population.

It is not surprising, then, that many Chicana writers explore their racial and sexual experience in poetry, narrative, essay, testimony, and autobiography through the evocation of indigenous figures. This is a strategy that Gloria Anzaldúa uses and calls "La herencia de Coatlicue/The Coatlicue state." The "state" is, paradoxically, an ongoing process, a continuous effort of consciousness to make "sense" of it all. Every step is a "travesía, a crossing," because "every time she makes 'sense' of something, she has to 'cross over,' kicking a hole out of the old boundaries of the self and slipping under or over, dragging the old skin along, stumbling over it" (Anzaldúa 1987, 48, 49). The contemporary subject-in-process is not just what Hegel would have us call the *Aufhebung*–that is, the effort to unify consciousness "is provided by the simultaneous negation and retention of past forms of consciousness within a radical recomprehension of the totality" (Warren 1984, 37)–as Anzaldúa's passage also suggests. The complex effort to unify, however tenuously, Chicanas' consciousness, which is too readily viewed as representing "postmodern fragmented identities" entails not only Hegel's *Aufhebung* with respect to Chicanas' immediate personal subjectivity as raced and sexed bodies but also an understanding of all past negations as communitarian subjects in a doubled relation to cultural recollection, and re-membrance, and to our contemporary presence and non-presence in the sociopolitical and cultural milieu. All of which together enable both individual and group identity as oppressed racialized women. In order to achieve unification, the Chicana position, previously "empty" of meanings, emerges as one who has to "make sense" of it all from the bottom through the recodification of the native woman. As such, the so-called postmodern decentered subject–a decentralization which implies diverse, multiply constructed subjects and historical conjunctures–insofar as she desires liberation must move towards provisional solidarities, especially through social movements. In this fashion, one may recognize the endless production of differences to destabilize group or collective identities, on the one hand, and the need for group solidarities to overcome oppressions through an understanding of the mechanisms at work, on the other (McLaughlin 1990; Kauffman 1990).

The strategic invocation and recodification of "the" native woman in the present has the effect of conjoining the historical repression of the "non-civilized" dark woman–which continues to operate through "regulative psychobiographies" of good and evil women, such as that of Guadalupe, Malinche, Llorona, and many others–with the present moment of speech that counters such repressions (Spivak 1989, 227). It is worth-while to remember that the historical founding moment of the construction of *mestiza(o)* subjectivity entails the rejection and denial of the dark Indian Mother as Indian, which has compelled women to often collude in silence against them-selves and to actually deny the Indian position even as that position is visually stylized and represented in the making of the fatherland. Within these blatant contradictions, the over-valuation of Europeanness is constantly at work. Thus, Mexico constructs its own ideological version of the notorious Anglo-American "melting pot" under the sign of *mestizo(a)*. The un-masking, however, becomes possible for Chicanas as they are put through the crisis of the Anglo-American experience, where ("melting pot") whiteness, not *mestizaje,* has been con-structed as the Absolute Idea of Goodness and Value. In the Américas, then, the native woman as ultimate sign of the po-tential reproduction of *barbarie* (savagery) has served as the sign of consensus for most others, men and women. Women, under penalty of the double-bind charge of "betrayal" of the fatherland (in the future tense) and the mother tongues (in the past tense), are often compelled to acquiesce with the "civiliz-ing" new order in male terms. Thus, for example, the "rights" of women in Nicaragua disappear vis-à-vis the democratizing forces of the U.S., the church's "civilizing-of-women" project, and traditional sexisms notwithstanding Sandinista intentions (Molyneux 1985). In this scenario, to speak at all then, "the" native woman has to legitimize her position by becoming a "mother" in hegemonic patriarchal terms, which is near to impossible to do unless she is "married" or racially "related" to the right men (Hurtado 1989). As a result, the contempo-rary challenge to the multiple negations and rejections of the native racialized woman in the Américas is like few others.

For Chicanas, the consideration of the ideological construc-tions of the "non-civilized" dark woman brings into view a most sobering reference point: The overwhelming majority of the workers in maquiladoras, for example, are *mestizas* who have been forcefully subjected not only to the described pro-cesses but to many others that await disentanglement. Many of those workers are "single," unprotected within a cultural order that has required the masculine protection of women to ensure their "decency," indeed to ensure that they are "civilized" in sexual and racial terms. In fact, as Spivak and others have suggested, "the new army of 'permanent casual' labor working below the minimum wage–[are] these women [who today] represent the international neo-colonial subject paradigmatically" (Spivak 1989, 223). These women (and some men) who were subjected to the Hispanic New World "feudal mode of power" (which in Mexico gave way to the construction of *mestizo* nationalism), and who were subjected to an Anglo-American "feudal mode of power" in the isolation of migrant worker camps and exchange labor (which in the U.S. gave rise to Chicano cultural nationalism of the 1960s), in the 1990s find themselves in effect separated in many instances from men who heretofore had joined forces in resistance. Though work in the fields continues to be done with kinship groupings, the "communal mode of power" under the sign of the cultural nationalist family may be bankrupt, especially for female wage-workers. Although, of course, the attempt to bring men and women together under the conservative notions of the "family" continues as well. In this instance "family" may be a misnaming in lieu of a search for a more apt name for community solidarity.

Whether working as domestic servants, canners, or in the service industry in the United States, or as electronic assemblers along the U.S./Mexican border, these "new" women-subjects find themselves bombarded and subjected to multiple cross-cultural and contradictory ideologies–a maze of discourses through which the "I" as a racial and gendered self is hard put to emerge and runs the risk of being thought of as "irrational" or "deluded" in her attempt to articulate her oppression and exploitation. In the face of Anglo-European literacy and capitalist industrialization, which interpellates them as individuals, for example, and the "communal mode of power" (as mode of defeudalization) (Spivak 1989, 224), which interpellates them as "Mothers" (the bedrock of the "ideal family" at the center of the nation-making process, despite discontinuous modes of its construction), the figure and referent of Chicanas today is positioned as conflictively as Lyotard's "differend." She is the descendant of native women who are continuously transformed into *mestizas*, Mexicans, émigrés to

Anglo-America, "Chicanas," Latinas, Hispanics—there are as many names as there are namers.

Lyotard defines a differend as "a case of conflict, between (at least) two parties, that cannot be equitably resolved for lack of a rule of judgment applicable to both arguments. One side's legitimacy does not imply the other's lack of legitimacy" (Lyotard 1988, xi). In appropriating the concept as a metonym for both the figure and referent of the Chicana, for example, it is important to note that though it enables us to locate and articulate sites of ideological and discursive conflict, it cannot inform the actual Chicana differend engaged in a living struggle as to how she can seize her "I" or even her feminist "We" to change her circumstances without bringing into play the axes in which she finds herself in the present—culturally, politically, and economically.

The call for elaborated theories based on the "flesh and blood" experiences of women of color in *This Bridge Called My Back* (Anzaldúa and Moraga 1983) may mean that the Chicana feminist project must interweave the following critiques and critical operations: (1) multiple cross-cultural analyses of the ideological constructions of raced "Chicana" subjects in relation to the differently positioned cultural constructions of all men and some Anglo-European women; (2) negotiations of strategic political transitions from cultural constructions and contestations to "social science" studies and referentially grounded "Chicanas" in the political economy who live out their experiences in heterogenous social and geographic positions. (Though not all women of Mexican/Hispanic descent would call themselves Chicanas, I would argue that it is an important point of departure for critiques and critical operations (on the hyphen/bridge) that keep the excluded within any theory-making project. That is, in the Mexican-descent continuum of meanings, Chicana is still the name that brings into focus the interrelatedness of class/race/gender into play and forges the link to actual subaltern native women in the U.S./Mexico dyad.) In negotiating points one and two, (3) how can we work with literary, testimonial, and pertinent ethnographic materials to enable "Chicanas" to grasp their "I" and "We" in order to make effective political interventions? This implies that we must select from the range of cultural productions, in dialogue with women, those materials that actually enable the emergence of "I/We" subjectivities (Castellano 1990).

Given the extensive ideological sedimentation of the (Silent) Good Woman and the (Speech-producing) Bad Woman that enabled the formations of the cultural nationalist "communal modes of power," Chicana feminists have an enormous mandate to make "sense" of it all, as Anzaldúa desires. It requires no less than the deconstruction of paternalistic "communal modes of power," which is politically perilous, since often it appears to be the "only" model of empowerment that the oppressed have, although it has ceased to function for many women as development and post-industrial social research indicates. Also, it requires the thematization and construction of new models of political agency for women of color, who are always already positioned cross-culturally and within contradictory discourses. As we consider the diffusion of mass media archetypes and stereotypes of all women, which continuously interpellate them into the patriarchal order according to their class, race (ethnicity), and gender, the "mandate" is (cross-culturally) daunting. Yet, "agent provocateurs" know that mass media and popular cultural production are always open to contestations and recodifications which can become sites of resistance (Castellano 1990).

Thus, the feminist Chicana, activist, writer, scholar, and intellectual has to, on the one hand, locate the point of theoretical and political consensus with other feminists (and "feminist" men), and on the other, continue with projects that position her in paradoxical binds. For example, breaking out of ideological boundaries that subject her in culturally specific ways, and not crossing over to cultural and political areas that subject her as "individual/autonomous/neutralized" laborer. Moreover, to reconstruct differently the raced and gendered "I's" and "We's" also calls for a rearticulation of the "You's" and "They's." Traversing the processes may well enable us to locate points of differences and identities in the present to forge the needed solidarities against repression and oppression. Or, as Lorde (1984) and Spivak (1988) would have it, locate the "identity-in-difference" of cultural and political struggle.

Author's Note

I would like to thank Gloria Anzaldúa, Rosa Linda Fregoso, Francine Masiello, and Margarita Melville for their reading and comments on this essay. Responsibility for the final version is, of course, mine.

Works Cited

Acuña, Rodolfo. 1972. *Occupied America: The Chicano's Struggle Toward Liberation.* San Francisco: Canfield Press.

Alarcón, Norma. 1989. "Traddutora, Traditora: A Paradigmatic Figure of Chicana Feminism." *Cultural Critique* 13.

___. 1990. "The Theoretical Subject(s) in *This Bridge Called My Back* and Anglo-American Feminism." In *Haciendo Caras/Making Face Making Soul,* edited by Gloria Anzaldúa. San Francisco: Spinsters/Aunt Lute.

Allen, Paula Gunn. 1988. "Who Is Your Mother? Red Roots of White Feminism." In *The Graywolf Annual Five: Multicultural Literacy,* edited by Rick Simonson and Scott Walker, 13-17. Saint Paul, Minn.: Graywolf Press.

Anzaldúa, Gloria. 1987. *Borderlands/La Frontera: The New Mestiza.* San Francisco: Spinsters/Aunt Lute.

Anzaldúa, Gloria, and Cherríe Moraga, eds. 1983. *This Bridge Called My Back: Writings By Radical Women of Color.* New York: Kitchen Table/Women of Color Press. (Published initially in 1981 by Persephone Press, Watertown, Mass.)

Barrera, Mario, et al. 1972. "The Barrio as Internal Colony." In *People and Politics in Urban Society,* edited by Harlan Hahn, 465-498. Los Angeles: Sage.

Castellano, Oliva. 1990. "Canto Locura y Poesía: The Teacher as Agent-Provocateur." *The Women's Review of Books* 8 (5): 18-20.

Córdova, Teresa, et al., eds. 1986. *Chicana Voices: Intersections of Class, Race, and Gender.* Austin, Tex.: Center for Mexican American Studies.

Giménez, Martha. 1989. "The Political Construction of the Hispanic." In *Estudios Chicanos and the Politics of Community,* edited by Mary Romero, and Cordelia Candelaria, 66-85. Boulder, Colo.: National Association for Chicano Studies.

Hurtado, Aída. 1989. "Relating to Privilege: Seduction and Rejection in the Subordination of White Women and Women of Color."

Signs: Journal of Women and Culture and Society 14 (4): 833-855.

Kauffman, L. A. 1990. "The Anti-Politics of Identity." *Socialist Review* 1: 67-80.

Lorde, Audre. 1984. *Sister/Outsider.* Trumansburg, N.Y.: Crossing Press.

Lyotard, Jean-Francois. 1988. *The Differend: Phrases in Dispute.* Translated by Georges Van den Abbeele. Minneapolis: University of Minnesota Press.

McLaughlin, Andrée Nicola. 1990. "Black Women, Identity, and the Quest for Humanhood and Wholeness: Wild Women in the Whirlwind." In *Wild Women in the Whirlwind,* edited by Joanne Braxton and Andrée McLaughlin, 147-180. New Brunswick: Rutgers University Press.

Melville, Margarita, ed. 1980. *Twice a Minority: Mexican American Women.* St. Louis: C. V. Mosby.

Mies, Maria, et al., eds. 1989. *Women: The Last Colony.* London: Zed.

Molyneux, Maxine. 1985. "Mobilization Without Emancipation: Women's Interests, The State, and Revolution in Nicaragua." *Feminist Studies* 11 (2): 227-254.

Mora, Magdalena, and Adelaide R. del Castillo, eds. 1980. *Mexican Women in the United States: Struggles Past and Present.* Los Angeles: Chicano Studies Research Center, University of California.

Muñoz, Carlos. 1989. *Youth, Identity, Power: The Chicano Movement.* London: Verso.

Rojas, Guillermo. 1989. "Social Amnesia and Espistemology in Chicano Studies." In *Estudios Chicanos and The Politics of Community,* edited by Mary Romero and Cordelia Candelaria, 54-65. Boulder, Colo.: National Association for Chicano Studies.

Ruiz, Vicki L., and Susan Tiano, eds. 1987. *Women on the U.S.-Mexican Border: Responses to Change.* Winchester, Mass.: Allen & Unwin.

Spivak, Gayatri C. 1988. "Can the Subaltern Speak?" In *Marxism and the Interpretation of Culture,* edited by Cary Nelson and Lawrence Grossbery. Chicago: University of Illinois Press.

___. 1989. "The Political Economy of Women as Seen by a Literary Critic." In *Coming to Terms: Feminism, Theory, Politics,* edited by Elizabeth Weed, 218-229. London: Routledge.

Trinh T. Minh-ha. 1989. *Women/Native/Other.* Bloomington: Indiana University Press.

Warren, Scott. 1984. *The Emergence of Dialectical Theory: Philosophy and Political Inquiry.* Chicago: University of Chicago Press.

Zavella, Patricia. 1987. *Women's Work and Chicano Families: Cannery Workers of the Santa Clara Valley.* Ithaca: Cornell University Press.

The Politics of Sexuality in the Gender Subordination of Chicanas

Aída Hurtado

> The sense of submission and docility that we see is not about that, it's about survival . . . a powerful mechanism. It's like when you're in the ocean and a shark is coming; if you stay still, it'll go right by you. If you can stay still enough, and you survive it, then you can go on, and do what you have to do. But the nuances and the dynamics are intricate. It's like a dance in a person's life, and it's a continuous conflict about which it is tremendously difficult to make conclusive remarks. (Interview with Ana Castillo, writer and artist, Navarro 1991, 132)

One of the challenges for feminist theory is to begin the documentation of culturally specific ways that gender subordination is imposed. If subordination is relational, then so is power. However, this is not to be confused with structural power which is institutionalized and independent of the actors that are cast as its inheritors. But in order to understand the specificity of the subordination of women, and before a multicultural feminism can be built, it is necessary to examine different ethnic/racial groups in the United States. The opportunity for this shift in the research lens comes from the development of many feminisms (Marks and de Courtivron 1981; Collins 1991; Anzaldúa 1990; hooks 1984, 1990; Cotera 1977; Brant 1984; Sandoval 1991; Segura 1994; Pesquera 1994; de la Torre and Pesquera 1993; Zavella 1994a; Fernández 1994). Gender is now conceptualized by many feminist theorists as the result of power relations between the sexes rather than as a binary biological category. This theoretical shift away from biological determinism provides an aperture to theorize about how race and class affect gender relations in our society because it allows for diversity in the expression of the "essential" natures of women and men. That is, every society has "normative conceptions of attitudes and activities appropriate for one's sex category" that help to "bolster claims to membership in a sex category" (West and Zimmerman 1987, 127). Not all groups in U.S. society ascribe to the same definitions of "womanhood" and "manhood" (Brod 1987; Stoltenberg 1993; Connell 1995; Zavella 1994a, 206). There is systematic variation according to race and class (Hurtado 1989; hooks 1981, 1989). White feminist theorists have made impressive contributions to the understanding of gender as manifested among white middle class people (Jaggar 1983). The incisiveness of their analysis has also advanced our understanding of the lives of all women regardless of race and class. Only recently, however, have feminist theorists begun to explore the socioculturally specific ways in which gender is accomplished and ultimately used to allocate privilege and to impose subordination (West and Fenstermaker 1993, 151-174). Some feminist theoreticians propose that women of Color are triply oppressed by their race, class, and gender (Zavella 1987; Pesquera 1985; Segura 1984; hooks 1984) and we now need to elucidate the intragroup relations that restrict women's spheres of action.

There is a growing body of feminist theory produced by women of Color, although as a group they have not had as much access as white feminists to traditional forms of theorizing. However, feminist thought has also been generated by women of Color through everyday verbal interaction and through creative production such as poetry and song. Consequently, the broadening of the paradigm of how gender is conceptualized also requires that other materials besides conventional academic production be used to theorize about women of Color. Patricia Hill Collins (1986) proposes the use of oral histories to uncover feminist thought in African American communities, and Alvina Quintana (1989, 189) advocates the use of literary texts to see Chicanas as "their own ethnographers." I propose to use a combination of both of these suggestions. In this chapter I use the analysis of the oral histories collected by Yolanda Broyles (1986, 1994) that chronicle the role of women in El Teatro Campesino and poetry written by Chicanas and Chicanos to elucidate how *intragroup* sexism is imposed within structurally subordinated Chicano communities. I intertwine the oral histories of Chicanas in El Teatro Campesino and the conflicts generated by gender issues among the actors with the use of poetry to further elucidate how gender subordination is imposed on Chicanas by members of their own group. I do not analyze the actual portrayals of Chicanas in El Teatro Campesino, mostly because the plays were primarily written by Luis Valdez from a man's perspective. I am interested in how the women in El Teatro Campesino dealt with Valdez's constructions and how they struggled with the male actors in trying to broaden El Teatro Campesino's portrayal of women. When I turn to the use of literary texts, I do use poetry written by men to contrast how they see women and then how women see themselves. Unfortunately, there was no simultaneous production of plays by women in El Teatro Campesino, so I am unable to use this device to further elucidate the gender dynamics in this arena.

The Beginnings of El Teatro Campesino

El Teatro Campesino is a theatrical group that was formed in 1965 by Luis Valdez in Delano, California. Its initial purpose was to support César Chávez and the farm workers' unionization struggle by performing improvised political skits urging farm workers to join the United Farm Workers Union (UFW) (Sánchez 1985). Although it severed its ties with the UFW in 1967, El Teatro Campesino currently operates as an independent theatrical company producing plays written by Luis Valdez and exploring new avenues of artistic expression (Diamond 1977). Its most recent accomplishments include the play (and eventual film) *Zoot Suit* and the film *La Bamba.*

From the beginning, El Teatro Campesino's goal was to represent the collective social vision of Chicanos and to reflect all that is valued in these communities: family ties, preservation of the Spanish language, Chicano culture, and political mobilization.[1] The main dramatic device developed by El Teatro was *el acto*–short, one-act skits with rapid dialogue, sharp wit, incorporating a critique of the day's events. The purpose of *el acto,* in Luis Valdez's words, was to "inspire the audience to social action. Illuminate specific points about social problems. Satirize the opposition. Show or hint at a solution. Express what people are feeling" (Valdez 1971, 6).

The emphasis of *el acto*, unlike that of other dramatic forms, was not to express the individual vision of Luis Valdez as a dramatist and an artist but the collective social vision of Chicano communities. As such, the characters in *el acto* are archetypes that are supposed to be representative of *La Raza*[2] and therefore particularly helpful in uncovering the collective representations of gender in Chicano communities. It is not surprising that El Teatro Campesino's treatment of intimacy, cultural nationalism, and political goals reproduces the intragroup gender dynamics found in Chicano communities.

The Stage as Metaphor

Of the many analyses of El Teatro Campesino (Frischmann 1982; Ramírez 1974; Morton 1974; Xavier 1983; Broyles 1986; Bruce-Novoa 1988; Yarbro-Bejarano 1985, 1986; Huerta 1982), only a few (Broyles 1986, 1994; Yarbro-Bejarano 1985, 1986) focus on the position of Chicanas within the troop. Broyles's (1986) analysis, in particular, shows that "the stereotyped roles found in the work of El Teatro Campesino are in many ways related to the stereotyped views of Chicanas found within society at large" (164). More succinctly, art imitates life.[3] Using El Teatro Campesino as metaphor–and in particular the stage where the plays get acted out–I explore how Chicanas experience gender subordination.

The Definition of Chicana Sexuality

The construction of Chicanas' sexuality is at the core of the gender dynamics that results in sexism in Chicano families and communities (Pérez 1993, 51-71; Zavella 1994a, 206). By and large, the women characters in El Teatro Campesino are cast into one of two roles: whores or virgins (putas/vírgenes). In the interstices of the bipolar conception of Chicanas' sexuality is the *neuter woman*–one who does not fit either sexual pole. In Teatro, this *neuter* role takes the form of allegorical characters that are neither men or women like *la Muerte* (Death) or *el Diablo* (the Devil).[4] In Chicano communities, the neuter woman is represented by what Abelardo Delgado (1978) calls the femme-macho, the woman who is attractive to men because she is strong and powerful but not a whore or meek like a wife. In fact, her psychological characteristics are grotesquely exaggerated, so much so that none of them are human. The femme-macho's sexuality, in particular, is so accentuated and objectified that she is in effect neutered.

In El Teatro Compesino, as in Chicano communities, the assignment into the categories of "virgins" or "whores" is based largely on physical characteristics and a woman's assertiveness and strength. The *virgin* is the woman who is small, fragile, fair-skinned, and has a pretty face.[5] In El Teatro, she is referred to as "soft." The potential *whore* is an Indian-looking woman who speaks up and is "difficult." Broyles (1986) says that this rigid dichotomy reflects *offstage* judgment of the female actors. Socorro Valdez (Luis Valdez's sister), a longtime actor in Teatro Campesino, describes the "rigidification process" as follows:

> As it were, the actresses that were "soft" offstage and just *muy buenas, muy buenas* [very nice, very nice] got the "soft roles." And the ladies that were *medias cabronas* [tough] and had a beer and a cigarette hanging out of their mouth, well you know what role they got . . . I always ended up with that other stuff. I know those choices. And I know there were moments in the group when there was to be a "girlfriend." Well, can Socorro be the girlfriend? No, Socorro can't be the girlfriend. Socorro is either the old lady or she's the jokester. But I was never in this company as a "soft" woman, because they confuse softness and hardness and they attach those two things to strength or weakness. But there is no such thing in my mind. You can't put those two things together like that. They fluctuate. (Broyles 1986, 171)

The femme-macho, unlike the virgin or the whore, can either be attractive or unattractive. A strong personality is what characterizes her. The strength of the femme-macho does not lie in her racial/physical appearance but rather on remaining emotionally uninvolved, though sexually active. The man's challenge is to deflower the femme-macho emotionally; the power of the femme-macho is to remain an emotional virgin. The Achilles' heel of the femme-macho is her emotions. However, she will only be punished for showing particular emotions. The femme-macho can be sarcastic, funny, outrageous, aggressive, mean, or belligerent, but she cannot be tender, loving (except in a political/abstract sense), frightened, or insecure. In fact, femme-machos are always in mortal combat with men to emasculate them and overpower them. Although femme-machos are able to express a wider range of emotions than other kinds of women—and therefore obtain some sense of freedom—they are still emotionally trapped because they are never allowed weakness.

Many Chicanas, struggling to escape the narrow confines of the whore/virgin dichotomy, embrace the femme-macho characteristics as a form of liberation. A prototype of this adaptation is the *persona* cultivated by the popular Mexican movie star María Félix (Taibo 1985). Whereas María Félix came from a working-class background, had no education, was not very talented but was decidedly beautiful, she was able to forge a career in Mexican cinema and reached international acclaim and wealth. There were many beautiful actors in the 1940s and 1950s when María Félix was at the height of her popularity but few who were femme-machos. In fact, most of María Félix's movies consisted of a formula where she was an arrogant, indomitable, and belligerent woman who eventually was tamed by a strong man, like Katherine, in Shakespeare's *The Taming of the Shrew*. However, although most of her movies ended with her submission, in public life she never submitted and instead flaunted her freedom, including her economic independence and her shrewd sense for business (Taibo 1985).[6] The femme-macho also plays with the notion of bisexuality— her taunting is attractive to men because of the morbid curiosity in the potential of watching women make love to each other. María Félix, as a femme-macho, is reported to have had an affair with Frida Kahlo which further enhanced her power because of her defiance of established sexual conventions (Herrera 1983).[7] She even committed the ultimate sin of keeping emotional distance from her only son and did not exalt her motherhood (Fuentes 1967).[8] Carlos Fuentes dramatized this relationship in his novel *Zona Sagrada* (*Sacred Zone*) (1967). In his novel, loosely based on María Félix's life and her relationship with her son, he details the characteristics of the femme-macho. In the novel, the mother goes so far as to emasculate her son by denying her approval (usually the relationship depicted between a powerful father and his son). In the novel, the main character also teases about her potential bisexuality as a further way to threaten men.

Sandra Cisneros (1994, 112) in her poem "Loose Woman" also exalts the characteristics of the femme-macho as a form of liberation:

Loose Woman

They say I'm a beast.
And feast on it. When all along
I thought that's what a woman was.

They say I'm a bitch.
Or witch. I've claimed
the same and never winced.

They say I'm a macha, hell on wheels,
viva-la-vulva, fire and brimstone,
man-hating, devastating,
boogey-woman lesbian.
Not necessarily,
but I like the compliment.

The mob arrives with stones and sticks
to maim and lame and do me in.
All the same, when I open my mouth, they
    wobble like gin.

Diamonds and pearls
tumble from my tongue.

Or toads and serpents.
Depending on the mood I'm in.

I like the itch I provoke.
The rustle of rumor
like crinoline.
I am the woman of myth and bullshit.
(True, I authored some of it.)
I built my little house of ill repute.
Brick by Brick. Labored,
loved and masoned it.

I live like so,
Heart as sail, ballast, rudder, bow.
Rowdy. Indulgent to excess.
My sin and success—
I think of me to gluttony.

By all accounts I am
a danger to society.
I'm Pancha Villa.

I break laws,
upset the natural order,
anguish the Pope and make fathers cry.
I am beyond the jaw of law.
I'm la desperada, most-wanted public enemy.
My happy picture grinning from the wall.

I strike terror among the men.
I can't be bothered what they think.
¡*Que se vayan a la ching chang chong*![9]
For this, the cross, the Calvary.
In other words, I'm anarchy.

I'm an aim-well,
shoot-sharp,
sharp-tongued,
sharp-thinking,
fast-speaking,
foot-loose,
loose-tongued,
let-loose,

woman-on-the-loose
loose woman.
Beware, honey.
I'm Bitch. Beast. Macha.
¡Wachale!
Ping! Ping! Ping!
I break things.

The poet uses hyperbole to exalt the appropriation of the femme-macho gender adaptation. Every single characteristic of the femme-macho is covered in this poem. If women are thought of as less human than men, the poet outright claims her bestiality ("I'm a beast . . . I'm a bitch."). If women are thought of as dangerous because they cannot control their passions (as animals often cannot) and they devour men, the poet "feasts" on the notion and claims herself "a danger to society," a "desperada," who "breaks laws" all the while her "happy picture [is] grinning from the wall." She defies patriarchal power and usurps a male identity for herself by becoming "Pancha Villa"–the only Mexican hero to openly defy the U.S. army at the turn of the century–furthering her transgression by feminizing the name Pancho to Pancha. She rebels against all authority and violates all sacred boundaries, including that of heterosexuality ("[que] viva-la-vulva")and defies the holy father by "anguish[ing] the Pope" as well as "mak[ing] fathers cry." She has fashioned herself into a crime of nature and rejoices in her transgression ("man-hating, devastating, boogeywoman lesbian"). She does not regret, apologize, or otherwise feel anything but passion and power ("Diamonds and pearls/ tumble from my tongue./Or toads and serpents./Depending on the mood I'm in./I like the itch I provoke"). Her emotion is not tempered by sympathetic response to anybody but instead thinks of no one but herself "to gluttony." She relishes her selfishness and laughs out loud at how she is the creator of her own image (not real but made out of bullshit through the appropriation and mockery of hegemonic masculinity). She laughs deep and she laughs hard and at the end only she is left standing because all her accusers have run away in fear ("The mob arrives with stones and sticks/to maim and lame and do me in./All the same, when I open my mouth, they wobble like gin"). And all the while she claims, sarcastically, with an implied wicked smile, this is what she thought "a woman was."

Whereas the femme-macho has her will—her source of strength—whores have no volition. As Emma Pérez (1993, 61) indicates, "For [Octavio] Paz, *la india* personifies the passive whore, who acquiesced to the Spaniard, the conqueror, his symbolic father—the father he despises for choosing an inferior woman who begot an inferior race and the father he fears for his powerful phallus." In El Teatro Campesino's portrayals, whores are not women who give themselves willingly in exchange for a predetermined amount of goods. Instead, they are fallen women and by definition, damaged merchandise. Most important, Chicana *putas* are traitors—traitors to the essence of *la cultura.* As *putas,* Chicanas betray all that is sacred to Chicano/Mexicano culture. At the root of the image of the *puta* is Chicanos' dread of the symbolic meaning of sexual penetration, especially the equation of penetration and the Spanish conquest of México (Paz 1985; Alarcón 1981; Del Castillo 1974; Pérez 1991, 67).

Historically, La Malinche, a woman, is the ultimate traitor of México. La Malinche supposedly facilitated Hernán Córtés's conquest of the Aztec empire by acting as translator between the Spanish and the different Mixteca tribes. From this betrayal modern México is born both figuratively and literally, since La Malinche converted to Catholicism *and* bore the children of Hernán Córtés's soldier Jaramaillo.[10] Thus began Mexican *mestizaje.*[11] La Malinche's betrayal was both *cultural* and *sexual.* El Teatro Campesino's version of La Malinche has emphasized *cultural betrayal.* In *Los Vendidos* [*The Sell-outs*], the antagonist is an assimilated Chicana, Miss Jimenez (pronounced *Jim*enez on stage), who acts as La Malinche by being a tool of the Reagan Administration—the symbolic conqueror Hernán Córtés of California. In *No Saco Nada de la escuela* [*I Don't Get Anything Out of School*], Malinche is Esperanza, who denies her Mexican heritage and wants to "pass" as Hawaiian (Brown 1980). More to the point of cultural betrayal, is the La Malinche in *La Conquista de Mexico* [*The Conquest of Mexico*], who is described for didactic purposes as:

Piedra:[12] This woman was to become infamous in the history of Mexico. Not only did she turn her back on her own people, she joined the white men and became assimilated serving as their guide and interpreter and generally assisting in the conquest. She was the first Mexican-American. (Valdez 1978, 58)

La Malinche in this play further underscores her cultural betrayal by also wanting to "pass" as she distanced herself from the other Indians about to be branded by Hernán Córtes "so I can tell you [them] apart." La Malinche chimes in, "son Indios estúpidos" (they are stupid Indians). When one of the Indians questions her distancing herself from other Indians by calling her a *prieta* (darkie), she replies, "Yo no soy India, I'm Spanish" ("I'm not Indian, I'm Spanish") (Valdez, 58).

Chicana feminists have reinterpreted La Malinche's role in the conquest of México from a traitor to that of a brilliant woman whose ability to learn different languages was unsurpassed by any of her contemporaries. There is historical evidence that demonstrates that la Malinche believed the Spanish would deliver many of her people from the cruelty of the Aztec religion that required human sacrifice. In contrast, Catholicism offered love and compassion as a philosophy of life. She was just as shocked as the rest of her people when the Spanish massacred thousands as they approached the conquest of México City.[13]

However, this recent reinterpretation has not yet displaced the old analysis. For example, Paz (1985) proposes that the conquest of México is a violation and La Malinche represents the violated mother country because she is the mistress to the leader of the conquest. *Mestizos* are "*hijos de la Chingada*"[14] or "the offspring of violation." La Malinche is *la chingada* because she consented to be opened and conquered by Córtes:

The *Chingada* is the Mother forcibly opened, violated or deceived. The *hijo de la Chingada* is the offspring of violation, abduction or deceit. If we compare this expression with the Spanish *hijo de puta* (son of a whore) . . . To the Spaniard, dishonor consists in being the son of a woman who voluntarily surrenders herself: a prostitute. To the Mexican it consists in being the fruit of violation . . . The *Chingada* is the mother who has suffered—metaphorically or actually—the corrosive and defaming action implicit in the verb that gives her name. (Paz, 1985, 79-80, 75)

Although the word *chingar* has many meanings in the Spanish-speaking world, according to Paz (1985, 76-77):

> The verb denotes violence, an emergence from oneself to penetrate another by force . . . *Chingar* . . . is to do violence to another. The verb is masculine, active, cruel: it stings, wounds, gashes, stains. And it provokes a bitter, resentful satisfaction . . . The *chingón*[15] is the macho, the male; he rips open the *chingada*, the female, who is pure passivity, defenseless against the exterior world. The relationship between them is violent, and it is determined by the cynical power of the first and the impotence of the second. The idea of violence rules darkly over all the meanings of the word, and the dialectic of the "closed" and the "open" thus fulfills itself with an almost ferocious precision.

The victim of the violence, *la Chingada*, is not deserving of pity or compassion but is worthless. When virginity, the only gift women have to offer men, is gone, women join the ranks of *las Chingadas*. According to Paz, even if a woman willingly partakes in the act of lovemaking, the fact that she is "penetrated" constitutes a violation. Because woman is conceptualized as not fully human but rather as property (Trujillo 1991, 188) that can be damaged by sexual violation, nothing she does is perceived as a choice (Alarcón 1981, 184). Only femme-machos, who are not really women but a hybrid of *man/woman*, can, to a *certain extent*, have a will. But theirs is not a *human* will (and therefore male) but rather an animalistic will that needs to be tamed. Femme-machos are also the only women who are allowed sexual pleasure. Virgins and wives are not supposed to feel sexual desire but rather see it as a necessary evil to accomplish the higher goal of becoming a mother. As Espín (1984) states:

> To shun sexual pleasure and to regard sexual pleasure as an unwelcome obligation toward her husband and a necessary evil in order to have children may be seen as a manifestation of virtue. In fact, some [Latina] women even express pride at their own lack of sexual pleasure and desire.

The enjoyment of sexual pleasure is particularly threatening in lesbians because they are asserting their sexuality by explicitly choosing the sexual object–other women (Trujillo 1991, 191). Any wife or girlfriend who seems to "enjoy sex" too much is suspect of potentially betraying her possessor (Castillo 1991, 28).

Thus, in Chicano culture, as in many other cultures, women are the possessions of men (Castillo 1991, 28; Navarro 1991, 115) whose virginity determines their property value (Alarcón 1981, 184).[16] Courtship and marriage include very specific rules for measuring the degree to which a woman is damaged merchandise. The least damaged is the virgin, followed by the once-married with children, then the divorced woman with no children (no evidence of having been opened), then the woman who lives with a man. The most damaged is the woman who sleeps with different men, regardless of her motivations for doing so.[17] However, the ultimate violation is committed by women who are opened by other women–lesbians (Trujillo 1991). Once a woman opens herself to another woman, she can never again redeem herself; not even through motherhood. Trujillo (1991, 190) indicates that Chicana lesbians who choose to become mothers are perceived as aberrations of the traditional concept of motherhood.[18] Within Chicanos' cult of virginity, Chicanas have to maneuver to be less rather than more *chingada*.[19] As Alma Villanueva (1978) laments:

> (mamacita)
> when a man opens a woman, she
> is like a rose, she
> will never close
> again.
> ever.

Their redemption as women is possible only through celibacy and, to a lesser extent, marriage because women's potential for betrayal is present from birth. It is in the very fact of being a *woman* that she is suspect and therefore in need of redemption. Redemption through celibacy is obvious because a woman has never been opened; redemption through marriage at least assures that she is open only to spew forth children in the image of *el Chingón.*[20] Femme-machos can to *some degree* escape this categorization but only through a constant battle of wills and wits. They must be prepared to lose strength, to then recover and to keep fighting. A femme-macho who does not fight back also joins the ranks of *Chingadas.*

Not surprisingly, these different sexual categories do not apply to white women. They are not the descendants of La Malinche and therefore do not have the potential for subverting the mestizo race (Pérez 1991, 169). Although lesbians of all races are derogated, the rules about virginity are suspended when white women are evaluated. If anything, white women, as a group, are thought of as sexually immodest because of "their culture." Even though attitudes towards white/Chicano intermarriage are extremely complex, white women are not held accountable as Chicanas to the same standards of proper sexual conduct. Take for example the poem by Mario Garza (1976, 98):

Tus Jefitos
Pobre Chicano
tus jefitos have
  been victimized by
    the gabacho racism.
When you went out
  with a gabacha feminist,
  she neglected you for
    her anglo friends.
She tried to castrate
  your manhood.
Tus jefitos would say,
  "Es gringuita
  es muy linda."
When you went out
  with your second ga-
    bacha,
  she fucked around with
    your best friends.
Tus jefitos would say,
  "Es gringuita
  es muy buena."

Your Parents
Poor Chicano
your parents have
  been victimized by
    white racism.
When you went out
  with a white feminist,
  she neglected you for
    her anglo friends.
She tried to castrate
  your manhood.
Your parents would say,
  "She's a little white one,
  so beautiful."
When you went out
  with your second white
    woman,
  she fucked around with
    your best friends.
Your parents would say,
  "She's a little white one,
  she's very nice."

Now you have a chicana	Now you have a chicana
Chicana like yourself	Chicana like yourself
she loves you	she loves you
she cares for you	she cares for you
she cleans for you	she cleans for you
she cooks for you	she cooks for you
she worries for you	she worries for you
Chicana like yourself	Chicana like yourself
But sometimes	But sometimes
she drinks and dances.	she drinks and dances.
Tus jefitos say,	Your parents say,
"Es chicana	"She's chicana
es muy puta!"	she's a whore!"

The male narrator in this poem is aware of the different, and unfair, standards that his parents apply to Chicanas in comparison to white women. However, the narrator is a mere observer with no apparent role in responding to the accusations, although he benefits from the relationships with these women. Also, the object of the analysis are the women, not his conduct, so there is no way for the reader to judge *in response* to what is the white woman "fucking" around with his best friends, nor do we know whether the Chicana's domestic behavior is a fair exchange in their relationship. Instead, the reader can only assess the behavior of both white and Chicana women as disembodied stereotypes who exist in relationship to an omnipotent and neutral Chicano male. More to the point of the discussion here, however, is the rigid perception of Chicana women—she is the *girlfriend* (who can potentially enter the other rigid role of wife if she behaves accordingly: cleans, cooks, and worries for the implicitly perfect male), who transgresses by acting like a potential whore by drinking and dancing. All her previous "girlfriend" behavior is defaulted by crossing the rigid line through drinking and dancing. Chicanas are effectively fenced in by the threat of accusation of being whores— sexual intercourse outside the protected boundaries of a monogamous heterosexual relationship. The transgression is not the drinking or dancing but the potential of unsanctioned sex.

Interestingly, Andrea Dworkin (1987), a white feminist, also conceptualizes sexual intercourse as violation. However, in her analysis, the Chicano meaning of sexual intercourse is turned on its head. Whereas for Chicanos, abstention from sexual intercourse is a mechanism used to control and subordinate Chicanas, in Dworkin's paradigm, abstention from sexual intercourse is–for white women–a revolutionary step towards liberation.

The outcome of sexual penetration outside of marriage for the value of Chicana womanhood is the same whether it happens by force or consent. Symbolically, women are always the potential enemy, even when they are most adored. A pampered, valued daughter can easily be disowned by her parents if she consents to be penetrated without the benefit of marriage. Overnight, the parents' devotion turns to strong hatred that will not subside until the ever-elusive family honor is repaired through marriage or revenge. If *la hija despojada* (the damaged daughter) remains within the family and has offspring, they too are judged as not legitimate.

The reward for women who save their virginity until marriage is to enter the revered status of wife, and eventually mother and grandmother. Mothers and grandmothers have legitimate realms of authority within Mexicano/Chicano culture, as they do in many other cultures. However, the family centeredness that characterizes Mexicano/Chicano culture idealizes motherhood.[21] Also, the respect that is supposed to be accorded to older people in general also facilitates the potential authority of mothers as they become grandmothers and great-grandmothers. Mothers are supposed to be superhuman beings who can perform miraculous deeds on behalf of their families. Their comforts and rewards are to see their children grow up and to support their husbands. Mothers and grandmothers are the nurturant warriors who heal the wounds inflicted by an oppressive, racist society (Zinn 1975a). As such, they have been mythologized in much of the Chicano literature produced in the 1960s. Consider José Montoya's poem "La Jefita" (1979):[22]

When I remember the campos	When I remember the fields
Y las noches and the	And the nights and the
sounds	sounds
of those nights en carpas o	of those nights in tents or

Bagones I remember my
        jefita's
Palote
Clik-clok; clik-clak-clok
Y su tocesita.

(I swear, she never slept!)
Reluctant awakenings a la
        media
Noche y la luz prendida,
PRRRRRRINNNNGGGGGGG!
A noisy chorro missing the
        Basin.
Que horas son, ama?
Es tarde mi hijito. Cover up
Your little brothers.
Y yo con pena but too
        sleepy.
   Go to bed little mother!
A maternal reply mingled with
The hissing of the hot planchas
Y los frijoles de la hoya
Boiling musically dando
        segunda
A los ruidos nocturnos and
The snores of the old man
   Lulling sounds y los perros
Ladrando–then the familiar
Hallucinations just before sleep.
   And my jefita no more.
But then it was time to get up!
My old man had a chiflidito
That irritated the world to
Wakefulness.
       Wheeeeeeeeeet!
         Wheeeeeeet!

Arriba, cabrones chavalos
Huevones!

train cars I remember my
        mother's
 Rolling pin
Clik-clok; clik-clack-clok
And her little cough.

(I swear, she never slept!)
Reluctant awakenings in the
        middle of the
Night and the light on,
PRRRRRRINNNNGGGGGGG!
A noisy drip missing the
        Basin
What time is it mom?
It's late my little son. Cover up
Your little brothers.
And I with embarrassment
        but too sleepy.
   Go to bed little mother!
A maternal reply mingled with
The hissing of the hot iron
And the homemade beans
Boiling musically singing
        backup
To the night noises and
The snores of the old man
   Lulling sounds and the dogs
Barking–then the familiar
Hallucinations just before sleep.
   And my little boss no more.
But then it was time to get up!
My old man had a little whistle
That irritated the world to
Wakefulness
       Wheeeeeeeeeet!
         Wheeeeeeet!

Get up, goddam kids,
Lazy!

Y todavia la pinche	And still the goddam
Noche oscura	Night was pitch black
Y la jefita slapping tortillas.	And my little boss slapping tortillas.
Prieta! Help with the lonches!	Dark one! Help with the lunches!
Calientale agua a tu 'apa!	Heat up the water for your dad!
(Me la rayo ese! My jefita never slept!)	(I'll be damned! My little boss never slept!)
Y en el fil, pulling her cien	And in the field, pulling her one hundred
Libras de algoda se conreis	Pounds of cotton
Mi jefita y decia,	My little boss
That woman—she only complains	That woman—she only complains
in her sleep.[23]	in her sleep.

The mother in this poem is rendered central to the family by her ability to nurture, care, be the voice of reason, and keep the family functioning. She performs household chores while the rest of the family sleeps and then works side by side with them picking cotton in the fields. According to the son, the narrator, she does not express needs, pains, or frustrations. Her silence is a direct measure of her sainthood. Her capacity to give is infinite, she expects no reward other than seeing her family survive. In fact, the father in this poem is portrayed as insensitive to the children and the mother. The family survives because the mother's saintly behavior is the glue that keeps all the family members together. This portrayal is not uncommon. In the film *La Bamba* the mother is dedicated to her children and especially to her son Ritchie's success.[24] Also, in El Teatro Campesino's *Soldado Razo* the father is a hard-drinking, authoritarian individual, while his wife is the "traditional long-suffering Latin mother figure" (Brown 1980). In this idealization of motherhood, the Indo-Hispanic notion of devotion is equated with obedience (Alarcón 1981, 186). *La Madrecita* (The Little Mother) enacts and inculcates the cultural ideals of respect, devotion, and the legitimacy of gender hierarchies (regardless of how little she believes or follows them). As Abelardo Delgado proclaims, "as long as women obey we make saints of them" (Delgado 1978, 34); and as Carla Trujillo reaffirms, "Martyrdom, the cloth of denial, transposes itself into a gown of cultural beauty" (Trujillo 1991, 188).

This poem strikes a cord of truth for many working-class Chicanas and Chicanos because the survival of the group has been possible precisely because of women's constant work, at home and in the fields (Trujillo 1991, 189). However, *La Jefita* is converted into the *other*, and in her objectification, she is dehumanized.[25] By contrast, the project of Chicana feminists, especially Chicana poets, is to allow the *other* to speak. Contrast "La Jefita" with Alma Villanueva's stanzas from her poem "Mother, May I" (Villanueva 1978):

18
and then began the years
of silence, the years
my mouth would open
and no words would speak,
my mouth locked tight.
and a loneliness grew
that I couldn't name.
19
I looked for it
in my husband's eyes.
I looked for it
in my children's eyes.
I looked for it
in supermarkets.
I looked for it
in the oven.
I looked for it
in the dustpan.
I looked for it
in the sink.
in the tv.
in the washing machine.
in the car.

in the streets.
in the cracks
on my linoleum.
I polished
and cleaned and cared for everything silently. I put on my
masks, my costumes and posed for each occasion. I
        conducted myself
well, I think, but an emptiness grew
that nothing could fill. I think
I hungered for myself.

This poem almost seems to be a mother's reply to the son in "La Jefita." The droning work has a cost for La Jefita–the loss of a voice with which to speak of her pain. The loss of her voice results in a loss of herself because nobody, no matter how noble their intentions, can live entirely for others. More importantly, the son in "La Jefita" *expects* her to live for others. I argue that it is this expectation that subordinates and controls Chicanas.[26] If La Jefita were to stop the rolling of tortillas and look up and say to the son, "I think I hungered for myself," the arrangement between Chicanos and Chicanas would collapse. Silence is imperative to maintain the image of mothers as self-sacrificing saints.

As Chicanas acquire political consciousness about gender subordination, they become aware of the restricted social constructions of Chicana womanhood. Socorro Valdez expresses her consciousness of the restricted definition of women within Teatro Campesino:

> It was like walking the same path over and over. There was the mother, the sister, or the grandmother or the girlfriend. Only four. You were either the *novia, la mamá, la abuela, o la hermana.* And most of the time these characters were passive. The way those females are laid out are for the most part very passive and laid back, *y aguantaban todo.* I think that is what really chewed me up at the time. (Broyles 1986, 166)

The comment that the female characters *aguantaban todo* (withstood everything) is pivotal in understanding the gender subordination of Chicanas. The structural position of Chicanos, as a group, has not permitted many of its women to be passive because physical survival is at stake. Historically, there have always been strong women leaders within the Chicano/ Mexicano community, from las *soldaderas*[27] who fought in the Mexican revolution of 1910 to Emma Tanayuca, famous labor leader in Texas. As a community, the fact that there is a type of adaptation–femme-macho–that allows for the expression of *will,* leaves an aperture for Chicana women to enforce their power. For women in El Teatro Campesino, their freedom of expression took the form of allegorical characters; for some Chicanas in the outside communities, it took the form of taking positions of leadership in the political struggles on behalf of their group. Therefore, the apparent "passivity" is much more complex and may, in fact, disguise a tremendous amount of strength and *will.* Many Chicanas are passive, yet strong enough to withstand (Castillo 1991, 35). Their subordination lies in this contradiction between having strength and refusing to use it on those who obviously oppress them.

Chicana poets have embraced the hybrid image of human/ animal to exalt their liberation. This appropriation sabotages the negative image of the femme-macho and turns it into a celebration of the breaking with gender boundaries. Consider the poem "Lizard" by Elba Sánchez (1992):

LAGARTIJA

aquí me ves
lagartija contenta
paso los días
panza al sol
cuerpo extendido
sin miedo
al filo
de mis imperfecciones
soy quien soy
desperté
de un largo sueño
me comó las telarañas
que antes me enredaban

LIZARD

here I am
contented lizard
I spend my days
stretching out
belly to the sun
without fearing
the dagger
of my imperfections
I am who I am
I awoke
from a long dream
ate the spiderwebs
that entangled

las pestañas	my eyelashes
vendándome los ojos	blindfolding me
ahora ya no como	I do not eat
moscas	flies any more
ni soy de sangre fría	nor am I cold blooded
yo misma	I am
mi propia partera	my own midwife
luciendo escamas	showing off scales
de cobre terrenal	of earthen copper
de cabeza a cola	from head to tail
me doy a luz	give birth to myself

Here the poet takes the image of a *lagartija*, not only an animal, but a cold-blooded reptile and a hermaphrodite to represent herself. In fact, the indigenous beliefs about the lizard are that "it is a sexual animal, snake-like and obsessed with the physical" (Huerta 1982, 98). *La lagartija* is antithetical to the warm-blooded nurturance that is expected of motherhood. Instead of supporting her man and her children, like La Jefita, she literally gives birth not to the husband's offspring but rather to herself–and even more blasphemous, she celebrates her liberation. Furthermore, the lizard-poet teases with the edges of sexual propriety by lying "belly to the sun," implying a sexually available pose which makes her open to violation by the "dagger." However, the lizard-poet has demystified the "dagger," representing penetration, and realizes that it is not sexual intercourse that "entangled [her] eyelashes" but rather the "imperfections" that she internalized and that blindfolded her. She no longer eats those "flies" or dictums of who she is. By disentangling herself, she can remain a lizard but not consider herself cold-blooded because now she celebrates who she is by "showing off scales/of earthen copper/from head to tail." The lizard-poet's focus on herself, her sexual availability, her acceptance of her cold-bloodedness, and her refusal to eat flies are defiant acts that embrace all those images that have been used against Chicanas to dispute they are worthwhile women. The lizard-poet is not hard at work like La Jefita, she does not "hunger for herself" as the narrator in "Mother, May I," she simply is—with the placid abandonment of a lizard lying in the sun enjoying itself.

But even the femme-macho's power is constructed with built-in limitations because femme-machos still are at the mercy of most Chicanos' conception of Chicana womanhood, which is highly restricted according to women's sexual behavior. Whatever liberation the femme-macho experiences by crossing gender boundaries and appropriating some "masculine" characteristics, such as assertiveness, it is only temporary. As Broyles (1986, 178) observes Socorro Valdez's trajectory within Teatro Campesino:

> Given the extraordinary acting skill of Socorro Valdez, it would be no exaggeration to speak of her as a leading figure in the history of El Teatro Campesino. In the entire history of her work with the Teatro Campesino, however, Socorro Valdez has never played a lead female part, only numerous male leads. This is a startling fact considering not only Socorro's almost legendary talents as a performer but also her yearning to explore more roles. Yet the stereotyped casting within the company eliminated her, and other women who look like her, from various female lead roles. There is sadness in her voice when she indicates that she never was allowed to play La Virgen de Guadalupe in *La Virgen del Tepeyac.*[28]
>
> I never even got close to it. They wouldn't let me . . . could never have the role . . . because Luis doesn't see me that way. They see the Virgen de Guadalupe as a soft, demure, peaceful, saintly, ingenue type. The really incredible part was when it turned out that I have too many teeth. I was told "You got too many teeth. The Virgen didn't have that many teeth." It appears the Virgen de Guadalupe had no teeth. I thought to myself: "That is the stupidest thing I ever heard of!" *Apoco estaba molacha la Virgen de Guadalupe?* (Don't tell me the Virgen of Guadalupe was toothless!)

Broyles (1986) concludes that the truth of the matter was that Socorro Valdez did not meet Western standards of beauty—she had *indígena*[29] features and very dark brown skin.[30] Women who looked like Socorro either played male parts or the allegorical characters who were "sexless" and were usually played under heavy makeup or under heavy costume, thus hiding the "real" gender of the actor: "The sexless roles became numerous, and they were pursued as a creative outlet for women to escape the confinement of female roles" (Broyles 1986, 178).

The restricted definition of Chicanas' sexuality—and therefore of their womanhood—within Teatro and within Chicano communities, stems from many men's inability to conceive of women who are fully human. But, as Broyles (1986, 168) points out, a more complex aspect of that narrowness in the perception of Chicanas by Chicanos is linked to the narrowness in mostly men's self-perceptions, as she quotes Socorro Valdez: "He [Luis] can't experience women any other way except as a man. And no one else can do that either, unless they are willing to *stretch their own image of themselves.*" Therefore, it was no coincidence that Luis Valdez could only write plays casting women as "types," because to describe women characters that are fully human would require that he also expand what it is to be a man. The gender liberation of Chicana women is intertwined with the gender liberation of Chicano men. Therefore, it would require the restructuring of deeply held values about sexuality, family, and community.

The Community as Familia—What Binds Chicanas to the Stage

Chicano/Mexicano culture is communal culture with deep historical roots in the tending for and caring of the land. The division of labor between women and men is an integral part of the social arrangements sustained by the culture (Mirandé and Enriquez 1979). However, Chicanos' colonization gave way to a devaluation of the work performed outside the home, mostly by Chicano men, and a focus on interpersonal relationships as a source of nurturance and validation of personhood. Social events such as *bailes, bautismos, lotería, bar-b-ques, fiestas de cumpleaños, misa, posadas, quinceañeras, velorios*[31] all became central to Chicano men and women in valuing themselves as *human beings* because of the enormous economic and social constraints they faced as a result of white racism. Many Chicanos as well as Chicanas feared the public sphere and avoided it at all costs. The Chicano community became the refuge from the harshness of the outside world (Barrera 1991, 122). Valdez himself has described Chicanos' complex feelings about their barrios:

> The barrio is not a ghetto, though there are ghettos in the barrio. It is a microcosm of a Chicano city, a place of dualities: a liberated zone and a prison; a place of love and warmth, and place of hatred and violence, where most of La Raza live out their lives. So it is a place of weddings, *bautismos, tardeadas, bailes, velorios*,[32] and patriotic enchilada dinners. It is a place of poverty and self-reliance, of beloved *ancianos* [the old ones], of *familias* [families], of *compadres* [godparents]. (Valdez 1972, 145)

For Chicanos, the basic unit of community organization has been *la familia* (the family) (Zavella 1988). *La familia*, which is patriarchal in nature, is considered a social support group, a source aiding migration, and a catalyst for political mobilization (Hurtado 1995; Zinn 1975b). *La familia* is the community and the symbolic head of the family is the father (Zavella 1987; Orozco 1986, 12; Frischman 1982, 264). *La familia es la cuna de la cultura*–the cradle where Chicano culture gets reproduced.

El Teatro Campesino's organizational structure is also based on family and on the cultivation of land.[33] Members of El Teatro Campesino live and work communally and the relationship between members of the ensemble is defined as a familial one. In addition, Teatro Campesino moved to San Juan Bautista, California, a rural community, to farm and raise livestock to underscore their philosophical position that "ultimate freedom for the farm worker means ownership of the land he [sic] works. We are now planting and building and raising animals in our forty acres . . . Our art grows out of our way of life. We call it *Agrarismo Chicano*" (Bruce-Novoa 1978).[34]

El Teatro Campesino's organization is headed by Luis Valdez, who is symbolic father as well as writer and director. The actors in the company are typically much younger than Luis Valdez. He is of course a benevolent father who has been very influential in the development of Chicano arts, encouraging and supporting the development of young Chicano artists. He has also tried to portray Chicanos, especially poor Chicanos, with dignity and depth–at least the men in his plays.

But, however benevolent a father might be, if his authority is based on his privilege as a man, it will result in the oppression of women. For example, as writer and director, Luis Valdez creates the women characters and decides which women enact which parts. Broyles's (1986) discussion of how roles are created and assigned in El Teatro Campesino in many ways reflects the scripts which Chicanas have been assigned outside the theater. In Chicano communities the legitimacy of patriarchal power also results in controlling the "acceptable scripts" that Chicanas may live.

Some Chicanas are *convinced* by Chicanos that group survival is dependent on acceptance of scripts delineated by patriarchy. Chicano familism is extended to the group *as a whole* and is embodied in the notion of *carnalismo*–brotherhood and sisterhood (Zinn 1975b).[35] The collective political commitment to group survival is supposedly threatened if Chicanas refuse to enact their ascribed "roles." This is the essence of the hold Chicano patriarchal power has on many Chicanas.

Women's roles in El Teatro Campesino have remained fairly constant throughout its history. Women characters typically engage in activities which are accessory to those of men. Never is the world seen through the eyes of women (Broyles 1986, 164). In Broyles's interviews with Teatro women, they placed these limited roles within the context of their own personal development. In the 1970s, Chicanas who joined El Teatro inherited the women's stereotyped roles as givens. At that time, most did not question these roles because they themselves were very young. Diane Rodríguez, who joined El Teatro at fifteen years of age, states:

> Somehow at that point we didn't have the consciousness and we played these cardboard roles. Or maybe we did have some consciousness but we didn't know how to get it on stage. (Broyles 1986, 165)

The limited roles given to women characters were also a result of a historical factor. Broyles (1986, 165) notes that during the 1960s in Teatro Campesino "the efforts to address *raza*[36] and the reality of *raza* as a *whole* somehow precluded a special consideration of women's roles and problems." During this

time, it was a common practice among leftist groups to exclude "women's" issues. What was happening with women's
roles in El Teatro paralleled the experiences of Chicana feminists in the 1960s within the Chicano movement (Sánchez 1985,
3-6). Chicano activists used two types of rhetoric to keep
Chicana feminists from raising women's issues within the movement: one that focused on the divisive nature of considering
them and another that implied joining the white feminist movement was betrayal (Zavella 1988, 125; Trujillo 1991, 188). The
fact that the white feminist movement was middle class in its
origins, ideology, and practice convinced some Chicanas that
indeed it did not speak to their specific position in this society.
Most Chicana feminists also felt that white feminism did not
address itself to political struggles which included race and class
(Hurtado 1989). In the 1960s, the response of many politically
progressive Chicano men to Chicana feminist demands was
not unlike that of their white counterparts: appeals to reason
("Yes, there are problems, but changes can come only incre-
mentally"); cries of confusion ("What is it that you want?");
requests of prescription ("Tell us what to do"); and finally outright anger (*"El problema no es el macho es el gabacho!"* [The problem is not the macho, it is the white man!]) (Orozco 1986, 12).

The Teatro women's dissatisfaction with women's character roles led to one of the longest and deepest struggles in the
development of El Teatro Campesino. In El Teatro Campesino,
men met women's challenge to expand their roles on the stage
with passive resistance. Men perceived this action as an un-
necessary provocation instead of as a challenge to expand El
Teatro's creativity. Whereas Teatro Campesino as well as the
Chicano Movement have been at the forefront of progressive
political action (unionization of farm labor, voter registration,
and prison reform) both have consistently been unwilling to
confront sexism. The men in El Teatro did not meet the
women's challenge and instead suggested that women create
their own theater company. Eventually the women did leave
and proceeded to write, produce, and act in their own plays.
For example, Olivia Chamucero started theater work with children of migrant workers and conducted a program of drama
workshops for women in battered women's centers and for
youth in drug prevention centers. However, as Broyles (1986,

168) indicates, "Clearly the collective spirit suffered a collapse when gender roles were questioned. Suddenly an individual solution was suggested for what was a collective problem."

It is important to understand that Chicanas' loyalty to Chicanos derives not from the hope of economic security but rather from their desire to gain *respectable* entry into the Chicano community. The Chicano community is the Universe for Chicanos who encounter hostility outside their segregated barrios. Attachment to a man is not merely for economic insurance but for their very inclusion in social and cultural life. That is the crux of the hold that Chicanos have on Chicanas, the threat of the universe collapsing—in Teatro terms, *El Fin del Mundo* [*The End of the World*], the title of the last play by Teatro Campesino, which was performed in Europe. The fear is that the Chicano way of life will disappear if Chicanas step outside the boundaries of the narrow stage set for them by Luis Valdez and other symbolic fathers.

Like the women characters in El Teatro Campesino, Chicanas in general are trapped on the stage of life, playing scripts which they have very little responsibility for creating and confined on a narrow stage that spotlights men (Cotera 1977, 24). Chicanas are assigned the task of waiting in the wings to pick men up, support them, and enhance them. Chicanas have always been part of the backdrop, not only on the stage but also in life. To refuse to be the backdrop is to destroy the play. The male actor cannot be the hero; there is no play if there is no framework, no backdrop, no extras to highlight the centrality of the main actor. Even if it is only a penumbra, there has to be a background or there is no universe. As women, Chicanas have carried the burden of knowing that they are essential, *no importa cuanto las maltraten* (it doesn't matter how much they are mistreated). Most Chicanas are socialized to believe that men cannot exist without them, and that has tied them to a stage which they might otherwise abandon. *Esta es la esencia de la madrecita sufrida* (This is the essence of the suffering mother).

When Chicanas in El Teatro Campesino questioned their gendered scripts, the response of the men was to say, "Write your own plays." But as a group, Chicanas are not socialized to separate from the group in that way (Zinn 1975b), and it is not because they lack strength or skills. Therefore, Chicana feminists and activists have resolved the dilemma by separating only in some areas. For example, Chicana academics created their own professional organization, Mujeres Activas in Letras y Cambio Social (MALCS)–Women Active in Scholarship and Social Change–in response to men's domination of the National Association for Chicano Studies (NACS). Yet, many of the MALCS members participate in NACS. Chicana feminists have never proposed to boycott or otherwise disengage from NACS. Instead, there have been a series of confrontations over the exclusion of women and absence of gender issues in the annual meetings of NACS. Chicana feminists do not want to be separate from the group that simultaneously constitutes their community and oppresses them.

El Fin del Mundo[37]–Chicanas Walk off the Stage

In 1980, Chicanas in El Teatro Campesino walked off the stage. El Teatro Campesino ended as a collective enterprise and the members of the ensemble went their separate ways. El Teatro Campesino still exists under Luis Valdez's direction but it is now dedicated to "mainstreaming" its productions and, as *La Bamba* shows, it even has had an effect on Hollywood.

Contemporary Chicana feminists, in and out of El Teatro Campesino, have wrested from men the right to invent themselves, and they have done so through many avenues, including creative and academic production. Undoubtedly, oppression always results in casualties but a by-product is the ability of some of its survivors to further the group's collective consciousness. The ability of some Chicanas to move between many worlds and many perceptions has resulted in the creation of a new consciousness about gender relations that is class and race specific–the result of the cultural and historical evolution of Chicanos.[38] In Maria Lugones's (1992, 7) words:

> [T]he liberatory experience lies in this memory, [of] these other people [who] have intentions one understands because one is fluent in several "cultures," "worlds," realities. One understands herself in every world in which one remembers oneself. This is a

strong sense of personal identity, politically and morally strong. The task of remembering one's other selves is a difficult liberatory task. Mystification is one of the many forms of control of our memory of our other selves. All oppressive control is violent because it attempts to erase selves that are dangerous to the maintenance of domination over us.

The crossing-over into many social realities results in recognition of the arbitrary nature of social categories as well as the arbitrary nature of the authority that creates them. As Gloria Anzaldúa puts it, "*Soy un amasamiento*, I am an act of kneading, of uniting and joining that not only has produced both a creature of darkness and a creature of light, but also a creature that questions the definitions of light and dark and gives them new meanings" (Anzaldúa 1987, 81). Chicana feminists theorize practically and academically from their position as part of the background for the play. Having been part of the penumbra gives Chicanas an advantage. They have seen men while men were not seeing themselves (Lugones 1992, 6-7). As Lugones (1992, 13-14) notes, Chicanas inhabit the *limen*, meaning they stand "betwixt and between successive lodgments in jural political systems . . . aside not only from [their] own social position but from all social positions . . . formulating unlimited series of social arrangements."[39] Inhabiting the limen provides the potential for liberation because it furnishes the social, psychological, and philosophical space to conceive of alternatives to oppression—alternatives that are inconceivable in structured social worlds where oppression is essential to the maintenance of the social and economic order. To inhabit the limen and understand its liberatory potential is to experience oneself as multiple, and therefore these "limen creatures" are extremely threatening to any world that requires "unification, either psychologically, morally, politically or metaphysically" (Lugones 1992, 9). Chicana poets have been especially powerful in delineating the contours of the liberatory potential of the limen:

> To live in the Borderlands means you
> are neither *hispana india negra española*
> *ni gabacha*,[40] *eres mestiza*,[41] *mulata*,[42] half-breed
> caught in the crossfire between camps

while carrying all five races on your back
not knowing which side to turn to, run from;

To live in the Borderlands means knowing
that the *india* in you, betrayed for 500 years,
is no longer speaking to you,
that mexicanas call you *rajetas*,[43]
that denying the Anglo inside you
is as bad as having denied the Indian or Black;

Cuando vives en la frontera[44]
people walk through you, the wind steals your voice,
you're a *burra, buey*,[45] scapegoat
forerunner of a new race,
half and half—both woman and man, neither—
a new gender;

To live in the Borderlands means to
put chile[46] in the borscht,
eat whole wheat tortillas,
speak Tex-Mex[47] with a Brooklyn accent;
be stopped by la migra[48] at the border checkpoints;

Living in the Borderlands means you fight hard to
resist the gold elixir beckoning from the bottle,
the pull of the gun barrel,
the rope crushing the hollow of your throat;

In the Borderlands
you are the battleground
where the enemies are kin to each other;
you are at home, a stranger,
the border disputes have been settled
the volley of shots have shattered the truce
you are wounded, lost in action
dead, fighting back;

To live in the Borderlands means
the mill with the razor white teeth wants to shred off
your olive-red skin, crush out the kernel, your heart

pound you pinch you roll you out
smelling like white bread but dead;

To survive the Borderlands
you must live *sin fronteras*[49]
be a crossroads.
    (Anzaldúa 1987, 195)

Anzaldúa (1987) does not use the term limen but Borderlands [*La frontera*] to denote that space where antithetical elements mix not to obliterate each other or to get subsumed by
a larger whole but rather to combine in unique and unexpected ways. The limen/borderland is where individuals can
put chile in their borscht and speak Tex-Mex with a Brooklyn
accent. It is a space some women of Color, specifically
Chicanas, can inhabit because of their ability to maintain
multiple selves without feeling incoherence. In the limen it is
possible to develop a "forerunner of a new race,/half and half—
both woman and man, neither–/a new gender."

> "There is something inside us that makes us different from other
> people. It is not like men and it is not like white women." (Parker
> 1979, interview with Toni Morrison)

A New Gender

White feminist theorists have written extensively about white
women's capacity to perceive multiple realities (Spender 1980).
However, Chicanas' multiple realities are not the same as white
women's and, in fact, some white women are guilty of objectifying them. Lugones (1992, 10) describes the interaction between a white woman and her maid:

> In the case of people who dominate others, they may not re-
> member the person they are in the reality of the dominated. For
> example, many times [white] people act in front of their maids
> as if there were no one in the room. They say things and behave
> in ways that one can only imagine as said or done in private.
> When people behave this way, they do not see themselves as the

maid sees them and they do not want to remember or recognize the person who is seen by the maid, of whom the maid is a witness. The maid can only testify in the world of the dominated, the only world where that testimony is understood and recognized. The employers do not remember themselves as maids know them for many reasons. One of these reasons concerns their own sense of moral integrity since as they are witnessed by the maid they lack it. So phenomena such as self-deception become very important in this way of seeing things.[50]

Obviously, not all white women have maids and not all maids are Chicanas. But this description shows how women can objectify other women. The hope for a comprehensive theory of liberation lies in delineating the different limen that are possible, and from those interstices, theorize about potential solutions for oppression. As Lugones (1992, 10) proposes:

[M]erely remembering ourselves in other worlds and coming to understand ourselves as multiplicitous is not enough for liberation: collective struggle in the reconstruction and transformation of structures is fundamental.

To be sure, there is overlap between the perceptions of different oppressed groups, but it is not complete. This fact is what has only recently been recognized by white feminists (Spelman 1988; Hurtado 1989; West and Fenstermaker 1993). One possible solution is to increase "dialogue among multiplicitous persons who are faithful witnesses of themselves and also testify to and uncover the multiplicity of their oppressors and the techniques of oppression afforded by ignoring that multiplicity" (Lugones 1992, 10). For example, Chicana theorists are struggling to claim their independence and to challenge traditional definitions of what is culturally appropriate for women. Much of Chicana feminist writing tries to redefine the virgin/puta dichotomy since "virginity (mental, physical, or whatever it may mean . . .) is more an obsession created by and for the use of men than an actual feminine state of being" (Del Castillo 1974, 144). The sweeping redefinition of Chicana womanhood includes the erasure of negative views of homosexuality, conventional familial roles for women and men, and Chicanos' own racism in rejecting their Indian heritage:

416 Aída Hurtado

Over the years, the confines of farm and ranch life began to chafe. The traditional role of la mujer was a saddle I did not want to wear. The conceptions "passive" and "dutiful" raked my skin like spurs and "marriage" and "children" set me to bucking faster than rattlesnakes or coyotes. I took to wearing boots and men's jeans and walking about with my head full of visions, hungry for more words and more words. Slowly I unbowed my head, refused my estate and began to challenge the way things were. But it's taken over thirty years to unlearn the belief instilled in me that white is better than brown—something that some people of color never will unlearn. And it is only now that the hatred of myself, which I spent the greater part of my adolescence cultivating, is turning to love. (Anzaldúa 1987, 202)

To love oneself as woman is therefore a revolutionary act. The reclaiming of self has come for Chicana feminists through self-love—not narcissistic, selfish involvement but as a political act of valuing what patriarchy has devalued. Chicana feminists proclaim that redemption does not come through men but rather comes from giving up the illusion of security and safety coming from being chosen by a man. It is, as Gloria Anzaldúa writes, "Letting Go":

> Nobody's going to save you.
> No one's going to cut you down
> cut the thorns around you.
> No one's going to storm
> the castle walls nor
> kiss awake your birth,
> climb down your hair,
> nor mount you
> onto the white steed.
>
> There is no one who
> will feed the yearning.
> Face it. You will have
> to do, do it yourself.
> (Moraga and Anzaldúa 1981, 200)

Chicana feminism does not advocate separatism from Chicano men or from the Chicano community. Chicana feminists, like other feminists of Color, are struggling to develop a truly inclusive political consciousness that embraces all who have been rejected and does not lead to the abandonment of hope, even in those who reject it. To refuse to separate from Chicano men and to understand their oppression does not mean excusing their brutality (Anzaldúa 1987, 83). What Chicana feminists advocate is a head-on engagement with Chicanos and with other members of their communities to achieve positive change for all parties involved.

Recently, Socorro Valdez was asked by Luis Valdez to return to El Teatro Campesino to play in his award-winning television special "Corridos." Socorro Valdez agreed under the condition that she play the woman lead for the first time in her career. In her words:

> I didn't want makeup on my face. I didn't want lipstick. I didn't want false eyelashes or fake boobs or nothing. I just wanted to be myself up there, just wanted to be the Indian person that I am . . . I came back to him [Luis Valdez], but I said: "That's it. No more masks, no more calavera face [skull mask], no more calavera bones on my face. None of that shit. I'll go out there in a plain cotton dress and I'll have those people going." (Broyles 1986, 182)

Just as Socorro Valdez wanted to keep her home in her theater community, Chicana feminists also want to remain in their communities and make their struggle as women part of the struggle that affects all oppressed peoples. Like Socorro Valdez, their presence will have to be on their own terms.

Notes

1. For a summary that communicates the purpose and spirit of the beginnings of Teatro Campesino, see Valdez 1971 (115-119).
2. Several scholars have highlighted the function of characters as archetypes in the representations of Teatro Campesino. For example, see Frischmann 1982, 260; Ramirez 1974; and Morton 1974.
3. Several analyses of Teatro Campesino indicate that Valdez explicitly wanted his plays to highlight in his fiction what he saw as the reality in Chicano communities. As Manuel de Jesús Vega states, "El Teatro Campesino es a la vez 'afirmación de la vida' y 'espejo de

la realidad' . . . Si la obra del Teatro está ligada estrechamente a la vida, esto quiere decir que hemos de encontrar allí una visión total de la misma; tanto el presente como el pasado y el futuro deben aparecer reflejados en la obra." [El Teatro Campesino is at the same time the 'affirmation of life' and 'the mirror of life' . . . If the project of El Teatro campesino is intimately tied to life, this means we should find in it a complete vision of it; not only in the present but the past and the future should be reflected in the plays] (Vega 1983, 350).

4. These characters appear in the play *La Carpa de los Rasquachis* [*The Tent of the Underdogs*].

5. This definition of femininity is highly influenced by hegemonic definitions in the United States.

6. The only celebrity that comes close to this adaptation in the United States is Madonna. She exhibits all the characteristics of a femme-macho and that is why cultural theorists have been intrigued with her blasting of sexual, gender, racial, and class boundaries. However, the main difference between Madonna and Chicana/Mexican femme-machos is the fact that in the United States there is no cultural space for her that fits into our conception of womanhood, whereas for Chicanos, femme-machos (successful ones, anyway) are watched with amusement and at times revered if they are willing to pay the price of their adaptation.

7. Madonna too has mainstreamed bisexuality and plays visually with "deviant" sexual behavior. However, in the United States sexual repression is so strong that there is no public space for handling this visual play with humor. And unlike Chicano/Mexicano culture, where the virgin/whore/femme-macho tripartite allows for *playing* with the edge of "propriety," no such playfulness exists in the United States without going over the edge. For example, Madonna's sexual play crosses over the accepted boundaries of sarcastic Chicano/Mexican humor when she implies in a skit on the television show Saturday Night Live an attraction to Chelsea Clinton rather than Hillary or Bill. Implied pedophilia is one boundary that even a femme-macho cannot cross.

8. María Félix, with her wicked sense of humor, considered playing the part on film of the principal character in *Zona Sagrada* with her son, also an actor, playing opposite.

9. This is a play on the word *chingar* which means to go fuck yourself.

10. Emma Pérez (1993, 61) indicates that Hernán Córtés did not feel Malintzin (or Malinche) was worthy of marriage because she was the "*other*, the inferior, disdained female" and when he was finished with her he passed her on to his soldier.

11. The mixture of European and Indian races.

12. The word *piedra* literally means stone in Spanish. The character "Piedra" in this *acto* was actually the Aztec Calendar made of stone placed in front of a bright red cloth screen. La Piedra served as the main narrator in the play.

13. See Alarcón (1981) for an in-depth analysis of this reinterpretation of la Malinche's role in the conquest of México.

14. Chingada literally means in Spanish the one who has been *fucked.*

15. El chingón literally means in Spanish the fucker, or the one who has the ability to fuck, implying the possession of a penis which is the instrument used to fuck.

16. Although sexual attitudes and sexual behaviors are one of the most underresearched areas for Chicanos (Almaguer 1991), the emergent literature indicates that there are strong attitudes that support what Patricia Zavella calls "the cult of virginity" (Zavella 1994b). For example, Padilla and Baird (1991, 100-101) find that among a sample of Mexican American adolescents between the ages of fourteen and nineteen years, a full 80 percent of all participants in the study agreed that women should be virgins when they marry, but only 37 percent of the respondents thought men should do the same. Men felt more strongly about this than women, but not significantly so.

17. Padilla and Baird (1991, 102) find that most of the Mexican American adolescents they studied did not approve of sex without love; young men were more likely to believe this was acceptable (45 percent) than young women (22 percent).

18. Chicana lesbians, like Malinche, are also characterized as "*vendidas* [sell-outs] to the race" because they have caught white women's sexual disease (Trujillo 1991, ix).

19. Emma Pérez (1993, 61) also denounces Octavio Paz's analysis of Chicanas as traitors because of their sexuality's potential for betrayal: "We dispute a historically specific moment that denigrates us, immortalizes us as 'the betrayer' for all time, eternally stuck in an image, la puta (the whore). Long before the arrival of the Virgen de Guadalupe, we were La Chingada. The metaphor cuts to the core of each Chicana; each mestiza is flouted as *la india*/whore. Worse yet is that *la india* is our mother, and Paz slashes away at her beauty. He subordinates our first love object by violently raping her in historical text, in male language."

20. Padilla and Baird (1991, 101) note that "It is more important for the males (94 percent) to have boy children than it was for the females (68 percent). The male adolescents also want a median of two boys, whereas the females want a median of one boy." For a historical view of some of these norms in Mexican American communities see Ruiz 1993, 118-119.

21. Hortensia Amaro (1988, 11) indicates that 91 percent of Mexican American women in her study report that the role of mother is either extremely important or has an important place in their lives, whereas only 8.8 percent report that motherhood is somewhat important.

22. *La Jefita* is a term of endearment for mothers used among working-class Chicanos and Mexicans. It literally means "little boss."

23. Jose Montoya's poem is reprinted in Mirandé and Enriquez 1979, 165-166.

24. In *La Bamba,* the mother's dedication is reciprocated in different ways by each of her children. In fact, when Ritchie Valens is asked by his promoter to leave the rest of his band behind to record his first record, the only reason he agrees is, as he says, "his family." Ritchie also uses the royalties of his albums to buy his mother the "the home of her dreams" (see Fregoso 1993, 141).

25. In *La Bamba,* Rosalinda Fregoso notes, "Since the film's dominant tendency is to refuse the mother a subject role within the narrative at the same time that it disallows her any other interests or desires apart from Ritchie, the Ritchie Valens story advances an image of a sacrificial mother whose only object of desire is the 'good son'" (Fregoso 1993, 143).

26. In some extreme cases, if the expectation of submissiveness is violated it can result in violence against women, which further encourages compliance for fear of the consequences (Amaro 1988). Another effective threat used by some Chicanos to force Chicanas into compliance is to create competition among women and threaten to leave them for another partner.

27. Literally means female soldier. *Soldaderas* actually participated in battle during the armed struggle in 1910 to help democratize Mexico from a feudal country to one where land was distributed among peasants.

28. This particular play is of great significance to the women in El Teatro because La Virgen del Tepeyac is the Catholic version of the Aztec goddess Tonantzin. La Virgen del Tepeyac is the only Indian woman to be beatified by the Catholic Church. To women in El Teatro, the role of the Virgen represented a tribute to female potentiality (see Broyles 1986, 171). La Virgen de Guadalupe also has significance outside of El Teatro Campesino. Manuel de Jesús Vega (1983, 378-380) not only agrees with this assessment but also quotes Paz to reinforce his point: "No puede hablarse de la religiosidad del mexicano sin hacer mención de la importancia que tiene en su vida la Virgen de Guadalupe. Recordemos que César Chávez y el sindicato que dirige siempre marchan trás de un estandarte con la imagen de la Virgen . . . 'La Virgen es el consuelo de los pobres, el

escudo de los débiles, el amparo de los oprimidos. En suma es la Madre de los huérfanos.'" [It is not possible to speak of Mexicans' religiosity without the mention of the importance to their lives of the Virgen of Guadalupe. Let us remember that César Chávez and the union he directs always walk behind a banner with the image of the Virgen . . . "The Virgen is solace for the poor, the shield of the weak, the protector of the oppressed. In summary, she is the Mother of all orphans."]

29. *Indígena* means Indian in Spanish.

30. Ironically, El Teatro members' internalized racism helped to re-write history by casting La Virgen as a white Madonna, when the significance of the character is precisely that she is *Indian*! bell hooks (1994) makes a similar point about the beauty standards in society at large as well as in Black communities where "the images of black female bitchiness, evil temper, and treachery continue to be marked by darker skin . . . We see these images continually in the mass media whether they be presented to us in television sitcoms (such as the popular show "Martin"), on cop shows, (the criminal black woman is usually dark), and in movies made by black and white directors alike" (179).

31. Dances, baptisms, Mexican bingo, bar-b-ques, birthday parties, mass, Christmas celebrations, fifteen-year old birthdays for young women, funerals.

32. Baptisms, afternoon gatherings, dances, wakes.

33. The interconnectedness of Teatro Campesino's position on family, community, and the ownership of land is summarized in their statement that "we are family . . . who live communally. We are all brothers and sisters because we have a Common Father . . . He created us, He who uplifted us, Our Father of the Astros, GOD THE FATHER" (Morton 1974).

34. The importance of *la tierra* (earth) is also manifested in Teatro Campesino's artistic production. See for example, *Bernabé* and the analysis of this play by Donald H. Frischmann (1982, 264-269).

35. *Carnalismo* is derived from the word *carne* which literally means one's flesh as in the biological ties that are the result of being from the same flesh.

36. Raza refers to José Vasconcelos's notion of a unified "cosmic race" in North America and Latin America that would result in a new social order combining the best elements of all cultures. Chicanos adopted this term, *raza*, to refer to the ties Chicanos feel as a group (see Vasconcelos 1979).

37. *El Fin del Mundo* [*The End of the World*] was the last play produced by El Teatro Campesino. Like most of the productions by El Teatro Campesino, *El Fin del Mundo* went through various stages in its four-

year evolution which began in 1974. The fourth and last version was created under Valdez's guidance and was directed by his sister Socorro Valdez in l978 (Huerta 1982, 209). *El Fin del Mundo* showed the evolution of El Teatro Campesino by this mixed-gendered collaboration and the sympathetic portrayal of a Chicana lesbian.

38. Zavella (1994a, 201, 207) rightly indicates that the crossing of borders by Chicanas is not an easy journey that is accomplished by all, and that in fact material conditions as well as cultural restrictions more often than not work against women crossing borders.

39. Lugones (1992) takes the concept of limen from Turner 1974.

40. *Gabacha*–a Chicano term for a white woman.

41. *Mestiza*–of mixed race.

42. *Mulata*–of African American and white race heritage.

43. *Rajetas*–literally, "split," that is, having betrayed your word.

44. When you live in the borderlands.

45. *Burra*–donkey; *buey*–oxen.

46. *Chile*–hot sauce.

47. Tex-Mex is a speech style particular to Texas, where Chicanos (and some Anglos) mix English and Spanish to create a dialect. It is creative language because new combinations can constantly be made, and has been used by Chicano poets as emphasizing Chicano cultural expression. Some expressions include *troca*–truck; *parkearse*– to park; *watcha*–to watch.

48. *Migra*–slang word use by Chicanos for the INS (Immigration and Naturalization Service).

49. *Sin fronteras*–without borders.

50. Lugones (1992, 10) makes explicit she is referring to white women in another part of her manuscript, although it is not explicit in this quote.

Works Cited

Alarcón, Norma. 1981. "Chicana's Feminist Literature: A Re-vision Through Malintzin/or Malintzin: Putting Flesh Back on the Object." In *This Bridge Called My Back: Writings by Radical Women of Color*, eds. Cherríe Moraga and Gloria Anzaldúa, 182-190. Watertown, Mass.: Persephone Press.

Almaguer, Tomás. 1991. "Chicano Men: A Cartography of Homosexual Identity and Behavior." *differences: A Journal of Feminist Cultural Studies* 3 (2): 75-100.

Amaro, Hortensia. 1988. "Women in the Mexican-American Community: Religion, Culture, and Reproductive Attitudes and Experiences." *Journal of Community Psychology* 16 (January): 6-20.

Anzaldúa, Gloria, ed. 1990. *Making Face, Making Soul: Haciendo Caras: Creative and Critical Perspectives by Women of Color*. San Francisco: Aunt Lute.

___. 1987. *Borderlands–La Frontera: The New Mestiza*. San Francisco: Spinsters/Aunt Lute.

Barrera, Marta. 1991. "Café con Leche." In *Chicana Lesbians: The Girls Our Mothers Warned Us About,* ed. Carla Trujillo, 80-83. Berkeley: Third Woman Press.

Brant, Beth, ed. 1984. *A Gathering of Spirit: Writing and Art of North American Indian Women*. Montpelier, Vt.: Sinister Wisdom Books.

Brod, Harry, ed. 1987. *The Making of Masculinities: The New Men's Studies*. Boston: Allen & Unwin.

Brown, Edward G. 1980. "The Teatro Campesino's Vietnam Trilogy." *Minority Voices* 4 (1): 29-38.

Broyles, Yolanda Julia. 1994. *El Teatro Campesino: Theater in the Chicano Movement*. Austin: University of Texas Press.

___. 1986. "Women in El Teatro Campesino: ¿Apoco Estaba Molacha La Virgen de Guadalupe?" In *Chicana Voices: Intersections of Class, Race and Gender*, ed. Ricardo Romo, 162-187. Austin: Center for Mexican-American Studies, University of Texas at Austin.

Bruce-Novoa, Juan. 1988. "De Los Actos a La Bamba: La Evolución de Valdez." Paper presented at the Third International Conference on the Hispanic Cultures of the United States, Barcelona, Spain, June 7-10.

___. 1978. "El Teatro Campesino de Luis Valdez." *Texto Crítico* 4 (10): 65-75.

Castillo, Ana. 1991. "La Macha: Toward a Beautiful Whole Self." In *Chicana Lesbians: The Girls Our Mothers Warned Us About,* ed. Carla Trujillo, 24-48. Berkeley: Third Woman Press.

Cisneros, Sandra. 1994. *Loose Woman*. New York: Alfred A. Knopf.

Collins, Patricia Hill. 1991. *Black Feminist Thought*. New York: Routledge.

___. 1986. "Learning from the Outside Within: The Sociological Significance of Black Feminist Thought." *Social Problems* 33, no. 6: 14-32.

Connell, R. W. 1995. *Masculinities*. Berkeley: University of California Press.

Cotera, Marta. 1977. *Chicana Feminism*. Austin, Tex.: Information System Development.

de la Torre, Adela, and Beatriz M. Pesquera, eds. 1993. *Building with our Hands: New Directions in Chicana Studies*. Berkeley: University of California Press.

Del Castillo, Adelaida. 1974. "Malintzin Tenépal: A Preliminary Look into a New Perspective." *Encuentro Femenil* 1 (2): 58-77.

Delgado, Abelardo. 1978. "An Open Letter to Carolina . . . or Relations Between Men and Women." *Revista Chicano-Riqueña* 6 (2): 33-41.

Diamond, Betty Ann. 1977. "Brown Eyed Children of the Sun: The Cultural Politics of El Teatro Campesino." Ph.D. dissertation, University of Wisconsin.

Dworkin, Andrea. 1987. *Intercourse.* New York: Free Press.

Espín, Oliva. 1984. "Cultural and Historical Influences on Sexuality in Hispanic/Latin Women." In *Pleasure and Danger: Exploring Female Sexuality,* ed. Carol S. Vance, 149-163. London: Routledge and Kegan.

Fernández, R. 1994. "Abriendo-Caminos in the Brotherland-Chicana Writers Respond to the Ideology of Literary Nationalism." *Frontiers: A Journal of Women Studies* 14 (2): 23-50.

Fregoso, Rosa Linda. 1993. "The Mother Motif in *La Bamba* and *Boulevard Nights.*" In *Building with our Hands: New Directions in Chicana Studies,* eds. Adela de la Torre and Beatriz M. Pesquera, 130-145. Berkeley: University of California Press.

Frischmann, Donald H. 1982. "El Teatro Campesino y su Mito Bernabé: Un Regreso a la Madre Tierra." *Aztlán* 12 (2): 259-270.

Fuentes, Carlos. 1967. *Zona Sagrada.* México: Siglo Veintiuno Editores.

Garza, Mario. 1976. *Un Paso Más, One More Step: Collected Poems.* Lansing, Mich.: El Renacimiento Publications.

Herrera, Hayden. 1983. *Frida: A Biography of Frida Kahlo.* New York: Harper & Row.

hooks, bell. 1994. *Outlaw Culture: Resisting Representations.* New York: Routledge.

___. 1990. *Yearning: Race, Gender, and Cultural Politics.* Boston: South End Press.

___. 1989. *Talking Back: Thinking Feminist, Thinking Black.* Boston: South End Press.

___. 1984. *Feminist Theory from Margin to Center.* Boston: South End Press.

___. 1981. *Ain't I a Woman? Black Women and Feminism.* Boston: South End Press.

Huerta, Jorge A. 1982. *Chicano Theater Themes and Forms.* Ypsilanti, Mich.: Bilingual Press/Editorial Bilingue.

Hurtado, Aída. 1995. "Variations, Combinations, and Evolutions: Latino Families in the United States." In *Understanding Latino Families: Scholarship, Policy, and Practice,* ed. Ruth E. Zambrana, 40-61. Thousand Oaks, Calif.: Sage Publications.

___. 1989. "Reflections on White Feminism: A Perspective from a Woman of Color." In *Social and Gender Boundaries in the United*

States, ed. Sucheng Chan, 155-186. Lewiston, N.Y.: The Edwin Mellen Press.

Jaggar, Alison. 1983. *Feminist Politics and Human Nature.* Totowa, N.J.: Rowman & Allanheld.

Lugones, Maria C. 1992. "Structure/Antistructure and Agency under Oppression." Unpublished manuscript, Carleton College.

Marks, Elaine, and Isabelle de Courtivron, eds. 1981. *New French Feminisms: An Anthology.* New York: Schocken Books.

Mirandé, Alfredo, and Evangelina Enríquez, eds. 1979. *La Chicana: The Mexican-American Woman.* Chicago: University of Chicago Press.

Montoya, José. 1979. "La Jefita." In *La Chicana: The Mexican-American Woman*, eds. Alfredo Mirandé and Evangelina Enríquez, 165-166. Chicago: The University of Chicago Press.

Moraga, Cherríe, and Gloria Anzaldúa, eds. 1981. *This Bridge Called My Back: Writings by Radical Women of Color.* Watertown, Mass.: Persephone Press.

Morton, Carlos. 1974. "La Serpiente Sheds Its Skin–The Teatro Campesino." *Drama Review* 18 (4): 71-76.

Navarro, Marta A. 1991. "Interview with Ana Castillo." In *Chicana Lesbians: The Girls Our Mothers Warned Us About*, ed. Carla Trujillo, 113-132. Berkeley: Third Woman Press.

Orozco, Cynthia. 1986. "Sexism in Chicano Studies and the Community." In *Chicana Voices: Intersections of Class, Race, and Gender*, ed. Ricardo Romo, 11-18. Austin: Center for Mexican American Studies, University of Texas.

Padilla, Amado M. and Traci L. Baird. 1991. "Mexican-American Adolescent Sexuality and Sexual Knowledge: An Exploratory Study." *Hispanic Journal of Behavioral Sciences* 13 (1): 95-104.

Parker, Bettye J. 1979. "Complexity: Toni Morrison's Women–An Interview Essay." In *Sturdy Black Bridges: Visions of Black Women in Literature*, eds. Roseanne Bell, Bettye Parker, and Beverly Guy-Sheftall. New York: Anchor/Doubleday.

Paz, Octavio. 1985. *The Labyrinth of Solitude.* Translated from the Spanish by Lysander Kemp, Yara Milos, and Rachel Phillips Belash. New York: Grove Press.

Pérez, Emma. 1993. "Speaking from the Margin: Uninvited Discourse on Sexuality and Power." In *Building with Our Hands: New Directions in Chicana Studies*, eds. Adela de la Torre and Beatriz M. Pesquera, 51-71. Berkeley: University of California Press.

–. 1991. "Sexuality and Discourse: Notes From a Chicana Survivor." In *Chicana Lesbians: The Girls Our Mothers Warned Us About*, ed. Carla Trujillo, 159-184. Berkeley: Third Woman Press.

Pesquera, Beatriz. 1994. "We're Still Tied to an Image: Chicana Workers and Motherhood." Paper presented at the 6th European Conference on Latino Cultures in the United States, Bordeaux, France, July 7-10.

—. 1985. "Work and Family: A Comparative Analysis of Professional, Clerical, and Blue-Collar Chicana Workers." Ph.D. dissertation, University of California, Berkeley.

Quintana, Alvina E. 1989. "Challenge and Counter-Challenge: Chicana Literary Motifs." In *Social and Gender Boundaries in the United States*, ed. Sucheng Chan, 187-203. Lewiston, N.Y.: The Edwin Mellen Press.

Ramírez, Elizabeth Cantú. 1974. "The Annals of Chicano Theater: 1965-1973." M.A. thesis, University of California, Los Angeles.

Ruiz, Vicki L. 1993. "'Star Struck': Acculturation, Adolescence, and the Mexican American Woman, 1920-1950." In *Building with our Hands: New Directions in Chicana Studies*, eds. Adela de la Torre and Beatriz M. Pesquera, 109-129. Berkeley: University of California Press.

Sánchez, Elba. 1992. *Tallos de Luna/Moon Shoots.* Santa Cruz, Calif: Moving Arts Press.

Sánchez, Marta E. 1985. *Contemporary Chicana Poetry: A Critical Approach to An Emerging Literature.* Berkeley: University of California Press.

Sandoval, Chela. 1991. "U.S. Third World Feminism: The Theory and Method of Oppositional Consciousness in the Postmodern World." *Genders* 10 (Spring): 1-24.

Segura, Denise. 1994. "Beyond Machismo: Chicanas, Work, and Family." Paper presented at the 6th European Conference on Latino Cultures in the United States, Bordeaux, France, July 7-10.

___. 1986. "Chicanas and Mexican Immigrant Women in the Labor Market: A Study of Occupational Mobility and Stratification." Ph.D. dissertation, University of California, Berkeley.

___. 1984. "Labor Market Stratification: The Chicana Experience." *Berkeley Journal of Sociology* 29: 57-91.

Spelman, Elizabeth. 1988. *Inessential Woman: Problems of Exclusion in Feminist Thought.* Boston: Beacon Press.

Spender, Dale. 1980. *Man Made Language.* London: Routledge, Chapman & Hall.

Stoltenberg, John. 1993. *The End of Manhood: A Book for Men of Conscience.* New York: Dutton Books.

Taibo, Paco Ignacio. 1985. *María Félix: 47 Pasos por el Cine.* México: J. Mortiz/Planeta.

Trujillo, Carla, ed. 1991. *Chicana Lesbians: The Girls Our Mothers Warned Us About.* Berkeley: Third Woman Press.

Turner, Victor. 1974. *Dramas, Fields, and Metaphors.* Ithaca: Cornell University Press.

Valdez, Luis. 1978. *Actos.* San Juan Bautista, Calif.: Menyah Productions.

___. 1973. "El Teatro Campesino: Notes on Chicano Theater." In *Guerrilla Street Theater,* ed. Henry Lesnick, 190-194. New York: Avon Books.

___. 1972. "Life in the Barrios." In *Aztlán: An Anthology of Mexican American Literature,* eds. Luis Valdez and Stan Steiner. New York: Vintage Books.

___. 1971. "El Teatro Campesino—Its Beginnings," in *The Chicanos: Mexican American Voices,* eds. Ed Ludwig and James Santibañez, 115-119. Baltimore: Penguin Books.

Vasconcelos, José. 1979. *The Cosmic Race/La Raza Cósmica.* Los Angeles: Centro de Publicaciones, Dept. of Chicano Studies, California State University.

Vega, Manuel de Jesús. 1983. "El Teatro Campesino Chicano y La Vanguardia Teatral: 1965-1975." Ph.D. dissertation, Middlebury College.

Villanueva, Alma. 1978. *Mother, May I.* Pittsburgh: Motheroot Publications.

West, Candace and Sarah Fenstermaker. 1993. "Power, Inequality and the Accomplishment of Gender: An Ethnomethodological View." In *Theory on Gender/Feminism on Theory,* ed. Paula England, 151-174. New York: Aldine.

West, Candace, and Don H. Zimmerman. 1987. "Doing Gender." *Gender and Society* 1 (2): 125-51.

Xavier, Roy Eric. 1983. *Politics and Chicano Culture: A Perspective on El Teatro Campesino.* Berkeley: Chicano Studies Library Publications, University of California.

Yarbro-Bejarano, Yvonne. 1986. "The Female Subject in Chicano Theatre: Sexuality, 'Race,' and Class." *Theatre Journal* 38 (1): 389-407.

___. 1985. "Chicanas' Experience in Collective Theatre: Ideology and Form." *Women and Performance* 2 (2): 45-58.

Zavella, Patricia. 1994a. "Reflections on Diversity Among Chicanas." In *Race,* eds. Steven Gregory and Roger Sanjek, 199-212. New Brunswick: Rutgers University Press.

___. 1994b. "Playing with Fire: The Gendered Construction of Chicano/Mexican Sexuality." Paper presented at the 6th European Conference on Latino Cultures in the United States, Bordeaux, France, July 7-10.

___. 1988. "The Problematic Relationship of Feminism and Chicana Studies." *Women's Studies* 17: 123-134.

_____. 1987. *Women's Work and Chicano Families: Cannery Workers of the Santa Clara Valley.* Ithaca: Cornell University Press.

Zinn, Maxine Baca. 1975a. "Chicanas: Power and Control in the Domestic Sphere." *De Colores* 2 (2): 19-31.

Zinn, Maxine Baca. 1975b. "Political Familism: Towards Sex Role Equality in Chicano Families." *Aztlán: Chicano Journal of the Social Sciences and the Arts* 6 (1): 13-26.

Listening to the Silences in Latina/Chicana Lesbian History

Yolanda Chávez Leyva

My kitchen window faces the west. Sometimes in the mornings I stand at the sink, cafesito in hand, looking out that window, eyes searching for the movement of *gente*, listening for
the noises that tell me the neighborhood is beginning another
day. Last spring, while the smell of *azares* still clung to the not-
yet-so heavy desert air, I looked out my window and saw her.
Norma García–sixty years old with a still-trim body, man's
haircut, and jeans. I had heard all about her. I knew the story
of how forty years earlier she loved a woman named Dora.
Everyone knew. *Pero nadie decía nada.* The silence surrounding her love was broken only by the sounds of the songs she
dedicated to Dora every Sunday afternoon, Mexican songs
about love that could or would never be. Songs about broken
hearts. Songs that made Norma's eyes well with tears. That
day I started to think about silences in a different way. I stopped
imagining silence as the absence of something. Rather I started
to listen for what silences held within them.[1] For lesbianas
Latinas, silence has been an enigma, a survival strategy, a wall
which confines us, the space that protects us.[2]

The choice to speak or not–it is a decision that we face
every day. Mariana Romo-Carmona writes in the introduction to *Compañeras: Latina Lesbians*:

> When we weigh the benefits of being silent and saving other people
> from the shock, or ourselves from the pain, we internalize the
> hatred against us. In essence, we begin to believe that our lives
> are less important, and we continue to hide a part of ourselves.[3]

She continues, asserting that the only way to truly live is
by speaking out:

How many daughters, mothers, sisters, godmothers and grandmothers, aunts, cousins, and best friends have lived and died
unknown? Each woman's forced silence was a denial of her existence, as if she never loved another woman, never rejoiced in
their union, or cried for her, or waited for her to come home.[4]

The urgency for lesbianas Latinas to speak out is undeni-
able.

From Carla Trujillo's challenge to Chicana lesbians to "fight
for our own voices as women"[5] to Emma Pérez's declaration
that "marginalized groups must have separate spaces to inaugurate their own discourses, *nuestra lengua en nuestro sitio*,"[6] the
call to create our language, to name ourselves, becomes a critical task of survival. But if, in the present day, our political and
cultural survival calls for the breaking of the silence, we must
come to terms with the meanings of that silence, today as well
as historically.

How do we begin to understand the many silences in the
lives of Chicana and Latina lesbians? As a people who have
passed on our historia through the sharing of *historias*,
storytelling itself provides a basis for unraveling the multiple
meanings of silence.[7] As one Chicana-identified lesbiana answered in response to my question about how to best maintain my commitment to community while continuing my academic work, "You engage in people's lives. You take down
their histories and put it down on paper and you work your
ass off to get it into libraries."[8] This essay is a call to answer
her challenge.

Nineteen seventy-four: I'm sitting in a parking lot waiting.
Waiting for "la Sylvia." Chaparita. And butch. With one of
the warmest smiles I've ever seen. She lives in a little three-
room house, set back from the street by a large, square courtyard. She lives there with her girlfriend. Their neighbors are
viejitas in bargain basement housedresses. Chavalitos with legs
dusty from chasing each other in the dirt. Young couples just
married. I've heard about la Sylvia even before I see her at
the local gay bar. The kids call her Mom and hang out in front
of her house. Everyone in the neighborhood just "knows" about
la Sylvia and her girlfriend. No one says anything. This is the
silence of knowing, of imagining. It is the silence that Carmen,

a lesbiana Cubana, describes when she says, "*Yo nunca le dije a [mi mama] que yo soy lesbiana, pero ella se lo imaginaba.*"[9]

In the 1970s, in the west Texas town where I grew up there was a gay bar, the Pet Shop. During the day, hundreds of downtown shoppers passed its padlocked door, unaware that each night, when the street emptied of cars and buses, a transformation took place. Down a narrow, always-unlit flight of stairs, descended drag queens in high heels, butches in western boots and leather jackets, young gay men who lived with their parents in pleasant, middle-class homes. They entered a dark, smoky room with two pool tables in the corner, a dance floor lit by flashing multicolored lights. Charlie went there every weekend. She dressed in men's clothing—usually western shirts and jeans. Her black hair, combed back, framed a lean, hard brown face. Always a beer in one hand, a cigarette in the other, she'd sit at a table, talking about how she really knew how to make love to a woman. Then she'd laugh at her own line, her expression becoming tender for just a second. It was the only time she ever talked about it, on those long and smoke-filled Friday and Saturday nights. She lived with her family—they never talked about "it." But they knew.

Alicia, a 45-year-old Puertorriqueña who came out in 1959, remembered that coming out:

> was very easy, because it was something that I enjoyed. I think the only hard part was in hurting my mom. I think that's about the only thing I've regretted . . . When I was sixteen I ran away from home. I just couldn't bring myself to say, "Mom, you know, I'm like this." It was kind of hard for her also. At that time as I was growing up I was very stubborn, very stone butch. I not only dressed like a man, I used a chest flattener, a band, anyway. And I used to get in a fight all the time . . . I never had the gall to tell her, "Mom, you know this is me," so I ran away from home.

When Alicia found out that her mother was very ill, she:

> called her and told her, "Look, I don't want to come home." My brother was on the other line. "I don't want to hurt you and I don't want to embarrass you." I think what made it better was her response. So she says, "*Tu eres mi sangre, seas buena o seas mala, yo te quiero.*" And my brother repeated her words. And I came

home. You know, right away she spoiled me, had my food on
the table and what not. Basically, you know, she doesn't like my
way of life so we don't talk about it. She respects me, she loves
me, she spoils me. But it's something we just don't discuss. I
think I don't do it out of respect for her, and she doesn't do it out
of respect for me.[10]

Alicia's story represents the complexity of silence. For Alicia and her mother, not discussing "it" became a way to put love first, to reconcile very different expectations, a way not only for the daughter to defer to her mother, but also a way for the mother to show respect for her daughter. In Alicia's story, there is also a language within the silence that does not rely on words. Alicia, dressed as a man, was a stone butch in the New York City of the early 1960s. What does silence mean when your looks say everything?[11]

Twenty years ago, Hilda Hidalgo and Elia Hidalgo Christensen conducted a study on "Puerto Rican Lesbians and the Puerto Rican Community." The lesbianas interviewed believed that there existed a "silent tolerance" for their lesbianism. The authors write that "families [knew] of their gayness but treat[ed] it as an unspoken truth."[12] It is a truth that is silent.

Silence has its own contours, its own texture. We cannot dismiss the silences of earlier generations as simply a reaction to fear. Rather than dismiss it, we must explore it, must attempt to understand it. We must learn to understand the ways it has limited us and the ways it has protected us.

This is not, however, a call to continue the silence, nor to justify it. Naming ourselves, occupying our spaces fully, creating our own language, is essential to our continued survival, particularly in these times of increasingly violence against us as Latinas and lesbianas. This is a challenge to explore the contradictions of silence within Latina lesbian history, to understand the multiple meanings of silence, to uncover the language of silence. A language without words whose meanings are found in the plaintive sounds of Mexican love songs shared between women, whose meaning are found in the day-to-day acts of women living together in places *donde todos saben pero no se dice nada*, a language without words whose meanings are found in the tough look of a Latina butch on a New York Street. And it is also a call to take seriously our *historias*, to turn to the storytellers in our community to understand the past.

Notes

1. Pseudonyms are used throughout this essay for the protection of the women. Thanks to María C. González and Julia Schiavone Camacho for challenging me always to write. Also to the women of Lesbianas Latinas de Tucson (Tucson, Arizona) and Lesbianas Latinas Sin Fronteras (El Paso, Texas) for listening. To the women who continue to share their stories of silence with me, knowing I'll break that silence by putting their stories down on paper. And, of course, to Magdalena Trujillo, for everything.

2. I've had the opportunity to read this essay to numerous formally and informally organized groups over the past year. The groups have included both lesbians and straight women, gay and straight men, Chicanas and others. What has been consistent in their response is the great desire to discuss silence and its meanings. The second thing that has been consistent is the amount of emotion which this topic brings to the surface. I think that as a people, and because of our experiences as queer people of color, Chicana lesbians have much to share about silences and the construction of silence. I hope that we continue these discussions, exploring continually what is not said in our lives.

3. Mariana Romo-Carmona, "Introduction," in Juanita Ramos, ed. *Compañeras: Latina Lesbians*, New York Latina Lesbian History Project, 1987, p. xxiii.

4. Romo-Carmona, "Introduction," *Compañeras*, p. xxiii.

5. Carla Trujillo, "Chicana Lesbians: Fear and Loathing in the Chicano Community," *Chicana Lesbians: The Girls Our Mothers Warned Us About*, ed. Carla Trujillo. Berkeley: Third Woman Press, 1991, p. 193.

6. Emma Pérez, "Irigaray's Female symbolic in the Making of Chicana Lesbian Sitios y Lenguas," *The Lesbian Postmodern*, ed. Laura Doan. New York: Columbia University Press, 1994, p. 109.

7. I do not think that it is a coincidence that in Spanish the word for story and the word for history are the same. As Ruth Behar writes in *Translated Woman*, her informant/comadre Esperanza Hernández, a sixty-year-old Mexican woman from Mexquitic, understood that the border between her life historias and historia itself was a fluid one.

See Behar's discussion in "Introduction: The Talking Serpent" in *Translated Woman: Crossing the Border with Esperanza's Story.* Boston: Beacon Press, 1993.
8. Interview with Susanna V., San José, California, March 1993. Interview was conducted by Yolanda Leyva as part of the Latina Lesbiana Archival project.
9. Carmen, "!No, no, yo me voy! (Historia oral)," *Compañeras*, p. 58.
10. Interview with Alicia B., Tucson, Arizona, December 1994. Interview conducted by Yolanda Leyva and Julia Schiavone Camacho.
11. We need to explore the combination of verbal silence with visual "noise." By visual noise, I'm referring to the ways in which lesbianas make obvious their otherness. One Chicana I interviewed, for example, came out in the early 1960s. She tried to discuss it with her family, but they wouldn't listen to her. So she went to a barber and got a crew cut. Her family may have tried to silence her, but they couldn't stop her visual "noise." (Interview with Pat C., spring 1995, Tucson, Arizona.)
12. Hilda Hidalgo and Elia Hidalgo Christensen, "Puerto Rican Lesbians and the Puerto Rican Community," *Journal of Homosexuality*, vol. 2 (2), Winter 1976-77, p. 118.

Mother's Day

Barbara Renaud González

She crossed the Río Grande from Mexico when she was just eighteen. She won't tell me how she did it. She was escaping a bad marriage and my old-fashioned grandmother. She was to be my mother.

How she dreamed of having me, her first-born, a daughter. After five years of marriage to my father, she could not conceive, and so she began to search for me. I was in her *caldo*, that succulent vegetable-beef soup that is said to start a baby. She sipped me in the bouquets of tea that promise children from the curanderas. Potions, *yerbitas*, prayers, and devotions to the holiest mother of all. Yes, my mother made her pleas to the blessed Virgen de Guadalupe so that she too would become a perfect mother.

No eres madre, I tease her today. *Eres una fábrica. Mami,* you are a baby factory. After all, she had eight children in thirteen years. *You,* Barbara, she would say as we gathered around the kitchen table before Daddy came home. The same table where he would ridicule her supper, her petite body, her English, her Mexican ways.

You, Barbara, she would begin her dreaming. *You must travel and write. Leticia, teacher, you have patience. Jorge Antonio—lawyer—keep the rest out of jail. Susanita, the middle child. Be the boss once and for all. Daniel, the sick one. You will keep the family together. Carlitos, the charmer, a politician. Roberto, we need a doctor in the family. Esteban, the baby in diapers, you can be the artist and rebel all you want.*

My mother took us to church every Sunday and even to Vacation Bible School in the summers. Every year it was a different religion, because she was looking for the answer, and she couldn't seem to find the questions that I would ask her. Believe in God, she would tell us. Have faith. And I will take you to the library next week.

She wanted me to be so different. *You don't have to learn to make tortillas,* she would tell me, *when you know how to buy bread.* Though Daddy would claim to be the real brains of the family, it was my mother who confronted his lack of ambition with her own. Take care of your brothers, and watch the *caldo de res* she would say, as she rushed to her night job as a nurse's aide. They are men, after all.

She let me date early, and encouraged me to have a rich social life in contrast to the restrictions of the girls around me. She showed me diagrams to my questions of sex. *Here it is,* she would say. *Don't. Men will never respect you. Believe me, I know. And have a good time.*

My mother surprised me with my first suitcase when I went away to college. *Remember,* she said. *You are no beauty like your sisters. So you must learn to be independent of men. Men don't like smart women.*

When my mother crossed the border in search of a better life, she didn't realize what she had done. She, who believes in the tradition of family, now lives alone, divorced after a marriage of twenty-eight years. She says that she will never marry again. She says that if she were to do it all over, she would have left my father in her thirties and that she was afraid of nothing after all.

Now she goes dancing on Saturday nights, and to church on Sunday mornings. She has a wall of college diplomas from her children. She has survived a son's death and another's imprisonment. She has seen a daughter return from prostitution, and she worries about *la feminista* and is shocked at the one who is lesbian and both. We are not what she expected, after all. Maybe if my father Roberto had been a real father, it would be different, she says. Maybe it is her fault.

My mother says that she may not live long enough to see the youngest, *Esteban,* receive his Ph.D. She trembles when she says this. Her hands look like wine-soaked bread.

I am the child of my mother's passion, the embodiment of her wildest hopes, and for that she fears what I have become. I know that she is still searching, and that it is up to me to find it. To do that, I will have to cross even more borders. She is me, but I can never be her.

Come home *mijita*, she says in the middle of her loneliness. I will make your favorite *caldo de camarón.*

You have forgotten me.

Contributors

Norma Alarcón is professor of Ethnic/Chicano/Women's Studies at the University of California, Berkeley. She is the author of many essays on Chicana writers and feminist theory and co-editor of the forthcoming book, *Between Woman and Nation*, to be published by Duke University Press. She is the founder and publisher of Third Woman Press.

Gloria Anzaldúa is a queer Chicana Tejana feminist patlache poet, fictionist, and cultural theorist from the Rio Grande valley of south Texas. She is the author of *Borderlands/La Frontera* and two bilingual children's books, *Friends From the Other Side* and *Prietita y la Llorona*, and coeditor of the classic anthology of writings by women of color *This Bridge Called My Back*. Forthcoming is a book theorizing the production of art, knowledge, and identity.

Antonia I. Castañeda is a Chicana feminist historian, born in Crystal City, Texas, and raised in Washington's Yakima Valley, where she lived at the Golding Hop farm labor camp and attended rural schools. She is a professor in the Department of History at St. Mary's University, San Antonio, Texas, and is the author of numerous articles on gender and colonialism, and is working on a book-length manuscript on *Native Women in California*. Her current projects include a bilingual critical edition of nineteenth-century California narratives and a social history of Tejana farmworkers in Washington State.

Sandra Cisneros is a novelist, poet, short-story writer, and essayist whose work gives voice to working-class Latino and Latina life in America. She is the author of *The House on Mango Street, Woman Hollering Creek and Other Stories, Hairs/Pelitos, Bad Boys, My Wicked Wicked Ways,* and *Loose Woman*. She is currently working on a novel entitled *Caramelo*. She is the recipient of numerous awards and honors, such as the PEN Center West Award for Best Fiction of 1991, the Lannan Foundation

Literary Award, the Before Columbus Foundation's American Book Award, and the prestigious MacArthur Foundation Fellowship (1995). She has received an honorary Doctor of Letters and various honored lectureships and fellowships. Born in Chicago, she currently resides in San Antonio, Texas.

Teresa Córdova is a professor in Community and Regional Planning at the University of New Mexico. Her publications focus on gentrification, affordable housing, community-based organizations in development, the impact of restructuring on Latino communities, and the formation of urban agendas. She is the author of "Roots and Resistance: Twenty Years of Chicana Feminist Writings," in a volume edited by Felix Padilla, and she co-edited *Chicana Voices: Intersections of Class, Race, and Gender*. Her current work focuses on the relationship of transnational corporations to local communities, and grassroots activists in the environmental and economic justice movement.

Yvette G. Flores-Ortiz is a professor of Psychology in Chicana/o Studies at the University of California, Davis. She is also a member of the U.C. Davis Chicana/Latina Research Center and a practicing psychologist with specialization in family therapy with abusive families and feminist psychotherapy with incest survivors. She has published extensively in the areas of family therapy, domestic violence, mental health, and feminist psychology. Her work also examines substance misuse and HIV prevention among ethnic minority adolescents. She was born in Panama, raised in Costa Rica until her adolescence, and recently received a Fulbright Senior Lecturer Award to teach in Panama. Her current work examines the impact of violence on the lives of Latinas through the collection of personal narratives.

Alicia Gaspar de Alba, a native of the El Paso-Juárez border, is a novelist, poet, essayist, and professor at the University of California, Los Angeles. She is the author of *Chicano Art Inside/Outside the Master's House: Cultural Politics and the CARA Exhibit*; "Beggar on the Córdoba Bridge," which appears in the volume *Three Times a Woman: Chicana Poetry*; *The Mystery of*

Survival; as well as a forthcoming novel on Sor Juana Inés de la Cruz entitled *Tenth Muse.* Her work has been anthologized in various publications, including several French, German, and Mexican anthologies of Chicana/o literature. She is the recipient of the "Premio Aztlan" in 1994, an annual prize given to Chicano/a writers of fiction at the beginning of their publishing careers. She lives in Southern California with her lifemate, Deena González.

Barbara Renaud González is a homeless writer traveling in Mexico and el Sur, thanks to the kindness of her accomplished friends. She is a Tejana, raised in the Panhandle, and a graduate of "Tortilla Tech," aka UT-Pan American University, on the Texas frontera in Edinburg. She got lucky and thanks to the grace of the Civil Rights movement, went to the University of Michigan at Ann Arbor, where she earned an M.S.W. (Social Work). She writes a monthly column for the San Antonio Express-News, and the New York Times "New American Voices" syndicate. She also writes occasional commentary for National Public Radio on Latino issues. Currently she is writing a novel about el Sur and the American Dream.

Deena J. González received her Ph.D. in history from the University of California at Berkeley in 1985. She is Associate Professor of History at Pomona College and Chair of Chicano Studies at Claremont. *Refusing the Favor: The Spanish-Mexican Women of Santa Fe, 1820-1880* is forthcoming from Oxford University Press. *The Dictionary of Latinas in the U.S.* is forthcoming from Garland Press. She has authored numerous articles in Chicana Studies, nineteenth-century frontier history, and in Chicano history.

Maya González is a working artist currently residing in San Francisco. She has a number of bilingual children's books published, including *Prietita and La Llorona* written by Gloria Anzaldúa. Prints of the cover art are available through Galleria de la Raza/Studio 24 in San Francisco.

Verónica Guerra is a professor in the Department of English at Texas A & M University. She teaches classes in Linguistics and Women's Studies. She was born in Brownsville, Texas, and received her doctorate in Applied Linguistics from the University of Houston in 1984. In addition to teaching, her work also encompasses being the project director for a Hispanic Serving Institution Title III grant and principal investigator for three additional grants. She is currently the only Chicana in the English Department and in the College of Arts and Humanities. She is one of only four Chicana professors in the entire university.

Aída Hurtado is Professor of Psychology at the University of California, Santa Cruz. Dr. Hurtado's research focuses on the effects of subordination on social identity. She is especially interested in group memberships like ethnicity, race, class, and gender that are used to legitimize unequal distribution of power between groups. Dr. Hurtado's expertise is in survey methods with bilingual/bicultural populations. She has published on issues of language, social identity, and feminist theory. Dr. Hurtado received her B.A. in Psychology and Sociology from the University of Texas-Pan American in Edinburg, Texas, and her M.A. and Ph.D. in Social Psychology from the University of Michigan.

Yolanda Chávez Leyva is a Chicana lesbian from the Texas-Chihuahua border. She believes in the power of memory and works to keep our stories alive by teaching, writing, listening, and remembering. She has been a member of the History Department faculties at New Mexico State University and the University of Texas at El Paso. She shares her life and her dreams with her compañera, Magdalena Trujillo, and her son, José Miguel.

Josefina López's writing career began at the age of seventeen when she wrote her first play, *Simply María or the American Dream*, which was a winner of the California Playwright's Project in San Diego, and was later produced for PBS. The PBS production went on to win an Emmy for Entertainment, a Media Award from the Conference of Christians and Jews for "promoting cultural understanding," and a Gold Award from the Corporation for Public Broadcasting. Soon after she attracted the attention of Luis Valdez's Teatro Campesino and they toured her play around the country. Her next play, *Real Women Have Curves*, has had sixteen productions around the the country, and is the basis of a situation comedy now titled The Chávez Family, which she created with Norman Lear's Act III Productions. Presently, her most current play, *Confessions of Women From East LA*, is touring California. Her goal, as a Chicana playwright/writer/actress, is to shatter the negative representation of Latinos in the theater and in Hollywood.

Elizabeth "Betita" Martínez is an activist and author who has published five books and many articles on social movements coming out of her own participation over the past thirty years. Her most recent book is the bilingual *500 Years of Chicano History in Pictures*. A former Books and Arts editor of *The Nation*, she currently serves as an editor of *CrossRoads* magazine and writes on Latino issues for various publications. She has been a part-time instructor in Ethnic Studies and Women's Studies at various California colleges and universities, and works with groups in the San Francisco Bay area including the Women of Color Resource Center and several Latino youth projects.

Lara Medina is completing her doctoral studies in History/American Studies at the Claremont Graduate School. Her research focuses on the religious history and spirituality of Chicanas/Latinas. Her dissertation will consider the religious agency of Chicanas across generations. She currently teaches at California State University, Northridge.

Cherríe Moraga is a poet, playwright, and essayist and the co-editor of *This Bridge Called My Back: Writings by Radical Women of Color*. She is the author of numerous plays, including *Shadow of a Man*, winner of the 1990 Fund for New American Plays Award, and *Heroes and Saints*, winner of the 1992 Pen West Award. Her most recent book is a collection of poems and essays entitled *The Last Generation*. Moraga is also a recipient of the National Endowment for the Arts' Theatre Playwrights Fellowship and an artist in residence at Brava Theatre Center in San Francisco. Brava Theatre produced her latest play, *Watsonville*, in the Spring of 1996. *Watsonville* won the 1995

Fund for New American Plays Award.

Mónica Palacios is a writer, playwright, actor, and comedian. A native Californian, her one-mujer shows have toured throughout the U.S. and her writings have been published in various anthologies. She also contributes to *LA Weekly, Ten Percent, Frontiers*, and has a column in *The Lesbian News*. She works as a co-producer in Los Angeles of two highly acclaimed annual events: *Fierce Tongues*, a three-day affair of powerful Latina artists, and *Chicks and Salsa*, an evening featuring outstanding Latina Lesbian artists. She is a lecturer at the University of California, Los Angeles, and co-produces performance and art shows with VIVA, Lesbian and Gay Latino Artists.

Emma Pérez, historian, critical theorist, and writer, teaches at the University of Texas at El Paso. She has also taught at the History of Consciousness Board at the University of California at Santa Cruz. She was awarded a Rockefeller Fellowship at the Center for Studies on Ethnicity and Race in America at the University of Colorado at Boulder in 1994-1995. She is the author of the novel *Gulf Dreams* (Third Woman Press, 1996).

Chéla Sandoval is an assistant professor of Cultural Theory in the Department of Chicana/o Studies at the University of California, Santa Barbara. Her book, *Rhetorics of Rebellion*, will be published in the Theory Out of Bounds series by the University of Minnesota Press. Her most recent article, "Re-Entering CyberSpace: Sciences of Resistance," is published in *Dispositio/n: Journal of Cultural Histories and Theories*.

María-Socorro Tabuenca C. (Coquis) is a fronteriza from the Juárez-El Paso area. At present, she is a researcher at El Colegio de la Frontera Norte in Juárez, where she also works as the regional director. She is a doctoral candidate from SUNY Stony Brook, and her disertation focuses on women's literature of México's northern border. Her interests of study also include Latin American women's literature, Chicana/o-Latina/o literature and Testimonial literature. She has published articles on Border Literature in *Discourse* and *Puentelibre*, and she has also published essays on Rosario Sanmiguel, Rosina Conde, Sandra Cisneros, and Gloria Anzaldúa in Mexican

and Chicana/o anthologies and revistas de cultura.
Carla Trujillo was born in New Mexico and received a Ph.D.
in educational psychology from the University of Wisconsin,
Madison. She is the editor of *Chicana Lesbians: The Girls Our
Mothers Warned Us About*. The anthology is now in its third
printing and won the LAMBDA Book Award for Best Lesbian Anthology and the Out/Write Vanguard Award for Best
Pioneering Contribution to the field of Gay/Lesbian Lifestyle
Literature in 1991. Trujillo is also the author of various articles
on identity, sexuality, and higher education. She works as an
administrator in diversity education and advocacy and as a
lecturer at the University of California, Berkeley. She is currently working on a novel about identity and survival.

Yvonne Yarbro-Bejarano is a professor who teaches in the
Spanish and Portuguese Department at Stanford University.
She is the author of *Feminism and the Honor Plays of Lope de Vega*
(1994), co-editor of *Chicano Art: Resistance and Affirmation* (1991),
and has published numerous articles on Chicana/o literature
and cultural studies, especially on theater and women writers.
Her collected essays on Cherríe Moraga are forthcoming from
the University of Texas Press. She is currently working on a
new book offering a comparative analysis of Chicana culture,
including writing, visual art, film and video, performance, and
popular culture.

Acknowledgments

Susan Bergholz Literary Services, for "A Woman of No Consequence/Una Mujer Cualquiera," by Sandra Cisneros, first presented as a keynote speech at the Third Annual Conference of the National Lesbian and Gay Journalists Association, with a portion of the essay published in *SI Magazine*, number 1, © 1995.

Columbia University Press, for "Irigaray's Female Symbolic in the Making of Chicana Lesbian *Sitos y Lenguas* (Sites and Discourses)," by Emma Pérez, first published in *The Lesbian Postmodern*, edited by Laura Doan, © 1994.

Esperanza Peace and Justice Center, for "History and the Politics of Violence Against Women," by Antonia Castañeda, adapted from a talk at the Take Back the Night Rally in Santa Barbara, Calif. in 1992, and published in abridged form in *La Voz de Esperanza: The Voice of Peace and Justice in San Antonio*, © 1995.

The University of Michigan Press, for "The Politics of Sexuality in the Gender Subordination of Chicanas," from *The Color of Privilege*, by Aída Hurtado, © 1997.

Cherríe Moraga, for "Free at Last," from *Waiting in the Wings: Portrait of a Queer Motherhood*, by Cherríe Moraga, published by Firebrand Press, © 1997.

Oxford University Press, for "Mestizaje as Method: Feminists-of-Color Challenge the Canon," by Chéla Sandoval, portions of which were published under the title "U.S. Third World Feminism" in *The Oxford Companion to Women's Writing in the United States*, edited by Cathy N. Davidson, and Linda Wagner-Martin, © 1995.

Books available from Third Woman Press

MÁSCARAS edited by Lucha Corpi. The top fifteen U.S. Latina writers discuss the historical, linguistic, political, economic and cultural realities that have shaped them as women and writers of color in the U.S. ISBN 0-943219-14-0, $16.95

LATINAS ON STAGE: PRACTICE AND THEORY edited by Alicia Arrizón and Lillian Manzor. Plays, performance pieces, interviews and critical essays by nineteen contributors. The only book of its kind focusing on U.S. Latinas. ISBN 0-943219-17-9, $24.95

GULF DREAMS by Emma Pérez. A powerful, gripping, and disturbing novel of lesbian passion and betrayal, survival and vengeance, compulsion and resilience, told in a fragmented, dreamlike narrative. ISBN 0-943219-13-2, $12.95

CHICANA (W)RITES: ON WORD AND FILM edited by María Herrera-Sobek and Helena María Viramontes. The strength, beauty and vigor of Chicana creative writing and filmmaking are analyzed in this anthology of sixteen authors. ISBN 0-943219-10-8, $16.95

LAS FORMAS DE NUESTRAS VOCES: CHICANA AND MEXICANA WRITERS IN MEXICO edited by Claire Joysmith. Thirteen Chicana and Mexicana authors and critics discuss their work. A co-publication with the Universidad Nacional Autónoma de Mexico, in Spanish and English. ISBN 9-683648-01-0, $24.95

DICTÉE by Theresa Hak Kyung Cha. A remarkable mixed media text that combines autobiographical and biographical fragments, photographs, historical narrative, calligraphy, and lyric prose poetry in a complex, discontinuous weave. ISBN 0-943219-12-4, $12.95

WRITING SELF/WRITING NATION edited by Elaine Kim and Norma Alarcón. Five Asian American women celebrate *Dictée* while offering reconstructions of ethnicity, feminism and nationalism. ISBN 0-943219-11-6, $12.95

CHICANA LESBIANS: THE GIRLS OUR MOTHERS WARNED US ABOUT edited by Carla Trujillo. Winner of numerous awards, including the Lambda Literary Award for Best Lesbian Anthology, and the Out/Write Vanguard Award. Now in its third printing. ISBN 0-943219-06-X, $12.95